A Pictorial Record of
GWR ABSORBED ENGINES

THIS WORK IS DEDICATED TO
A. C. (TONY) STERNDALE
FOR WHOSE HELP IN THE LOAN OF PHOTOGRAPHS,
THE CHECKING OF THE MANUSCRIPT AND A MASS
OF GENERAL INFORMATION, I AM, INDEBTED.

A Pictorial Record of

GREAT WESTERN ABSORBED ENGINES

by J.H. Russell

Oxford Publishing Co.

ISBN 0 902888 74 9

A FOULIS-OPC Railway Book

© J.H. Russell and Oxford Publishing Co. 1978
Reprinted 1987

Published by:
Haynes Publishing Group
Sparkford, Near Yeovil, Somerset. BA22 7JJ

Haynes Publications Inc.
861 Lawrence Drive, Newbury Park, California 91320, USA

The publishers wish to point out that many of the line illustrations are taken from official drawings and due to the age of these, the reproduction is not as clear as they would wish.

FOREWORD

The steam locomotives of the Great Western Railway fell naturally into two groups, first, those which were the pure products of Swindon and Wolverhampton, and second, all the engines which were added to the stock when the Welsh and M.S.W.Jc railways merged into the GWR at the grouping of the railways in 1922/3.

Before this date, the railways of South Wales were many and various, as indeed were their respective locomotives. But the Railways Act of 1921 brought about the fusion of all these smaller private companies, into a greater Great Western Railway Company of 1923.

So it was that, at a stroke, an extra 700 assorted steam locomotives of all makes and sizes, were brought into the enlarged parent body of the GWR. The very diversity of the engines makes an interesting study, but the fact which many people, myself included, find so fascinating, is the way this heterogeneous collection of locomotives were eventually rebuilt, converted, and refitted at Swindon factory, to be eventually returned to service on their home lines, as almost unrecognisable versions of their original designs.

Being an enthusiast of all things Great Western, and in particular the steam engines, I have made a collection of many of these interesting conversions, and have committed many of them to print herein, hoping that fellow railway devotees might also find the subject worthy of a glance. Where possible, I have shown in picture and diagram, the engines of the various companies, as they were on their home lines, and again, as they emerged from Swindon Works after a major refit, sometimes with new boilers and old fittings, or old boilers with new fittings. It would seem that every kind of permutation was tried, but always, the converted engines which emerged seemed to have that little extra something which personified the GWR.

It has been said that, take any wheel arrangements, any type of boiler, with any kind of coal bunker and water tanks, choose your own chimney and safety valve, plus a little imaginative designing, and for sure, one such engine could be found amongst the hundreds of 'Absorbed' locomotives from South Wales.

This work is only a cross section of the vast amount of stock which was absorbed from 1922 onward, indeed there were many taken into the GWR before this date, but I have endeavoured to restrict this collection to those locomotives which were taken over at the Grouping and not before. These include not only the Welsh companies, but also the Midland and South Western Junction, The Cleobury Mortimer & Ditton Priors, and the Weston, Clevedon & Portishead. Mention is also made of the R.O.D. engines, and those locomotives which were borrowed during the War period, and saw service on the Great Western.

It is a vast subject, and I have only been able to scratch the surface, but for greater detail and a fuller account, I would recommend the reader acquiring a copy of Part 10 of the R.C.T.S's superb work *The Locomotives of the Great Western Railway*, from which I have drawn so much inspiration and a great deal of knowledge.

This book is intended as a companion volume to my previous work *A Pictorial Record of G.W.R. Engines* published by Oxford Publishing Co., and is designed primarily as a prompt and guide to all those railway modellers, who, like myself, find relaxation in the search for material towards the construction of model railways, especially with the 'Western' flavour. If historians and other enthusiasts find it of interest, then the project will indeed have been worthwhile.

Jim Russell

INTRODUCTION

The Locomotives of the old Great Western Railway Company were, in the main, constructed at either Swindon or Wolverhampton workshops, to the design of the six successive engineers Gooch, Armstrong, Dean, Churchward, Collett and Hawksworth. All the engines carrying the proud insignia of the GWR bore a distinct family likeness to one another throughout the 113 years of the Company's existence. However, many other strange locomotives found their way on to the Great Western stock lists, particularly after the grouping of the railways, when, under the Act of 1921, the GWR was enlarged considerably by the addition of the Welsh companies and several other small lines on the western side of the British Isles.

The companies concerned were six constituents and twelve subsidiary, being alphabetically:—

The Alexandra Docks & Railway
The Barry Railway
The Cambrian Railway
The Cardiff Railway
The Rhymney Railway
The Taff Vale Railway

The Brecon & Merthyr Railway
Burry Port & Gwendraeth Valley Railway
Cleobury Mortimer & Ditton Priors Light Railway
Gwendraeth Valleys Railway
Llanelly & Mynydd Mawr Railway
Midland & South Western Junction Railway
Neath & Brecon Railway
Port Talbot Railway
Rhondda & Swansea Bay Railway
South Wales Mineral Railway
Swansea Harbour Trust
Powlesland & Mason

In addition to these companies and their locomotive stock, other foreign engines taken on the Great Western stock were the R.O.D. engines bought from the War Department, the American engines lent to the GWR in the Second World War, and those of the SR, LMS and LNER which saw service on the old GWR.

The photographs in this work are from many sources, collected over the years by the author. Special acknowledgements are due to . . . British Rail; R. Carpenter; A.C. Sterndale; Real Photos and the P. Reed Collection, by courtesy of John Reed.

GREAT WESTERN RAILWAY.

The ALEXANDRA (NEWPORT & SOUTH WALES) DOCKS and RAILWAY

The Alexandra (Newport) Dock Company of 1865 was originally founded to construct Docks at Newport, with a railway to link them to the Great Western. It took 10 years for the first dock to be built, and the opening took place on 10th April 1875. Three years later in 1878, another small company, The Pontypridd Caerphilly & Newport Railway came into being for the purpose of conveying coal from the Rhondda & Aberdare mines to Newport for shipment. To get to Newport, the P. C. & N. had to use running powers over both the Rhymney and Brecon & Merthyr railways via Penrhos Junction, Caerphilly and Bassaleg. Eventually the P. C. & N. was taken over by the Alexandra Dock Company in 1897 which consisted then of approximately 100 miles of docks and harbour sidings at the one end, and a 9¼ mile section of running line from Pontypridd Tram Road to the junction with the Rhymney at Penrhos. The A. D. & Railway had owned a motley collection of locomotives totalling some 56, plus two rail motors, but at the grouping when the company became a constituent of the GWR the stock consisted of 39 numbered consecutively from 1 to 37 with *Trojan* and *Alexandra* completing the total.

Builder	Alex. Docks No.	New No. by GWR	Type	Diagram	Withdrawn
R. Stephenson	1	674	0-6-0T	A72	1929
,,	2	675	,,	,,	1926
,,	3	676	,,	,,	1929
,,	4	677	,,	,,	1929
,,	5	678	,,	,,	1925
Beyer-Peacock	6	1207	2-6-2T	V	1932
,,	7	1208	,,	VY	1929
,,	8	1209	,,	V	1929
,,	9	1211	,,	,,	1929
,,	10	1201	,,	,,	1929
,,	11	1204	,,	V(Z)	1929
R. W. Hawthorn	12	664	0-6-0T	A67	1930
,,	13	665	,,	,,	1926
GWR	14	1426	0-4-2T	J(K)	1934
R. Stephenson	15	668	0-6-0T	A69	1929
Hawthorn Leslie	16	671	,,	A71 (B41)	1937
,,	17	672	,,	,, ,,	1924
Peckett	18	679	,,	A73 (B1)	1929
,,	19	680	,,	,, ,,	1948
R.Stephenson	20	669	,,	A70 (B8)	1925
,,	21	670	,,	,, ,,	1926
Beyer-Peacock	22	1344	0-6-4T	A	1923
,,	23	1345	,,	,,	1923
,,	24	1346	,,	A(D)	1927
Kitson	25	1199	2-6-2T	U	1931
Worcester. E. Co.	26	663	0-6-2T	A14 (A28)	1926
GWR	27	1679	0-6-0T	A98	1926
,,	28	1683	,,	,,	1926
Andrew Barclay	29	190	0-6-2T	X(A25)	1948
,,	30	191	,,	,,	1934
,,	31	192	,,	,,	1946

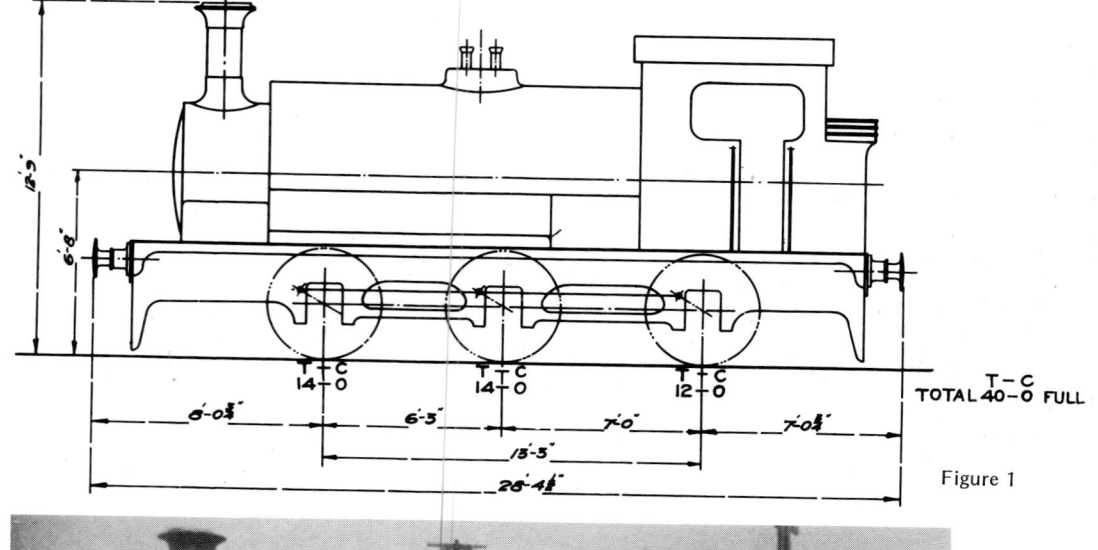

Figure 1

Builder	Alex. Docks No.	GWR No.	Type	Diagram	Withdrawn
Fletcher Jennings	32	1356	0-6-0T	Y	1923
GWR	33	993	"	A97	1930
Kerr Stuart	34	666	"	A68 (B13)	1955
"	35	667	"	"	1954
Hawthorn Leslie	36	1205	2-6-2T	W	1956
"	37	1206	"	"	1951
Avonside E.	Trojan	1340	0-4-0T	K (P)	1932
"	Alexandra	1341	"	L(S)	1946

Five engines numbered 1-5 were purchased from R. Stephenson & Co., two in 1898 and three more in 1900. These engines replaced earlier second-hand locomotives which had carried these numbers. They were all six wheel coupled saddle tanks with 4' 0½" diameter wheels, set at 6' 3" + 7' 0" wheelbases. The boilers were pressed for 140 lbs with a firegrate area of 13.5 sq ft and a weight of 39 tons 12 cwt. All five were rebuilt by the A.D. Railway between 1912-19 but only numbers 1 and 3 went to Swindon for refitting, returning to traffic in 1926 with new smokeboxes, chimneys and bunkers. After only three years work on the parent line No. 1 (renumbered GW 674) was sold to Hodroyd Coal Co. where it once again became (H.C.C.) No. 1, and No. 3 went to the Ashington Coal Co., both lasting out until the 1940's. A.D.'s No. 2 only lasted until 1926. No. 4 went in 1929 and No. 5 as early as 1925. *Figure* 2 shows pre-GWR days and *Figure* 4 "lettered out" Great Western and numbered 675.

Figure 3

Figure 2

Figure 4

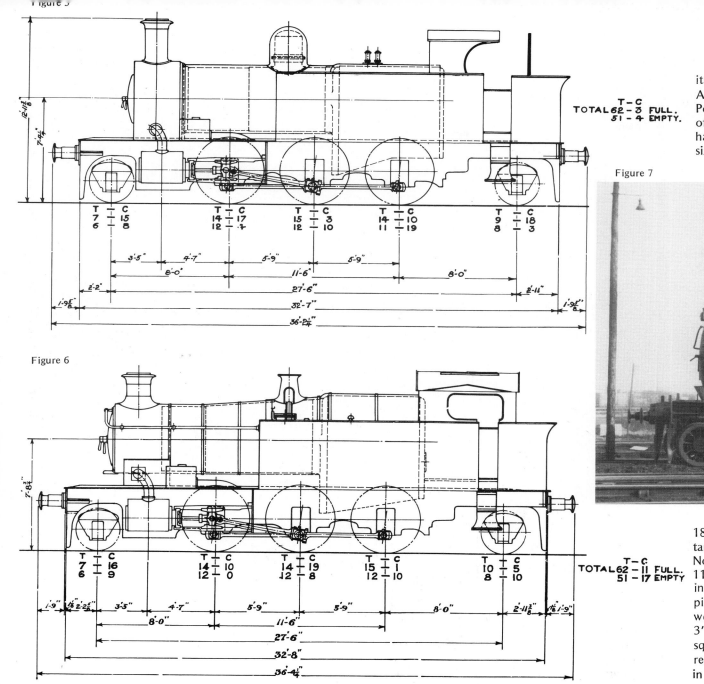

Figure 5

Figure 6

T—C
TOTAL 62—3 FULL.
51—4 EMPTY.

T	C
7	15
6	8

T	C
14	17
12	7

T	C
15	3
12	10

T	C
14	10
11	19

T	C
9	18
8	3

3'-5" 4'-7" 5'-9" 5'-9"
8'-0" 11'-6" 8'-0"
2'-2" 27'-6" 2'-11"
1'-9⅝" 32'-7" 1'-9⅝"
36'-2¼"

T	C
7	16
6	9

T	C
14	10
12	0

T	C
14	19
12	8

T	C
15	1
12	10

T	C
10	5
8	10

T—C
TOTAL 62—11 FULL.
51—17 EMPTY.

1'-9" 4½" 2'-2½" 3'-5" 4'-7" 5'-9" 5'-9" 8'-0" 2'-11¾" 6½" 1'-9"
8'-0" 11'-6"
27'-6"
32'-8"
36'-4¼"

In 1903 the Mersey Railway decided to go electric and so many of its steam locomotives were put up for sale. At the same time the Alexandra Dock Railway were concerned about the working of the Pontypridd — Newport trains, as the Taff Vale Railway had opted out of this duty. It was therefore most opportune to secure ten large second-hand tank engines at bargain prices from the Liverpool area. The first six engines were of the 2-6-2T classification built by Beyer-Peacock in

Figure 7

1887 and were equipped with condensing pipes into the side water tanks. When taken over by the A.D. Railway this gear was removed and Nos. 6-11 appeared as shown in *Figure* 5 to Diagram V. One engine, No. 11 (renumbered GWR 1204) was rebuilt at Swindon with a No. 3 boiler in 1922-3 and was used with a new Diagram 'Z' as at *Figure* 6 and a picture of the rebuild is to be seen in *Figure* 7. A few leading dimensions were: driving wheels 4' 7" at 5' 9" + 5' 9" centres, pony truck wheels 3' 0½", boiler 10' 2" + 4' 6" + 4' 4" pressed to 160 lbs, grate area 23.5 sq ft, a working weight of 62 tons 9 cwt. As can be seen from the register all these locomotives had a short life, Nos. 7-11 being withdrawn in 1929 and No. 6 lasting until 1932.

W5408

Figure 8

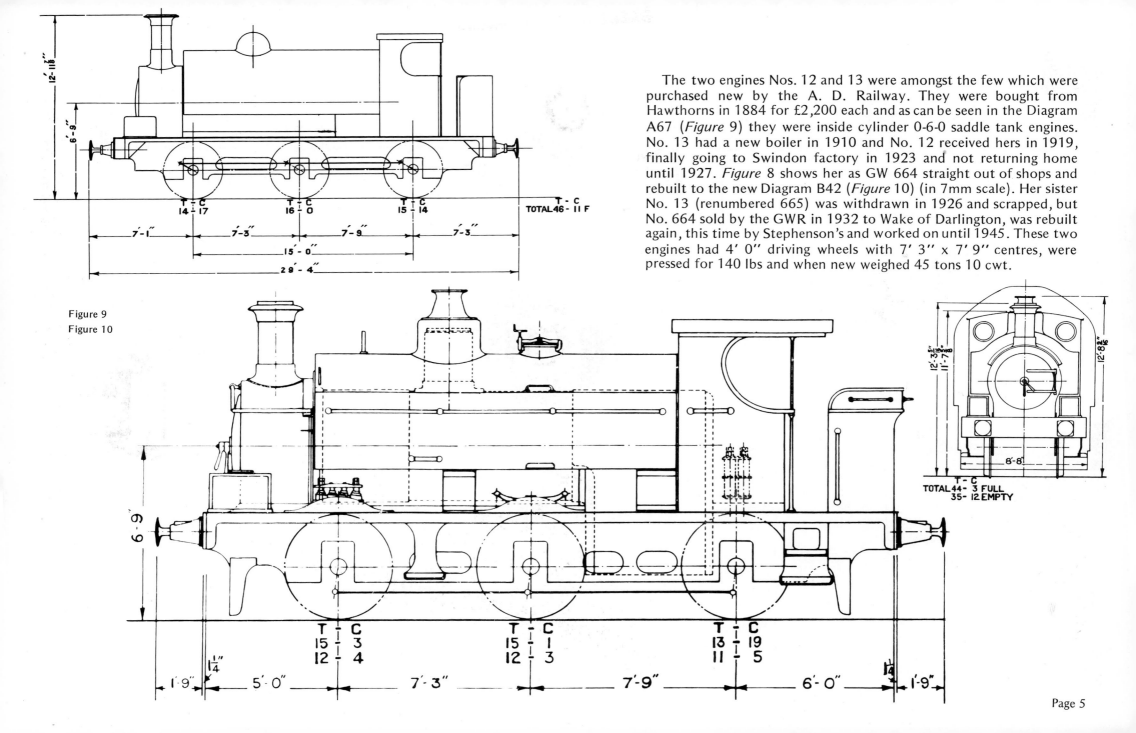

The two engines Nos. 12 and 13 were amongst the few which were purchased new by the A. D. Railway. They were bought from Hawthorns in 1884 for £2,200 each and as can be seen in the Diagram A67 (*Figure* 9) they were inside cylinder 0-6-0 saddle tank engines. No. 13 had a new boiler in 1910 and No. 12 received hers in 1919, finally going to Swindon factory in 1923 and not returning home until 1927. *Figure* 8 shows her as GW 664 straight out of shops and rebuilt to the new Diagram B42 (*Figure* 10) (in 7mm scale). Her sister No. 13 (renumbered 665) was withdrawn in 1926 and scrapped, but No. 664 sold by the GWR in 1932 to Wake of Darlington, was rebuilt again, this time by Stephenson's and worked on until 1945. These two engines had 4' 0" driving wheels with 7' 3" x 7' 9" centres, were pressed for 140 lbs and when new weighed 45 tons 10 cwt.

Figure 9
Figure 10

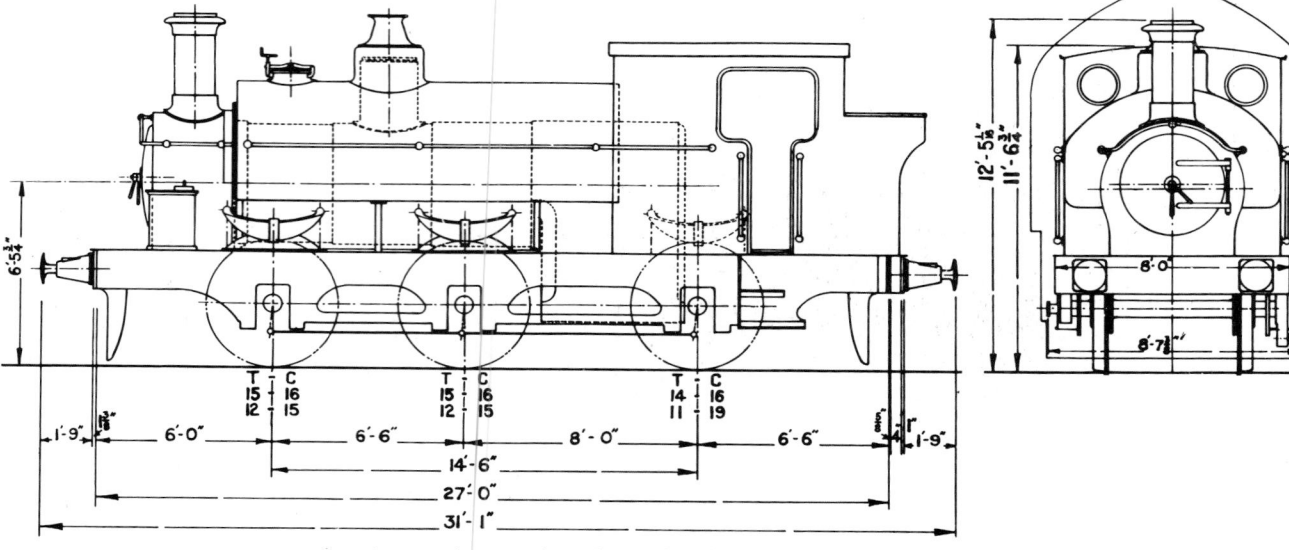

Figure 11

Figure 12

Another engine purchased new by the Company was No. 15 bought from R. Stephenson & Co. in 1885 for £1,540. She was a double framed saddle tank with six coupled wheels, and the small water tank only covering part of the boiler. 4' 6" driving wheels were fitted at 6' 6" x 8' 0" spacing and the boiler pressure was 140 lbs sq ft. The original diagram issued by the GWR was A69 (*Figure* 14) but upon being rebuilt with a new boiler, smokebox, tank, bunker and fittings between 1924-27 she emerged to Diagram B43 as at *Figure* 11. Placed on the sales list in 1929 she went to Ocean Coal Co. at Treharris, and carried on until 1947 under her original number 668. No. 21 whose diagram is shown in *Figure* 13 was another R. Stephenson engine, one of a pair purchased in 1894 for £3,708. These two, Nos. 20-21, became GW Nos. 669-70 and were similar to No. 15 (668), except that they had Ramsbottom safety valves instead of the spring balance type on No. 15. Ross pop valves were fitted when the boilers were changed in 1916/18. Both engines were withdrawn in 1925-6, No. 670 going also to the Ocean Coal Co. where she worked until 1947.

Figure 13

Figure 14

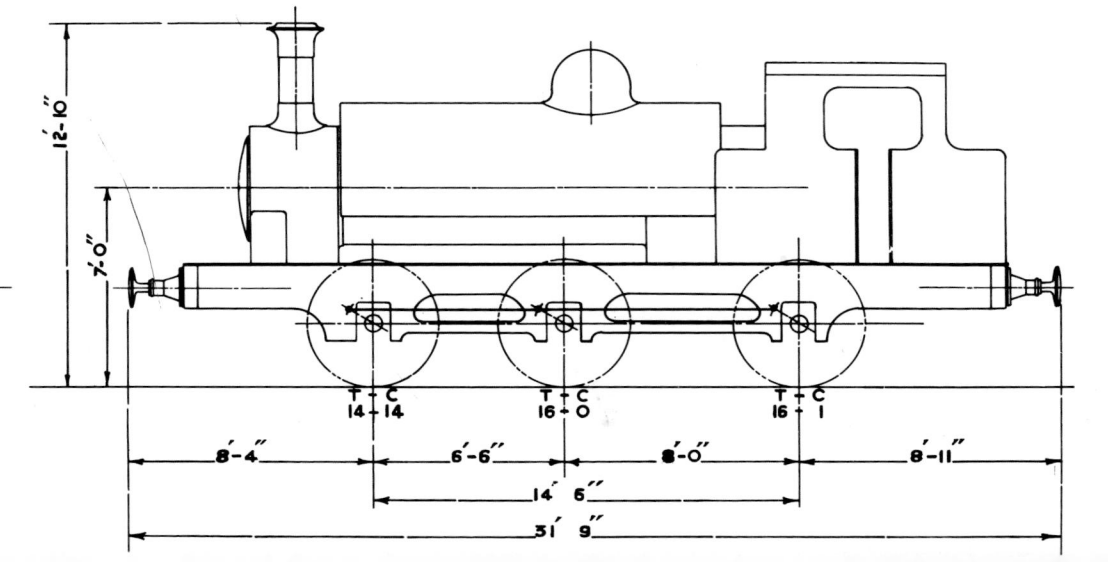

Figure 15

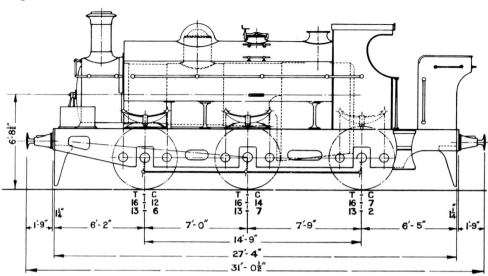

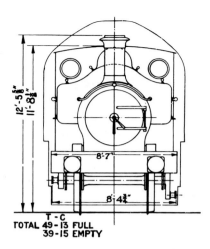

Hawthorn Leslie & Co. supplied Nos. 16 & 17 in 1889. They were again 0-6-0 saddle tank engines, the tanks having flattened sides with rounded tops. Double frames were used with access holes cut in the side plates. 4' 6" driving wheels were fitted and spaced at 7' 0" + 7' 9". Boiler pressure was 160 lbs with a weight of 50 tons. New boilers were installed in 1907 and their appearance upon entering the GWR stock is shown on Diagram A.71 (*Figure* 17). No. 17 (GW 672) only lasted until 1924 when she was stripped of her boiler and scrapped. The reconditioned boiler was passed to her sister No. 16 (GW 671) which then emerged in 1927 to the new Diagram B.41 seen in *Figure* 15. She was finally cut up in 1938.

Figure 16

Figure 17

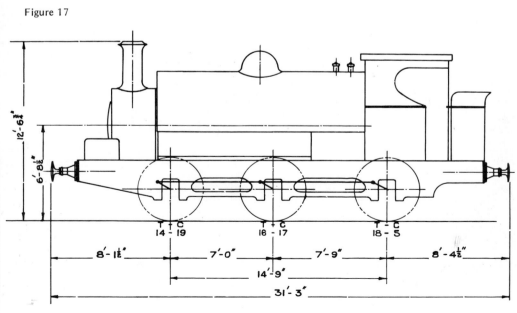

Figure 18

Amongst all other locomotive builders, Messrs Pecketts products were also represented on the A.D. Railway in the form of two small 0-6-0 saddle tanks. Purchased for £2,130 in 1890-91, these two became A.D. Railways No. 18 and 19 (eventually GW 679-80). Very small engines, only 23' over buffers, they were fitted with 3' 6" wheels set at 4' 10½" centres. Boiler pressure was 160 lbs and the weight was only 29 tons. Given the Diagram A.73 (*Figure 19*) by the GWR when taken over, they endured various modifications and eventually had a new Diagram B.1 (*Figure 20*) (notice the official diagram was redrawn on the tracing linen over the A.73 figure). No. 680 saw service at Oswestry in her Great Western days and No. 679 even had a spell on the dock line at Weymouth. She was sold out to a colliery in 1929 and worked on until 1953, No. 680 going five years earlier in 1948.

Figure 19

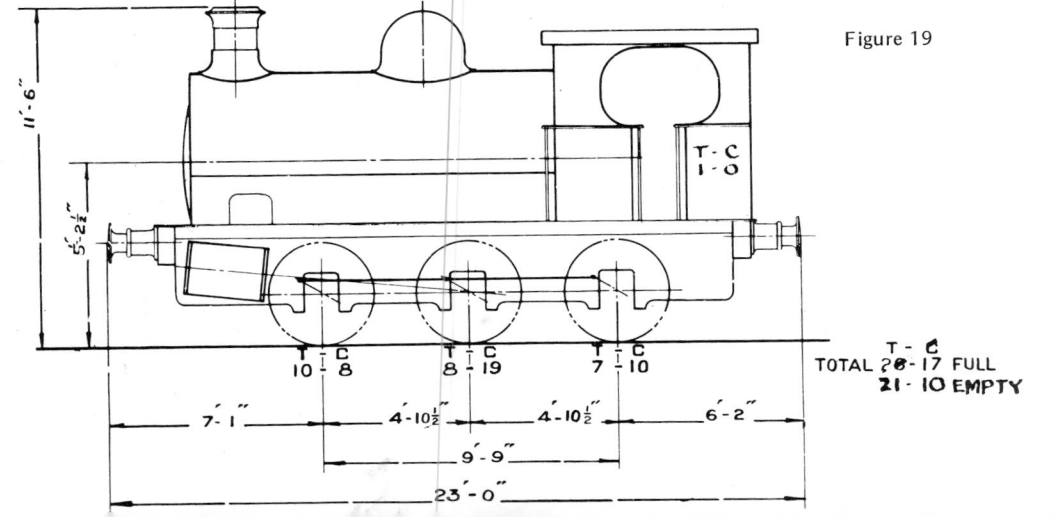

Figure 20

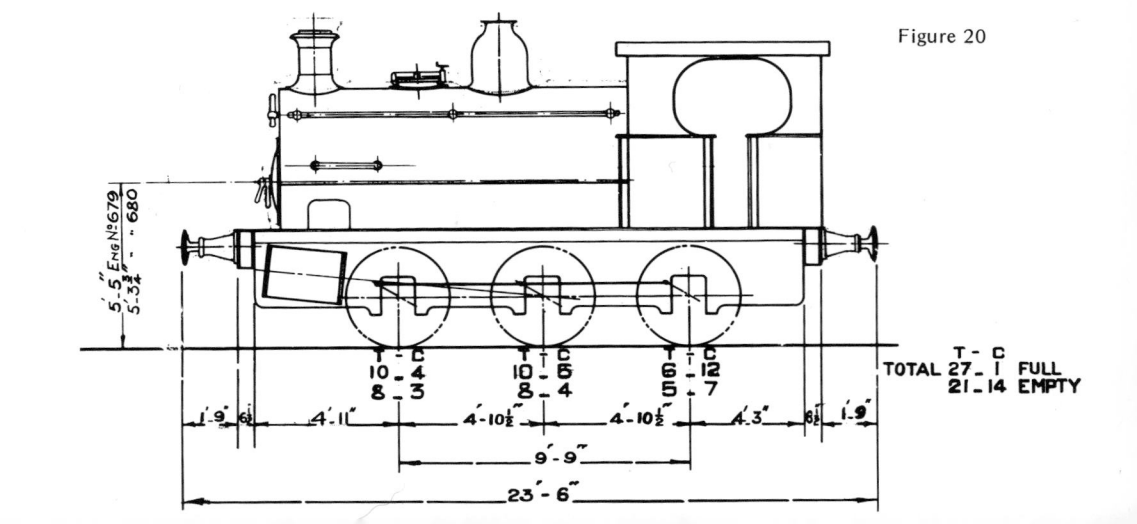

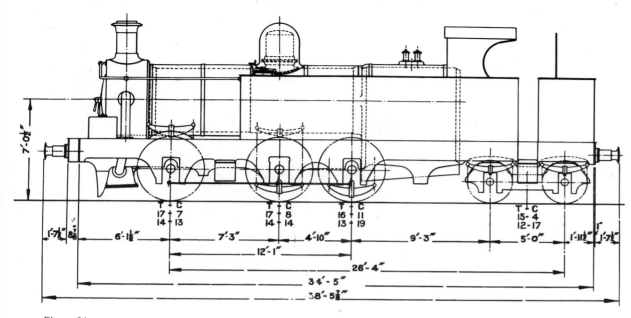

Figure 21

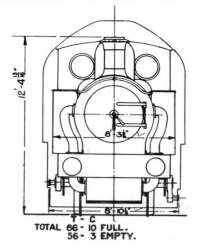

TOTAL 66-10 FULL.
56-3 EMPTY.

Three more large engines from the Mersey Railway were delivered to the A.D. Railway in January of 1905. These were also built by Beyer-Peacock in 1885 and were of the rather strange configuration 0-6-4T. Outside framing was used for the 4' 7" driving wheels, spaced at 7' 3" and 4' 10", whilst the small bogie of 5' wheelbase and 3' 0" wheels, had inside frames and bearings. As with their 2-6-2T sisters these engines were originally fitted with condensing gear and were named. No. 22 was *Fox*, No. 23 *Duke of Lancaster*, No. 24 *Earl of Chester*. They were rebuilt between 1910 and 1915 and allotted Diagram A (*Figure* 27) at the grouping. However, Nos. 22 and 23 were both withdrawn in 1923, and only No. 24 (GW No. 1346) survived to have a reconditioned boiler in 1924, so that with small changes she was turned out to a new Diagram 'D' shown at *Figure* 22. No. 1346, alias No. 24, was finally scrapped in 1928, having been on the sales list for 12 months and not sold.

Figure 22

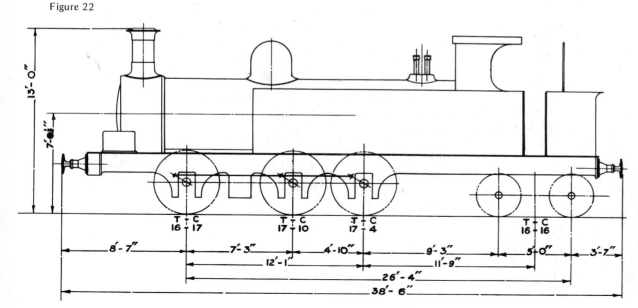

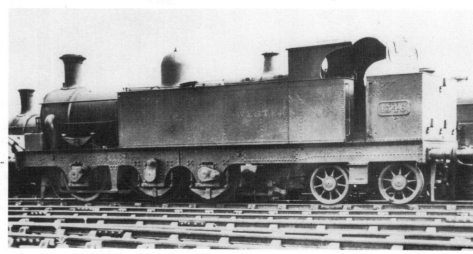

Figure 23

Figure 24

The final tank engine to come from Mersey Railway sale was the Kitson built *Burcot*, which became A.D. Railway No. 25. She was a 2-6-2T with outside cylinders, one of three similar built originally in 1892. The design was almost the same as the Beyer-Peacock 2-6-2T engines, except that in No. 25 the front and rear carrying wheels were on radial axles instead of pony trucks and the smokebox was extended beyond the saddles to form a drum head style.

Figure 26

The Diagram allotted was the Swindon U. and in the two *Figures* 25 & 26 it is possible to compare the diagram of the Kitson engine with No. 7 (GW. 1208), the photograph of the rebuilt Beyer-Peacock. After many modifications at Swindon No. 1199 (as No. 25 became) was finally withdrawn in 1931.

Figure 25

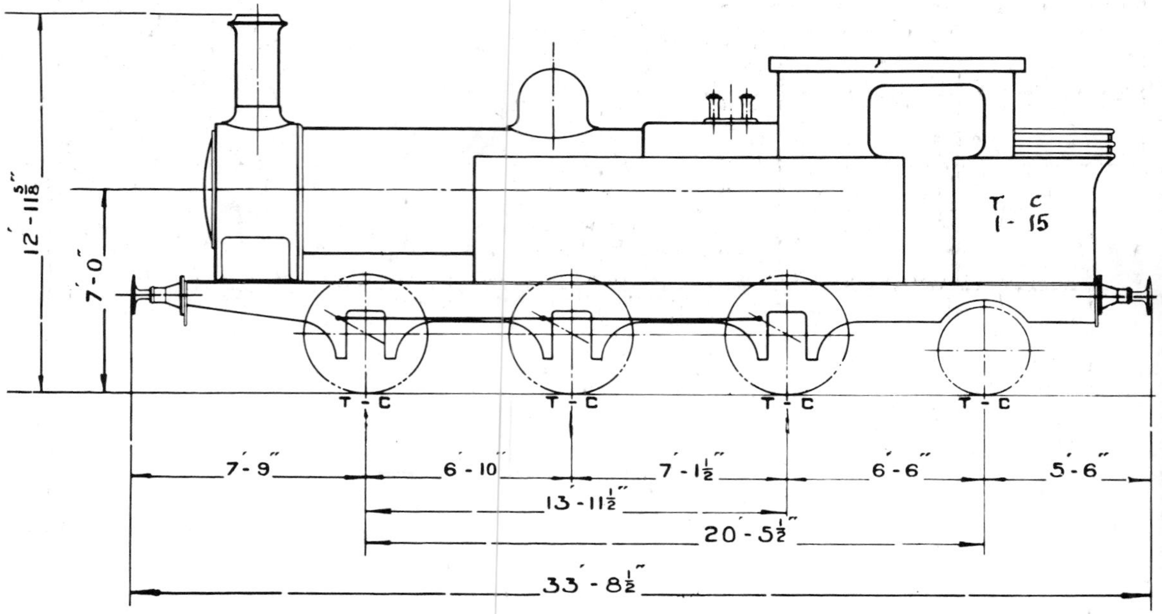

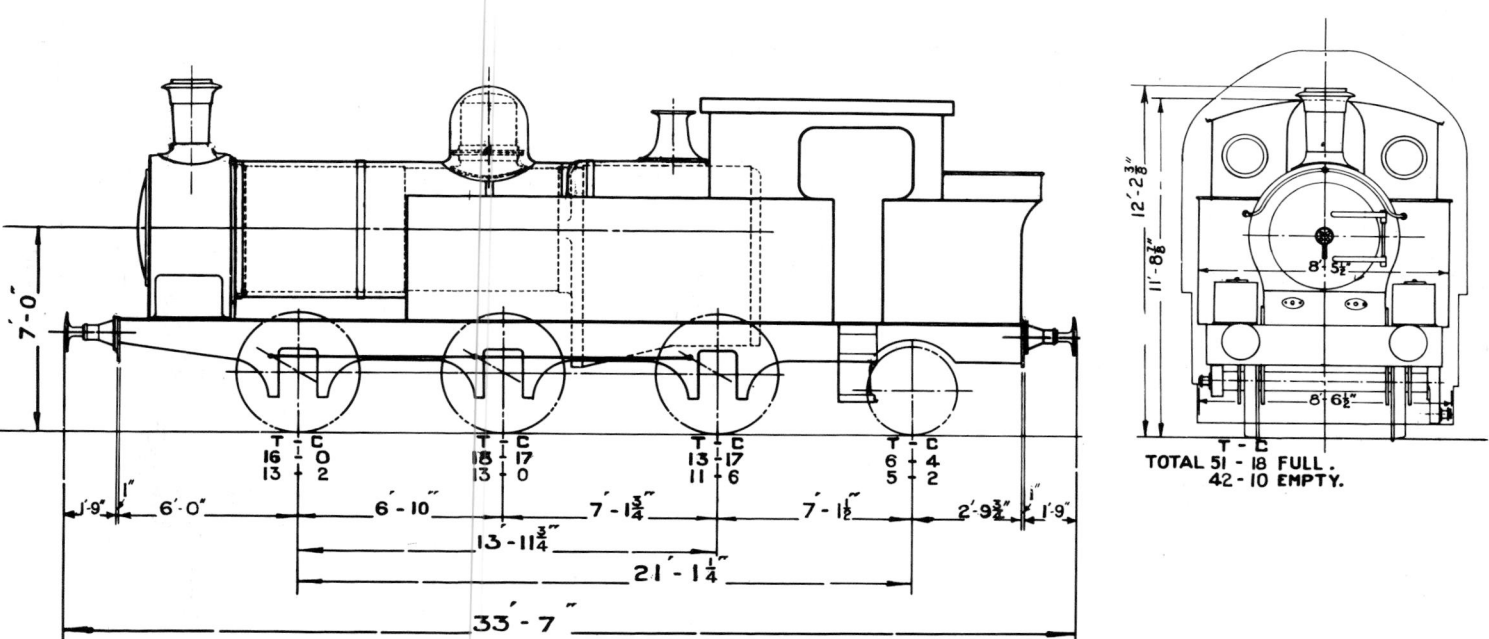

Figure 27

Figure 29

T C
1 - 15

12'-11⅝"
7'-0"

7'-9"   6'-10"   7'-1½"   6'-6"   5'-6"
13'-11½"
20'-5½"
33'-8½"

T-C   T-C   T-C   T-C

Figure 28

7'-0"

16   18   13   6
13   17   17   4
2   13   11   5   2
    0   6   2

1'-9" 6'-0"   6'-10"   7'-1¾"   7'-1½"   2'-9¾" 1'-9"
13'-11¾"
21'-1¼"
33'-7"

T C   T C   T C   T C

12'-2⅜"
11'-8⅞"
8'-5½"
8'-6½"
T-C
TOTAL 51 - 18 FULL.
42 - 10 EMPTY.

No. 26 (GW. 663) was an engine with a long history. She was built in 1868 by the Worcester Engine Co. for the Metropolitan Railway. She was at that time a double framed 0-6-0 side tank with 4' driving wheels, intended for an extension of the Metropolitan to Hampstead Village. As it turned out, the extension was abandoned, and this engine was eventually sold to the Sirhowy Railway in 1873. She was sold to the A.D. Railway Co. in 1879, rebuilt in 1891, renumbered to 26 in 1905, reboilered again in 1919 and in 1921 was sent to Hawthorn Leslie to be rebuilt as an 0-6-2T type with overall cab and longer bunker. In this condition, she was given the Diagram A.14 (*Figure* 27) and finally in 1924 Swindon modified her for the last time as seen in Diagram A.28, *Figures* 28 and 29. Put up for sale in 1926, there were no bidders and she was cut up in October 1928.

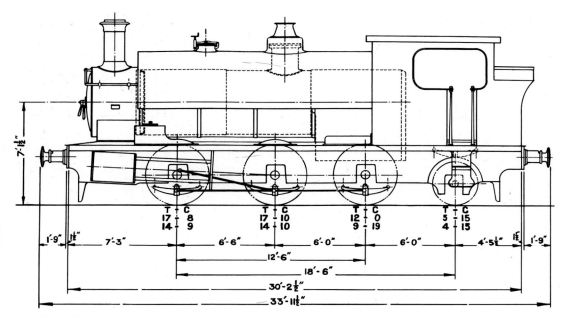

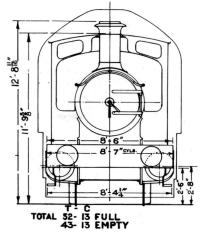

TOTAL 52-13 FULL
43-13 EMPTY

Figure 30

The need for heavy shunting tanks in 1908 to cope with the increased coal export traffic at the docks led to the purchase of three outside-cylindered 0-6-2 saddle tanks from Messrs Andrew Barclay & Co. Costing £2,120 each, they were delivered in December 1908 and numbered 29-31. They were heavy engines, weighing 53 tons with driving wheels of 4′ 3″ set at 6′ 6″ and 6 foot centres and with trailing wheels of 3′ 0″ diameter. Full length tanks were fitted and the GWR gave them Diagram X. When in 1923/4 they were taken into Swindon, given shorter tanks, GWR smokeboxes and adapted safety valve bonnets, the Diagram became A.25 and the engines were renumbered 190-2 (*Figure* 30). All three ran large mileages, No. 191 going first in 1934, whilst Nos. 190 and 192 lasted into the mid-1940s.

Figure 31

Figure 32

T - C
TOTAL 53-1 FULL.

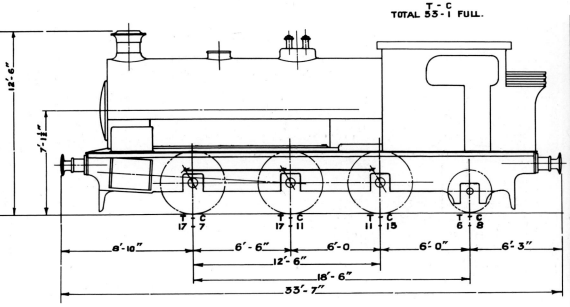

Figure 33

Figure 34

The three Andrew Barclay engines are seen here in Great Western ownership, No. 190 (ex A.D. No. 29) in *Figure* 33, No. 191 (ex A.D. No. 30) in *Figure* 34, and No. 192 (ex A.D. No. 31) in the lower illustration (*Figure* 35). Note the flat sided saddle tanks, and the square rear windows to the cabs.

Figure 35

This page shows the three stages of the Alexandra Dock 2-6-2T engines which were purchased from the Mersey Railway. In the upper photograph (*Figure* 36) one of these locomotives is shown running on the parent company's track the Mersey Railway, as their No. 13 *Brunlees*. The middle picture (*Figure* 37) shows No. 25 as she was on the Alexandra Dock Railway. The same engine is seen in the lower illustration (*Figure* 38) as GW 1199 in Great Western ownership.

Figure 36

Figure 37

Figure 38

Figure 39

Page 16

Figure 40

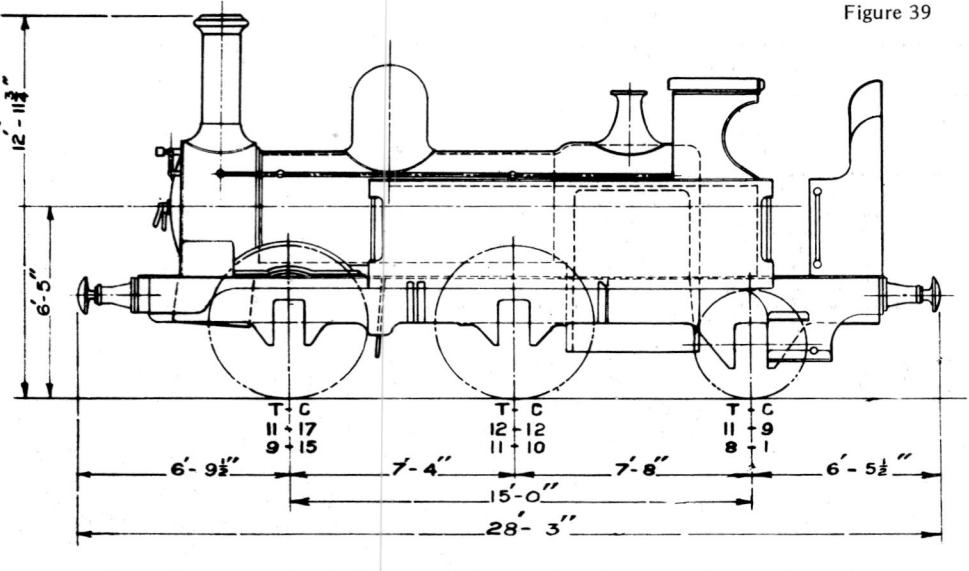

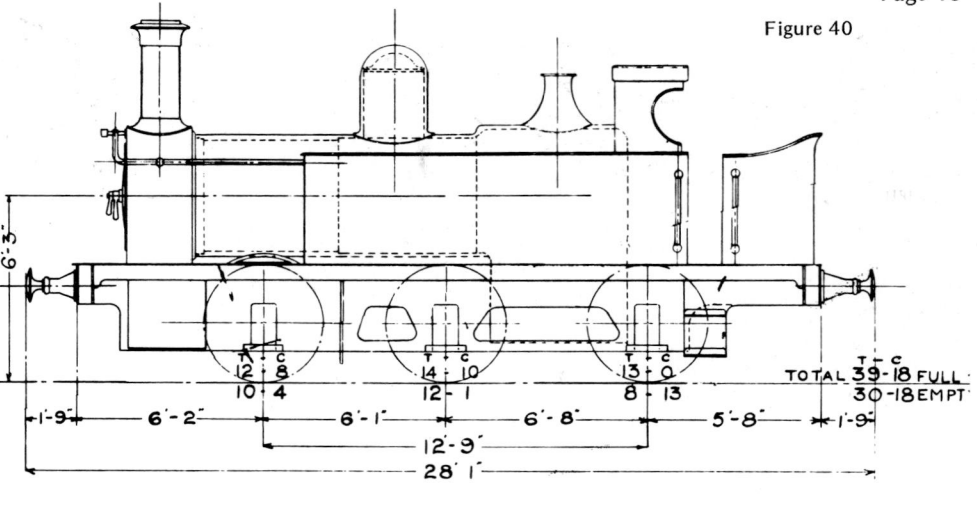

The Alexandra Dock Railway also purchased several locomotives from the Great Western Railway before the grouping, which meant that these engines, after a spell in the stock lists of the A.D. Railway finally came back into the ownership of their original builder. One of the first of these was one of the '517' class of 0-4-2T engines built at Wolverhampton. No. 1426 went to the A.D. Railway in 1911 and was given their number 14, which was changed back to her original '1426' in 1922 when once again in GWR hands. Her diagram is shown in *Figure* 39 as K. No. 32 was originally built by Fletcher Jennings for the Severn & Wye Railway in 1873. It was rebuilt at Swindon in 1896 and became No. 1356, the property of the Bute Works Supply Co. This little 0-6-0T carried the name of *Will Scarlett*, but when purchased by the A.D. Railway in 1912, she lost her name and became simply No. 32 (*Figure* 40). When restored to the GWR at the grouping, she again became 1356, and was withdrawn in 1923. No. 33, a Wolverhampton 0-6-0 saddle tank (*Figure* 41) of the '850' class, was purchased by the A.D. Railway in 1913. It was rebuilt with a large tank with a capacity of 1013 gallons and when coming back on to the GWR lists in 1922, had a diagram all to itself, namely A.97, and regained its original number 993. The engine eventually received pannier tanks and lasted until 1930. The other two Great Western engines purchased by the A.D. Railway were Nos. 1679 and 1683. Bought in 1906 for £800 each they became Nos. 27 and 28. These locomotives were of the '1661' class built at Swindon and like the other 'Western' engines before them, regained their old numbers at the grouping. Both lasted until 1926 and were allotted the Diagram A.98 (*Figure* 42).

Figure 41

Figure 42

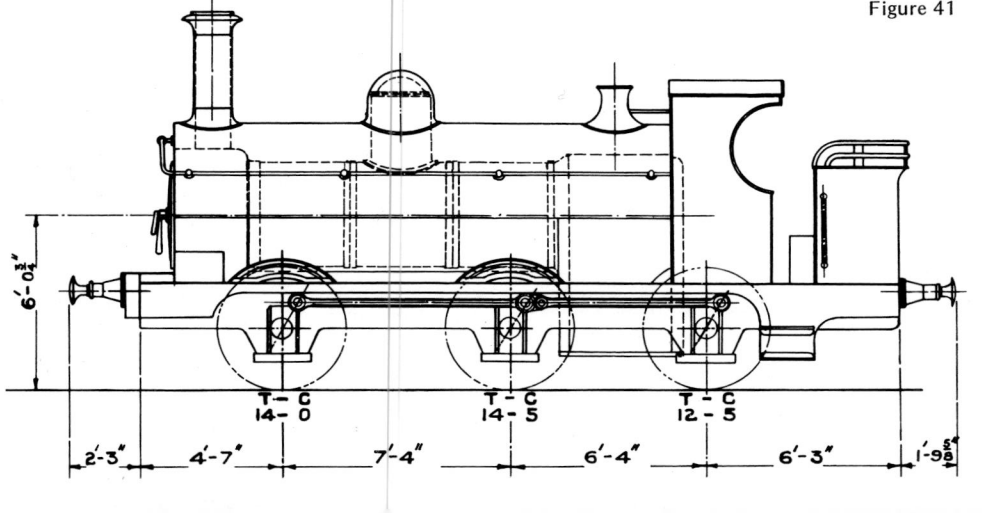

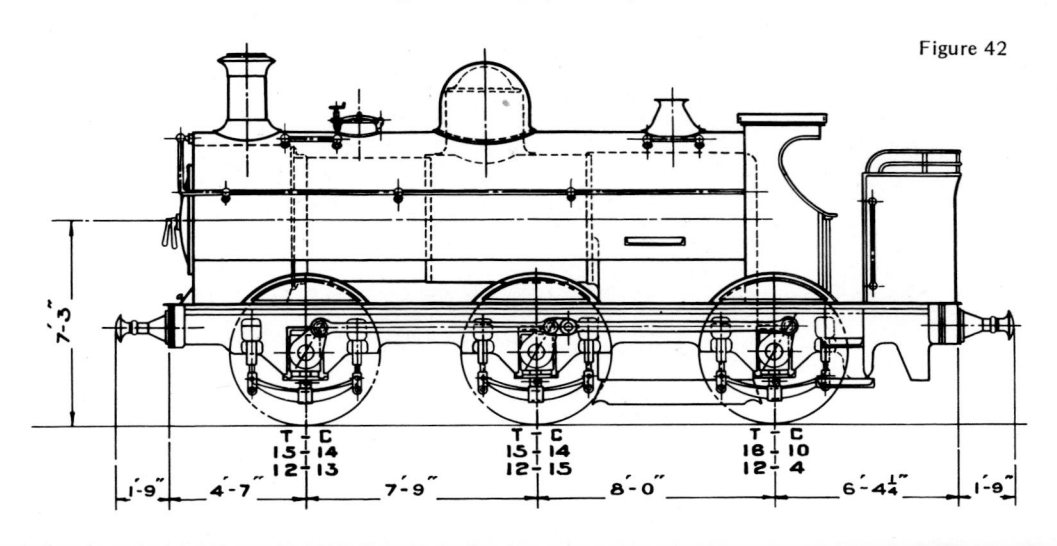

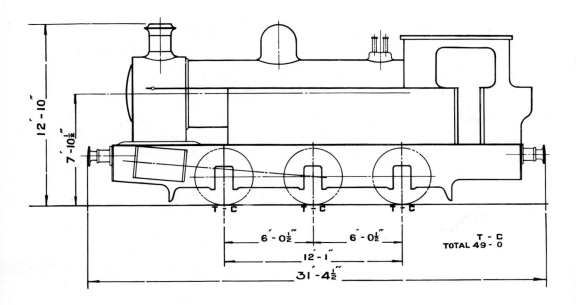

Figure 43

Figure 44

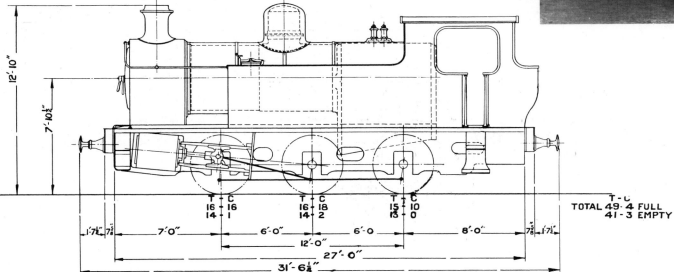

Figure 45

After the 1914-18 War two outside-cylindered 0-6-0 side tank engines were purchased from Messrs Kerr Stuart & Co. who built them to an order for the Railway Operating Division of The Royal Engineers. They had driving wheels of 4' 0" diameter set at 6' 0" and 6' 0" centres, with a weight of approximately 49 tons. Given numbers 34 and 35 by the A.D. Railway it was only three years before they were received on to the GWR list and were then renumbered 666 and 667. At first they were given the Diagram A.68 (*Figure* 43) but when altered slightly at Swindon in 1923/4 the diagram was changed to B.13 (*Figure* 44). Being comparatively modern engines, these two lasted right into British Railways ownership, No. 667 going in 1954 and 666 in 1955.

Figure 46

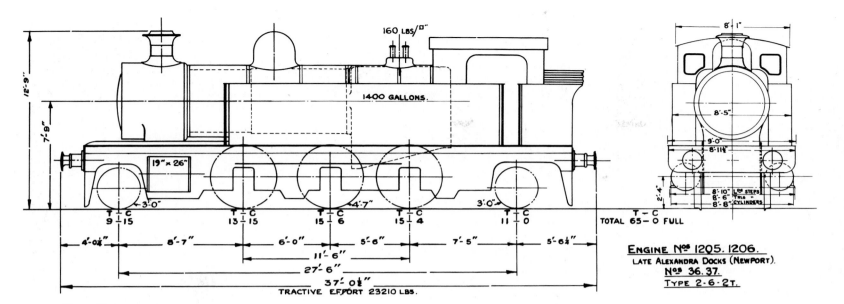

160 LBS/□"

1400 GALLONS.

19"×26"

12'-9"

7'-9"

3'-0"

4'-7"

3'-0"

T—C
9 — 15

T—C
13 — 15

T—C
15 — 6

T—C
15 — 4

T—C
11 — 0

T—C
TOTAL 65—0 FULL

4'-0¼" 8'-7" 6'-0" 5'-6" 7'-5" 5'-6¼"

11'-6"

27'-6"

37'-0½"

TRACTIVE EFFORT 23210 LBS.

Figure 47

8'-1"

8'-5"

9'-0"
8'-11¼"

2'-4"

8'-10" Lᵈ STEPS
8'-6" Tᴷˢ
8'-8" CYLINDERS

ENGINE Nᵒˢ 1205. 1206.
LATE ALEXANDRA DOCKS (NEWPORT).
Nᵒˢ 36. 37.
TYPE 2·6·2T.

The last engines built for the Alexandra Dock & Railway were a pair of 2-6-2T locomotives, based closely on the design of the Mersey Railway engines of 1887. These last two were ordered from Messrs Hawthorn-Leslie & Co. and delivered to Newport in 1920. As can be seen from the diagram and photographs, Belpaire fireboxes were fitted with Ross pop valves and the only major change the GWR made, was to replace the Ross pop valve with a Swindon pattern safety valve, shown in *Figure* 48. Both engines lasted into the 1950s. No. 36 (renumbered 1205) ended her days at Cardiff and Llantrisant whilst No. 37 (1206) saw the last of her service at Hereford Shed.

Figure 48

TROJAN

1340

Figure 49

Figure 50

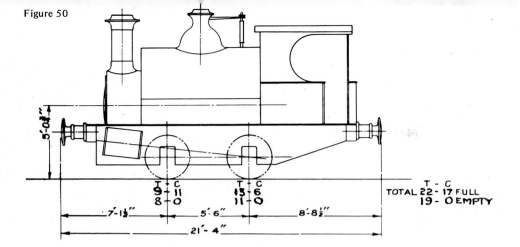

Figure 51

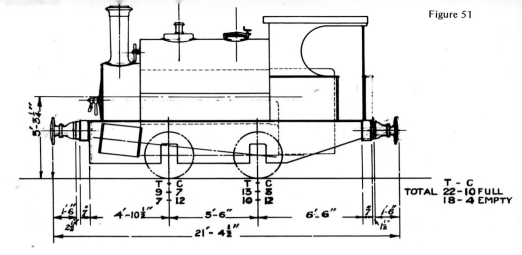

The two smallest, and perhaps the two most famous locomotives of the Alexandra Dock and Railway, were without doubt the unnumbered engines *Trojan* and *Alexandra*. Three such engines were purchased from Messrs Dunn & Shute in 1903, the third being named *Active*. These three had been used by Messrs Dunn & Shute in the construction of Newport's Town Dock, but the little Hunslet of 1882 *Active* was passed on in 1915 to the Newport & Abercarn Colliery at Crumlin. This left *Trojan* and *Alexandra* to be passed into GWR ownership in 1921. *Alexandra's* builders and origin are shrouded in mystery, see page 22 (*Figures 52 & 53*). All that can be stated is that driving wheels were 3' 0" diameter set at 6' 3" centres, outside cylinders 12" x 19" with a boiler of 8' 6" x 3' 5½"

and a total weight of 18 tons 8 cwt. She entered the factory in 1922 and spent three years there before being turned out with various changes. Wheels were shown as 3' 2" and the boiler contained 115 x 1" tubes instead of 82 x 2" as before and so on. These alterations made the little engine 1 ton heavier than before. Her name was removed and she was numbered 1341, working on until being scrapped at Caerphilly in 1946. Her sister *Trojan* was an Avonside Engine Co. of 1897 to the design seen in diagram K (*Figure 50*). She also had 3' 0" wheels but a shorter wheelbase of 5' 6" only. 1922 saw her at Swindon for an overhaul of six months duration and on returning to service she was allotted a new Diagram P (*Figure 51*). This well-known little tank roamed around extensively, not only in South Wales but also at Oswestry and in the late 1920s she worked at Park Royal and Greenford. She was sold in 1934 and moved to various collieries and was last heard of at Tamworth in 1965.

Figure 52

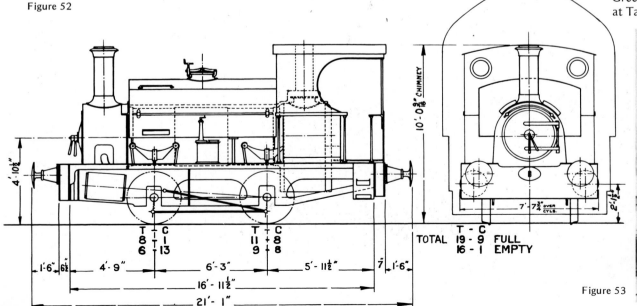

Figure 53

The BARRY RAILWAY COMPANY

The Barry Railway came into being under an Act of 1884 and started operating in 1888. The reason for its inception was the inability of the Taff Vale and Cardiff Railways to handle the vast coal exports to the Docks at Penarth and Cardiff. Firstly the colliery owners raised the capital necessary for the building of the new port facilities at Barry, and secondly, The Barry Dock & Railway Co. as it was called initially, was launched in order to connect these new docks with the collieries in the Aberdare & Rhondda Valleys. The main line of the Barry Railway ran from Cadoxton in a northerly direction to Trehafod Junction where it joined the Taff Vale branch between Pontypridd and Treherbert, a distance of 18¾ miles. A mineral branch ran from Tanteg Junction to Treforest Junction where a connection with the Taff Vale Railway was made. Another branch ran round to Barry Island and was used for passenger traffic and connected with the steamers there. The main line to the north crossed the GWR at St Fagans, and loops from north and south connected at this point. Together with running powers granted over the Brecon & Merthyr Railway and Cardiff more than 65 miles of route was obtained. To give some idea of the traffic conveyed by the Barry Railway, in 1913 11 million tons of coal were moved from the mines to the docks for shipment. To handle this a large locomotive stud was needed, and upon being merged into the GWR in 1922, the total stood at 148 arranged as follows.

Builder	Barry No.	GWR No.	Type	Diagram		Withdrawn
Sharp-Stewart	1- 5	699-700/2/3/6	0-6-0T	A80	(B9)	1926-32
,, ,,	6- 20	198-201/3/4/6-214	0-6-2T	Z	(A24)	1922-48
,, ,,	21- 22	1322-23	2-4-2T	M	(S)	1926-28
,, ,,	23- 32	223-32	0-6-2T	Z	(A24)	1932-47
Hudswell-Clarke	33- 34	781-82	0-6-0T	A82	(B5)	1932-39
Sharp-Stewart	35- 36	1387-88	0-8-0	A		1927-28
,, ,,	37	708	0-6-0T	A81	(B6)	1932
,, ,,	38- 46	233-5/8/40-44	0-6-2T	A1	(A21/24/36)	1932-48
,, ,,	47- 49	710-12	0-6-0T	A81	(B19)	1932-34
Hudswell-Clarke	50- 53	783-4/713/785	0-6-0T	A81/82	(B21)	1932-49
Vulcan Foundry	54- 63	245-254	0-6-2T	A1	(A21/36)	1932-49
,, ,,	64- 65	714-15	0-6-0T	A81	(B19)	1932-34
,, ,,	66- 69	2-4/9	0-4-4T	D		1925-29
Sharp-Stewart	70- 72	716-18	0-6-0T	A81	(B19)	1932-34
,, ,,	73- 78	255-60	0-6-2T	A1		1932-49
,, ,,	79- 85	1380-86	0-8-2T	C		1925-30
Hudswell-Clarke	86- 91	1311-16	2-4-2T	M	(T)	1926-30
Sharp-Stewart	92- 93	1389-90	0-8-0	A		1927-30
,, ,,	94- 98	1317-21	2-4-2T	M	(R)	1926-30
,, ,,	99-104	719-24	0-6-0T	A81	(B19)	1933-36
,, ,,	105-126	261-272/193-7/273-7	0-6-2T	A1Y	(A21)	1945-51
North British &	127-138	725-6/807/729/742/7	0-6-0T	A81	(B19)	1922-37
Hudswell-Clarke		754/76-80			(B6)	
Hudswell-Clarke	139-148	1347-1355/7	0-6-4T	B	(C)	1926

Figure 54

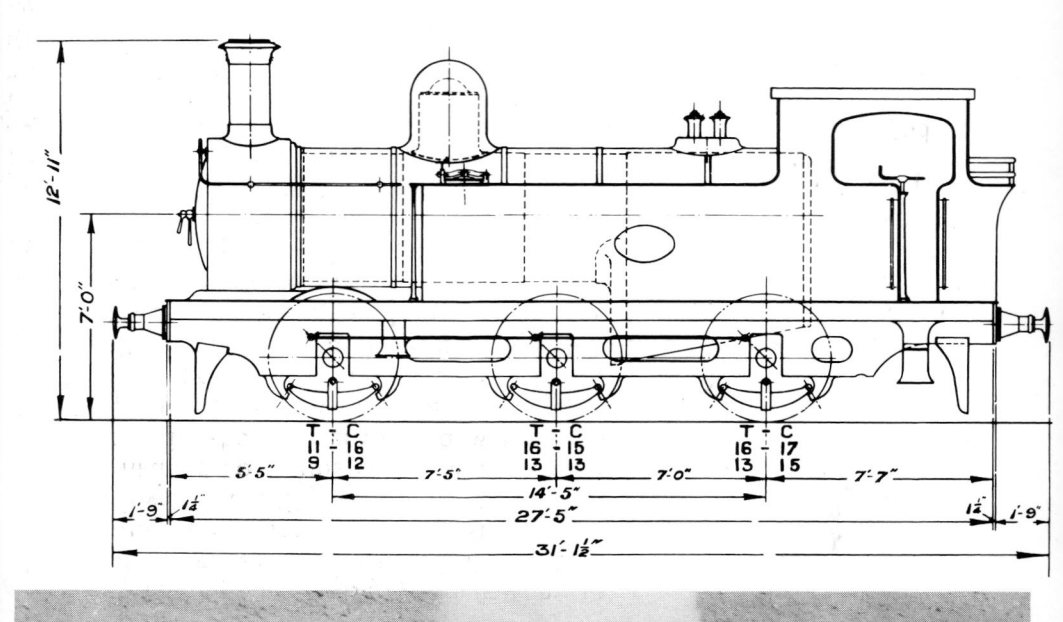

Figure 55

The first five locomotives delivered to the Barry Railway were Nos. 1-5 and were built by Sharp-Stewart & Co. to a design of John Wolfe Barry, one of the engineers concerned with the building of the Docks. These small side tanks had driving wheels of 4' 3" diameter set at 7' 3" and 7' 0" centres, and at first were responsible for the passenger service between Barry Docks and Cogan, but spent the rest of their Barry service at the Docks. On passing through Swindon shops Nos. 1, 3 and 5 received GW type smokeboxes and chimneys and as can be seen in *Figure 55*, No. 4 (later 703) was refitted with a taper chimney with capuchon. Renumbered 699/700/702/703/706 they were withdrawn between 1926 and 1931. No. 1 went to Coventry Colliery, No. 2 was sold to Dowlais Steelworks and No. 4 to Ocean Coal Co. *Figure 56* shows the latter at Ynysybwl before being scrapped in 1956. Whilst owned by the Barry Railway Co. this series of five was known as 'A' Class.

Figure 56

Figure 57

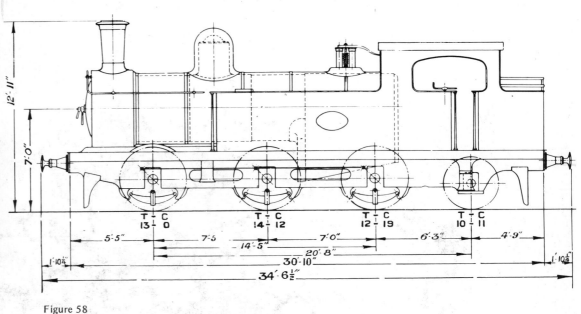

Figure 58

Figure 59

The 'B' Class of Barry Railway engines were a slightly larger version of the previous 'A' Class. Built by Sharp-Stewart also, a comparison will immediately reveal a strong family likeness in the outline. However the 'B's were of the 0-6-2 classification, to carry the slightly enlarged coal bunker with a capacity of 2 tons as compared with 30 cwt in the 'A' series, and with water capacity increased to 1400 gallons. Twenty five engines were built to this design between 1888-1890 and they were delivered in two batches. The first fifteen were 8" shorter in the front overhang than the subsequent ten. When absorbed into the GWR they were renumbered from 198 to 232 and several were rebuilt with the Swindon No. 9 boilers, together with the GWR type coal bunker. Swindon gave them the Diagram Z initially (*Figure* 58) and afterwards issued A.24 to cover the minor differences (*Figure* 60). *Figure* 59 shows No. 19 (GW 213) in 1948 with a Barry boiler fitted with GWR smokebox and chimney, whilst in *Figure* 57, No. 3 (GW 231) is seen in 1950 with the GWR standard Belpaire firebox, boiler, fittings and bunker.

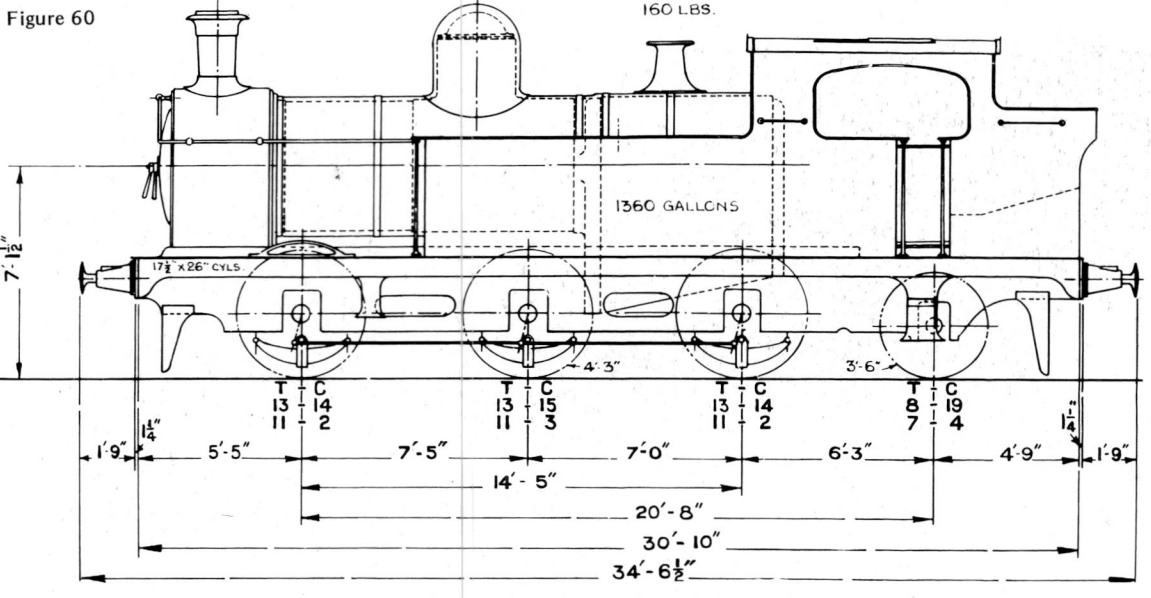

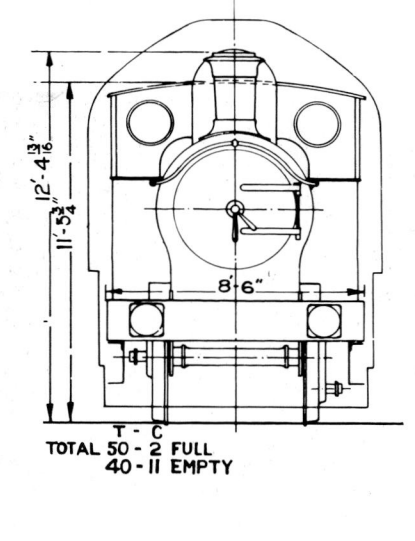

Figure 60

160 LBS.

1360 GALLONS

$17\frac{1}{2}$" x 26" CYLS.

$7'\text{-}1\frac{1}{2}$"

$1\frac{1}{4}$"

1'-9" 5'-5" 7'-5" 7'-0" 6'-3" 4'-9" 1'-9"

14'-5"

20'-8"

30'-10"

34'-$6\frac{1}{2}$"

T	C	T	C	T	C	T	C
13	14	13	15	13	14	8	19
11	2	11	3	11	2	7	4

4'-3" 3'-6"

$12'\text{-}4\frac{13}{16}$"

$11'\text{-}5\frac{1}{4}$"

8'-6"

T - C
TOTAL 50 - 2 FULL
40 - 11 EMPTY

The Swindon Diagram A.24 is seen in *Figure* 60 and follows closely the photograph in *Figure* 62 where No. 6 (GW 198) is seen at Swindon in 1948 showing the left hand side of the engine. To illustrate the opposite side and a little of the top detail No. 18 (GW 212) is seen at Swindon scrap yard in 1950 (*Figure* 61).

Figure 61

Figure 62

In these two pictures of the Barry 'B' Class taken in 1935 at Swindon, No. 29 (*Figure* 63) and No. 12 (*Figure* 64) are both seen, still with the Barry boilers that they received in 1901-2. At the time of the photographs these engines were on the sales list, but as no prospective buyers came forward, they were eventually scrapped. Note that the lettering can still be seen clearly on the side tanks and No. 12 has become GWR 206, and No. 29 is GWR 229.

Figure 64

Figure 63

Figure 65

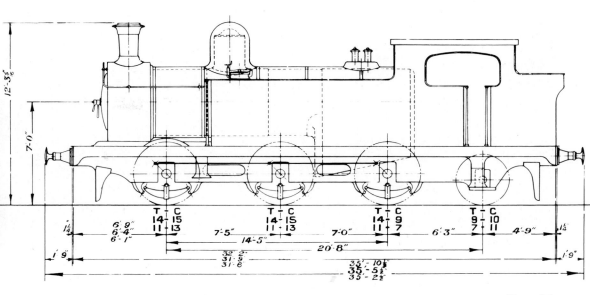

Figure 66

The next locomotives in size progression were known as the 'B1' series, being larger versions of the 'B' Class, as the 'B's were larger 'A' Class engines. The 'B1' Class was the most numerous on the Barry Railway, consisting as it did of 42 locomotives. The main difference between 'B' and 'B1' was in the water and coal capacities. The 'B1's water tanks held 230 gallons more than the 'B's, with 3cwt more coal space in the bunker. Messrs Sharp-Stewart made Nos. 38-46 in 1890 and Nos. 73-78 in 1894. Messrs Vulcan had the order for Nos. 54-63 in 1892, another batch Nos. 105-116 was built by Sharp-Stewarts in 1900, and five were constructed in Belgium in 1900 by Société Anonyme Franco-Belge, one of which, No. 126 was exhibited at the Paris Exhibition of that year. *Figure 65* shows No. 41 as GWR 238 in 1948 still carrying its Barry boiler, smokebox, chimney and coal bunker, but sporting a GWR safety valve bonnet. The whole class was renumbered by the GWR consecutively from 198 to 277 and the two diagrams were A.1 for the Barry boilered versions, and later A.36 (*Figure 67*) when fitted with Swindon No. 9 boilers.

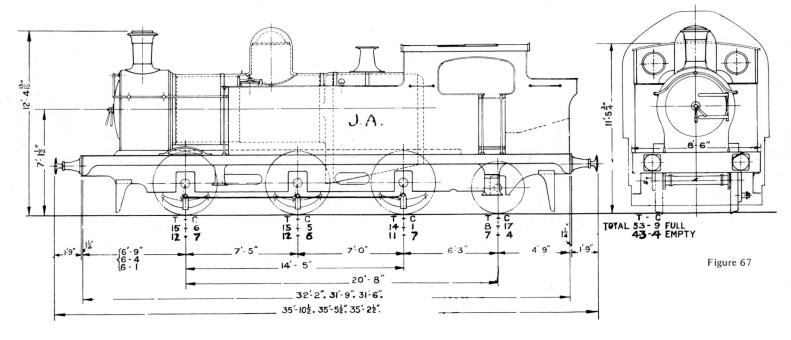

Figure 67

Figure 68   Figure 69

Figure 68 shows No. 45 (GW 243) carrying its own boiler, with GWR smokebox and capuchon fitted chimney at approximately 1936. No. 56 (GW 247) in *Figure* 70 also has its own boiler, smokebox and bunker, with GWR chimney, and whistles mounted alongside the safety valves! Completely refitted above the running plate, No. 59 (GW 250) is illustrated in *Figure* 69 looking thoroughly 'Westernized'. In this condition this engine lasted until December 1947 before being withdrawn.

Figure 70

Figure 71

No. 41 (GW 238) seen again (*Figure* 71) at Swindon just before being withdrawn in 1948, still retaining her own Barry boiler and fittings, but with the substitution of a 'Western' coal bunker in place of the original style. The 'B1' in *Figure* 72 is No. 76 (GW 258) which is in very similar condition to her sister above, but the Barry smokebox has been changed for the Swindon pattern. This engine lasted until the end of 1949 into British Railways ownership. Another of the class No. 109 (GW 265) also lasted into BR days, and she is seen, still retaining her own Barry bunker in 1950, on shunting duties at Swindon in the wagon yard (*Figure* 73).

Figure 72

Figure 73

Two pictures showing both sides of the 'B1' class at Barry shed in 1937. In *Figure 74*, No. 110 (GW 266) is seen in almost pure Barry condition, the only exception being the GW whistles sprouting out of the safety valve. In *Figure 75*, No. 40 (GW 235) is "almost Barry", but has the GWR chimney and dome cover mounted upon the Barry boiler.

Figure 75

Figure 74

On the next page are two final pictures of the 'B1' class 0-6-2T engines of the Barry Railway which were absorbed in the GWR in 1922. *Figure 76* shows Barry No. 78 which became GW 260 in 1935 at Swindon with GWR chimney and safety valve bonnet and smokebox, and *Figure 77* illustrates No. 124 (GW 275) one of the class which was built in Belgium in 1900. She is seen at Barry shed in 1937 fitted with Great Western standard No. 9 boiler, smokebox and fittings, plus GWR bunker. This engine worked on right into 1948.

▼

Figure 76

Figure 77

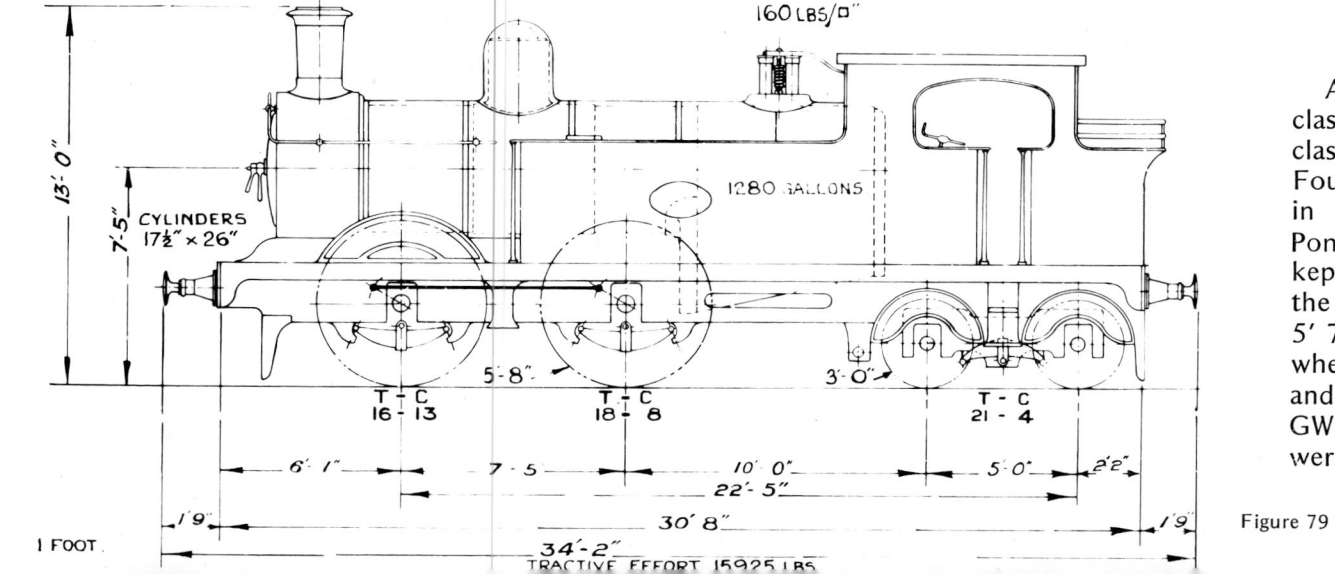

BARRY
67
RAILWAY

Figure 78

160 LBS/□

1280 GALLONS

13' 0"

7' 5"

CYLINDERS
17½" × 26"

5-8"

3' 0"

T - C
16 - 13

T - C
18 - 8

T - C
21 - 4

6' 1"

7' 5

10' 0"

5' 0"

2' 2"

22'-5"

1' 9"

30' 8"

1' 9"

1 FOOT

34'-2"

TRACTIVE EFFORT 15925 LBS

Figure 79

A small class of four engines numbered 66 to 69 formed the 'G' class of the Barry Railway. They were side tank engines of the 0-4-4T classification. Two, numbers 66-7 were products of the Vulcan Foundry in 1892, and the other pair 68-9 were from Sharp-Stewart in 1895; mainly used on the passenger service from Barry to Pontypridd, and Pontypridd to Cardiff. In their heyday they were kept in first class condition, with the polished brass domes setting off the reddish chocolate of the Barry livery. The driving wheels were 5' 7½", set at 7' 5" centres, with trailing bogie wheels of 3' having a wheelbase of 5' 0". Water capacity of the tanks was 1,400 gallons and 30 cwt of coal could be carried. They were renumbered by the GWR to 2, 3, 4 and 9, but little else was done to them, and all four were withdrawn by 1929.

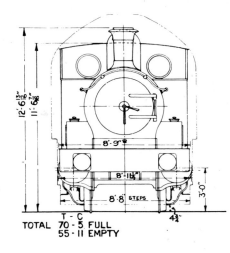

12'-6 13/16"
11'-6 5/16"

8'-9"

8'-1 1/2"

8'-8 STEPS

3'-0"

4 1/4"

T - C
TOTAL 70 - 5 FULL
55 - 11 EMPTY

1380 CLASS
TYPE 0-8-2T

LATE BARRY RLY "H" CLASS. Nos 79

The Barry Railway was the first Company in the British Isles to introduce the heavy 0-8-2 tank engines. Classified as the 'H' class these seven locomotives were built by Sharp-Stewart in 1896. They were weighty machines, scaling upwards of 74 tons, the wheels were the standard 4' 3" drivers, set at 5' 3" x 5' 2" x 5' 0" centres, with a pair of trailing wheels of 3' 6" diameter.

Figure 80

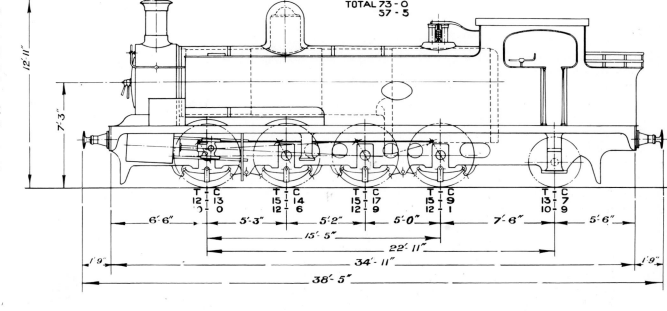

T - C
TOTAL 73 - 0
57 - 5

12'-11"

7'-3"

T - C
12 - 13
0 - 0

T - C
15 - 14
12 - 6

T - C
15 - 17
12 - 9

T - C
15 - 9
12 - 1

T - C
13 - 7
10 - 9

6'-6"   5'-3"   5'-2"   5'-0"   7'-6"   5'-6"

15'-5"

22'-11"

34'-11"

1'-9"   38'-5"   1'-9"

Figure 81

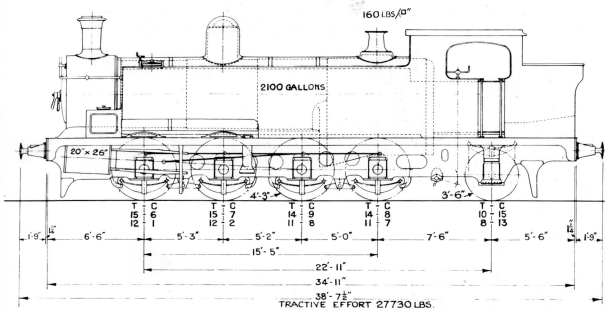

160 LBS/□"

2100 GALLONS

20" x 26"

4'-3"

3'-6"

T - C
15 - 6
12 - 1

T - C
15 - 7
12 - 2

T - C
14 - 9
11 - 8

T - C
14 - 8
11 - 7

T - C
10 - 15
8 - 13

1'-9" 1/4"   6'-6"   5'-3"   5'-2"   5'-0"   7'-6"   5'-6"   1/4" 1'-9"

15'-5"

22'-11"

34'-11"

38'-7 1/2"
TRACTIVE EFFORT 27730 LBS.

Although designed for working heavy trains over the Vale of Glamorgan line, their actual service was moving loaded coal wagons between the tip sidings at the docks and Cadoxton yard. Swindon issued two diagrams for these engines the first being 'C' seen at *Figure* 80 and 'D' in *Figure* 81 for the variations which were carried out at Swindon between 1922 on Nos. 79 and 82. Their Barry numbers were 79-85, but when adopted by the GWR they became 1380 to 1386. All seven had been withdrawn by 1930.

Figure 82

Figure 84

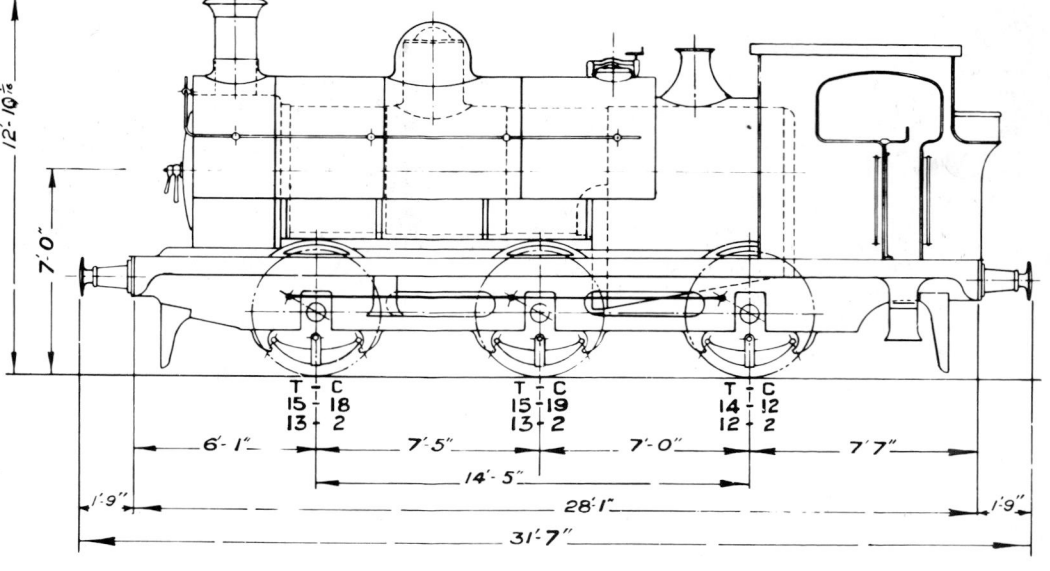

Figure 83

The Barry class F series, were saddle tank versions of the 'A' class 0-6-0 side tanks. There were 28 in all, built over 15 years by four different builders. Nos. 47, 48 and 49 were constructed by Sharp-Stewart in 1890; Nos. 70, 71 and 72 were constructed by Sharp-Stewart in 1894/5; Nos. 64 and 65 were constructed by Vulcan Foundry in 1892; Nos. 37, 52, 99 to 104 were constructed by Sharp-Stewart in 1900; Nos. 127 to 132 were constructed by North British Loco. in 1905, and Nos. 133 to 138 by Hudswell-Clarke in 1905. Driving wheels were as usual 4′ 3″ set at 7′ 5″ and 7′ 0″ centres and with the large saddle tanks with a capacity of 1,050 gallons, the weight of these engines was almost 50 tons. Upon coming in to the GWR stock list in 1922, the diagram given was A.81. Seen in *Figure 85*, a small series of modifications, which included the fitting of GWR pattern of safety valves, resulted in Diagram B.6 seen in *Figure 84*.

Figure 85

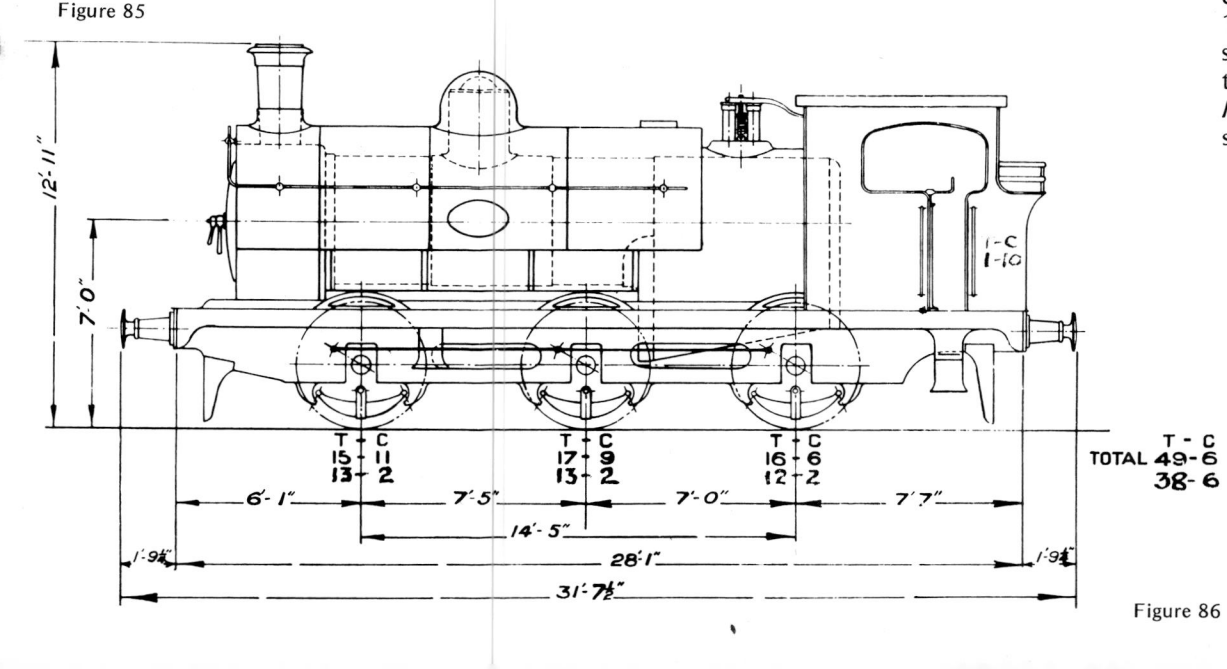

Figure 86

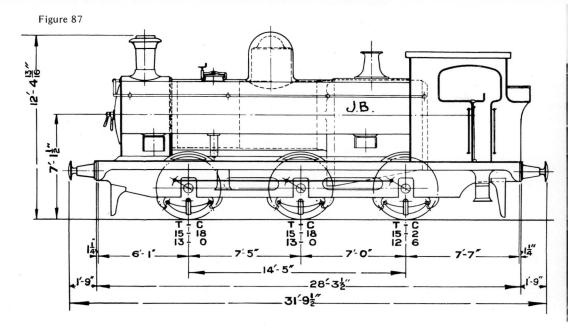

Figure 87

Figure 88

Later several class 'F's had standard No. 9 boiler and pannier tanks fitted and came under yet another diagram namely B.19 for the superheated version and the non-superheated engines were allotted to diagram B.60. All the class were withdrawn from GW service by 1937. Many were sold to collieries all over Britain continuing in service in several instances to the mid sixties. The GWR renumbering was as follows: No. 37 to 708; 47, 48, 49 to 710/11/12; 52 to 713; 64/5 to 714/5; 70/1/2 to 716/7/8; 99-104 to 719-724; 127/8 to 725/6; 130-138 to 729/42/47/54/76-80; and No. 129 to 807. *Figure* 88 shows No. 47 (GW 710) as rebuilt to B.60 diagram.

Figure 89

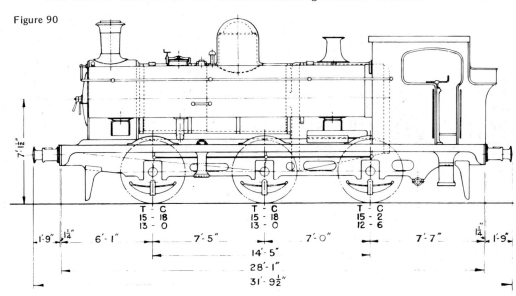

Figure 90

Figure 91

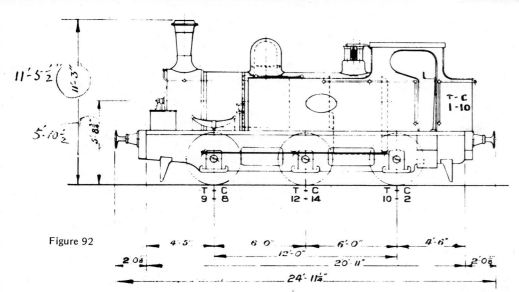

Figure 92

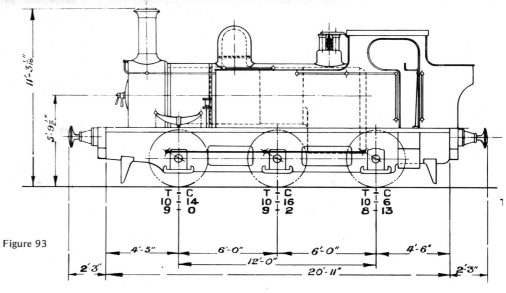

Figure 93

Access to the breakwater sidings at Barry Island, used to be through a small tunnel hewn from the solid rock. Clearances were short, and only a very light axle loaded engine could be allowed on this twisting track. Five little side tanks were built by Hudswell-Clarke in 1889-91 for working on the breakwater, and negotiating the sharp curves in the docks. They were known as the 'E' class, and given numbers 33/34/50/51/53. Small wheels of 3' 3½" were fitted at 6' centres, the little boilers were pressed for 140 lbs, 30 cwt of coal was the limit, and the tanks held only 660 gallons. Two of the class, Nos. 33 and 53 were at one time altered to 0-4-2T by removal of the trailing connecting rods, to act as a type of auto-car engine for passenger work, with a couple of non bogie carriages in each of two sets. The early design was to diagram A.82 as in *Figure* 92, and they became GW Nos. 781/85. Nos. 782 and 783 went to Swindon in 1922/23, 782 receiving a new smokebox and chimney and 783 getting a new boiler and chimney. The diagram for this rebuilding was B.21 (*Figure* 98) and another, B.5, (*Figure* 93) was prepared for No. 782 which showed removal of the sandboxes, new chimney and bunker, although in fact the latter was not fitted to any except No 783. Nos. 781, 782 and 785 were sold in the 1930s and lasted until the late '50s, the other two just seeing ownership in British Railways. *Figure* 91 (on page 38) shows No. 784 at Barry in 1937 still with her own fittings, note the wooden blocks on the buffer beams, for dealing with coal tubs at the docks.

Straight out of Swindon shops in 1923, No. 782 is seen in the official photograph *Figure* 94; it will be noticed that she has her new smokebox and chimney, but the original safety valves and bunker are still in place.

Figure 94

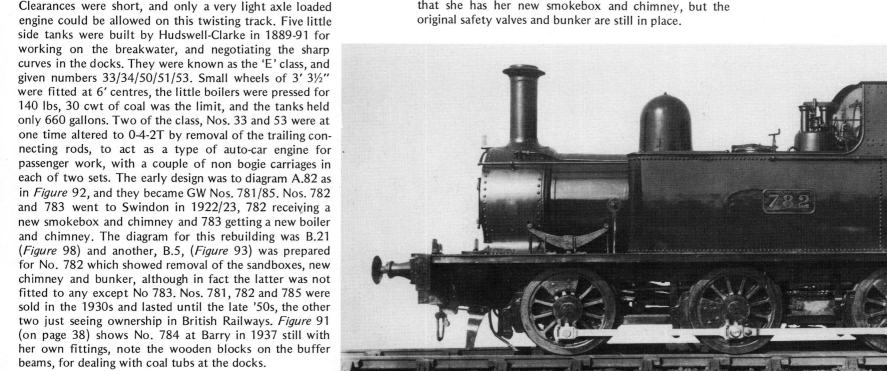

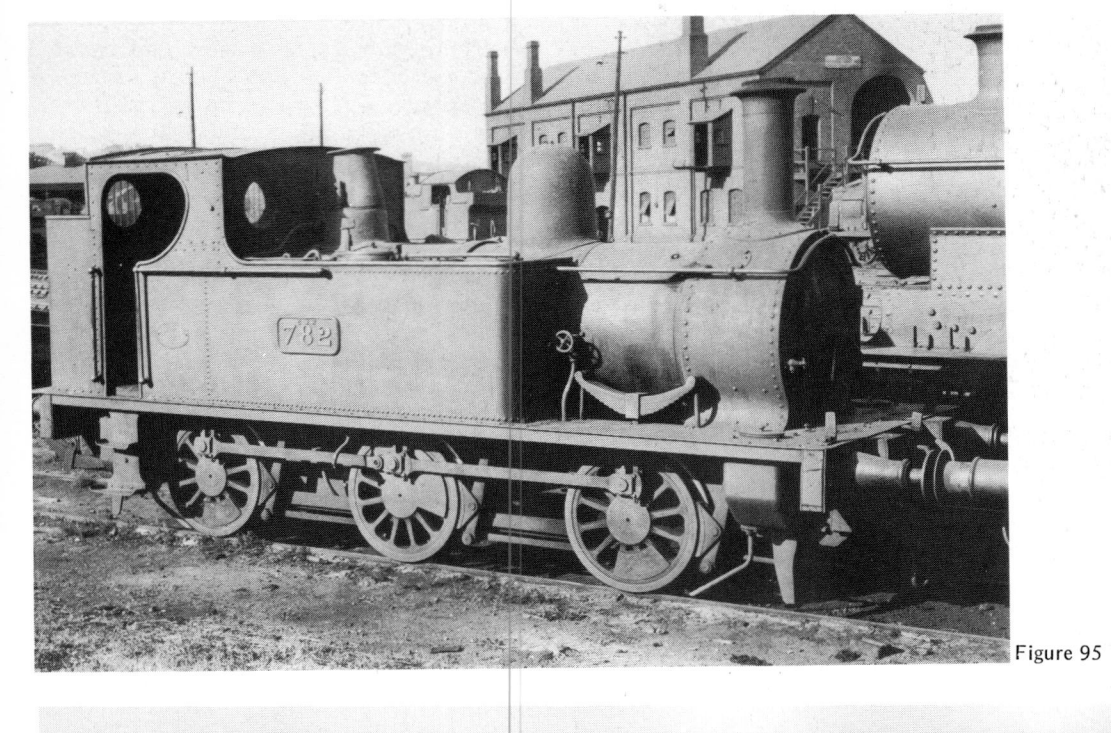

Figure 95

Figure 96

Three pictures of the 'E' class are shown on these pages. In *Figure 95* No. 782 is seen in the 1930s with a bonnet on her safety valve. The initial engine No. 33 or 781 as she became, can be seen in *Figure* 96 with her rods off at Swindon in 1932 awaiting movement to Robert Stephenson's of Darlington after being placed on the sales list and purchased by them in 1933.

Figure 98

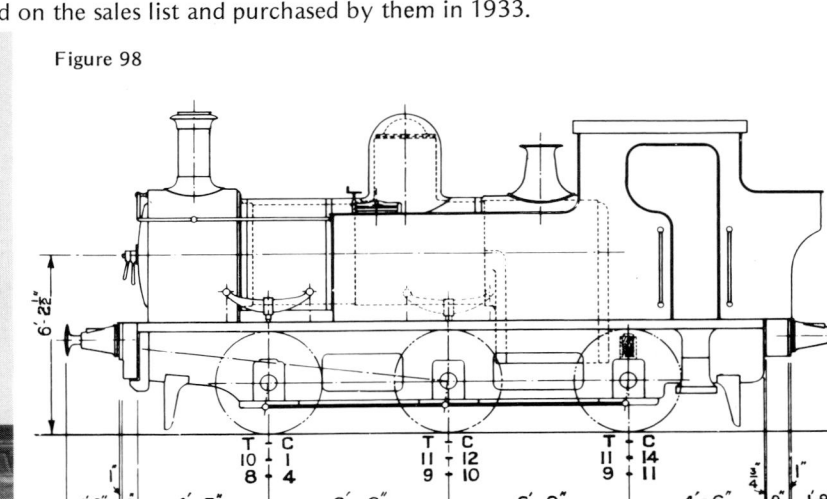

No. 783 was the only one of the class to be reboilered at Swindon, and to have a diagram (B.21) all to herself (*Figure* 98). *Figure* 97 shows her in full broadside, just out of the works in 1926, and *Figure* 99 is the usual official three-quarter shot the Swindon "studio" always took. Personally I think this rebuild of the 'E' class made a really delightful little engine.

GREAT WESTERN 783

Figure 99

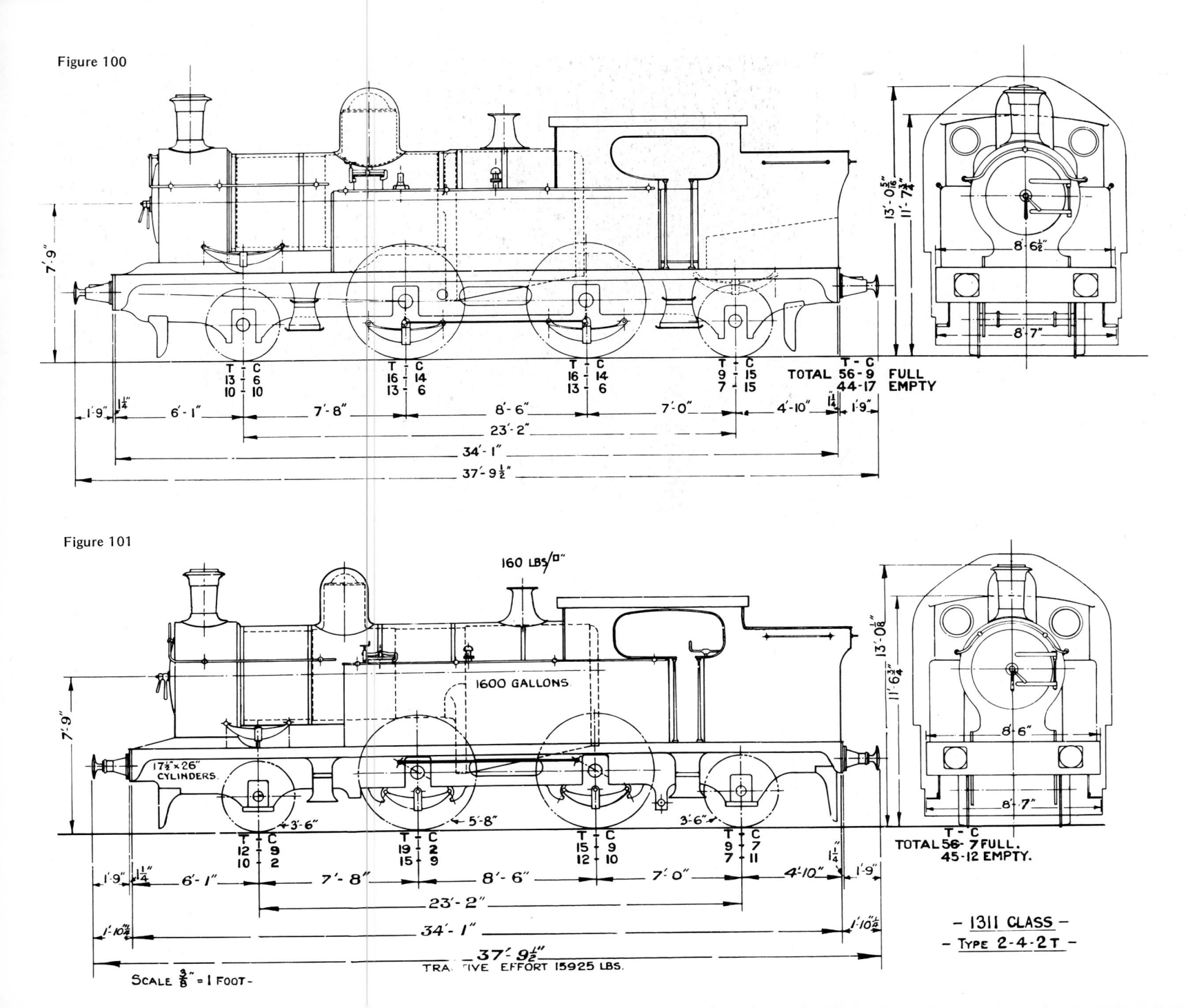

Figure 100

13' - 0 5/16"
11' - 7 1/4"

8' - 6 1/2"

8' - 7"

T - C
13 - 6
10 - 10

T - C
16 - 14
13 - 6

T - C
16 - 14
13 - 6

T - C
9 - 15
7 - 15

T - C TOTAL 56 - 9 FULL
44 - 17 EMPTY

7' - 9"

1' - 9" 1 1/4" 6' - 1" 7' - 8" 8' - 6" 7' - 0" 4' - 10" 1 1/4" 1' - 9"
23' - 2"
34' - 1"
37' - 9 1/2"

Figure 101

160 LBS/□"

1600 GALLONS.

13' - 0 1/8"
11' - 6 3/4"

8' - 6"

8' - 7"

17 1/2" x 26"
CYLINDERS.

3' - 6" 5' - 8" 3' - 6"

T - C
12 - 9
10 - 2

T - C
19 - 2
15 - 9

T - C
15 - 9
12 - 10

T - C
9 - 7
7 - 11

T - C TOTAL 56 - 7 FULL.
45 - 12 EMPTY.

7' - 9"

1' - 9" 1 1/4" 6' - 1" 7' - 8" 8' - 6" 7' - 0" 4' - 10" 1 1/4" 1' - 9"
1' - 10 3/4"
23' - 2"
34' - 1"
1' - 10 1/2"
37' - 9 1/2"

SCALE 3/8" = 1 FOOT

TRACTIVE EFFORT 15925 LBS.

- 1311 CLASS -
- TYPE 2-4-2T -

The 'J' class engine of the Barry Railway were passenger engines, and spent much of their working life in the Cardiff area. Looking very smart in the full livery and polished brassworks, Nos. 86, 87 and 88 were built by Hudswell-Clarke in 1897, and Nos. 89-91, 94-98 by Sharp-Stewart in 1898-9. There were slight differences in the two groups of engines, so that Sharp-Stewart series became 'J1's. Being of the 2-4-2T classification, they ran equally well with passenger trains either forwards or backwards, having 5' 7½" driving wheels at 8' 6" centres with carrying wheels fore and aft of 3' 6" diameter. Large capacity bunkers were fitted carrying 3½ tons, and the side tanks had a capacity of 1,600 gallons. As they came into the GWR fold they were allotted Diagram M seen in *Figure* 102. The class numbered 1311 to 1321 and four engines passed through Swindon in 1924, Nos. 1315/8/9/20 to have their own boilers brought up to Swindon standards, and fitted with GW boiler mountings and bunkers. In this condition they were allotted Diagram R seen in *Figure* 101. One other engine No. 1312 had a standard No. 9 boiler and Belpaire firebox in 1926, and for this Diagram T was prepared (*Figure* 100). These engines did not last long, and after being put on the Sales List, were all eventually cut up at Swindon by 1930.

Nos. 21 and 22 started their careers in 1889 as small 2-4-0Ts built by Sharp-Stewart, with two sisters, Nos. 37 and 52 joining them in 1890. Their work was with passenger trains between Barry and Cardiff until 1898, when Nos. 21 and 22 were altered to 2-4-2T configuration to increase their usage. Their sisters Nos. 37 and 52 were sold to the Port Talbot Railway also converted to 2-4-2Ts, but Nos. 21 and 22 stayed with the parent company and did duties on the handling of the V.I.P. inspection trips, as well as later acting as locomotives for the trailer cars on the Vale of Glamorgan workings. Swindon gave these two engines Diagram M in 1922 (*Figure* 103) and renumbered them GW 1322/3. Only No. 1322 went through the

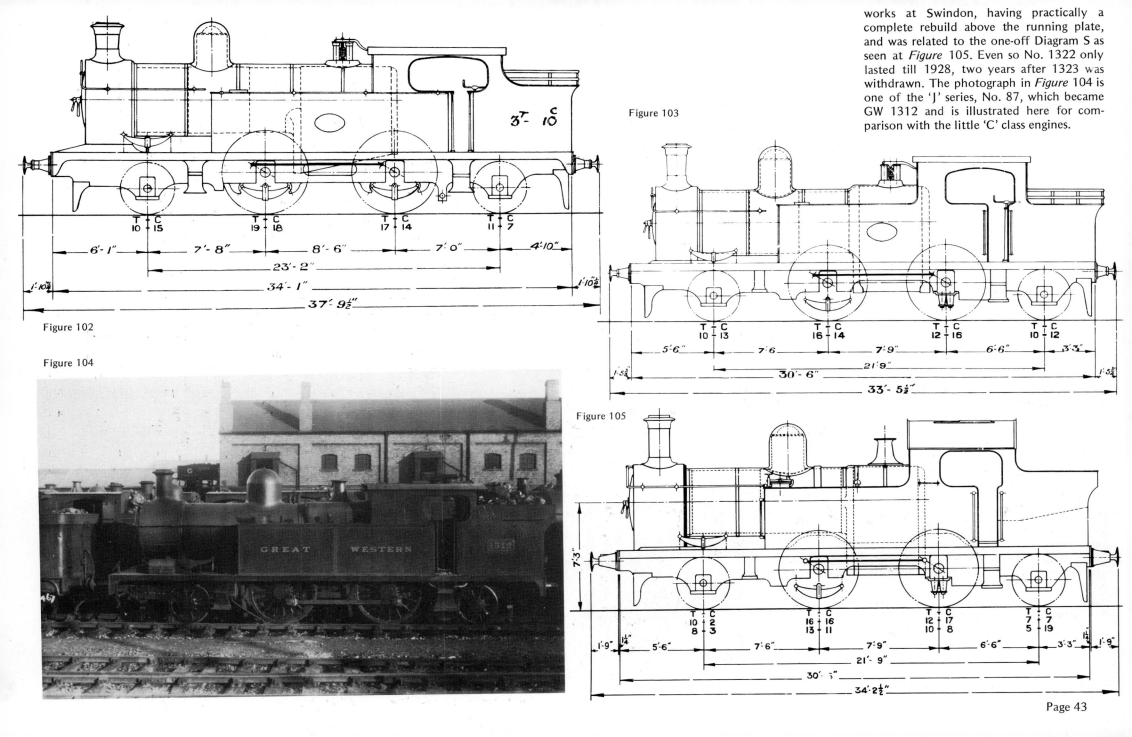

works at Swindon, having practically a complete rebuild above the running plate, and was related to the one-off Diagram S as seen at *Figure* 105. Even so No. 1322 only lasted till 1928, two years after 1323 was withdrawn. The photograph in *Figure* 104 is one of the 'J' series, No. 87, which became GW 1312 and is illustrated here for comparison with the little 'C' class engines.

Figure 102

Figure 103

Figure 104

Figure 105

The Barry Railway in all its history only had four tender engines on the locomotive stock list. These were Sharp-Stewarts Nos. 35/6 built in 1889 and Nos. 92/3 following in 1897. All four were originally intended for overseas but eventually found their way on to the Barry. The eight coupled wheels were 4′ 3″ diameter, with centres 5′ 3″ + 5′ 2″ + 5′ 0″ and the tenders were of the four wheeled type. When passing over to the GWR these engines were renumbered 1387-1390, the diagram A (*Figure* 107) being similar to the Barry drawing, and diagram B (*Figure* 108) was a Swindon allocation after No. 36 and 93 received the 'Western' treatment. Nos. 1387 and 1389 stayed at Barry, but all four were eventually scrapped by the GWR by 1930.

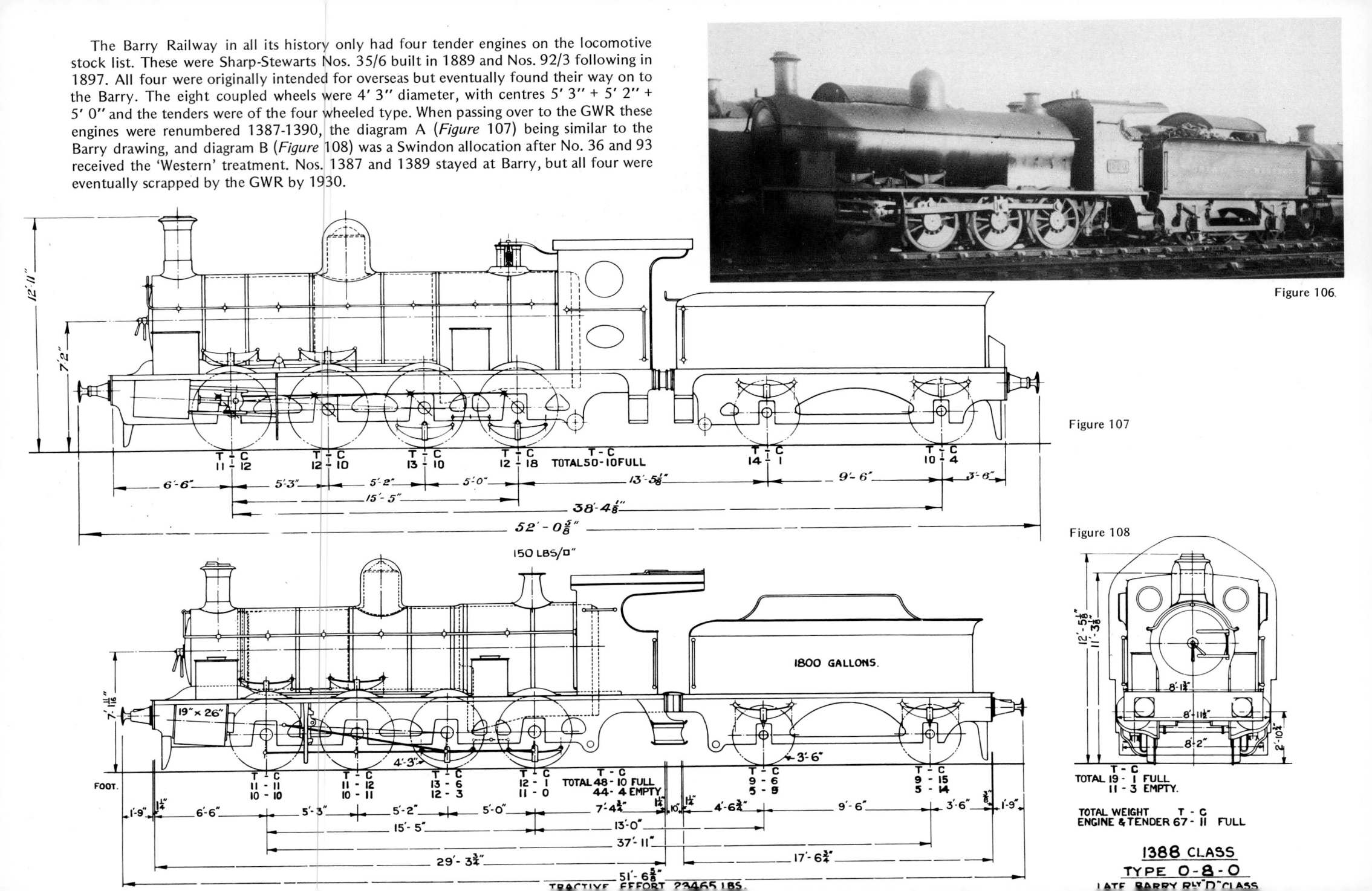

Figure 106.

Figure 107

Figure 108

150 LBS/□″

1800 GALLONS.

19″ × 26″

4′-3″

FOOT.

TRACTIVE EFFORT 23465 LBS.

TOTAL 19 - 1 FULL
11 - 3 EMPTY.

TOTAL WEIGHT   T - C
ENGINE & TENDER 67 - 11 FULL

1388 CLASS
TYPE 0-8-0
LATE BARRY Rⁿ "D" CLASS

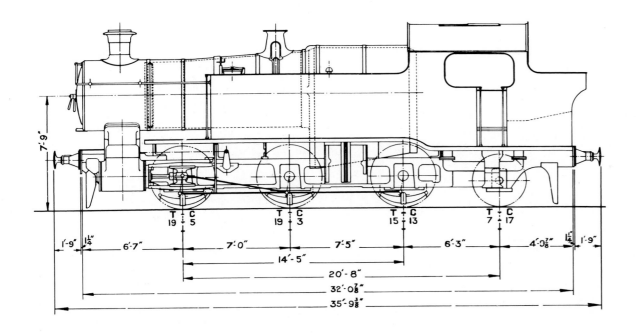

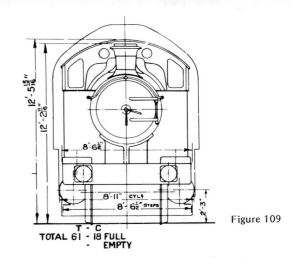

Figure 109

The 'Yankees' were a class of five engines of the 0-6-2T classification, which were built to Mr Hosgood's requirements in America for the Barry Railway, at a time when British locomotive builders were swamped with orders for engines of all kinds. Officially the 'K' class, they were ordered in the spring of 1899, and by the autumn of the year No. 118, the first to arrive, was unloaded in parts at Barry Docks, and before the year ended all five had been received, erected and were actually in service. The Barry numbering was 117-121, altered later in GW days to 193-197. As can be seen in Diagram Y, *Figure* 110, the rear end was typical Barry style, whilst the front, with its bar frames and Richardson balanced slide valves was pure American. Driving wheels were 4' 3" with thick tyres, with trailing truck wheels of 3' 6" diameter.

After the grouping Nos. 194 and 196 passed through Swindon works, and were practically rebuilt above the running plate, and returned to service in 1924 in the condition shown in *Figure* 111, with a new Diagram A.31 (*Figure* 109). Their lives however were comparatively short, all being cut up at Swindon between 1927 and 1932.

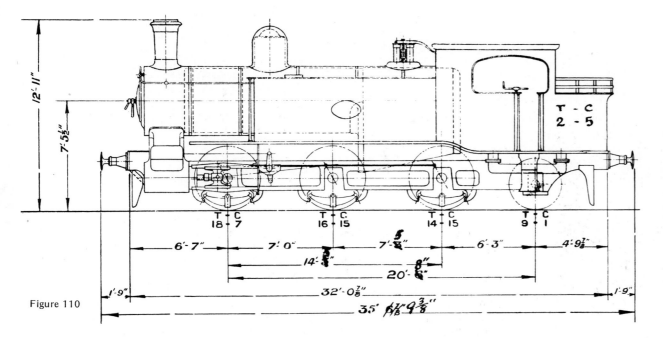

Figure 110

GREAT WESTERN 196

Figure 111

Figure 112

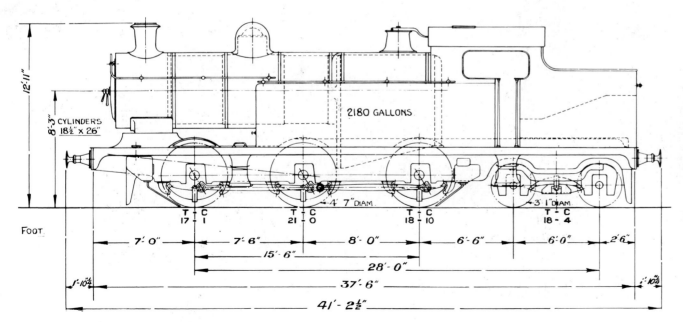

The last Barry engines to receive mention were the ten short lived 'L' class of heavy 0-6-4T's. They were inside cylinder side tanks, with a long wheelbase of 28' 0'' and it was the large overhang at the rear which caused much trouble in operating, derailments being frequent, and in one instance No. 147 turned right over on its side. They were built by Hawthorn, Leslie in 1914, and were numbered 139 to 148. The class received many modifications in 1917, and the Swindon Diagram B (*Figure* 113) shows the engines in this condition. Nos. 139/41/3/8 went to Swindon in 1922 followed in 1923 by No. 142. Extensively rebuilt, and renumbered, Nos. 1347/9/51/7 returned to their home territory in 1923 in the condition seen in *Figure* 114, and to the Diagram C (*Figure* 115). No. 1348 received only a new smokebox, chimney and safety valve, and No. 1350 was altered only by having GW pattern safety valve.

Finally after the General Strike of 1926, they were ordered to Swindon, and, it has been rumoured, cut up on mistaken instructions from the C.M.E's office. A sad end to a rather handsome and powerful class.

Figure 113

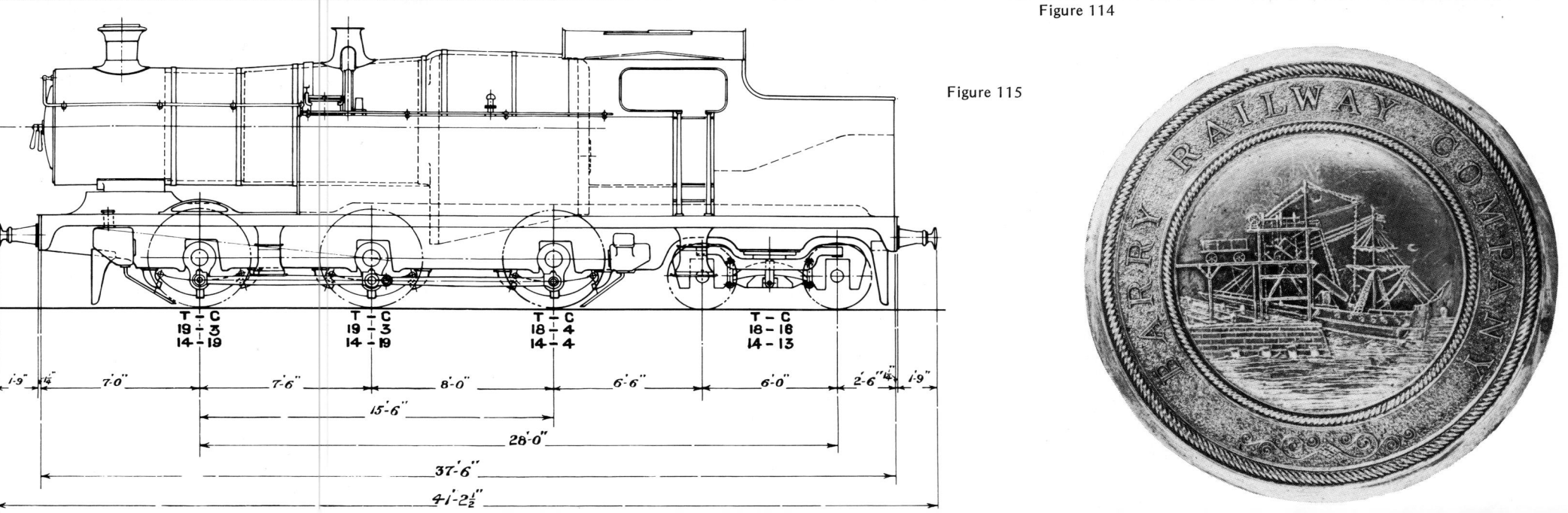

Figure 114

Figure 115

The CAMBRIAN RAILWAYS COMPANY

The Cambrian Railway came into being as a direct result of five Welsh companies amalgamating together in 1865 with the Mid Wales Railway joining in 1904. All of these small railways were situated in Mid Wales from Pwllheli in the north west to Talyllyn Junction in the south east and from Aberystwyth in the west to Whitchurch in the north east. Other smaller lines, including the narrow gauge Vale of Rheidol and Welshpool & Llanfair were also absorbed, so that when the GWR took over the Cambrian in 1922 as a constituent company, the system consisted of approximately 300 miles of mostly single track, passing through some of the finest scenic and sparsely populated country in the British Isles. The workshops of the Cambrian were located at Oswestry, and the locomotive stud at the take-over, including the narrow gauge, stood at 107. However the GWR in 1922 immediately condemned 23 of these, and so the total came down to 84. Naturally with a railway extending over such a large mileage the locomotives were many and varied, the majority being 0-6-0 and 4-4-0 tender engines to cope with the rural services. Engine livery from the early days of the Cambrian, was first green and then black, lined out blue-grey and thin red lines. The crest of the company appeared on the leading splashers from approximately 1888, but later the Prince of Wales plume was used with gold letters on each side, but in the last days before amalgamation the single word "Cambrian" in a pale blue-grey appeared on the tenders, without any crest whatsoever.

Locomotive sheds were spread around the system, there being 16 in 1898, the main depots being Aberystwyth, Machynlleth and Llandiloes, apart from the largest shed at Oswestry.

Cam. No.	GWR No.	Type	Maker	GWR Diagram	Cam. No.	GWR No.	Type	Maker	GWR Diagram
1	1329	2-4-0	GWR	A/4	29	849	0-6-0	Beyer Peacock	A/13
2	1129	4-4-0T	Beyer Peacock	E	30	824	0-6-0T	Manning Wardle	A/96 - B3
3	10	0-4-4T	Nasmyth Wilson	E H	31	855	0-6-0	Beyer Peacock	A/13 - A23
4	897	0-6-0	Sharp Stewart	A 16	32	1085	4-4-0	R. Stephenson	A/32
5	11	0-4-4T	Nasmyth Wilson	E	33	1131	4-4-0T	Beyer Peacock	E
7	15	"	"	"	34	1113	4-4-0	"	A/33
8	19	"	"	"	35	821	0-6-0T	Chapman & F	A/94 - B2
9	20	"	"	"	36	1114	4-4-0	Beyer Peacock	A/33
10	1328	2-4-0	GWR	A/3	37	1132	4-4-0T	"	F
11	1068	4-4-0	Cam Rlys	A/32	38	864	0-6-0	"	A/13
12	1130	4-4-0T	Beyer Peacock	E	40	899	"	Sharp Stewart	A/16
14	898	0-6-0	Sharp Stewart	A/16	41	1330	2-4-0	Sharp Stewart	A/5
15	844	"	Beyer Peacock	A/13	42	873	0-6-0	Beyer Peacock	A/13
16	1115	4-4-0	Sharp Stewart	A/34	43	1331	2-4-0	Sharp Stewart	A/5
17	1116	"	"	"	44	1190	2-4-0T	"	O
19	1082	"	Cam Rlys	A/32	45	900	0-6-0	"	A/16
20	1117	"	Sharp Stewart	A/34	46	901	"	"	"
21	1118	"	"	"	47	1086	4-4-0	R. Stephenson	A/32
23	21	0-4-4T	Nasmyth Wilson	E	48	908	0-6-0	Sharp Stewart	A/16
24	819	0-6-0T	Hunslet E. Co.	A/93	49	909	"	"	"
26	820	0-6-0T	Chapman & F	A/94-	50	1110	4-4-0	"	A/34

Figure 116

Cam. No.	GWR No.	Type	Maker	GWR Diagram
51	910	0-6-0	Sharp Stewart	A/16
52	911	,,	,, ,,	,,
53	1332	2-4-0	,, ,,	A/5
54	874	0-6-0	Beyer Peacock	A/13
55	1333	2-4-0	Sharp Stewart	A/5
56	1191	2-4-0T	,, ,,	0
57	1192	,,	,, ,,	P -T
58	1196	,,	,, ,,	,,
59	1197	,,	,, ,,	,,
60	1112	4-4-0	,, ,,	A/34
61	1088	,,	,, ,,	A/32
62	1090	,,	,, ,,	,,
63	1091	,,	,, ,,	,,
64	1093	,,	,, ,,	,,
65	1096	,,	,, ,,	,,
66	1097	,,	,, ,,	,,
67	1100	,,	,, ,,	,,
68	1101	,,	,, ,,	,,
69	1102	,,	,, ,,	,,
70	1103	,,	,, ,,	,,
71	1104	,,	,, ,,	,,
72	1105	,,	,, ,,	,,
73	875	0-6-0	Neilson	A/14
74	876	,,	,,	A/15
75	878	,,	,,	,,
76	879	,,	,,	A/14
77	880	,,	,,	A/15
78	881	,,	Vulcan	,,
79	882	,,	,,	,,
80	883	,,	,,	A/14
81	1084	4-4-0	Sharp Stewart	A/32
82	3521	,,	GWR	A/13
83	1106	,,	Sharp Stewart	A/32
84	1107	,,	,, ,,	,,
85	1108	,,	Stephenson	,,
86	1109	,,	,,	,,
87	884	0-6-0	Neilson	A/15
88	885	,,	,,	A/14
89	887	,,	Stephenson	A/13
90	888	,,	,,	,,
91	889	,,	,,	,,
92	891	,,	,,	,,
93	892	,,	,,	,,
94	1014	4-4-0	,,	A/31
95	3546	,,	,,	A/13
96	1029	,,	,,	A/31
97	1035	,,	,,	,,
98	1043	,,	,,	,,
99	893	0-6-0	Beyer Peacock	A/13
100	894	,,	,, ,,	,,
101	895	,,	,, ,,	,,
102	896	,,	,, ,,	,,

One of the first mixed passenger class of six locomotives to run on the new constituted Cambrian Railway was No. 7 *Llanerchydol* seen in *Figure* 116. Although much too early to be absorbed into the GWR she nevertheless finds a place here, if only to illustrate the style of engine to be found on the early Cambrian. She was built by Sharp-Stewart in 1860, one of their 0-4-2 design with 5' 0" driving wheels, and trailing wheels of 3' 1½". As can be seen, she sported a small four wheeled tender which carried just 3 tons of coal, and 1,200 gallons of water. She lasted for 34 years being withdrawn in 1894, just after being pictured at Towyn with the entire staff of that station.

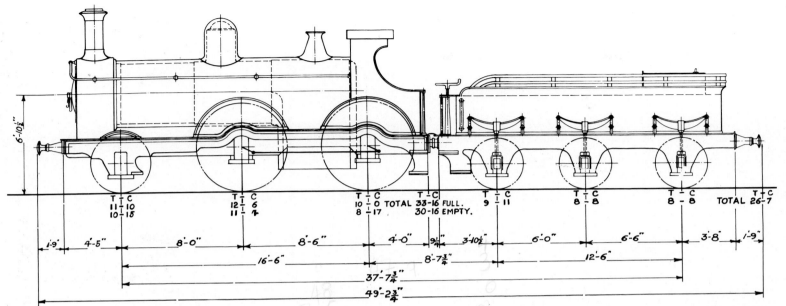

Curiously, Cambrian No. 1 was a Great Western engine (No. 212) built originally at Wolverhampton. She and the sister engine No. 10 (No. 213) were bought in 1921 from the Bute Works Supply Co. for £870 each. The only difference in the two locomotives, was that No. 1 seen in *Figure* 117 had a Belpaire boiler firebox, whereas No. 10 still retained the old round-top type of firebox.

Upon purchase, both engines were passed through the Company's workshops at Oswestry, repainted in the Cambrian livery and were rostered to work the coast line from Machynlleth. On returning to the GWR in 1922 they were renumbered 1328 and 1329, and in 1923 old No. 1 was rebuilt with a Standard Goods boiler, lasting only until 1927, her sister being cut up 12 months previously in 1926.

Figure 117

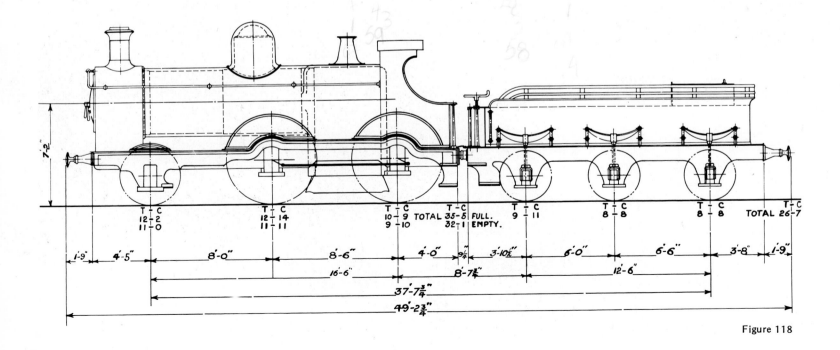

Figure 118

The picture in *Figure* 119 does not depict either No. 1 or No. 10, but is purely representational of the Wolverhampton class of 2-4-0 locomotives that these GWR engines originated from.

Figure 120

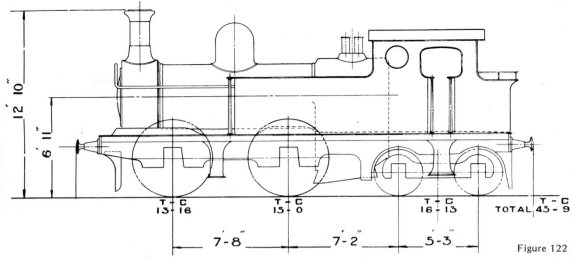

Figure 122

Figure 121

The small 0-4-4T class of six engines given the Cambrian Nos. 3, 5, 7, 8, 9 and 23 were designed and built by Nasmyth Wilson & Co. in 1895-99 for working the Ellesmere branch from Wrexham. They had 5′ 3″ driving wheels set at 7′8″ centres, with a trailing bogie having 3′ 1½″ wheels. Their unusual feature was the circular windows in the cab side sheets. Taken over by the GWR in 1922 they were renumbered 10, 11, 15, 19-21, but three of the six were in such bad shape that they were cut up at Swindon in that same year. Nos. 3 and 8 were overhauled and went back to work in 1925, No. 9 being refitted at Oswestry and worked on until 1928. *Figure* 121 shows No. 8 in Cambrian days when the engine was lined out, and No. 3 is seen in *Figure* 120 unlined and with one of the company's goods brake vans. The Diagram E was allotted to the unrebuilt engines (*Figure* 122) and when dealt with at Swindon given Diagram H (*Figure* 125) overleaf.

Figure 123

Figure 124

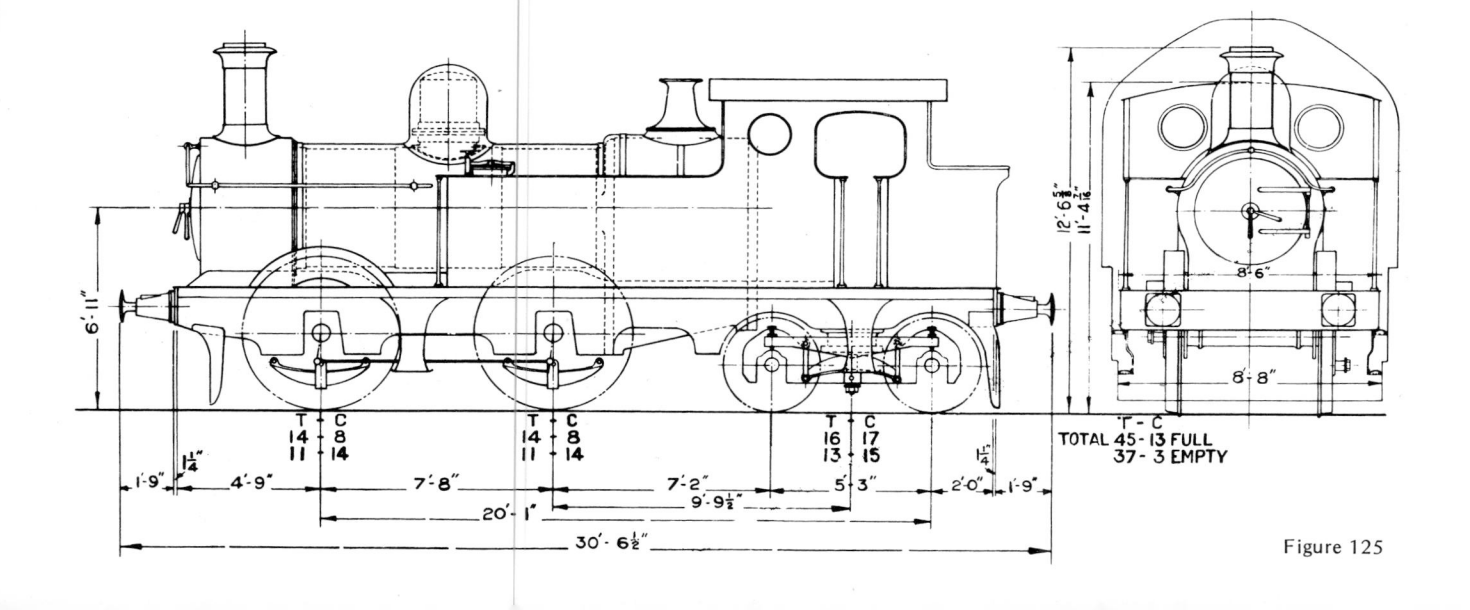

Figure 125

No. 9 is seen in *Figure* 124 bearing the GWR insignia, and in *Figure* 123, No. 7 is seen in early days fitted with coal rails.

In 1904 The Cambrian Railway purchased three small locomotives from the Lambourn Valley Railway. They were named *Eadweade*, *Ealhswith* and *Aelfred*, the first from Hunslet Engine Co. and the other two from Chapman and Furneaux of Gateshead. On being delivered to Oswestry the names were removed, and the engines were renumbered 24, 26 and 35. Although from two different builders, all three locomotives were very similar, having six coupled wheels of 3' 7" diameter, side tanks and outside cylinders. At the grouping Swindon gave No. 24 Diagram A.93 (*Figure* 126) and they fitted her out with many 'Western' items, finally isssuing another Diagram to suit, namely B.35 (*Figure* 127). All three were renumbered, 819, 820 and 821 and *Figure* 128 shows No. 24 as 819 just out of works in 1926.

Figure 126

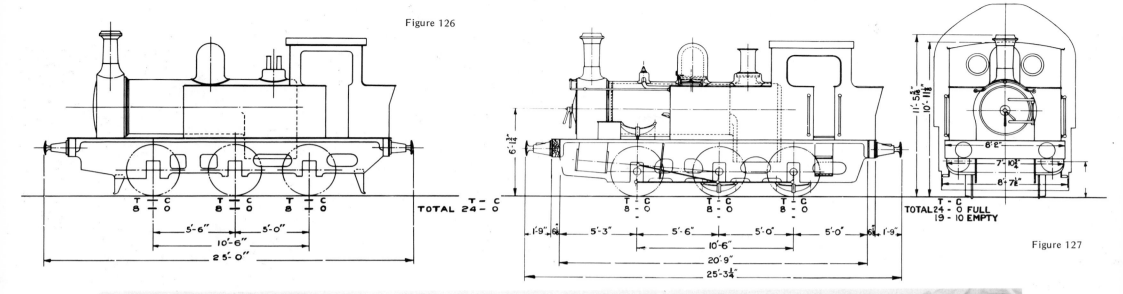

6'-1¾"

T - C
8 - 0

T - C
8 - 0

T - C
8 - 0

TOTAL 24 - 0

5'-6"   5'-0"

10'-6"

25'-0"

1'-9" 6¾   5'-3"   5'-6"   5'-0"   5'-0"   6¾ 1'-9"

10'-6"

20'-9"

25'-3¼"

T - C
8 - 0

T - C
8 - 0

T - C
8 - 0

11'-5⅝"

10'-11⅛"

8'-2"

7'-10¾"

8'-7½"

T - C
TOTAL 24 - 0 FULL
19 - 10 EMPTY

Figure 127

Figure 128

GREAT WESTERN   819

On this page are three diagrams of 0-6-0T engines of the Cambrian. *Figure* 129 shows Diagram A.94 which represented Nos. 26 and 35 at the grouping, and in *Figure* 130 as both engines were turned out from Swindon in 1922 and 1926 having the new Diagram B.2 Swindon Diagram A.96 (*Figure* 130A) illustrates the little No. 30 which was *Mawddwy* taken over with the Mawddwy Railway in 1911. No. 30 was built by Manning Wardle in 1865, one of two, her sister engine being *Disraeli* which was scrapped in 1912, and so was not absorbed into the GWR. No. 30 however became GW No. 824, received a refit at Swindon and worked along the Van branch until 1940 when she was withdrawn. At the bottom of the page, (*Figure* 131) No. 820 is illustrated in the 'Westernised' condition linking up with the Diagram B.2. The little engine is pictured at Mells Colliery in 1938, being finally scrapped by Cohens in 1948.

Figure 129

Figure 130

Figure 131

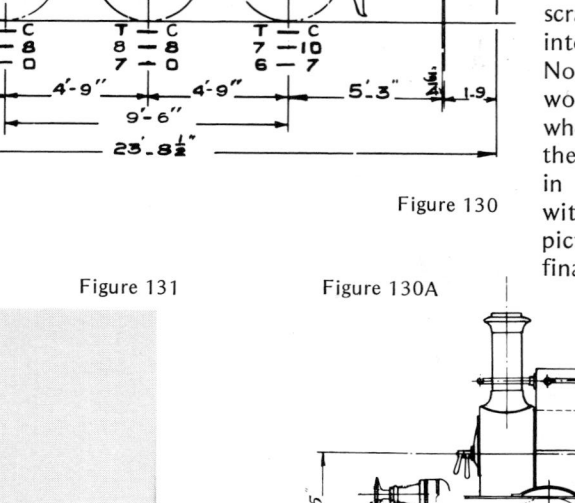

Figure 130A

Known as the 'Small Goods' class, a series of Sharp-Stewart 0-6-0 engines built between 1861 and 1865, were originally all given names. A class of sixteen, thirteen eventually belonged to the Cambrian, and three went to the Brecon & Merthyr. A further nine joined the thirteen between 1872-75, so that the class on the Cambrian was 22 strong. The small picture in *Figure* 132 shows No. 34A at Aberdovey in a very early condition. Only nine out of the class were taken over by the GWR, they were 4/14/40/45/46/48/49/51 and 52 and were given the Swindon Diagram A.16 (*Figure* 133). Renumbered by the Great Western they became 879/98/99/900/901/908/909/910/911 (*Figure* 135). All the class except No. 908 went to Swindon, but only three of these ever came into service again, Nos. 898, 900 and 910. The odd one out, No. 48, which became GW 908 after spending time at Oswestry, finally made the journey to Swindon shops in 1927 and was fitted with '2021' class boiler, emerging under a new Diagram Swindon A.26 (*Figure* 134).

Figure 132

Some of these engines ran with six wheeled tenders, and others like No. 908 had the small four wheel type. *Figure* 135 shows No. 900 at Swindon in 1938 fitted with the GW smokebox and chimney. She lasted out until 1945, a long life for this little engine with 4' 6'' driving wheels, which had been built back in 1864.

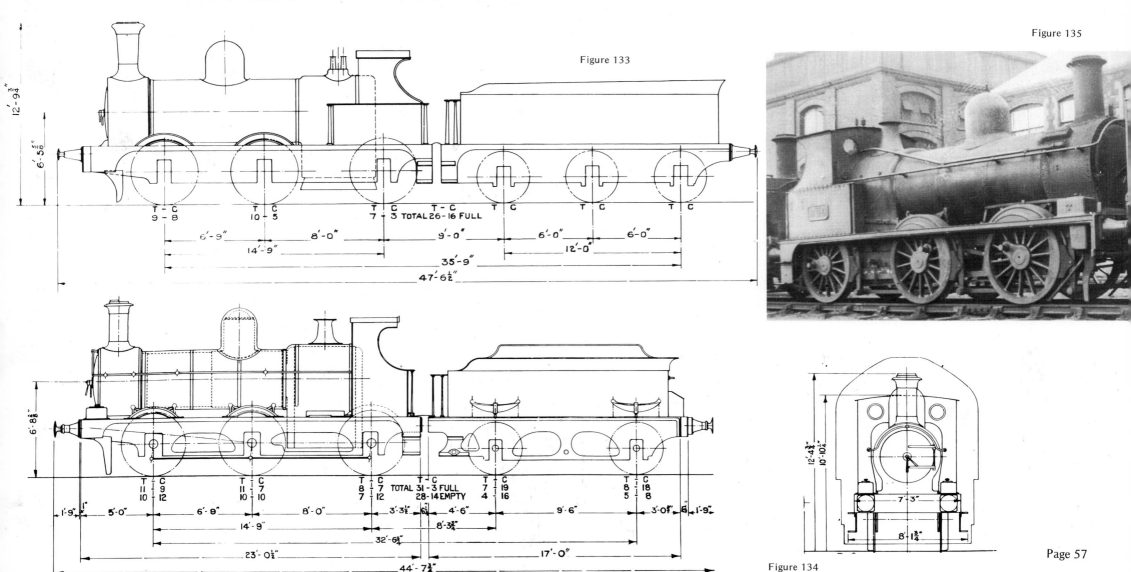

Figure 133

Figure 135

Figure 134

Page 57

Figure 136

Figure 137

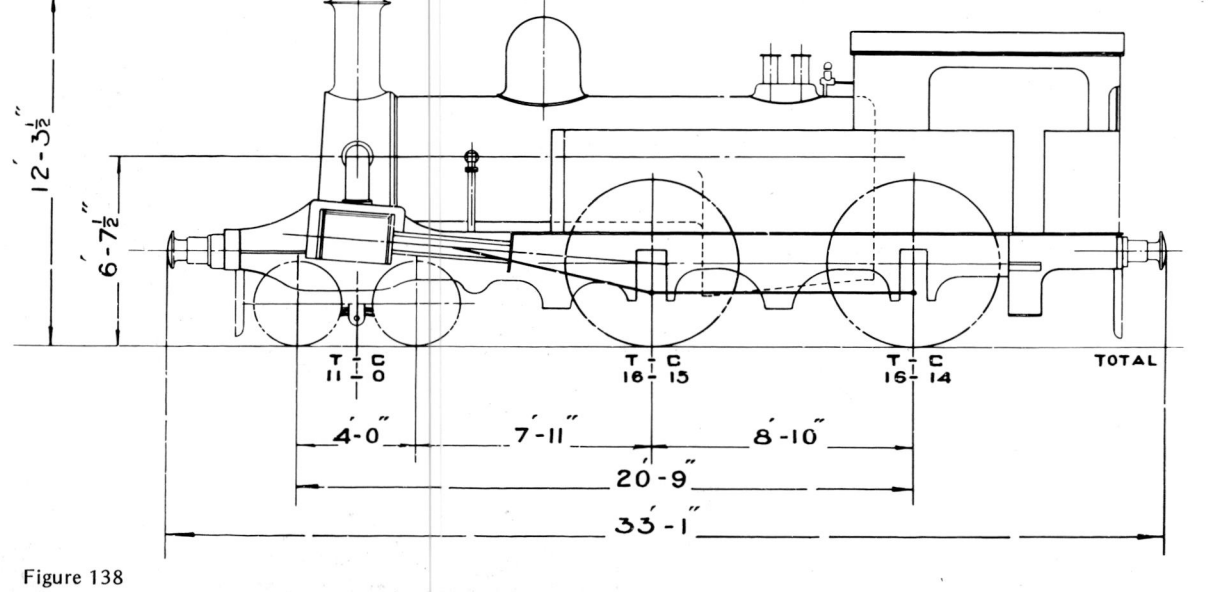

Figure 138

In 1905 The Cambrian Railway bought six Beyer-Peacock outside cylindered 4-4-0T engines from the Metropolitan Railway which at that time was changing over to full electrification. These engines had large wheels of 5' 10" being passenger engines, and most unsuitable to work on the Cambrian branch lines, and even on the main line runs had such small water and coal capacities that they proved to be a very poor purchase. Upon coming on to the Cambrian they were given the Nos. 2/12/33/34/36/37 and at the grouping took the GW numbers 1129/1130/1131/1113/1114/1132, but only No. 1130 actually carried the new number. Cambrian Nos. 34 and 36 even had the experience of being changed into tender engines, (see below) but all were scrapped by 1923, the GWR judging them to be unsuitable for any rebuilding. The diagram shown in *Figure* 138 is F which was issued for No. 37 only, and the photographs show No. 12 in *Figure* 136 and finally No. 37 in *Figure* 137 which relates to the diagram.

Figure 139

Figure 140

As referred to on the above page, two of the Metro engines were converted to tender engines, first No. 34, being sent to Beyer-Peacock's works in 1915, where the bunker was sliced off, a new drag box fitted behind the firebox, a different style of cab was substituted, and a six wheeled tender off the 'Small Goods' engine was added.

This resulted in an engine as shown in the Swindon Diagram A.33 (*Figure* 141). No. 34 proving successful, it was decided to rebuild No. 36 in a similar fashion, and this was completed at Oswestry in 1916. The two engines struggled on until the GWR took over, but were then immediately scrapped. The engine in *Figure* 139 is No. 34 seen at Machynlleth in her Cambrian livery, and just before being dispatched to Manchester for the transformation.

Figure 140 illustrated the next class to be described, namely the 'Small Passenger' series. Built in 1863/65, twelve came on to the Cambrian stud and were all named. No. 30 seen in this picture was originally *Albion* but did not survive in GWR days, being cut up in 1910.

Figure 141

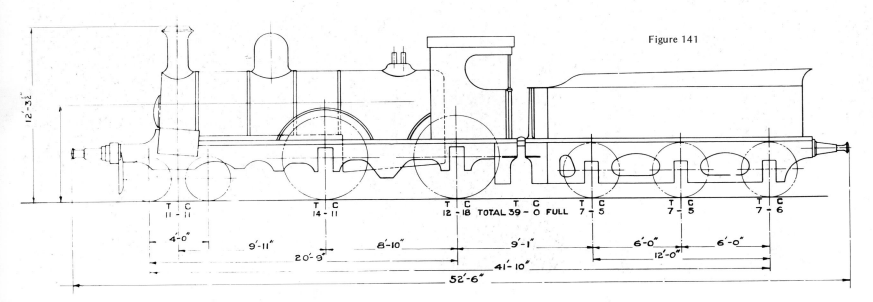

Figure 142

Figure 143

Figure 144

Figure 145

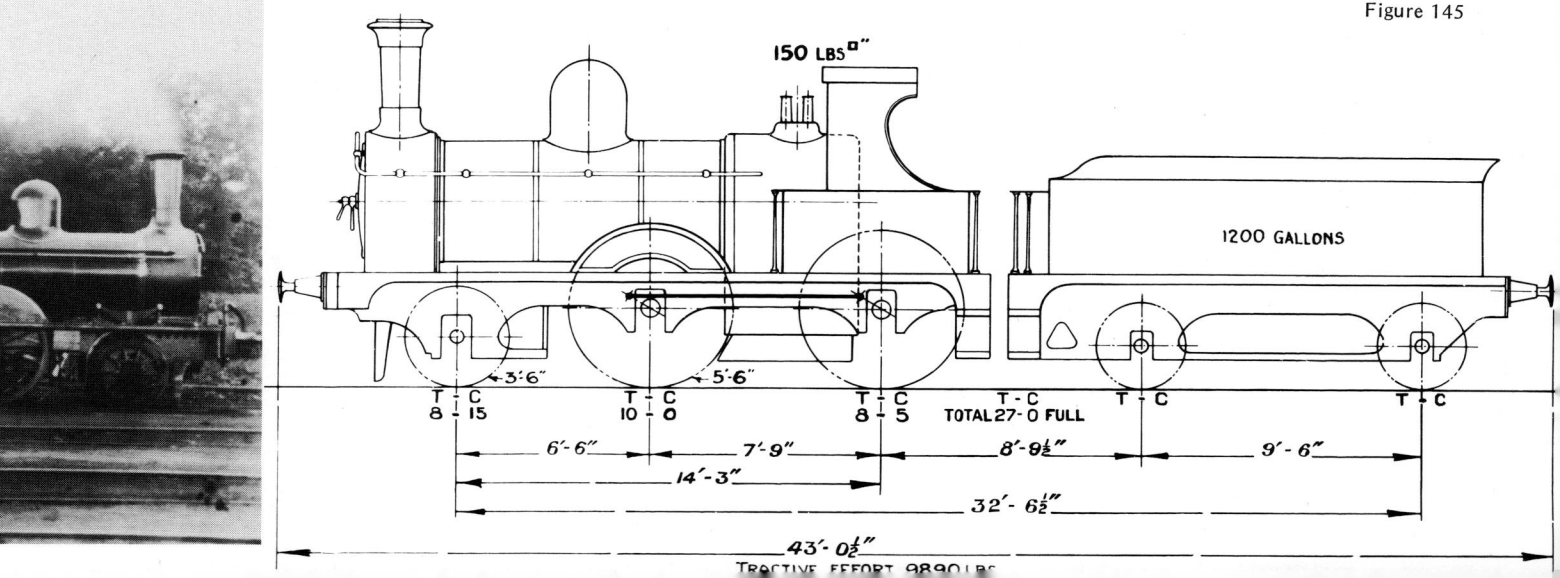

150 LBS□″

1200 GALLONS

3′-6″ 5′-6″

T - C   T - C   T - C   T - C   T - C   T - C
8 - 15   10 - 0   8 - 5   TOTAL 27- 0 FULL

6′-6″   7′-9″   8′-9½″   9′-6″

14′-3″

32′-6½″

43′-0½″

TRACTIVE EFFORT 9890 LBS

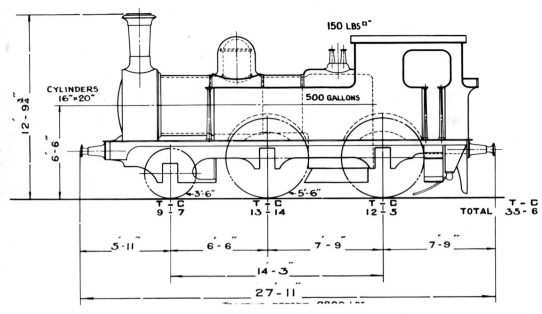

Figure 146

Figure 147

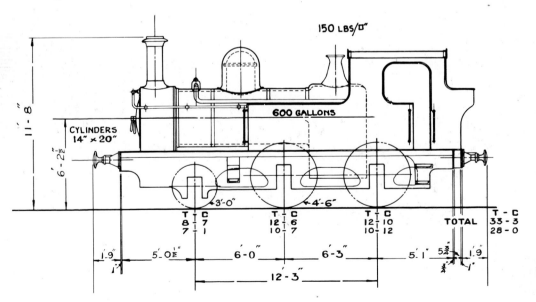

The 'Small Passenger' engines lost their names between the years 1884 and 1891, but retained their Cambrian numbers, which were cast into brass oval plates affixed to the cab side sheets. The series were Nos. 28-31, 41-44 and 53-56. They had 5' 6'' driving wheels set at 7' 9'' centres, with a pair of leading carrying wheels of 3' 6'' diameter.

A small 4 wheel tender was used which held 1,200 gallons of water, and the little engines were pressed for only 120lbs. being one of Sharp-Stewart's standard designs. This class of twelve small locomotives worked the Cambrian main line for 30 years or more, but only six survived to be absorbed by the GWR. These were Nos. 41/43/44/53/55/56 which were renumbered to GW 1330/1/1190/1332/1333/1191, but all six were withdrawn in 1922, including two, Nos. 44 and 56, which had been converted in 1907 into side tanks (see below). Although the 2-4-0's never actually worked on the GWR or even carried their new numbers, Swindon nevertheless issued Diagram A.5 to cover them (*Figure* 145). The left-hand side is seen of No. 43 in *Figure* 142 and *Figures* 143 and 144 show the right-hand sides of Nos. 55 and 56 respectively.

The Diagram in *Figure* 146 is the Swindon O which was allotted to the two 'Small Passenger' class of Cambrian engines Nos. 44 and 56 which were rebuilt at Oswestry in 1907 to a tank design. The tiny bunkers only held 30 cwt of coal and the side tanks 500 gallons of water. Used on the coast section at first, they were tried on various branches, finishing up at Machynlleth for the Mawddwy branch. They suffered the same fate as their sister tender engines, being cut up at Swindon in 1922 and never carried their GWR numbers 1190 and 1191. *Figure* 148 shows No. 44 proudly carrying the 'Prince of Wales' feathers on the water tank sides.

A very similar 2-4-0T engine class of the Cambrian was the 'Small Side Tank' of three engines, also Sharp-Stewart construction. These three not only survived into GWR ownership, but were also rebuilt at Swindon, and as rebuilt were issued with the Diagram T seen in *Figure* 147.

Figure 148

Figure 150

Figure 149

The next two pages concern these three small 2-4-0Ts which were the last engines ordered for the Cambrian Railway by Thomas Levin in the early 1860s. Sharp-Stewart of course were the builders and Nos. 57, 58 and 59 were given the names *Magnola*, *Gladys* and *Seaham*. All three are seen here in *Figures* 149, 150 and 151. Originally they had the single sheet cab cover as shown on *Seaham*, but eventually they were fitted with a box-like cab with side windows as depicted in *Figures* 149 and 150, and a rather better shaped chimney. The trio had long and varied careers, from working the Elan Valley line at Rhayader to the Tanat Valley and even trying the Ellesmere branch, all three arriving at Swindon in 1922 for rebuilding. The diagram at this time was Swindon P seen in *Figure* 152.

Figure 151

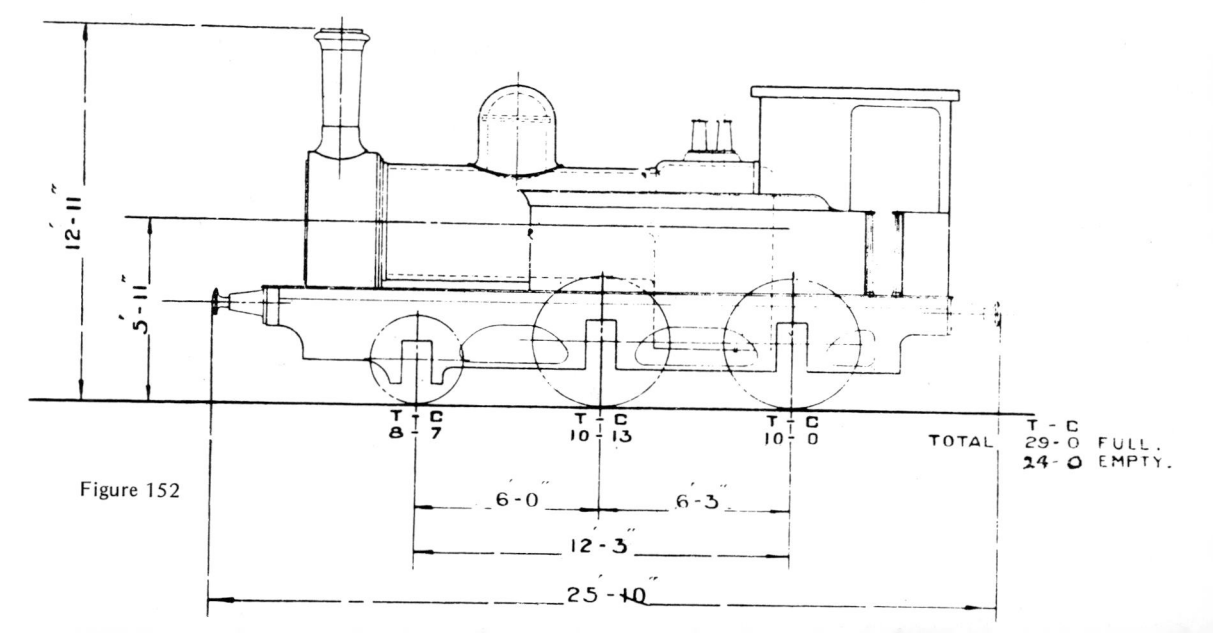

Figure 152

The reincarnation of the 'Small Side Tanks' at Swindon consisted of fitting new inner fireboxes and tubes to the Cambrian boilers, replacing the smokeboxes, chimneys and safety valves with 'Western' pattern items, trimming the curved valance off the side tanks, and replacing the cabs and bunkers with a larger style. Renumbered 1192/96/97 they were returned to the Cambrian area in 1923-4 looking very smart, neat and business-like. In 1927 No. 1192 went down to work the Hemyock branch, and was scrapped in 1929. Her sister 1196 also had a short spell in the Exeter Division, but returned to join 1197 again at Oswestry where they both remained until 1948, having each put in a remarkable million miles, for such small locomotives.

Figure 153 shows No. 1192 at Exeter during her Culm Valley days, and No. 1196, seen with her delightful little train of two four-wheelers on the Tanat Valley line, is shown in *Figure* 155. Finally No. 1197 in *Figure* 154 is depicted at Swindon wearing the GWR roundel on the side tanks.

Figure 153

Figure 155

Figure 154

The '73' class of 0-6-0 goods engines came into being in the 1890s owing to the need for a stronger series of locomotives to handle the increased traffic on the Cambrian at that time. Ten engines were ordered, three by Vulcan Foundry and seven from Neilson & Co. Eight were delivered between 1894/95 and the other two arrived in 1899. These tender engines had six wheels coupled of 5' 1½" diameter with wheelbases of 7' 5" and 7' 10" respectively, inside cylinders and frames, with 10' 3" parallel boilers with dome and Ramsbottom valves. Their numbers on the Cambrian list were 73-80, 87-88 and in 1922 they became GW 875-76 and 878-885. Swindon gave Diagram A.14 to reboilered engines Nos. 875/79/83/85 (*Figure* 158) and A.15 to those still with their original or reconditioned boilers (*Figure* 157).

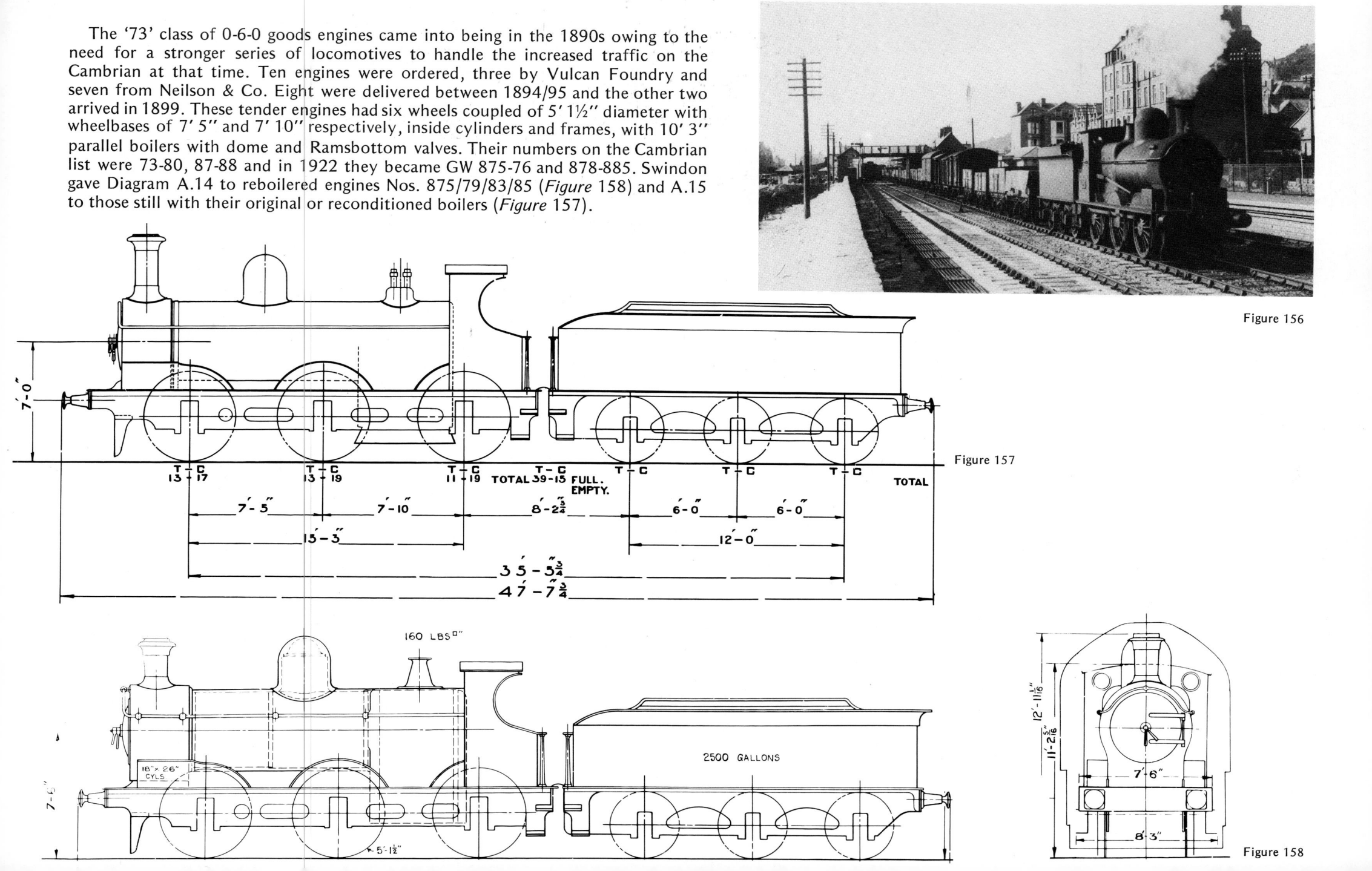

Figure 156

Figure 157

Figure 158

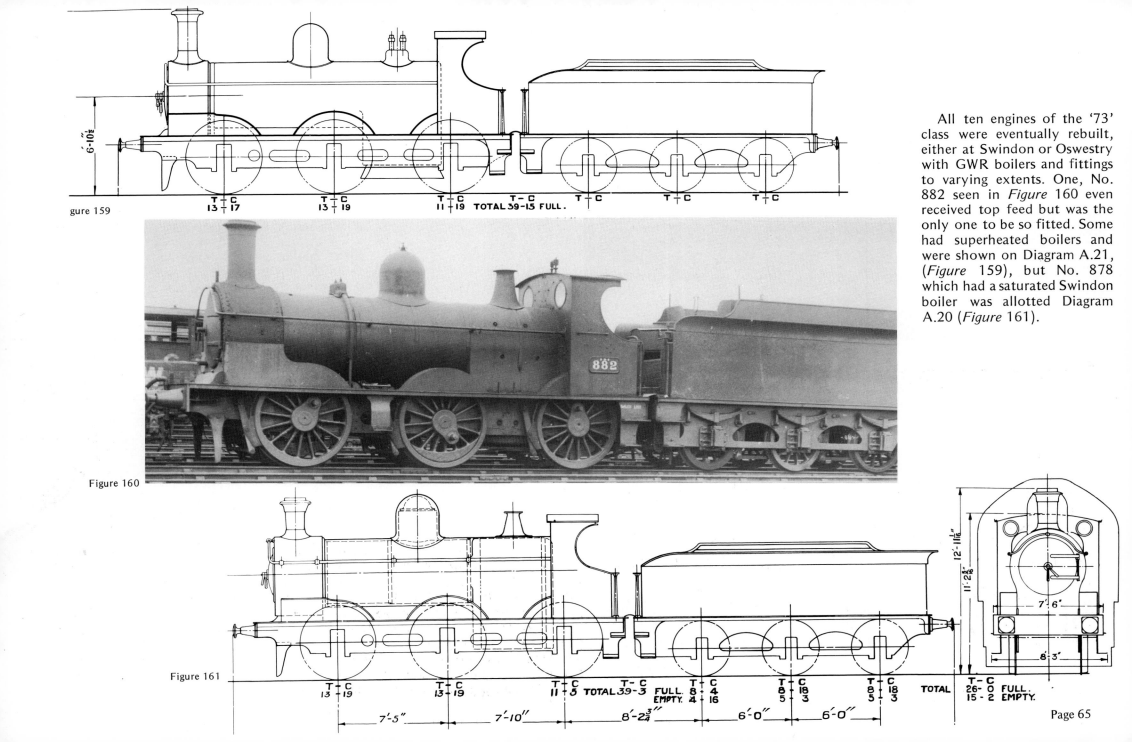

gure 159

T-C 13-17 T-C 13-19 T-C 11-19 TOTAL 39-15 FULL. T-C T-C T-C

6-10¾"

All ten engines of the '73' class were eventually rebuilt, either at Swindon or Oswestry with GWR boilers and fittings to varying extents. One, No. 882 seen in *Figure* 160 even received top feed but was the only one to be so fitted. Some had superheated boilers and were shown on Diagram A.21, (*Figure* 159), but No. 878 which had a saturated Swindon boiler was allotted Diagram A.20 (*Figure* 161).

Figure 160

882

Figure 161

T-C 13-19 T-C 13-19 T-C 11-5 TOTAL 39-3 T-C FULL. T-C 8-4 EMPTY 4-16 T-C 8-18 5-3 T-C 8-18 5-3 TOTAL T-C 26-0 FULL. 15-2 EMPTY.

7'-5" 7'-10" 8'-2¾" 6'-0" 6'-0"

12'-11⅙" 11'-2⁵⁄₁₆" 7'-6" 8'-3"

Page 65

The year 1903 saw the introduction on the Cambrian of the 'Large Belpaire Goods' series of 0-6-0 engines. Also known as the '15' class, eventually there were fifteen in all, five made by R. Stephenson & Co., and ten from Beyer-Peacock & Co. Building was spread over the years from 1903 until after the War in 1919. These fifteen were big engines, closely resembling the GWR Dean Goods.

Figure 162

No. 878 which fits the Diagram A.20 is shown in *Figure* 163 alongside the coal dump at Oswestry in 1937, coupled to one of the standard Cambrian tenders.

In *Figure* 162 No. 884 can be seen at Machynlleth shed just before the Second World War. The earliest to be withdrawn was 883 which was cut up in 1928, and the last was No. 884 which went in 1947.

Figure 163

The six coupled wheels were 5' 1½" diameter set at 7' 3" and 8' 3" wheelbases and the boiler with the Belpaire firebox was pressed to 160lbs. At the grouping in 1922 Swindon issued Diagram A.13 (*Figure* 164) to cover the class as absorbed, and of course the numbers were changed to fit the GW stock book. This renumbering was a little complicated, so a table is set out here to clarify.

However it should be noted that Nos. 90/91 and 92 never carried their new numbers, being scrapped at Swindon. The other twelve received various 'Western' modifications and many lasted until after nationalization. The Diagram issued to cover those with a saturated boiler was A.28 shown in *Figure* 167, and the two illustrations are of No. 887 in *Figure* 165 and 844 in *Figure* 166.

No.	15	became	GWR	No.	844
No.	29	,,	,,	No.	849
No.	31	,,	,,	No.	855
No.	38	,,	,,	No.	864
No.	42	,,	,,	No.	873
No.	54	,,	,,	No.	874
No.	89	,,	,,	No.	887
No.	90	,,	,,	No.	888

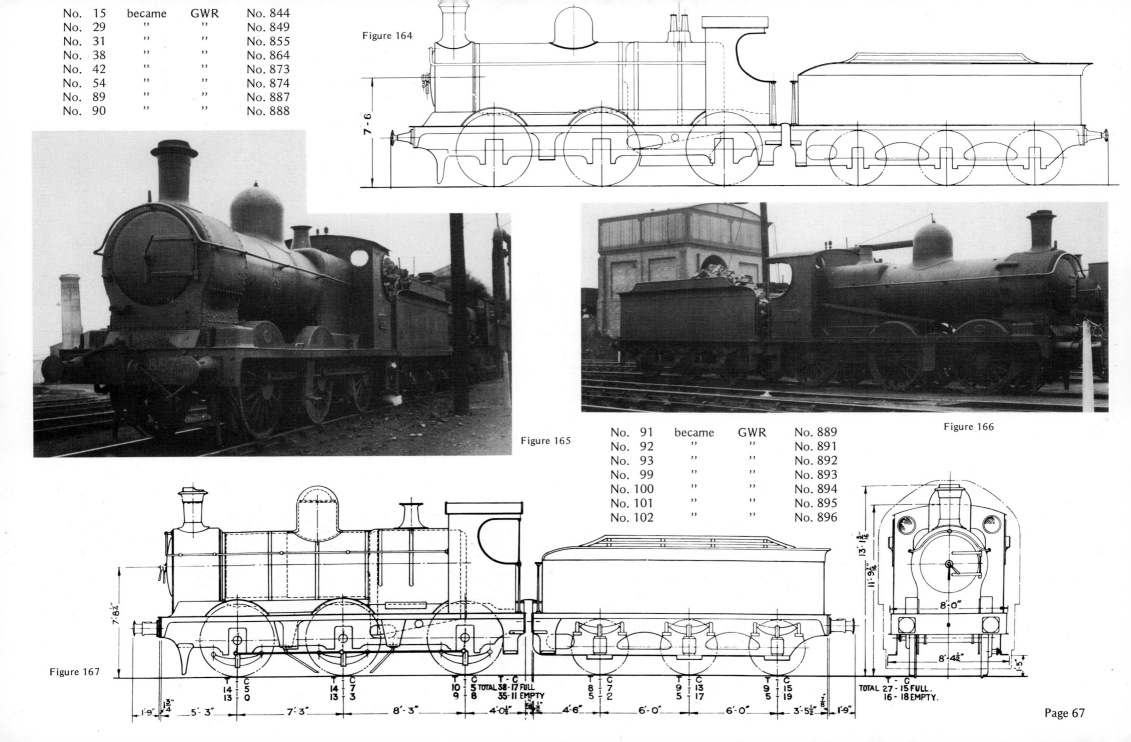

Figure 164

Figure 165

Figure 166

No.	91	became	GWR	No.	889
No.	92	,,	,,	No.	891
No.	93	,,	,,	No.	892
No.	99	,,	,,	No.	893
No.	100	,,	,,	No.	894
No.	101	,,	,,	No.	895
No.	102	,,	,,	No.	896

Figure 167

Figure 168

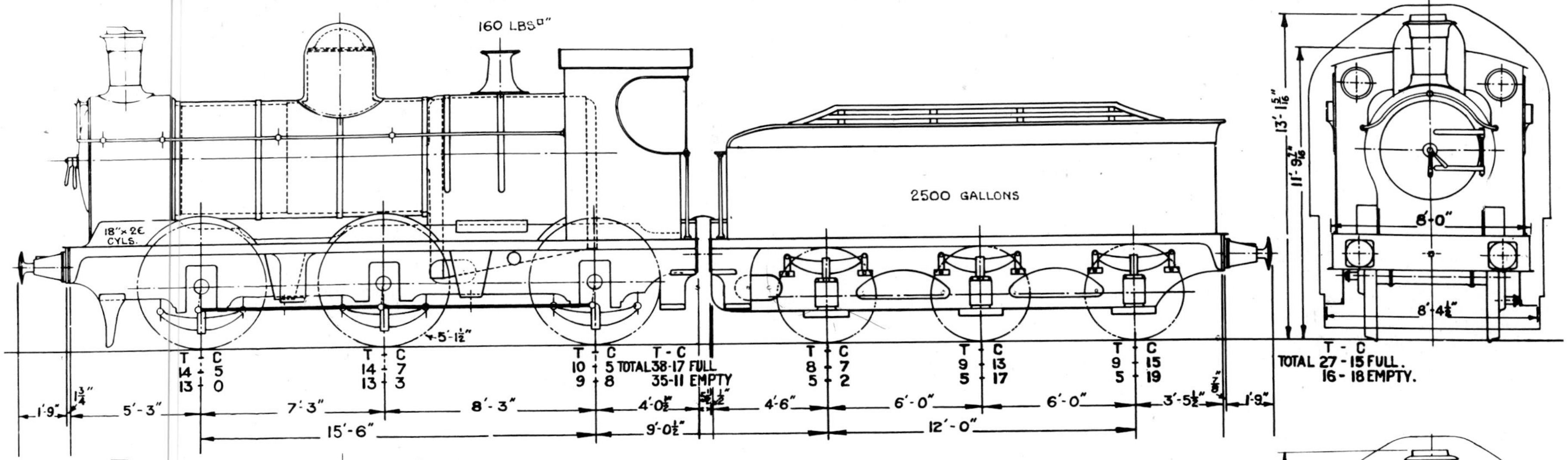

Figure 169

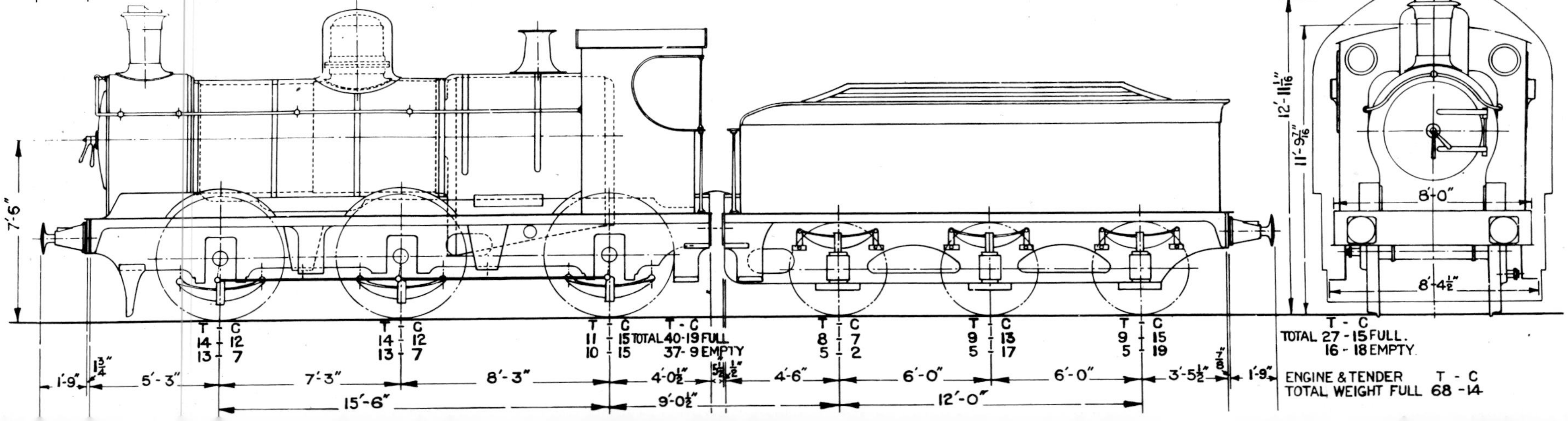

160 LBS□"

18"× 2E CYLS.

2500 GALLONS

13'-1⅛"
11'-9⅞"
8'-0"
8'-4½"

T	C
14	5
13	0

T	C
14	7
13	3

T	C
10	5
9	8

T-C TOTAL 38-17 FULL
35-11 EMPTY

T	C
8	7
8	5

T	C
9	13
9	5

T	C
9	15
9	5

T-C
TOTAL 27-15 FULL.
16-18 EMPTY.

1'-9" 1¾" 5'-3" 7'-3" 8'-3" 4'-0½" 5½" 4'-6" 6'-0" 6'-0" 3'-5½" ⅞" 1'-9"
15'-6" 9'-0½" 12'-0"

Figure 170

7'-5"

12'-11⁷⁄₁₆"
11'-9⁷⁄₁₆"
8'-0"
8'-4½"

T	C
14	12
13	7

T	C
14	12
13	7

T	C
11	15
10	15

T-C TOTAL 40-19 FULL
37-9 EMPTY

T	C
8	7
8	5

T	C
9	13
9	5

T	C
9	15
9	5

T-C
TOTAL 27-15 FULL.
16-18 EMPTY.

ENGINE & TENDER   T - C
TOTAL WEIGHT FULL 68 -14

1'-9" 1¾" 5'-3" 7'-3" 8'-3" 4'-0½" 5½" 4'-6" 6'-0" 6'-0" 3'-5½" ⅞" 1'-9"
15'-6" 9'-0½" 12'-0"

Figure 171

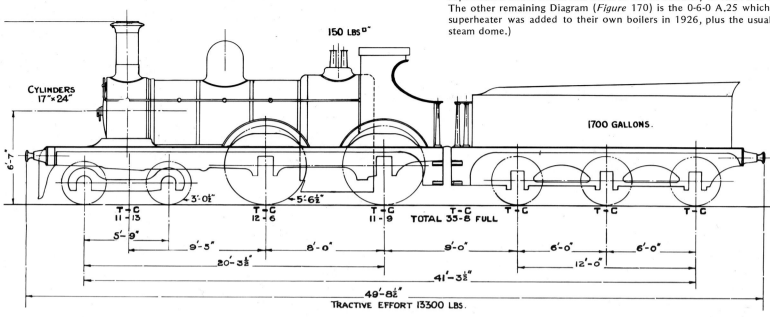

150 LBS □

CYLINDERS
17" x 24"

6'-7"

1700 GALLONS.

3'-0½"   5'-6½"

T-C   T-C   T-C   T-C   T-C   T-C   T-C
11-13   12-6   11-9   TOTAL 35-8 FULL

5'-9"
9'-5"   8'-0"   9'-0"   6'-0"   6'-0"
20'-3½"   12'-0"
41'-3½"
49'-8½"
TRACTIVE EFFORT 13300 LBS.

Seen at Worcester Shed in 1951 No. 895 (*Figure* 168) carries "British Railways" on the tender, and is carrying the same type of superheated boiler which was fitted to her at Oswestry in 1924 and which relates to the Swindon Diagram A.23 shown in *Figure* 169. The other remaining Diagram (*Figure* 170) is the 0-6-0 A.25 which was issued to cover Nos. 864 and 896 when a standard Swindon superheater was added to their own boilers in 1926, plus the usual GWR smokebox, chimney and safety valve. (Note the unusual steam dome.)

1878 saw the delivery of six more Sharp-Stewart engines to the Cambrian. This was the 'Small Bogie Passenger' class and consisted of six locomotives which were numbered 16/17/20/21/50/60. They were attractive little machines, having inside cylinders driving four-coupled wheels of 5' 6½" diameter at 8' centres, with a leading bogie having wheels of 3' 0½" diameter with a 5' 9" wheelbase. Boiler pressure was 140 lb and the loaded weight came to 35 tons 5 cwt. At the grouping Swindon gave the class the Diagram A.34 (*Figure* 171). No. 20 was cut up in 1922, but the other five received various bits and pieces and were renumbered 1115-18, 1110/12 (No. 1117 being allotted to the ill fated Cambrian No. 20). They completed their time in Great Western ownership, still on their home ground, but were gradually scrapped, the last, No. 21 (GW 1118), hanging on until 1930.

As previously mentioned, the years of 1890-92 brought a great increase in traffic on all the railways in the United Kingdom, not only for merchandise, but also for conveyance of passengers. At that time, and indeed ever since, the undulations and engineering difficulties of the Cambrian meant weight restrictions on the axle loading of the locomotives using the system, which in turn meant that there was a severe limit to the size of engines permitted on the line. Again Messrs Sharp-Stewart were asked to design a light locomotive which could handle this increased passenger traffic, and duly came up with the '61' class of 4-4-0 inside cylindered engine, having a maximum axle load of 15 tons on the leading driving wheels, in effect a larger version of the 'Small Bogie Passenger' class. Known as the 'Large Bogie Passenger' series, twenty two engines were built; 16 by Sharp Stewart's, 4 by Stephenson, and 2 more at Oswestry works in 1901 and 1904. *Figures* 172 and 173 show No. 47 and No. 11, two engines of the '61' class, practically as built, and one can see the similarity between these engines and their forerunner the 'Small Bogie' in the diagram above (*Figure* 171).

Figure 172

Figure 173

One of this '61' class was destroyed in the accident at Abermule in 1921, so that only 21 of the series came on to the GWR in 1922. Five were cut up in that year and four more in 1924, the other remaining twelve being fitted with various GWR items such as smoke-boxes, chimneys and safety valves, and giving service for several years. The final engine to be withdrawn was No. 83, and the year 1931. Their Cambrian numbers and the allocated GW numbers were as follows.

Cambrian	No.67	to	GWR	1100
"	No.71	to	GWR	1104
"	No.32	to	GWR	1085
"	No.85	to	GWR	1108
"	No.19	to	GWR	1082
"	No.61	to	GWR	1088
"	No.63	to	GWR	1091
"	No.65	to	GWR	1096
"	No.69	to	GWR	1102
"	No.84	to	GWR	1107
"	No.47	to	GWR	1086
"	No.86	to	GWR	1109
"	No.11	to	GWR	1068
"	No.62	to	GWR	1090
"	No.64	to	GWR	1093
"	No.66	to	GWR	1097

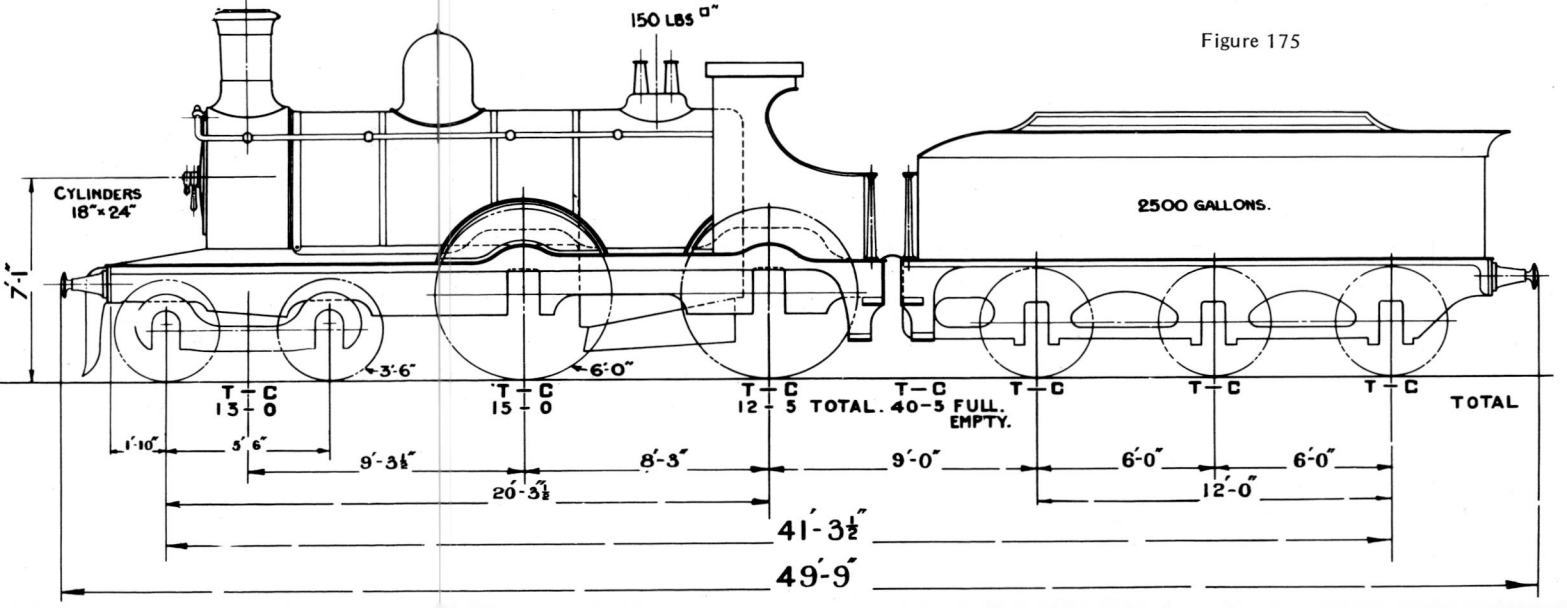

Figure 174

Figure 175

CYLINDERS 18"×24"

150 LBS

2500 GALLONS.

7′-1″

3′-6″   6′-0″

T—C 13—0   T—C 15—0   T—C 12—5 TOTAL. 40-5 FULL. EMPTY.   T—C   T—C   T—C   T—C   T—C   TOTAL

1′-10″   5′-6″

9′-3¾″   8′-3″   9′-0″   6′-0″   6′-0″

20′-3¾″   12′-0″

41′-3½″

49′-9″

Figure 174 illustrates No. 61 (GW 1088) the first of the class after an overhaul and new safety valve bonnet at Swindon, and the Diagram A.32 is that which was issued for the Cambrian 'Large Passenger' series (*Figure* 175).

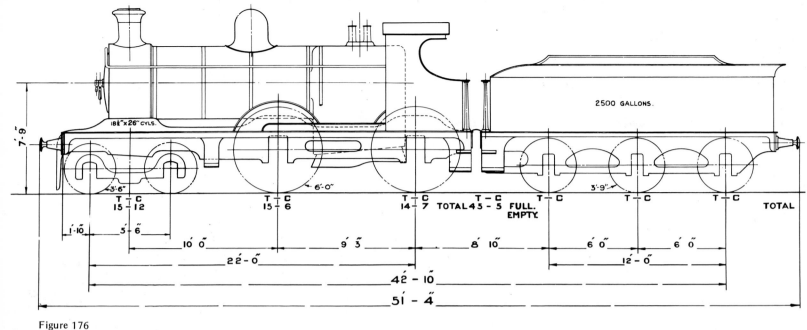

18½"x26" CYLS.

7'-9"

2500 GALLONS.

3'-6"

6'-0"

3'-9"

T — C
15 — 12

T — C
15 — 6

T — C
14 — 7 TOTAL 45 — 5 FULL.
EMPTY.

T — C

T — C

T — C

T — C

TOTAL

1'-10"   5'-6"

10'-0"

9'-3"

8'-10"

6'-0"

6'-0"

22'-0"

12'-0"

42'-10"

51'-4"

Figure 176

The last class of locomotives built for the Cambrian Railway was the 'Large Belpaire Passenger'. Only five engines were ordered and built by Stephenson & Co. in 1904. They were of the usual 4-4-0 classification but differed from the '61' class in being much larger all round. 6' 0" driving wheels were set at 9' 3" centres with bogie wheels of 3' 6" diameter. Boiler pressure was set at 170 lb and the weight scaled 45 tons 5 cwt. Cambrian numbers were 94-98 and like the previous class, one of the series No. 95 was involved in the head-on collision at Abermule and like No. 82 was a complete write-off. Therefore at the grouping only four engines went into the GWR and were renumbered 1014/1029/1035/1043. Swindon diagram A.31 was allocated (*Figure* 176) but the modifications to these engines were only minor, such items as smoke-boxes, chimneys and safety valves, although 1043 did receive a GWR superheater. *Figure* 177 shows No. 94 in the Cambrian days. *Figures* 178 and 179 (on next page) illustrate GW No. 1043 showing both left and right-hand sides of the same engine.

Figure 178

Figure 177

Figure 179

The CARDIFF RAILWAY COMPANY

The Cardiff Railway was first and foremost a Dock System. Bute West Dock, opened in 1839 by the second Marquis of Bute, was the sea outlet for the Bute Collieries, and these docks stayed with the Bute family until 1886 when the enterprise was formed into the Bute Docks Company. At first the Taff Vale Railway used their engines to work the Bute Docks, until in approximately 1860 the Marquis used his own steam locomotives for the shunting operations.

Penarth Dock opened in 1865, followed by the large Barry Dock in 1889, both of which took a lot of the coal trade from Cardiff and consequently the Bute Docks suffered. In the face of this opposition the Bute Docks Company decided to change its name to the Cardiff Railway Company which it achieved in 1897, and to justify the new grandiose title sought for fifteen years to extend their mileage. With about 120 miles of sidings at the docks, route mileage only amounted to approximately 8¾. This consisted of a line from Heath Junction on the Rhymney Railway to Rhydyfelin where it joined the Taff Vale. There were also many other short links, loops and deviations, all designed to facilitate the passage of coal from the pits to the Cardiff Bute Docks.

Cardiff No.	GWR No.	Type	Diagram	Cardiff No.	GWR No.	Type	Diagram
1	156	0-6-2T	H	19	697	0-6-0T	A78
2	693	0-6-0T	A77	20	151	0-6-2T	K
3	686	0-6-0T	A76	21	161	0-6-2T	K
4	687	0-6-0T	A76	22	152	0-6-2T	K
5	1338	0-4-0T	O	23	1676	0-6-0T	A99
6	1339	0-4-0T	O	24	698	0-6-0T	A79
7	685	0-6-0T	A75	25	1689	0-6-0T	A100(A29)
8	688	0-6-0T	A76	26	163	0-6-2T	O
9	157	0-6-2T	N(A20)	27	162	0-6-2T	M
10	158	0-6-2T	N	28	159	0-6-2T	M
11	160	0-6-2T	K(A19)	29	692	0-6-0T	A76
12	694	0-6-0T	A78	30	691	0-6-0T	A76
13	690	0-6-0T	A76	31	1667	0-6-0T	A99(A47)
14	681	0-6-0T	A74	32	684	0-6-0T	A74
15	695	0-6-0T	A78	33	153	0-6-2T	L
16	682	0-6-0T	A74	34	154	0-6-2T	L
17	683	0-6-0T	A74	35	155	0-6-2T	L
18	696	0-6-0T	A74	36	1327	2-4-2T	Q

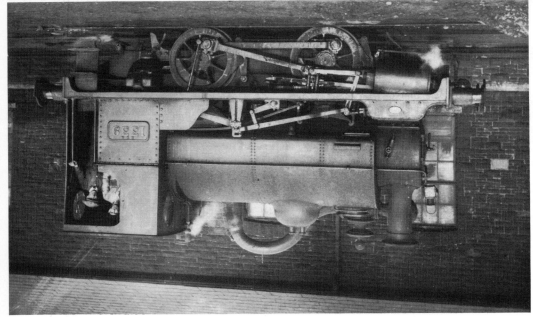

Figure 183

Figure 182

Figure 180

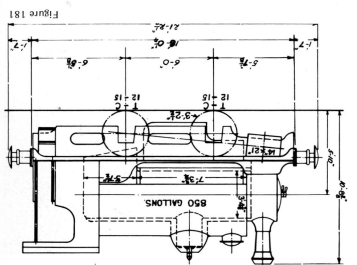

Figure 181

850 GALLONS.

Page 74

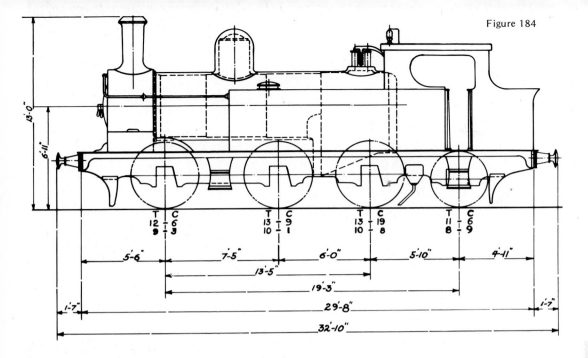

Figure 184

Two of the smallest engines of the Cardiff Railway were Nos. 5 and 6, both built by Messrs Kitson & Co. in 1898-99 of saddle tank design with just four coupled wheels of 3' 2½" diameter set at 6' 0" centres and an all-up weight of 25½ tons. The unusual feature of these two locomotives was the fitting of the Hawthorn Kitson valve gear, a form of Walschaerts, but with the link above the running plate instead of the more usual position, below. Also it should be noted that no coal bunker was fitted! Attention to the fire was either from a small quantity in the cab, or from a stock pile at the docks. In 1922 No. 5 became GW 1338, No. 6 became 1339 and Swindon issued Diagram O for the pair (*Figure* 181). No. 1339 was scrapped in 1934 (*Figure* 183) but No. 1338 shown in *Figures* 180 and 182 worked not only in the Cardiff area but also at Swansea and even Bridgwater Docks. She can still be seen in preservation.

Another Kitson engine design which the Cardiff Railway used, was the 0-6-2T of which No. 27 is a good example. She and her sister No. 28 were built in 1887. They had six coupled driving wheels of 4' 6" diameter with a trailing truck having wheels 3' 8¼" diameter. Both engines were rebuilt in 1904 and 1906 respectively and finally came into GW stock in 1922. One other, numbered 1, joined Nos. 27 and 28 and all three became GW Nos. 156/162/159. Two of these, Nos. 156 and 159 were sold out of the Great Western in 1931, and No. 162 was cut up at Swindon in 1935. The Diagram allotted was M (*Figure* 184), and the illustration of No. 162 shows her with her own boiler but fitted with GWR smokebox, chimney and safety valve (*Figure* 186).

Figure 186

Figure 185

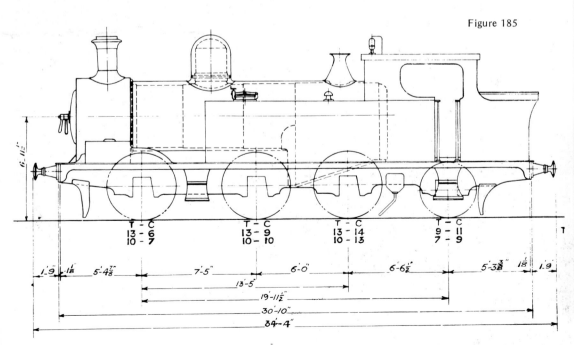

Figure 187

Figure 188

Figure 189

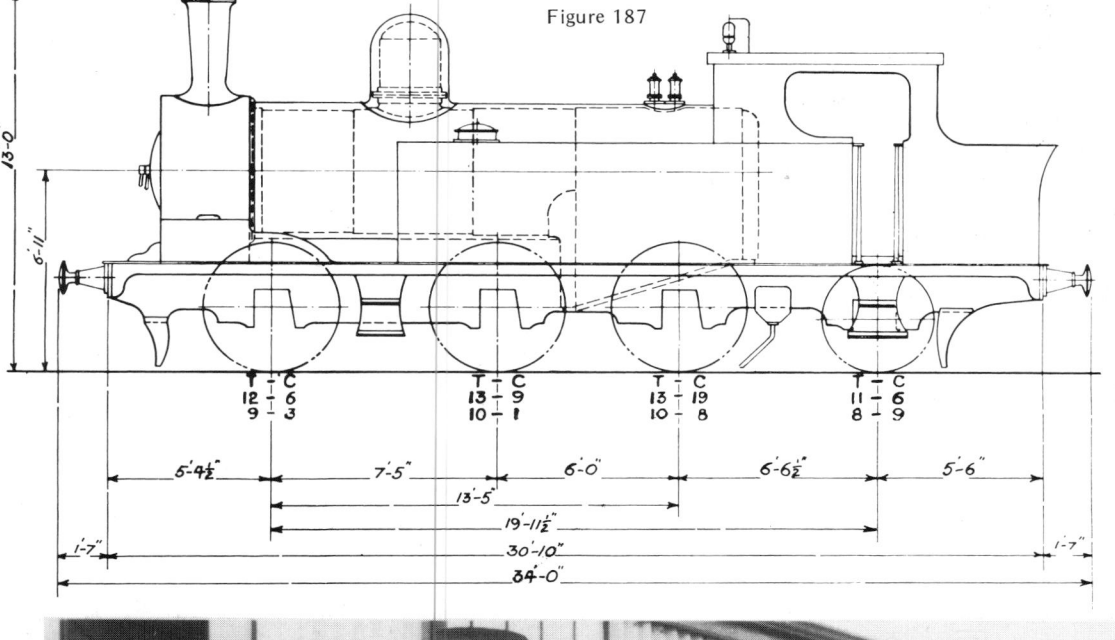

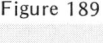

Two more similar locomotives were delivered to the Cardiff Railway in 1898, these were Nos. 9 and 10, and only differed from the previous three in that they had slightly larger bunkers, and consequently a longer wheelbase. Given GW numbers 157 and 158 in 1922 they were given Diagram N (*Figure* 187) and only 157 received the 'Western' treatment, emerging under Diagram A.20 in *Figure* 185. No. 157 went in 1928, but 158 worked on until 1932.

The two illustrations in *Figures* 188 and 189 show No. 10 before and after the grouping.

Four rather strange looking 0-6-2T engines were Nos. 11, 21, 20 and 22. Built by Kitsons, two in 1905, and two in 1919, they were unusual in having full length side tanks, extending from the cab to the front of the smokebox. *Figure* 190 shows No. 11 as delivered to the Cardiff Railway in 1905. They had driving wheels of 4' 7" diameter set at 7' 5" and 6' centres, with 3' 8¼" trailing wheels under the bunker which had a capacity of 3 tons. Quite heavy engines, they scaled 59 tons, in working order. The first pair, Nos. 11 and 21, had steam brakes and Ramsbottom safety valves, but the later pair Nos. 20 and 22 had Ross pop safety valves and were fitted with vacuum brakes. *Figure* 191 shows the Swindon Diagram K which was allotted to Nos. 20 and 22 renumbered to GW 151 and 152. Nos. 11 and 21 became GW 160 and 161. Only No. 160 was rebuilt with a Swindon boiler, the others making do with various boiler fittings. All four had been withdrawn by 1936, the first to go being No. 161 which was scrapped in 1929.

Figure 190

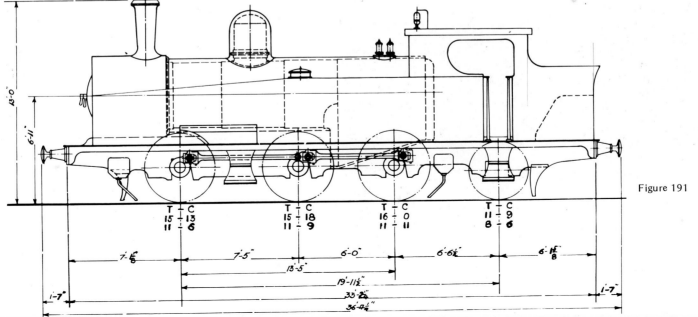

Figure 191

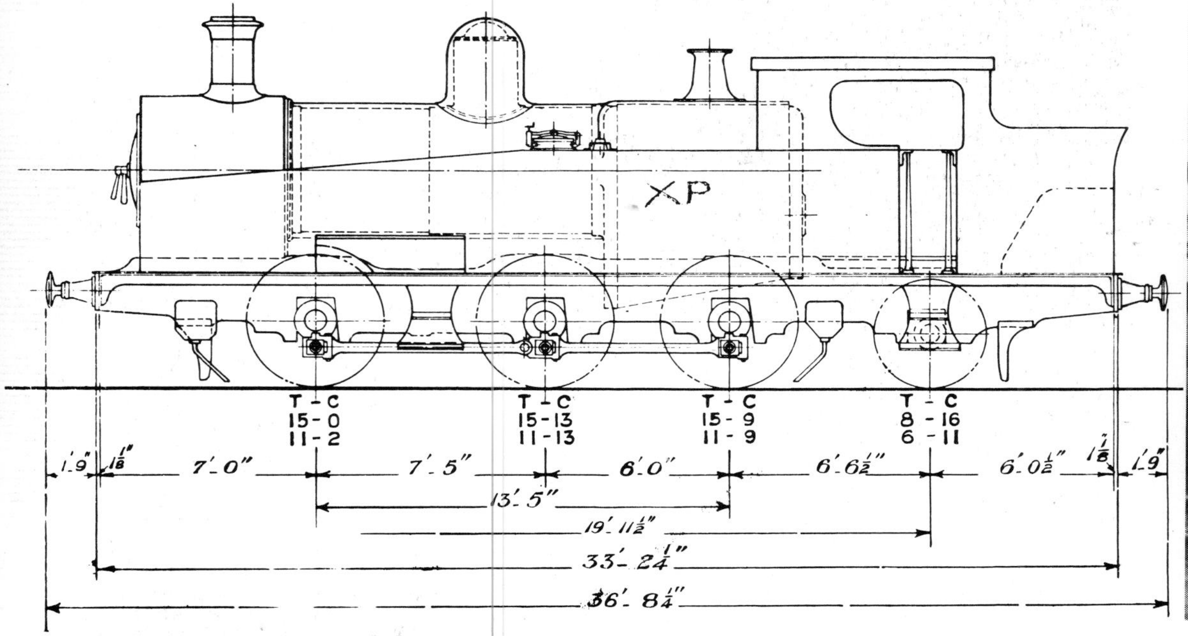

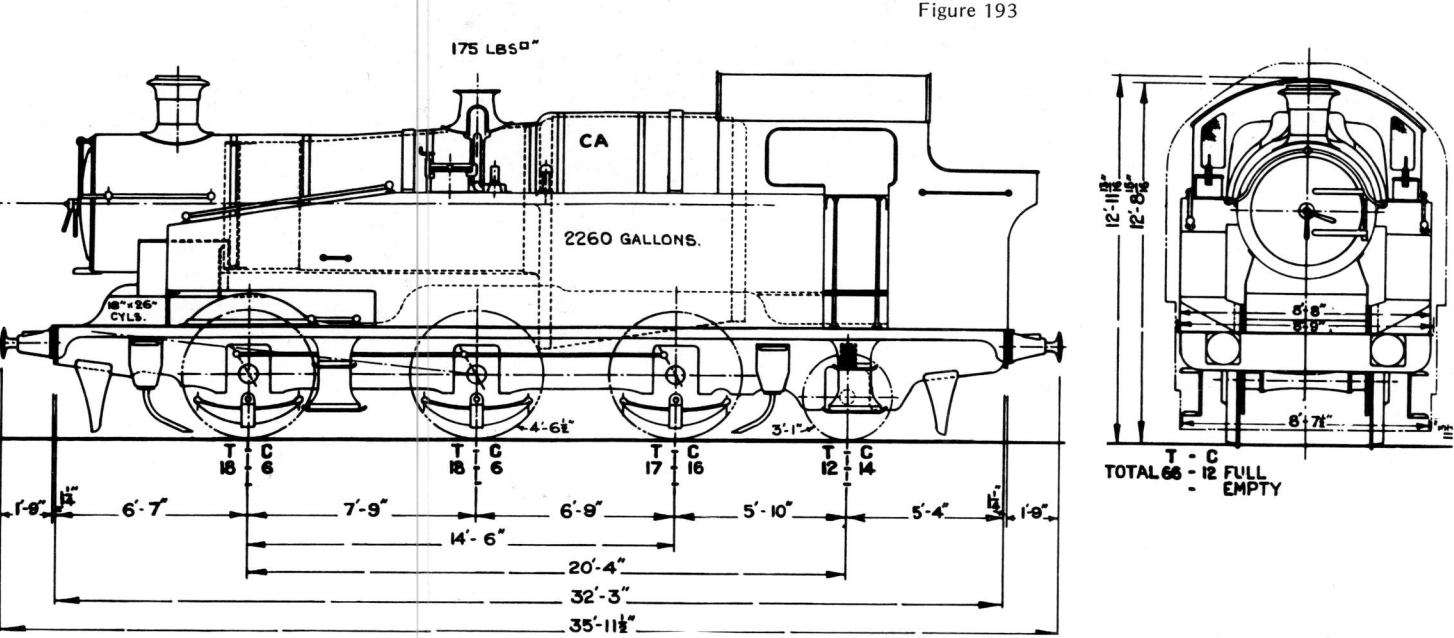

XP

T - C
15 - 0
11 - 2

T - C
15 - 13
11 - 13

T - C
15 - 9
11 - 9

T - C
8 - 16
6 - 11

1'-9" 1⅛"   7'-0"   7'-5"   6'-0"   6'-6½"   6'-0½"   ⅞" 1'-9"

13'-5"

19'-11½"

33'-2¼"

36'-8¼"

Figure 192

Figure 194

Figure 193

175 LBS□"

CA

2260 GALLONS.

18"×26"
CYLS.

T - C
18 - 6

T - C
18 - 6

T - C
17 - 16

T - C
12 - 14

4'-6¼"   3'-1"

1'-9" 1¼"   6'-7"   7'-9"   6'-9"   5'-10"   5'-4" ¼" 1'-9"

14'-6"

20'-4"

32'-3"

35'-11½"

12'-11⅛"
12'-8⅝"

5'-8"
6'-9"

8'-7⅛"

T - C
TOTAL 66 - 12 FULL
        - EMPTY

No. 152 which was Cardiff Railway No. 22 had her pop valves changed for GW type safety valves, and can be seen in this condition in *Figure* 194. The Diagram in *Figure* 192 is the Swindon A.19 which was drawn for No. 160, the only engine of the four to be converted at Swindon in 1922 with the GW Belpaire boiler.

In contrast to these long rather unwieldy looking engines, *Figure* 193 illustrates the 'Western' version of one of the three Kitson engines Nos. 33-35 which became GW Nos. 153-55. This was No. 155 rebuilt at Swindon in 1928 and was the only Cardiff engine to carry a Swindon taper boiler, the Diagram was A.41.

Figure 195

Figure 195 shows the front view of No. 153, one of the Kitson 1908 engines, and in Figure 196 No. 154 is seen with the GW safety valve and enlarged coal bunker, but otherwise as in her Cardiff condition. This engine was eventually sold to Hartley Main collieries and worked on until 1960.

Figure 196

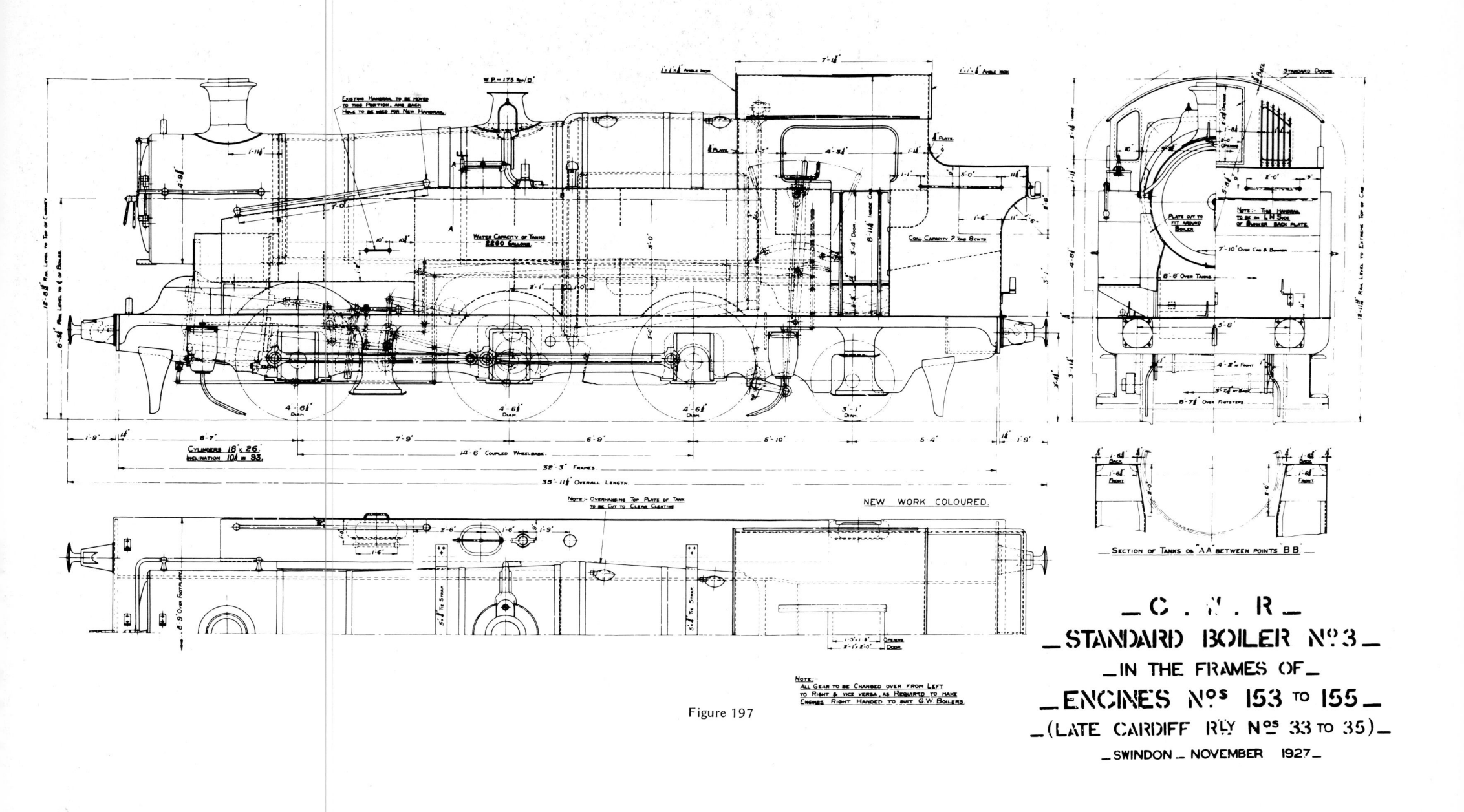

Figure 197

_ C . W . R _
STANDARD BOILER Nº 3
IN THE FRAMES OF
ENGINES Nºs 153 to 155
(LATE CARDIFF RLY Nºs 33 to 35)
_SWINDON _ NOVEMBER 1927_

In *Figure* 197 we show the Swindon drawing of 1927 which was made to illustrate the fitting of the Standard No. 3 boiler into the frames of the Cardiff Railway engines Nos. 33-35. These three became GW 153 to 155 as already mentioned, but only No. 155 actually carried the coned boiler, despite the text on the works drawing. The locomotive No. 155 is shown in *Figure* 198 just as depicted in the plans above, the date of the photo is 1948 and site is Swindon factory. Note that the engine still has her cast iron chimney at this date. In *Figure* 199 she is seen again at Swindon in 1949 but fitted now with the built-up chimney with copper top, plus the British Railways smokebox number plate. No. 155 remained at Cardiff East Dock until being withdrawn in 1953.

Figure 199

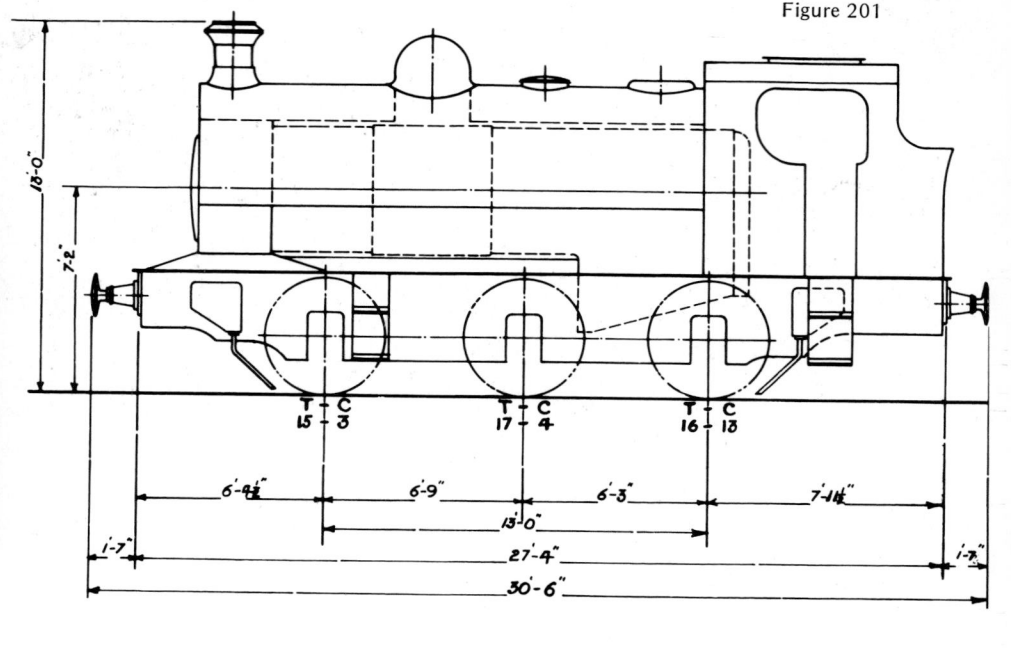

Figure 201

Figure 200

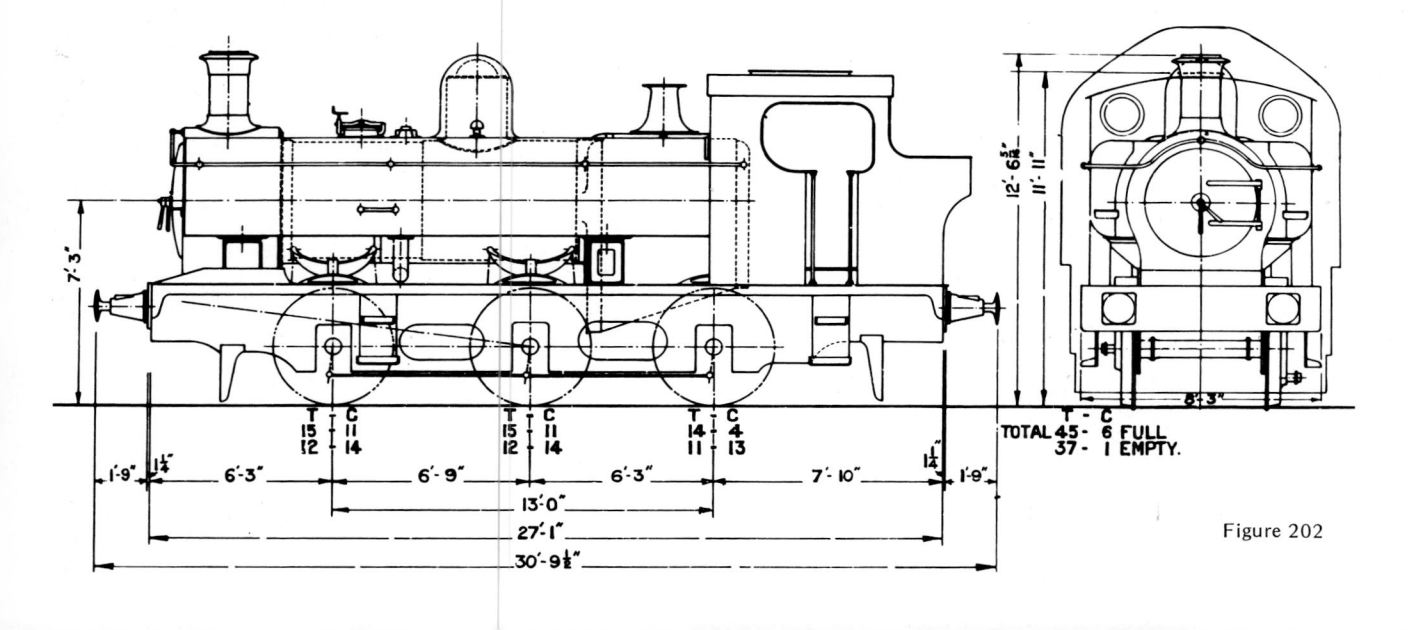

Figure 202

Four 0-6-0 engines built by Hudswell Clarke & Co. in 1920, were the last engines to be delivered to the Cardiff Railway before the company was absorbed into the GWR in 1922. Given the numbers 14, 16, 17 and 32 these four locomotives had full length saddle tanks with inside cylinders, and closed-in cabs. The driving wheels were 4' 1" set at 6' 3" centres and the working weight was 49 tons. No. 32 is seen in *Figure* 200 as she was built, with the Swindon Diagram A.74 illustrated in *Figure* 201. These four saddle tanks were renumbered GW 681-4 and between the years of 1926 and 1939 all were reconstructed at Swindon with a standard No. 11 boiler with GWR boiler fittings, a new bunker, and finally a pair of pannier tanks. Swindon Diagram B.36 represented the rebuild to this condition as is shown in *Figure 202*.

Figure 203

Some superb pictures on this page from the camera of A. E. Sterndale, show the rebuilt Hudswell Clarke engines of ex-Cardiff Railway stock. No. 17 (GW 683) in *Figure* 203 is seen at Cardiff Docks in 1951. In *Figure* 204 No. 32 (GW 684), also during 1951, basks in the evening sunshine at Cardiff, and No. 16 (GW 682) stands "dead" on the stop blocks in 1946 (*Figure* 205).

Figure 204

Figure 205

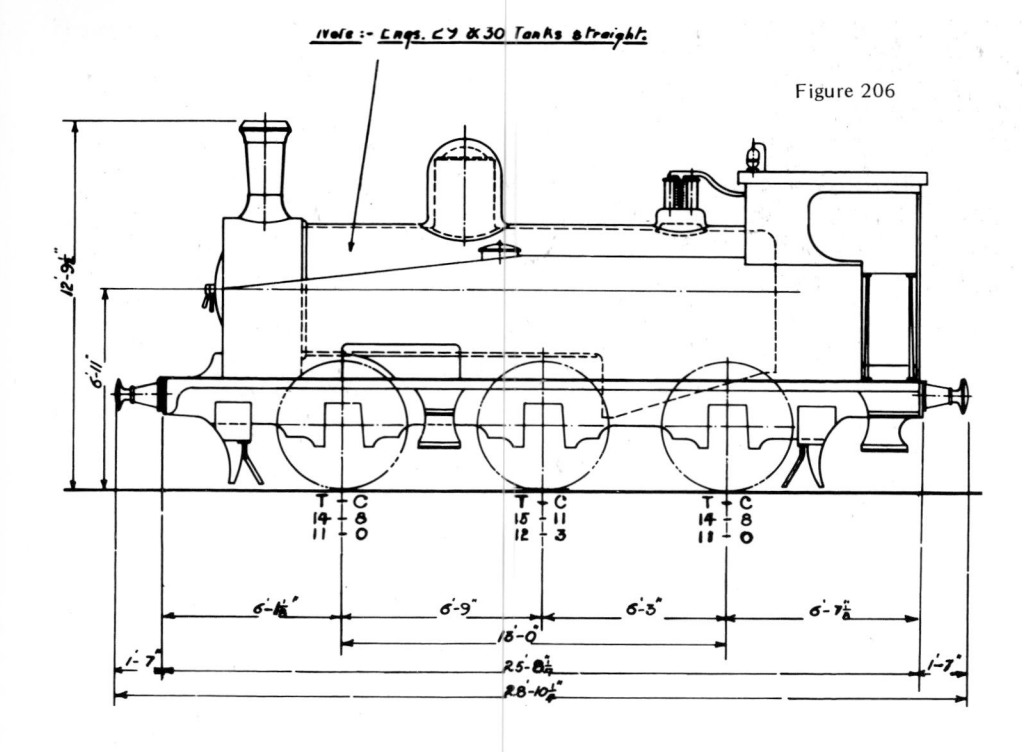

Note:- Engs. 29 & 30 Tanks straight.

Figure 206

Figure 207

Figure 208

Six smaller Kitson tank engines were taken on to the Cardiff locomotive stock between 1889 and 1899. These were 0-6-0T classification and had the sloping top side tanks which ran from cab to smokebox front. A hole was left to allow access to the motion for lubrication. There was no coal bunker fitted, just a flat back sheet to the cab with two spectacle plates therein. Any coal carried was lodged behind the left-hand side tanks! It was the normal practice in dockwork to replenish often from a specific coal stock. These six had an unusual range of numbers when in Cardiff ownership, being Nos. 29/30/3/13/4/8. The first two, 29 and 30, were slightly different from their sisters in that their side tanks did not slope downwards like the other four. 4' 6" driving wheels were fitted at 6' 9" and 6' 3" centres, and the working weight was 44½ tons. Renumbered into the GWR they became 692/91/86/90/87/88 and received the Swindon Diagram A.76 seen in *Figure* 206. Four were sold out of the GWR in 1927 and 1929 and Nos. 686 and 687 were withdrawn in 1925. *Figure* 207 shows No. 688 wearing the 'Great Western' lettering on the right-hand cab side and on the left-hand cab side in *Figure* 208. The other member of the class, No. 687, is depicted in *Figure* 209 at Cardiff Shed.

Figure 209

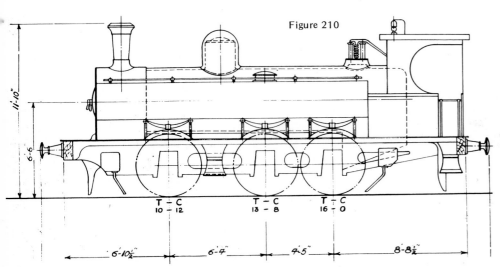

Figure 210

Figure 211

Three other engines of the Cardiff Railway are illustrated on the next two pages. In *Figures* 210 and 211 are diagram and picture of No. 2, one of the pannier tank 0-6-0T engines, built of course by Kitsons in 1882. As can be seen in the drawing (A.77) No. 2 had a very short wheelbase, coupled with a rather long overall length. The GWR changed her number to 693 but she was never rebuilt by the Swindon factory, being cut up at Leeds in 1925.

The small saddle tank shown in *Figures* 212 and 213 was one of thirteen similar built by Parfitt and Jenkins between 1869 and 1881. Only four survived to be absorbed into the GWR, these were 12/15/18/19 and they became 694-7. The last two, 696 and 697, were withdrawn in 1923 and 1925 respectively, but 694 and 695 although offered for sale, were not purchased, and were finally cut up in 1928.

Figure 212

Figure 213

Figure 214

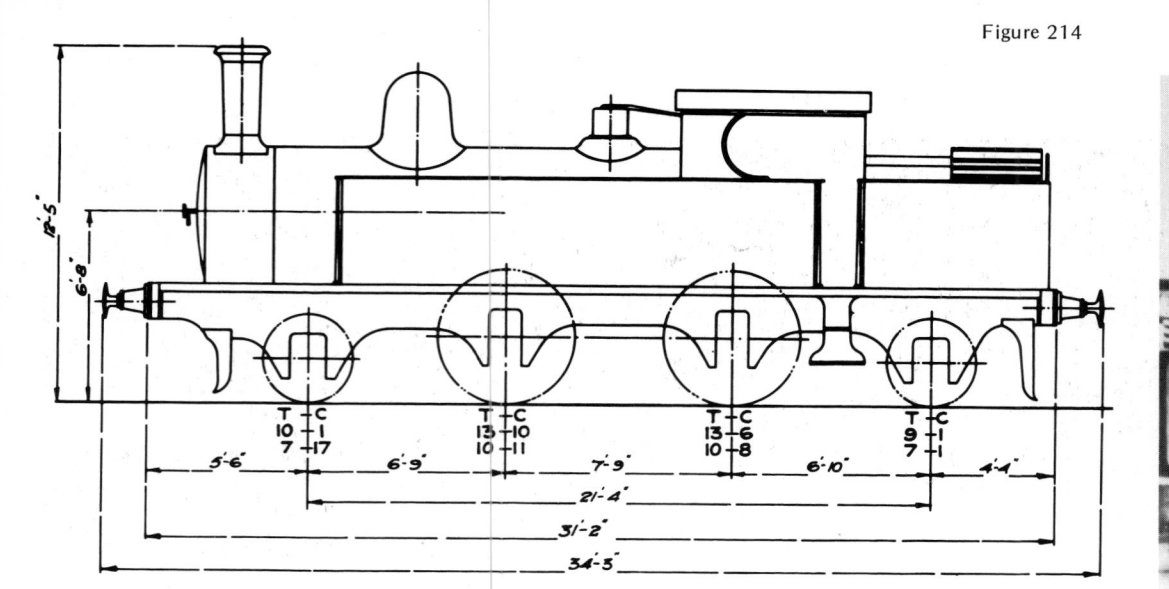

Figure 215

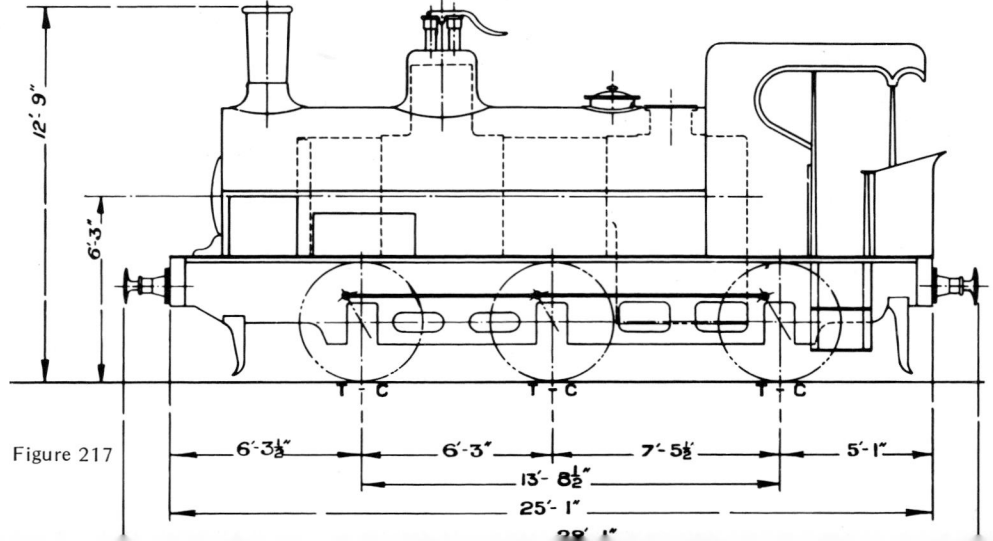

Figure 216

The 2-4-2T locomotive in *Figures* 214 and 215 is the LNWR tank which was named *The Earl of Dumfries*, being the only engine on the Cardiff Railway to carry a name. She came to the Cardiff in 1914 and was passed over to the GWR in 1922, who allotted Diagram Q to her and the number 1327 but she never carried the number, being cut up in that same year.

The last Cardiff engine to be illustrated is to the Swindon Diagram A.79 (*Figures* 216 and 217). The diagram shows the 0-6-0T engine which was No. 24. Her history is rather remarkable; thought to have been built by Beyer-Peacock to the 0-4-2T configuration, she was changed to 2-4-2ST in 1883 and was rebuilt again in 1885 as an 0-6-0T. By 1892 most of the engine was a rebuild from parts of other engines and she became Cardiff No. 24. Taken into the GWR she was renumbered according to records as 698, old No. 15 seen in the two pictures *Figures* 216 and 218 (next page) carrying the number GW 695!

Figure 217

Figure 218

COMMON SEAL OF THE CARDIFF RAILWAY COMPANY 1886·1897

WRTH DDWR A THAN

CARDIFF RAILWAY COMPANY
LOCOMOTIVE DATA

No.	Type	Builder	Date Built	Builder's No.	Cylinders Dia'r	Cylinders Stroke	Dia'r wheels Coupled	Dia'r wheels Radial	Wheel Base Fixed	Wheel Base Total	Length over Buffers	Extreme Width	Tractive Force @ 85% Present Boiler Pressure	Water Capy. Galls	Coal Capy. Cwt.	Weight Loaded Tons Cwt
					ins	*ins*	*Ft ins*	*Ft ins*	*Ft ins*	*Ft ins*	*Ft ins*	*Ft ins*	*Lbs*			
1	0-6-2	Kitson & Co	1894	3580	17½	26	4-6	3-8¼	13-5	19-3	33-0	8-7½	20054	1677	40	51-0
2	0-6-0	Do.	1882	2458	17	26	4-2½	–	10-9	10-9	29-4		17706			50-0
3	0-6-0	Do.	1895	3602	17½	26	4-6	–	13-0	13-0	28-10¼	8-8	20054	1350	23	44-7
4	0-6-0	Do.	1899	3871	17½	26	4-6	–	13-0	13-0	28-10¼	8-8	20054	1350	23	44-7
5	0-4-0	Do.	1888	3799	14	21	3-2½	–	6-0	6-0	21-2¼	8-3½	14539	850	15	25-10
6	0-4-0	Do	1899	3969	14	21	3-2½	–	6-0	6-0	21-2¼	8-3½	14539	850	15	25-10
7	0-6-0	Do.	1919	5182	17½	26	4-6	–	13-0	13-0	28-10¼	8-8	21307	1350	40	47-1
8	0-6-0	Do.	1899	3872	17½	26	4-6	–	13-0	13-0	28-10¼	8-8	20054	1350	23	44-7
9	0-6-2	Do.	1898	3869	17½	26	4-6	3-8¼	13-5	19-11½	34-0	8-7½	20054	1670	50	51-0
10	0-6-2	Do.	1898	3870	17½	26	4-6	3-8¼	13-5	19-11½	34-0	8-7½	20054	1670	50	51-0
11	0-6-2	Do.	1905	4333	18	26	4-6	3-8¼	13-5	19-11½	36-4¼	8-7½	19890	2300	60	59-0
12	0-6-0	Parfitt & Jenkins	1899		15½	22	4-0	–	13-4½	13-4½	26-10	7-9½	14975	1000	18	35-0
13	0-6-0	Kitson & Co	1895	3603	17½	26	4-6	–	13-0	13-0	28-10¼	8-8	20054	1350	23	44-7
14	0-6-0	Hudswell Clarke & Co	1920	1404	18	24	4-1½	–	13-0	13-0	30-6	8-3	23367	1250	40	49-0
15	0-6-0	Parfitt & Jenkins	1873		15½	22	4-0	–	13-4½	13-4½	26-10	7-9½	14975	1000	18	35-0
16	0-6-0	Hudswell Clarke & Co	1920	1405	18	24	4-1½	–	13-0	13-0	30-6	8-3	23367	1250	40	49-0
17	0-6-0	Do.	1920	1407	18	24	4-1½	–	13-0	13-0	30-6	8-3	23367	1250	50	49-0
18	0-6-0	Parfitt & Jenkins	1875		15½	22	4-0	–	13-4½	13-4½	26-10	7-9½	14975	1000	18	35-0
19	0-6-0	Do.	1875		15½	22	4-0	–	13-4½	13-4½	26-10	7-11	14975	1000	18	35-0
20	0-6-2	Kitson & Co	1919	5180	18	26	4-6	3-8¼	13-5	19-11½	36-4¼	8-7½	22542	2300	60	59-0
21	0-6-2	Do.	1905	4334	18	26	4-6	3-8¼	13-5	19-11½	36-4¼	8-7½	19890	2300	60	59-0
22	0-6-0	Do.	1919	5181	18	26	4-6	3-8¼	13-5	19-11½	36-4¼	8-7½	22542	2300	60	59-0
23	0-6-0	G.W.R. Co	1886	1676	18	26	5-1	–	15.9	15-9	29-7	8-7	20560	1100	40	47-0
24	*Sent to GWR Swindon May 1922*															
25	0-6-0	G.W.R. Co	1887	1689	18	26	5-1	–	15-9	15-9	29-7	8-7	17608	950	40	47-0
26	0-6-2	Kitson & Co	1886	2879	17½	26	4-6	3-8½	13-5	19-3	32-10	8-7½	17547	1600	45	51-1
27	0-6-2	Do.	1887	3069	17½	26	4-6	3-8¼	13-5	19-3	33-0	8-7½	18800	1677	40	51-0
28	0-6-2	Do.	1887		17½	26	4-6	3-8¼	13-5	19-3	33-0	8-7½	20054	1677	40	51-0
29	0-6-0	Do.	1889	3132	17½	26	4-6	–	13-0	13-0	26-10¼	8-8	18800	1350	23	44-7
30	0-6-0	Do.	1889	3133	17½	26	4-6	–	13-0	13-0	28-10¼	8-8	20054	1350	23	44-7
31	0-6-0	G.W.R. Co	1896	1667	18	26	5-1	–	15-9	15-9	29-7	8-7	20560	1100	40	47-0
32	0-6-0	Hudswell Clarke & Co	1920	1408	18	24	4-1½	–	13-0	13-0	30-6	8-3	23367	1250	40	49-0
33	0-6-2	Kitson & Co	1908	4595	18	26	4-6½	3-1	14-6	20-4	35-7½	8-9	23144	2300	38	66-5
34	0-6-2	Do.	1908	4596	18	26	4-6½	3-1	14-6	20-4	35-7½	8-9	23144	2300	38	66-5
35	0-6-2	Do.	1908	4597	18	26	4-6½	3-1	14-6	20-4	35-7½	8-9	23144	2300	38	66-5
36	*Sent to GWR Swindon May 1922*															

No.	BOILER: Working Pressure LBS Sq. in. Original	Present	Date Reduced	Tubes No.	Tubes Dia	Tubes Length	Heating Surface Sq. Ft.	Grate Area Sq. Ft.	RENEWALS & REPAIRS: New Boiler	New Tubes Date	New Tubes Material	New Cylinders	New Tyres	Last Overhaul (Heavy)
1	160	160	–	185	1¾	10-8¾	993.0	21-0	1915	May '15		May '15	Dec '20	December 1920
2	140	140	–	135	1¾	13-3	883.0	14-3	1902	Sept '21		Jan '14	Sept '21	September 1921
3	160	160	–	179	1¾	10-8½	947.13	18-7	1919	– '19		'19	'19	February 1920
4	160	160	–	179	1¾	10-8½	947.13	18-7	1920	July '20		Jan '20	July '20	July 1920
5	160	160	–	110	1¾	7-9¼	434.0	8-75	1918	Jan '18		–	Jan '18	January 1918
6	160	160	–	110	1¾	7-9¼	434.0	8-75	1916	Dec '16			Dec '16	December 1919
7	170	170	–	179	1¾	10-8½	947.1	18-7	–	Dec '21		Dec '21	'19	December 1921
8	160	160	–	179	1¾	10-8½	947.1	18-7	1921	Apl '21		1918	May '16	April 1921
9	160	160	–	185	1¾	10-8¾	993.0	21-0	1919	May '19		1922	Sept '14	May 1919
10	160	160	–	185	1¾	10-8¾	993.0	21-0	1921	Dec '21		Dec '21	Apl '18	December 1921
11	160	150	Nov '13	185	1¾	10-8 9/16	993.0	21-0	–	Dec '13		–	May '17	October 1920
12	160	160	–	141	1¾	9-6	641.3	12-12	1918	– '18		Dec '18	Dec '18	June 1921
13	160	160	–	179	1¾	10-8½	947.13	18-7	1916	Sept '16		–	Sept '16	September 1916
14	175	175	–	200	1¾	10-11½	1079.7	17-36	–	–		–	–	
15	160	160	–	141	1¾	9-6	641.3	12-12	1922	Apl '22		Apl '22	Apl '22	April 1922
16	175	175	–	200	1¾	10-11½	1079.7	17-36	–	–		–	–	
17	175	175	–	200	1¾	10-11½	1079.7	17-36	–	–		–	–	
18	160	160	–	141	1¾	9-6	641.3	12-12	1917	Oct '17		'94	May '19	May 1921
19	160	160	–	141	1¾	9-6	641.3	12-12	1921	Dec '21		'02	Jan '18	December 1921
20	170	170	–	185	1¾	10-8 9/16	993.0	21-0	–	Apl '19		–	Apl '19	
21	160	150	Apl '19	185	1¾	10-8 9/16	993.0	21-0	–	July '14		–	Jan '19	January 1919
22	170	170	–	185	1¾	10-8 9/16	993.0	21-0	–	Apl '19		–	Apl '19	
23	175	175	–	249	1⅝	10-10	1238.08	17-33	1922	Apl '22		–	Apl '14	May 1922
24														
25	165	150	(?)	233	1⅝	10-9	1154.42	15-45	X	Apl '21		–	'09	March 1921
26	140	140	–	187	1¾	11-2	1025.0	16-7	–	Feb '11		'98	May '17	October 1921
27	160	150	Feb '08	185	1¾	10-8¾	993.0	21-0	1904	Dec '14		'96	Mar '18	July 1921
28	160	160	–	185	1¾	10-8¾	993.0	21-0	1922	Oct '15		'18	Oct '15	November 1920
29	180	150	May '19	179	1¾	10-8½	947.13	18-7	1909	July '09		Aug '21	Feb '14	April 1921
30	160	160	–	179	1¾	10-8½	947.13	18-7	1908	Aug '20		Aug '20	Aug '20	March 1920
31	175	175	–	249	1⅝	10-8	1220.44	17-33	1922	Mar '22			Nov '18	March 1922
32	175	175	–	200	1¾	10-11½	1079.7	17-36	–	–		–	–	
33	175	160	Jan '19	229	1¾	11-7½	1301.0	21-0	–	–		–	'20	July 1920
34	175	160	Apl '19	229	1¾	11-7½	1301.0	21-0	–	–		–	Mar '17	March 1917
35	175	160	May '19	229	1¾	11.7½	1301.0	21-0	–	Apl '22		–	Apl '22	May 1922
36														

X = Second hand boiler from Swindon, 1922.

The RHYMNEY RAILWAY COMPANY

Taking its name from the town of Rhymney, the Rhymney Railway consisted of some 51 miles of route between Cardiff and Rhymney and many smaller branches. The first section laid was from Rhymney to Hengoed, then on down to Walnut Tree Junction where it joined the Taff Vale Railway, and managed at last to get running powers over the Taff Vale main line right into Cardiff, service being opened in 1858. In 1864 sanction was given to build a new direct line into Cardiff via Caerphilly and Llanishen, which was opened in 1871. Many other short lines were added, and running powers were granted here, there and everywhere, so that the Rhymney seemed to have access to a great majority of the collieries and industrial areas of South Wales. At the time of the 1922 grouping the Rhymney Railway passed 123 locomotives over to the GWR.

Rhymney No.	GWR No.	Type	Diagram
1	30	0-6-2T	A
2	31	0-6-2T	A
3	32	0-6-2T	A
4	82	0-6-2T	H (A37)
5	76	0-6-2T	F
6	83	0-6-2T	H
7	84	0-6-2T	I (A27)
8	85	0-6-2T	I
9	86	0-6-2T	I
10	52	0-6-2T	D
11	53	0-6-2T	D
12	54	0-6-2T	D
13	55	0-6-2T	E
14	56	0-6-2T	D
15	57	0-6-2T	E
16	33	0-6-2T	B
17	34	0-6-2T	A (A38)
18	58	0-6-2T	E
19	59	0-6-2T	E
20	60	0-6-2T	E
21	61	0-6-2T	E
22	62	0-6-2T	D
23	63	0-6-2T	D
24	64	0-6-2T	D
25	65	0-6-2T	D
26	66	0-6-2T	D
27	67	0-6-2T	D

Rhymney No.	GWR No.	Type	Diagram	Rhymney No.	GWR No.	Type	Diagram
28	68	0-6-2T	D	76	109	0-6-2T	I
29	69	0-6-2T	D	77	110	0-6-2T	I
30	70	0-6-2T	D	78	112	0-6-2T	I
31	77	0-6-2T	F	79	113	0-6-2T	I
32	604	0-6-0T	A 63	80	114	0-6-2T	I
33	605	0-6-0T	A 63	81	115	0-6-2T	I
34	606	0-6-0T	A 63	82	117	0-6-2T	I
35	78	0-6-2T	G	83	118	0-6-2T	I
36	79	0-6-2T	G	84	119	0-6-2T	I
37	80	0-6-2T	G	85	122	0-6-2T	I
38	81	0-6-2T	G	86	127	0-6-2T	I
39	35	0-6-2T	C	87	129	0-6-2T	I
40	36	0-6-2T	C	88	130	0-6-2T	I
41	37	0-6-2T	C	89	131	0-6-2T	I
42	38	0-6-2T	C	90	133	0-6-2T	I
43	39	0-6-2T	C	91	134	0-6-2T	I
44	40	0-6-2T	C	92	135	0-6-2T	I
45	41	0-6-2T	C	93	136	0-6-2T	I
46	42	0-6-2T	C	94	137	0-6-2T	I
47	43	0-6-2T	C	95	138	0-6-2T	I
48	612	0-6-0T	A 65	96	139	0-6-2T	I
49	614	0-6-0T	A 65	97	46	0-6-2T	A
50	618	0-6-0T	A 65	98	140	0-6-2T	I
51	619	0-6-0T	A 65	99	141	0-6-2T	I
52	622	0-6-0T	A 65	100	142	0-6-2T	I
53	625	0-6-0T	A 65	101	143	0-6-2T	I
54	629	0-6-0T	A 65	102	144	0-6-2T	I
55	631	0-6-0T	A 65	103	145	0-6-2T	I
56	657	0-6-0T	A 65	104	147	0-6-2T	I
57	87	0-6-2T	I	105	148	0-6-2T	I
58	88	0-6-2T	I	106	47	0-6-2T	B
59	89	0-6-2T	I	107	48	0-6-2T	B
60	90	0-6-2T	I	108	49	0-6-2T	B
61	91	0-6-2T	I	109	50	0-6-2T	B
62	44	0-6-2T	O	110	51	0-6-2T	B
63	149	0-6-2T	J	111	608	0-6-0T	A 64
64	150	0-6-2T	J	112	609	0-6-0T	A 64
65	1324	2-4-2T	O	113	610	0-6-0T	A 64
66	1325	2-4-2T	O	114	611	0-6-0T	A 64
67	97	0-6-2T	I	115	71	0-6-2T	E
68	98	0-6-2T	I	116	72	0-6-2T	E
69	99	0-6-2T	I	117	73	0-6-2T	D
70	100	0-6-2T	I	118	74	0-6-2T	E
71	101	0-6-2T	I	119	75	0-6-2T	E
72	105	0-6-2T	I	120	661	0-6-0	A 66
73	106	0-6-2T	I	121	662	0-6-0	A 66
74	107	0-6-2T	I	033	659	0-6-0	A 65
75	108	0-6-2T	I	036	660	0-6-0	A 65

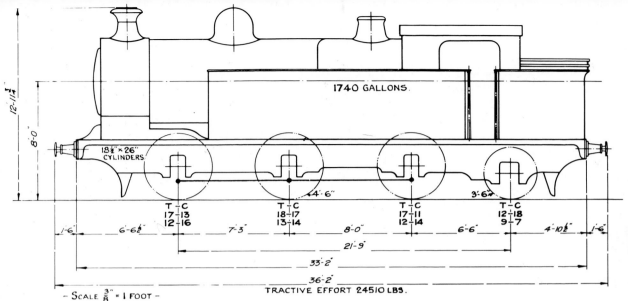

1740 GALLONS.

18½" × 26"
CYLINDERS

T-C 17-13 12-16
T-C 18-17 13-14
T-C 17-11 12-14
T-C 12-18 9-7

4'-6"   3'-6"

1'-6"   6'-6½"   7'-3"   8'-0"   6'-6"   4'-10½"   1'-6"

21'-9"

33'-2"

36'-2"

12'-11¾"   8'-0"

TRACTIVE EFFORT 24510 LBS.

— SCALE ⅜" = 1 FOOT —

Figure 219

Figure 221

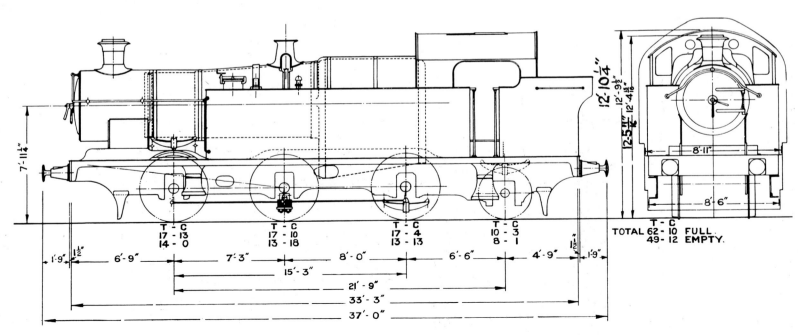

7'-11¼"

12'-10¼"
12'-9½"
12'-4½"
12'-5½"

8'-11"

8'-6"

T-C 17-13 14-0
T-C 17-10 13-18
T-C 17-4 13-13
T-C 10-3 8-1
T-C TOTAL 62-10 FULL 49-12 EMPTY.

1'-9"   1½"   6'-9"   7'-3"   8'-0"   6'-6"   4'-9"   1½"   1'-9"

15'-3"

21'-9"

33'-3"

37'-0"

Figure 220

The majority of the Rhymney Railway locomotive stud at the grouping was of the 0-6-2T type, and the first to be illustrated is the 'R' class. In 1907 three engines were delivered by Stephenson's, and numbered 1-3, two more were built in 1909 and took the numbers 17 and 97, and the class was added to by ten more in 1921, four from Hudswell Clarke, and six more from Beyer-Peacock taking the numbers 39 to 47 and No. 62. Strange to relate, the last two, Nos. 47 and 62, were taken into the Rhymney stock at the time of grouping with the GWR. The diagram issued for the first five engines was the Swindon A (*Figure* 219) and the prototype engine R.R. No. 1 is shown in *Figure* 221 in GWR days; note the carriage type ventilators set in the cab roof. In 1934 No. 17 was rebuilt at Swindon to the Diagram A.38 seen in *Figure* 220, with a Standard No. 2 taper boiler with GW fittings, a new Swindon bunker, and a high domed roof cab.

All were renumbered in 1922, being 30-32/34-44/46 and the whole class lasted right into British Railways days.

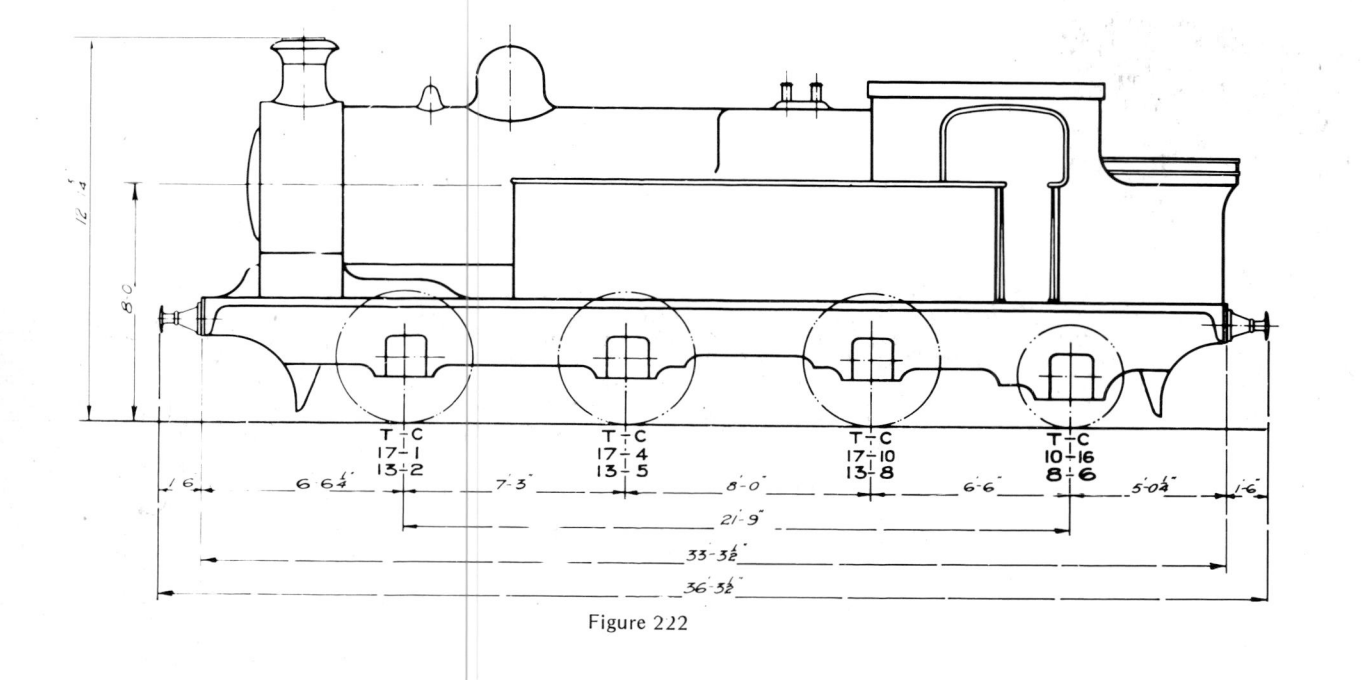

Figure 222

Known as the 'M' class, another series of 0-6-2T engines built by R. Stephenson's were delivered to the Rhymney Railway in 1904. Numbered 106 to 110 with the last one taking the number 16 instead of 111, so that it could replace an older engine and thus be charged to revenue. All six were fitted with Belpaire fireboxes, and had Ramsbottom valves mounted thereon. Driving wheels of 4' 6" diameter set at 7' 3" and 8' 0" centres, plus trailing wheels on a radial axle, cylinders were 18½" x 26¾", having balanced slide valves made for a sound locomotive which, like the class, became practically a prototype for the '5600' class of 0-6-2T built by and for the GWR from 1924 onwards. At the grouping Swindon issued Diagram B for these six engines (*Figure* 222) and they were renumbered 47 to 51, plus No. 16 which was renumbered 33. This engine features in both *Figure* 223 and 224 showing both the left-hand and right-hand sides of the locomotive.

Figure 223

Figure 224

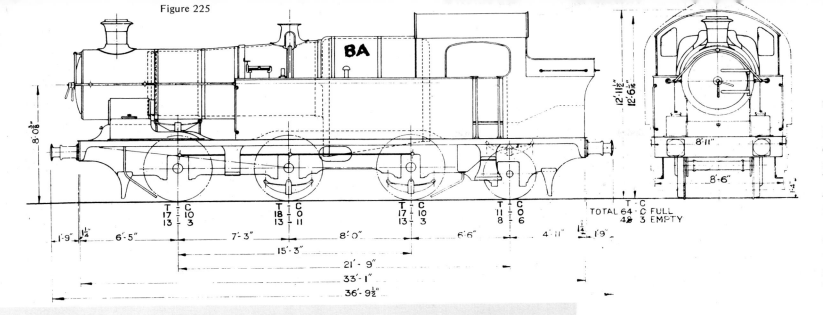

Figure 225

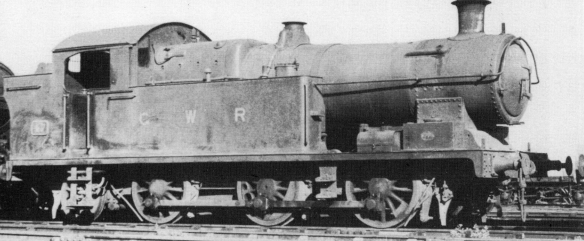

Figure 226

Figure 227

Only one engine in the 'M' series received a Swindon boiler and this was No. 47, being rebuilt with the Standard No. 2 taper boiler, together with the high domed roof and 'Western' bunker. This reconstruction can be seen in *Figure* 226. The Diagram prepared for the rebuilt No. 47 was A.44 and is shown in *Figure* 225. No. 51, seen in *Figure* 227, is as her Rhymney days but with the addition of a GWR safety valve bonnet. Incidentally she was the only one of the series to be scrapped at Caerphilly, all others meeting their end at Swindon.

Figure 228

Figure 229

Figure 230

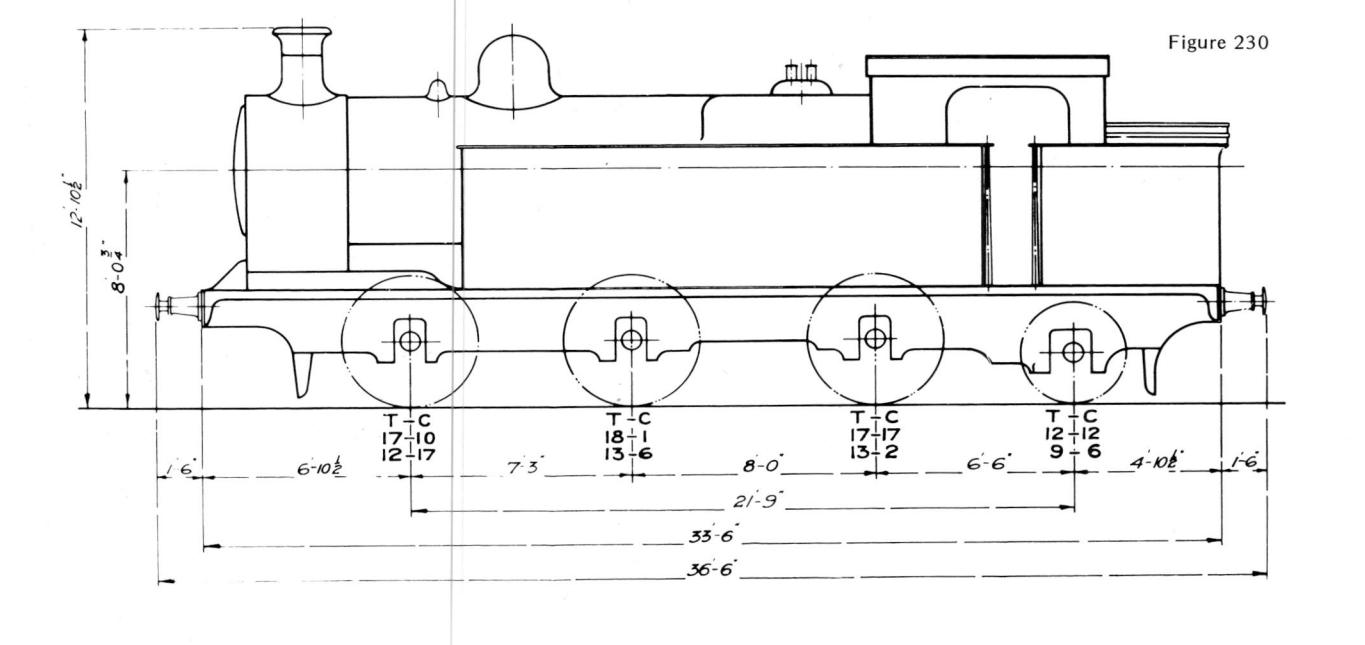

The second batch of class 'R' engines of the Rhymney Railway as already mentioned were delivered in 1921, and were numbered 39 to 47 and No. 62. The only difference between them and the original five engines was in the number of boiler tubes and heating surface.

Swindon gave the Diagram C (*Figure* 230) for these ten engines and this was only different from Diagram A in engine weight and pitch. *Figure* 228 at the top of the page shows R.R. No. 40 carrying her Westinghouse brake pump on the smokebox side, and in *Figure* 229 R.R. No. 39 is seen in GWR days as GW No. 35; she spent her last days as a stationary boiler at Worcester from 1957 to 1958.

Three more illustrations of the later 'R' class engines are shown below, two in Great Western days and No. 37 in *Figure* 231 at Cardiff Docks in 1951 with the BR emblem on the side tanks. No. 38 in *Figure* 232 is seen at Cardiff East Dock in 1951 and No. 42 stands in the sunshine for her photograph at Cardiff Docks in 1952 (*Figure* 233). Note the roof ventilators on both these last two engines. Perhaps it should be mentioned that these locomotives were often referred to as the 'AR' class, but officially they were still just plain 'R'

Figure 231

Figure 232

BRITISH   RAILWAYS

Figure 233

Figure 234

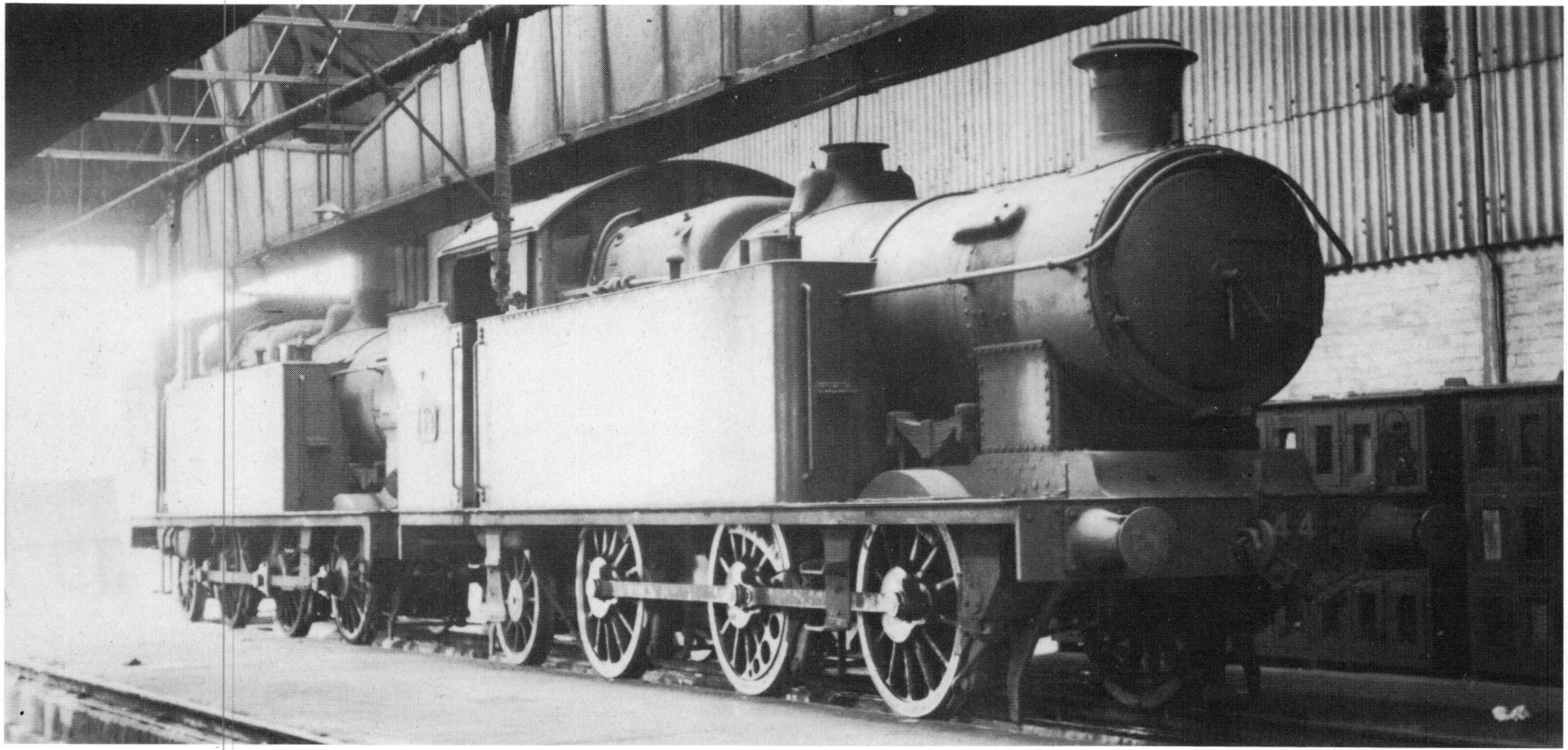

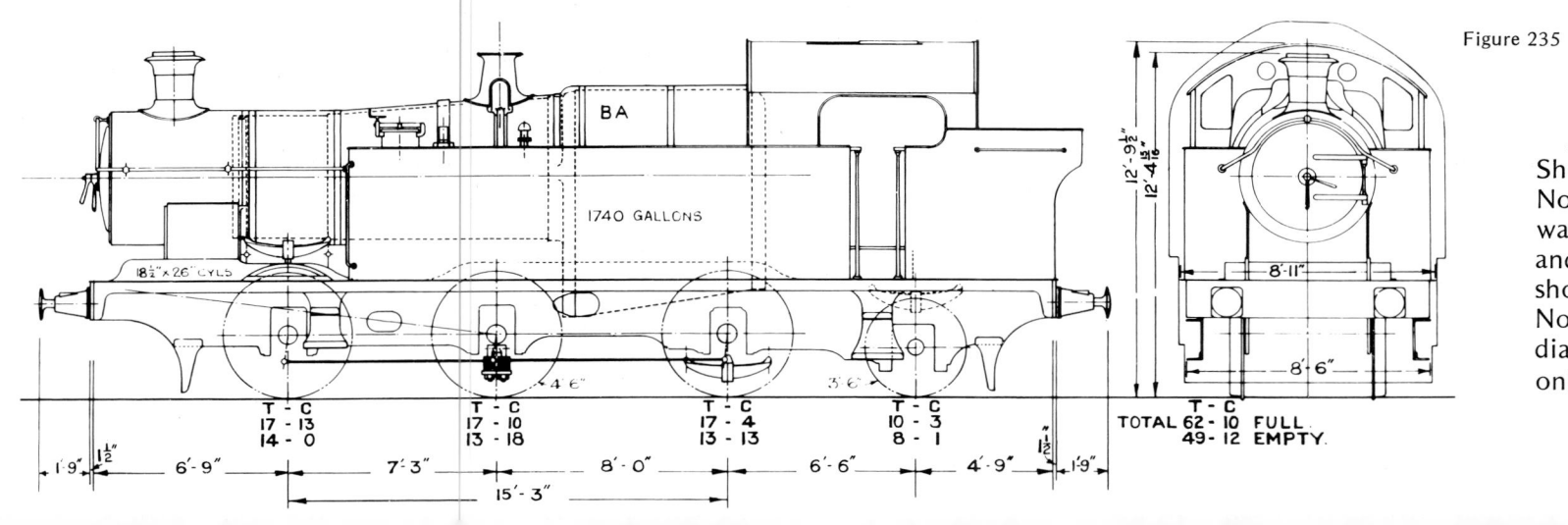

Figure 235

Figure 234 illustrates the inside of Radyr Shed in 1947 and the first engine in line is No. 44 which was the old R.R. No. 62. She was built in 1943 with the GWR coned boiler, and covered by the Swindon Diagram A.38 as shown in *Figure* 235. Her sister engine GW No. 40 (R.R. 44) was also rebuilt to this same diagram in 1949 after nationalization, but only lasted until 1954 (*Figure* 236).

Figure 236

Figure 237

The two locomotives shown on this page illustrate well the slight differences between the Rhymney 'R' class and the 'A1' series in Great Western ownership.

In *Figure* 237 GW No. 34 (R.R. 17), one of the 'R' class engines, is seen at Radyr in 1947. Note that this locomotive has been fitted with GWR '5600' class driving wheels. No. 30, which became GW 70, was one of the 'A1' class and in *Figure* 238 is seen at Margam in 1952. She was the only engine in the 'A1' series to be rebuilt with the Swindon high domed cab, and lasted until 1955 before being withdrawn.

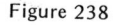
Figure 238

The 'A' — 'A1' class of Rhymney engines consisted of three batches. Nos. 10-14 and Nos. 115-119 were delivered in 1910; the second lot of six in 1911 from Hudswell Clarke were numbered 15, 18-22, and the last batch, which were fitted with Belpaire fireboxes were classed as 'A1' to distinguish them from the 'A' series. The last batch consisted of numbers 23-25 delivered in 1914, Nos. 26-27 in 1916, and Nos. 28-30 arrived in 1918 which made a total of eight engines in the 'A1' class. At the grouping Swindon issued two Diagrams for each type of the 'A's, the early series being allotted E as seen in *Figure* 239, and the Belpaire fireboxed 'A1's took the Diagram D shown in *Figure* 240. Over several years five of the 'A' class were refitted with Belpaire fireboxes and boilers which meant that Nos. 12/117/11/14 and 22 joined the ranks of the 'A1' class, so that there were 10 of the 'A' series and fourteen in the 'A1' class. No. 62 in *Figure* 241 is one of the 'A' class which as can be seen became 'A1'. For the GWR renumbering see Pages 89-90.

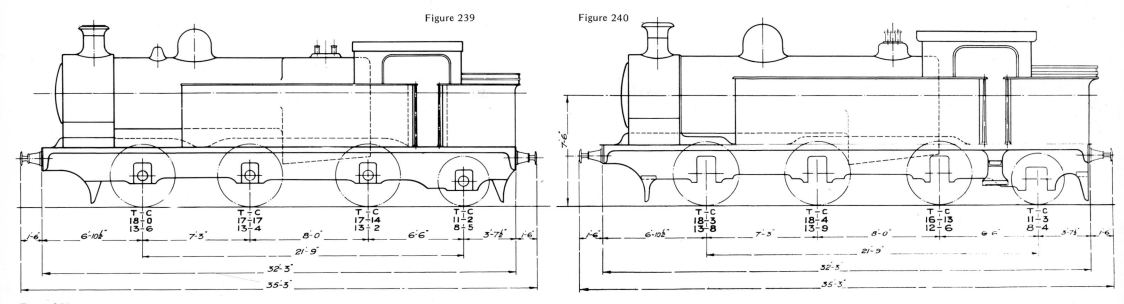

Figure 239

Figure 240

Figure 241

Figure 242

The saga of the 'A' and 'A1' class was rather complicated because when passing to the GWR two of the 'A1' class were given round top boilers, putting them back into the 'A' series! These were GW Nos. 63 and 65, and in 1930-32 the GWR converted three 'A' class to 'A1', these being Nos. 57/61/72. The three 'A1's illustrated on this page are from the camera of A.C. Sterndale, and show R.R. No. 15 as GW 57 at Cardiff Docks in 1951. Note that she has R.R. side tanks and boiler but has been fitted with a GW bunker (*Figure* 242). No. 53 (R.R. 11) is seen in *Figure* 243 at Cardiff East Dock in 1948 with her original boiler, but sporting a GW type safety valve and No. 68 (R.R. 28) is also at Cardiff in the same year (*Figure* 244).

Figure 243

Figure 244

Figure 245

Figure 246

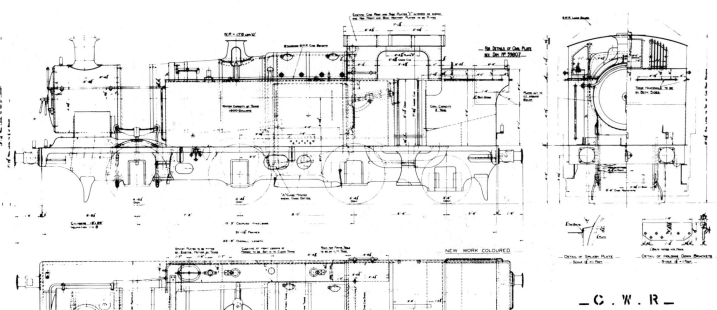

_C . W . R_
STANDARD BOILER Nº 10

Figure 247

Another 'A1' class of Rhymney engines is No. 64 (R.R. 24) seen in *Figure* 245 during the last visit to Swindon in 1950. It will be seen that she still retains her Rhymney outline, and the only 'Western' feature is the safety valve. Between the years of 1929-36 fifteen of the 'A' and 'A1' class were rebuilt at Swindon with the GW Standard No. 10 boiler. These were GW Nos. 52/55/56/71/74/ 75/58/59/60/62 from the 'A' class and GW Nos. 63/65/66/69/70 from the 'A1' series. GW No. 63 is seen in *Figure* 246 as fitted with the No. 10 taper boiler, fittings and bunker.

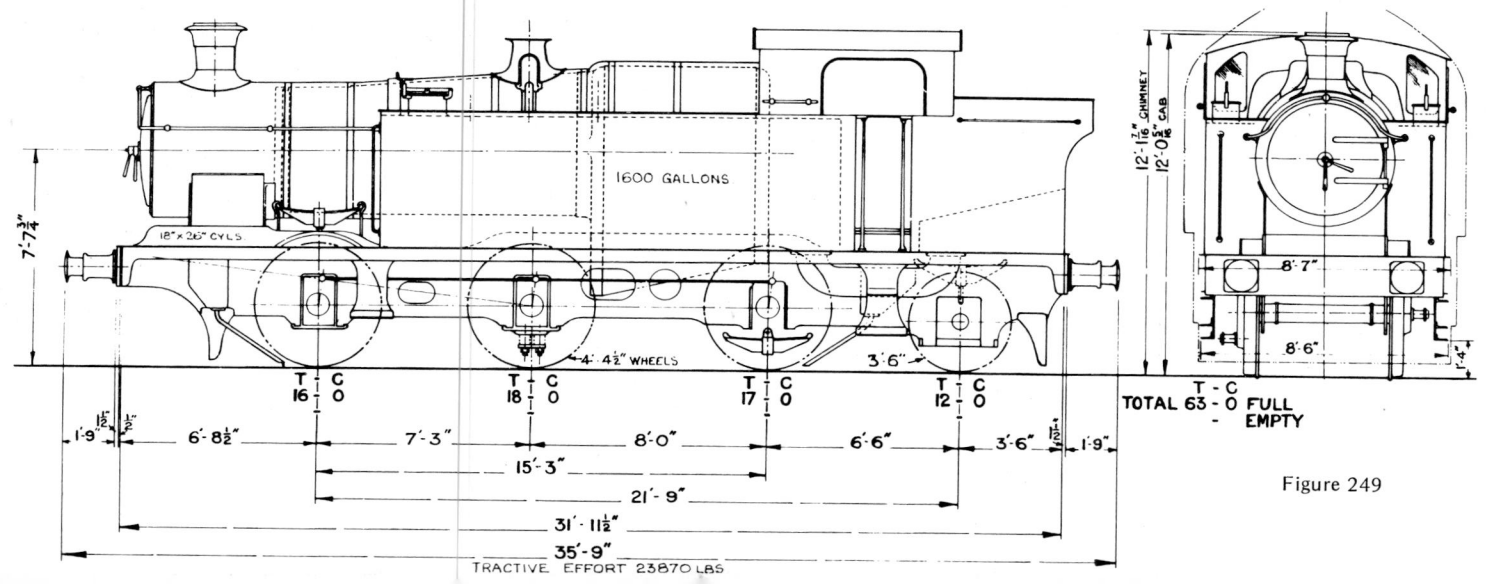

Figure 248

Figure 249

1600 GALLONS

18"x 26" CYLS

7'-7¾"

12'-7⁄₁₆" CHIMNEY
12'-0½" CAB

8'-7"

8'-6"

T C
16 O   T C
18 O   4'-4½" WHEELS   T C
17 O   3'-6"   T C
12 O

T-C
TOTAL 63-0 FULL
- EMPTY

1½"
1-9"   6'-8½"   7'-3"   8'-0"   6'-6"   3'-6" 1½" 1-9"

15'-3"

21'-9"

31'-11½"

35'-9"

TRACTIVE EFFORT 23870 LBS

Seen in British Railways ownership No. 59 (original R.R. No. 19) at Cardiff in 1951, has the Standard No. 10 boiler and fittings, plus the GW type bunker. She was at this time painted black with the straw coloured BR 'Lion' crest with the brass number on a red background; quite a handsome and powerful machine.

For this final rebuild Swindon issued Diagram A.42 shown in *Figure* 249; see also Works drawing on previous page (*Figure* 247).

Figure 250

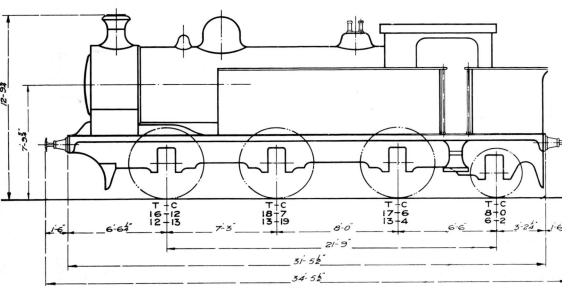

Figure 251

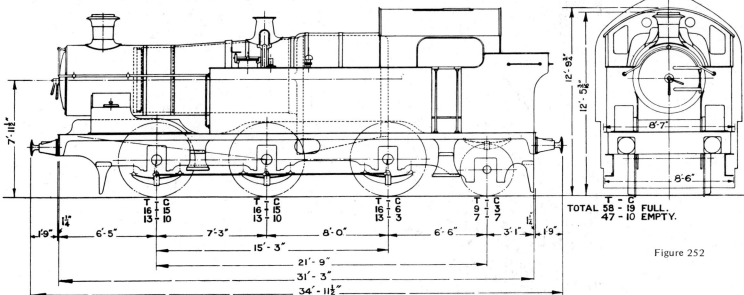

Figure 252

Rhymney 'P' class engines were 0-6-2T designs but with rather larger driving wheels to deal with the faster and lighter traffic of conveying passengers rather than the more usual movement of coal.

The first three locomotives ordered from Stephenson's in 1908 were numbered 4, 5 and 6 and were fitted with the usual round topped firebox as seen in the Swindon diagram H in *Figure* 251. In 1915 engine No. 5 was fitted with an 'A1' Belpaire boiler which made it into class 'P1'. The success of this rebuild resulted in one extra engine being built by Hudswell Clarke in 1917 to the 'P1' design, this became No. 31. Thus at the grouping there were four engines in this class, two 'P's and two 'P1's. R.R. Nos. 4 and 6 became GW 82 and 83 and R.R. Nos. 5 and 31 were given GW numbers 76 and 77. Eventually all four engines were rebuilt with Standard GWR No. 10 taper boilers, Nos. 82 and 83 to the Diagram A.37 seen in *Figure* 252. The picture of No. 83 in *Figure* 250, shown in Caeharris Shed in 1949, illustrates well the larger 5' 0'' diameter driving wheels and the overall 'Western' style this engine displayed after being rebuilt in 1939.

Figure 253

These two official photographs from the Swindon Gallery show No. 82 (R.R. No. 4) just out from the factory at Caerphilly in 1926, when she had just been rebuilt with the GW taper boiler and fittings and bunker. In addition the braking system had been changed from Westinghouse to Vacuum working.

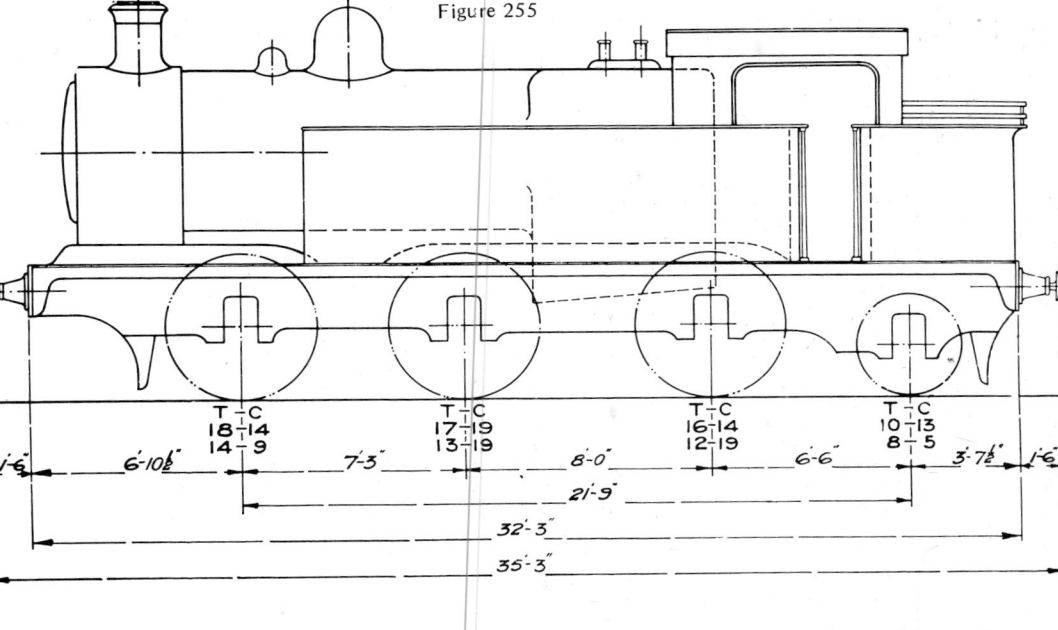

Figure 255

Figure 256

Diagram F seen in *Figure* 255 was issued for the Rhymney 'P1' class and it can be noted that this drawing's only difference to Diagram H is the Belpaire firebox. As with the rebuilding of Nos. 82 and 83, the other two engines Nos. 76 and 77 of the 'P1' were also to receive the Standard No. 10 taper boiler and fittings, and Swindon Diagram A.43 was issued for these two locomotives (*Figure* 257).

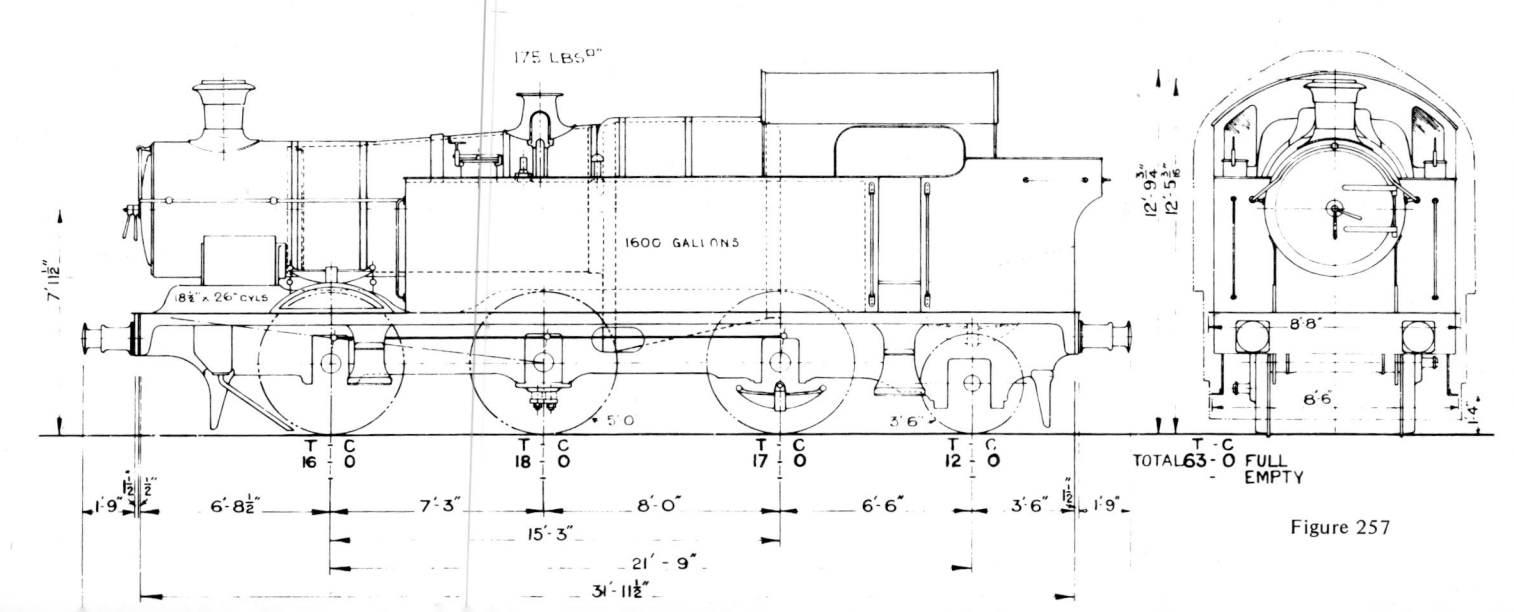

Figure 257

Following very closely to the 'P1' design, the last small class of 0-6-2T engines to be purchased for the Rhymney Railway before the grouping was a series of four engines built by Hudswell Clarke in 1921. Numbered 35, 36, 37 and 38 these four were very similar to the last 'P1' built (No. 31) with the addition of larger side tanks, and a more commodious bunker. The other unusual fitting for Rhymney engines was providing the 'AP' series, as they were known, with steam heating apparatus for the benefit of passengers, who, until 1920 still had to make do with foot warmers!

Swindon issued Diagram G (*Figure* 258) for these locomotives in 1922 and renumbered them 78 to 81. The first two to receive the GW Standard No. 10 taper boiler, were No. 80 in 1928, and No. 81 in mid-1929 both to the Diagram A.43 seen on this page. No. 78 and 79 kept their Rhymney boilers until 1949 although they did receive GWR bunkers and other fittings, as can be seen in *Figure* 259. *Figure* 260 is a copy of the Swindon works drawing, which was prepared to show the rebuilding of the 'P' and 'AP' class with the Standard No. 10 boiler.

Figure 258

Figure 259

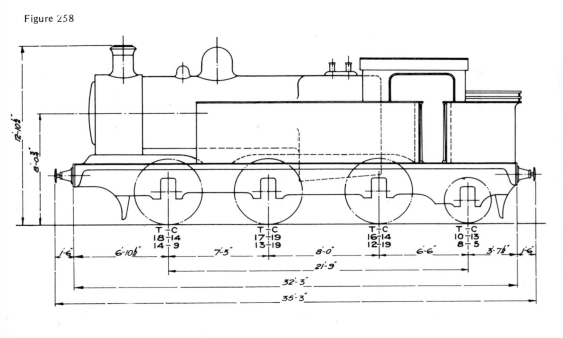

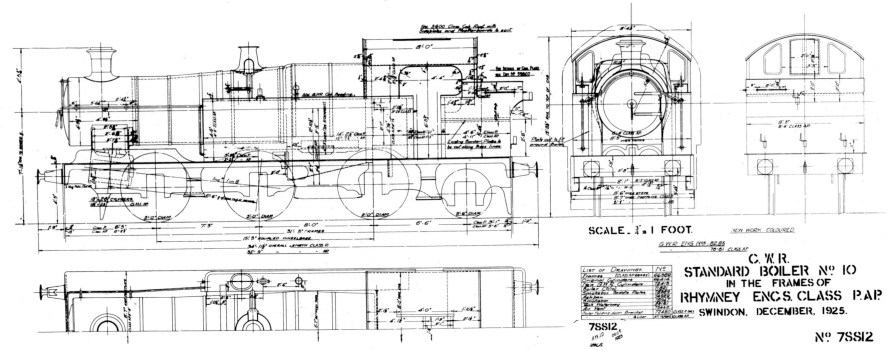

SCALE. ¾" = 1 FOOT.   NEW WORK COLOURED.

G.W.R.
STANDARD BOILER Nº 10
IN THE FRAMES OF
RHYMNEY ENGS. CLASS P.AP.
SWINDON, DECEMBER, 1925.

Nº 7SS12

Figure 260

Figure 261

Figure 262

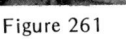

Figure 263

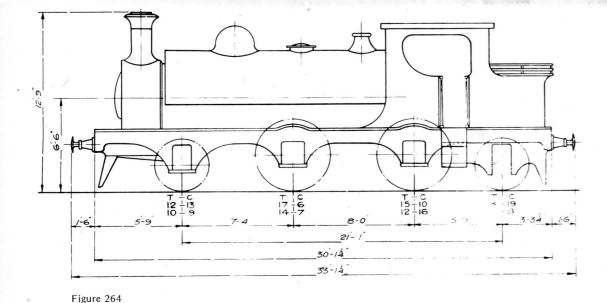

Three superb pictures illustrating the 'AP' class of Rhymney locomotives. In *Figure* 262 No. 78 is seen at Rhymney in 1952 after being fitted with the taper boiler. No. 38, which became GW No. 81, is shown in both *Figures* 261 and 263, showing the right-hand side of the engine standing "dead" on the stop block at Rhymney, and the left-hand front view at the bottom of the page shows No. 81 running in the Cardiff Queen Street with a passenger train in 1952.

Another small class of tank engine belonging to the Rhymney Railway which had the larger 5' 0" driving wheels meant for running passenger services, was the series of five Vulcan Foundry engines built to the design of 2-4-2 saddle tank. Numbered from 62 to 66 the five were added to the strength in 1891. The illustration in *Figure* 265 shows No. 65 as she looked when new, still in the works grey. In 1908 Nos. 62 and 63 were rebuilt to the 0-6-2T configuration and were classified as 'L1', and in 1911 No. 64 was also converted to an 0-6-2T which just left Nos. 65 and 66 in the 2-4-2T condition to be handed over to the GWR in 1922. Swindon gave them Diagram 'O' (*Figure* 264) but did little else to change them until withdrawal in 1928. *Figure* 266 shows No. 65 proudly displaying the R.R. on the saddle tanks.

Figure 264

Figure 265

Figure 266

Figure 269

Figure 268

Figure 267

Figure 270

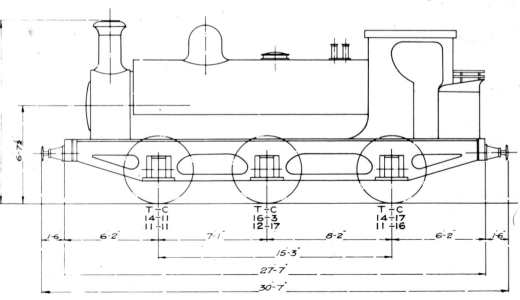

Figure 272

Three pictures of the 'L' class are shown above, two of No. 1325 and one of 1324. These were the numbers which the Great Western gave No. 66 and 65. In *Figure* 267 we can see No. 1324 with the Westinghouse pump mounted on the left-hand side of the smokebox. Incidentally these engines were driven from the left-hand side at first, and were only changed over in 1925-26. No. 1325 is seen in the other two illustrations, (*Figures* 268 and 269) wearing the GWR safety valve bonnet. Both engines were placed on the sales list in 1928, but, finding no buyers, were cut up in November 1929.

Although this is a collection of pictures and drawings of locomotives which were absorbed into the GWR in 1922, the two engines shown on this page, both of which had been scrapped before this date, are worth putting on record nevertheless. They show the parent design of the saddle tank engines of the Rhymney, and also illustrate the livery and lining of the R.R. in the nineteenth century. No. 31, seen in *Figure* 270, was one of a batch of ten engines built by Sharp-Stewart in 1872, followed by six more from Nasmyth Wilson in 1874 and a final six in 1878. They were numbered from 23-44. Only two survived to go on the Swindon stock list and by this time had been duplicated, so had an extra nought added to their Rhymney numbers becoming 033 and 036. Swindon altered their numbers again to 659 and 660 but they were never rebuilt, lasting only until 1925. The Diagram to cover these two engines was A.65 (*Figure* 272), this also referred to the 45-56 class series, seen on the next page.

No. 18, illustrated in *Figure* 271, was one of two outside cylinder saddle tanks, built by Vulcan Foundry in 1861 and rebuilt in 1884. The two engines Nos. 17 and 18 were classified 'F' in 1906, but were scrapped in 1909 and 1912 respectively.

Figure 271

Figure 274

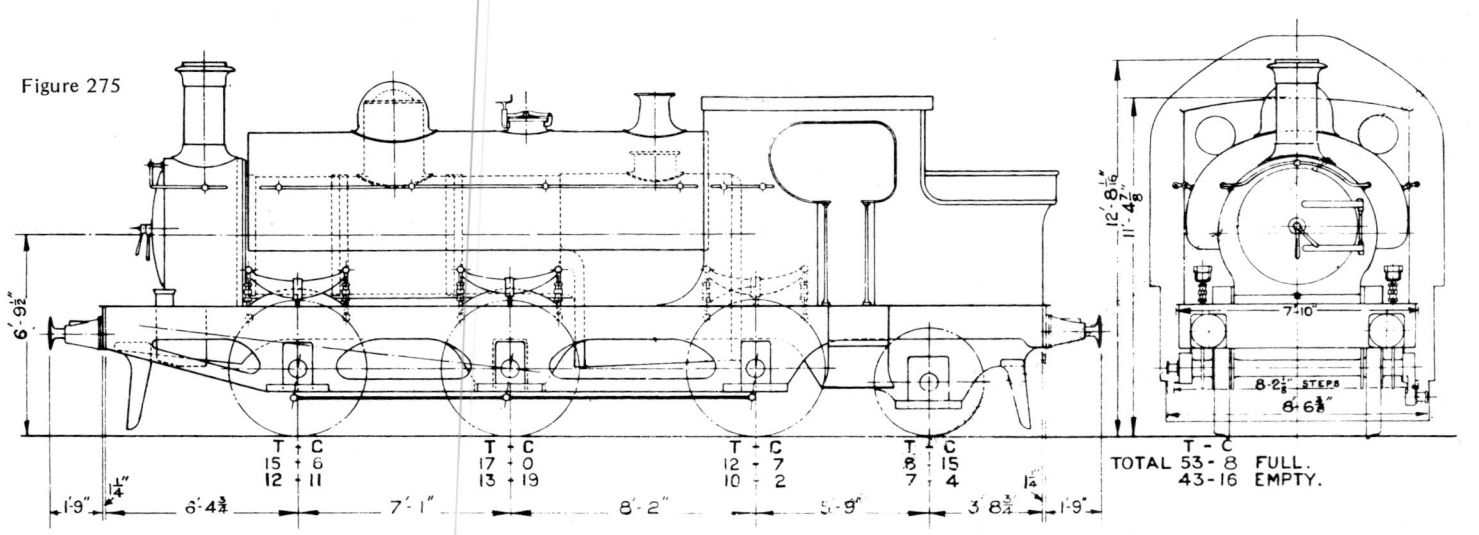

Figure 273

Figure 275

TOTAL 53-8 FULL.
43-16 EMPTY.

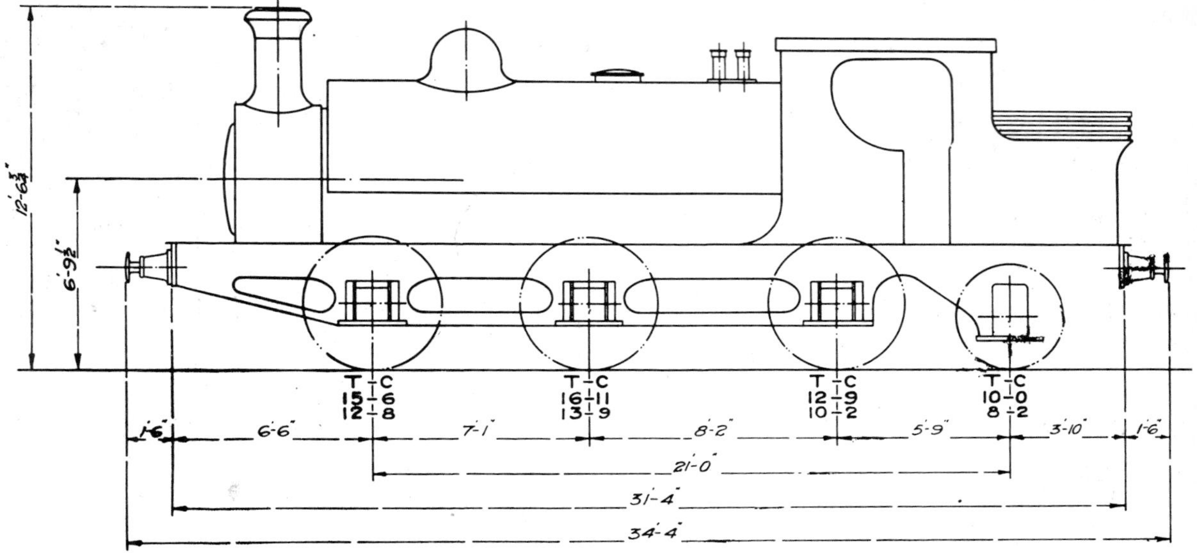

The photograph on this page shows No. 612, one of the 'J' class engines, a series of 12 locomotives built by Sharp-Stewart; numbered 45 to 56, only nine passed into GWR hands and these became 612/14/18/19/22/25/29/31/57. The Diagram A.65 (*Figure* 272 on previous page) was allotted for these engines.

The natural development of the Vulcan Foundry engines Nos. 17 and 18 rebuilt in 1884 was the creating of the '57' class, slightly larger, necessitating a pair of radial wheels under the bunker, a design which became so successful, that before 1900 there were 47 engines in this 0-6-2T class. At the grouping Swindon issued Diagram I to cover this class, which after 1906 became known as the 'K' class, *Figure* 274. After various modifications at Swindon, a new Diagram was issued and is illustrated in *Figure* 275, this was A.27.

Two official photographs of the 'K' class are portrayed on the next two pages. In *Figure* 276 GW No. 127 (R.R. 86) is seen with the coupling rods off, fitted with the short chimney, but minus the Westinghouse pump. The other 0-6-2T is GW No. 85 originally R.R. No. 8. She still has both the tall chimney and the brake pump on the smokebox. This class numbered forty six engines; for details and for the GW re-numbering see the beginning of the chapter on the Rhymney Railway.

Figure 276

Figure 277

Figure 278

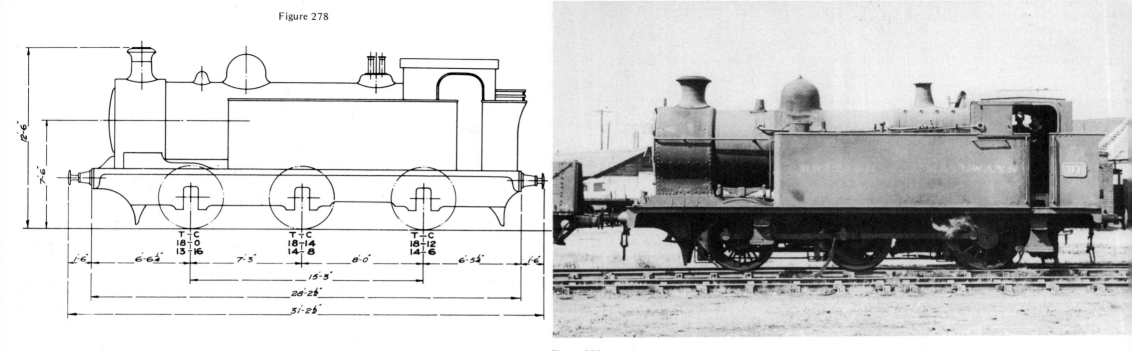

Figure 279

Figure 280

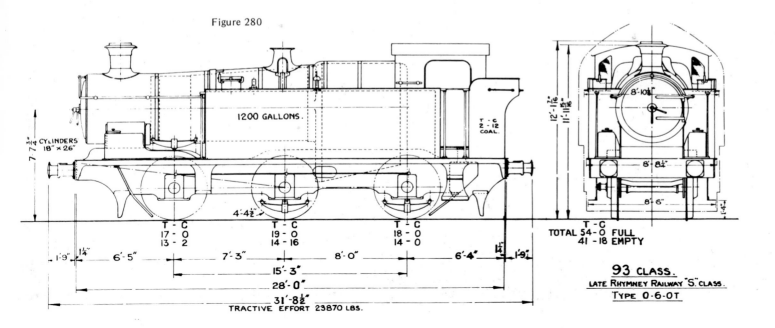

1200 GALLONS

T - C
2 - 12
COAL.

CYLINDERS
18" x 26"

8'-10⅛"

8' 8¼"

8' 6"

TOTAL 54 - 0 FULL
41 - 18 EMPTY

93 CLASS.
LATE RHYMNEY RAILWAY "S" CLASS.
TYPE 0-6-0T

TRACTIVE EFFORT 23870 LBS.

Known as the 'S' class, four 0-6-0T engines built by Hudswell Clarke were delivered to the Rhymney in 1908. Their numbers were 111 to 114 and they were side tank engines with round-top fireboxes, carried on six small driving wheels of 4' 4½" diameter, set at 7' 3" and 8' 0" centres. At the grouping these four were renumbered, and became GW 608 to 611. Swindon Diagram A.64 in *Figure* 278 shows the locomotives as taken over. In 1930 each engine was rebuilt with the GW Standard No. 10 boiler and a new Diagram B.57 (in *Figure* 280) was issued to cover. In 1946 they received new numbers in the renumbering scheme, becoming Nos. 93 to 96.

Figure 279 shows GW No. 91 in 1949, which previously had been No. 605 and prior to that R.R. No. 33; this engine was one of the 'S1' class, the series which followed the introduction of the 'S' class.

Figure 281

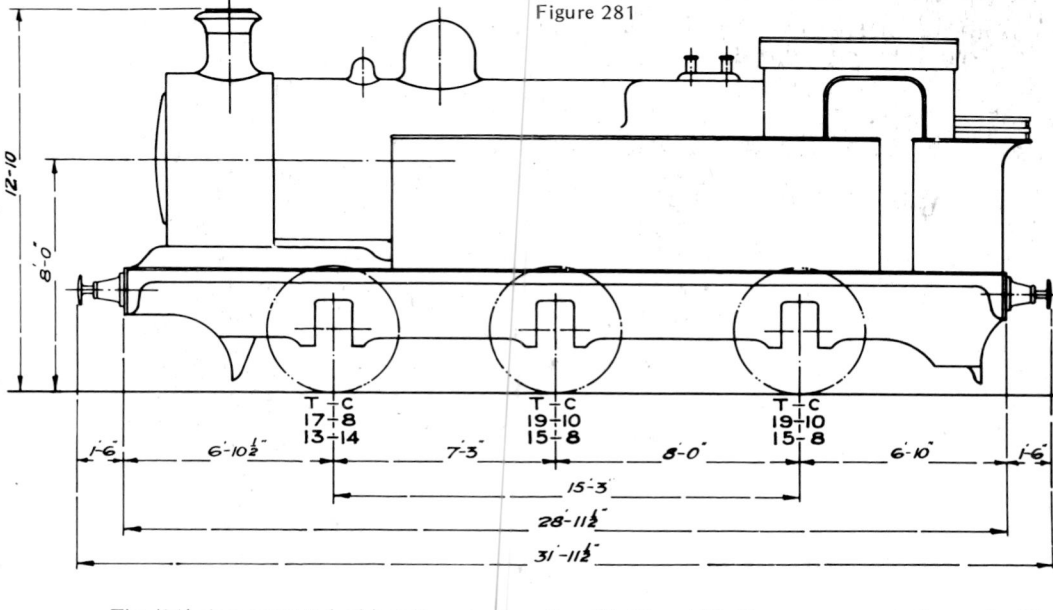

Figure 283

The 'S1' class consisted of just three engines, Nos. 32, 33 and 34. They were very similar to the 'S' series, but were improved by being built with Belpaire fireboxes instead of the round-top. When taken into the GWR in 1922 they were renumbered 604, 605 and 606 and Diagram A.63 (*Figure* 281) was issued. No. 604 is seen in *Figure* 283 as she was in Great Western days, because although Diagram B.58 (*Figure* 282) was prepared for the rebuilding of these engines with a Standard No. 10 boiler, in fact they were not fitted. They were renumbered in 1946 to Nos. 90 to 92. The large engine, GW No. 608, in *Figure* 284 was one of the rebuilt 'S' class mentioned on the previous page. She was eventually renumbered 93 in 1946.

Figure 282

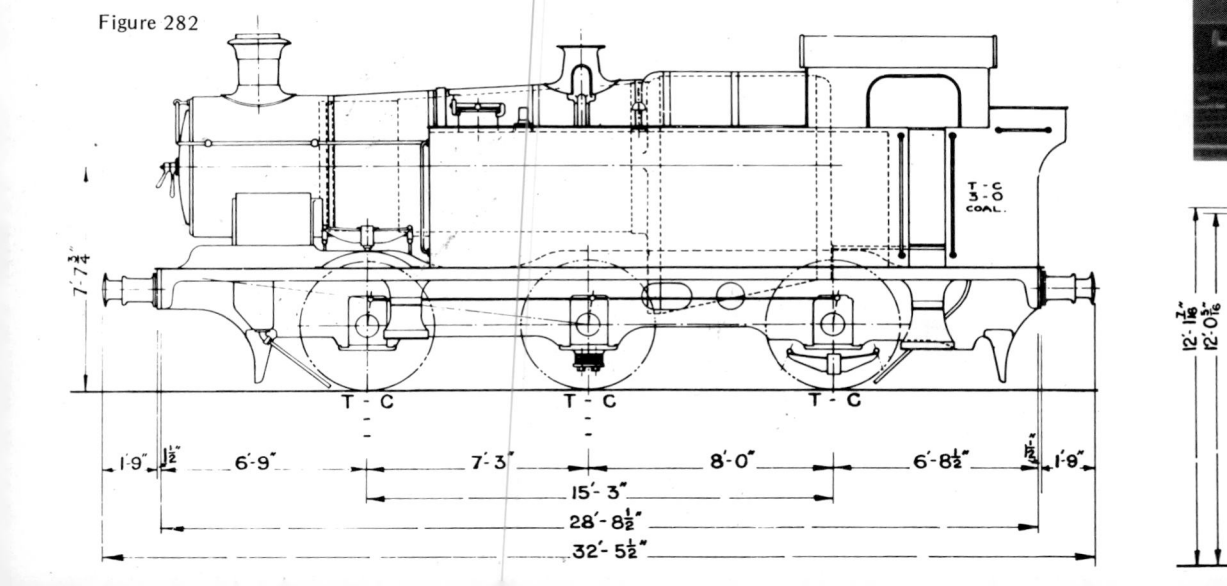

Figure 284

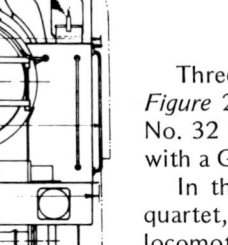

Three more studies from the collection of A. C. Sterndale. *Figure* 285 shows No. 90 (GWR numbering of 1946), ex-R.R. No. 32 seen in *Figure* 286 is the only one to have been fitted with a GWR bunker.

In the bottom illustration (*Figure* 287) another of the 'S' quartet, this is No. 96 seen at Cardiff Docks in 1951. This locomotive was previously GW 611 and started life as Rhymney No. 114. She was eventually scrapped in 1954.

Figure 285

Figure 286

Figure 287

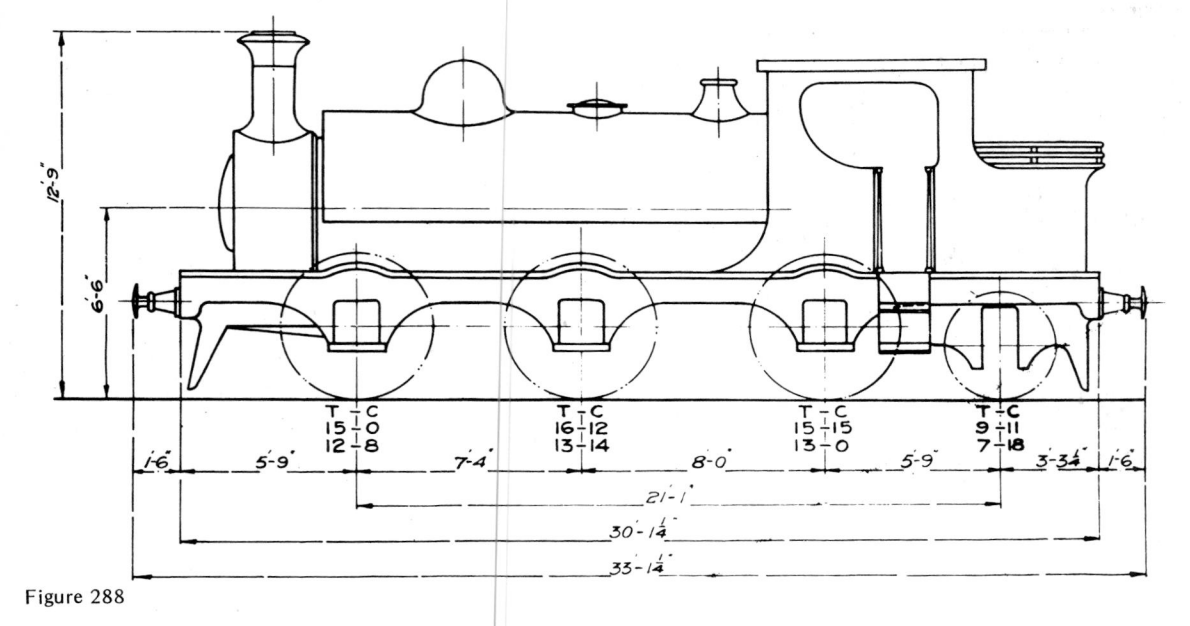

Figure 288

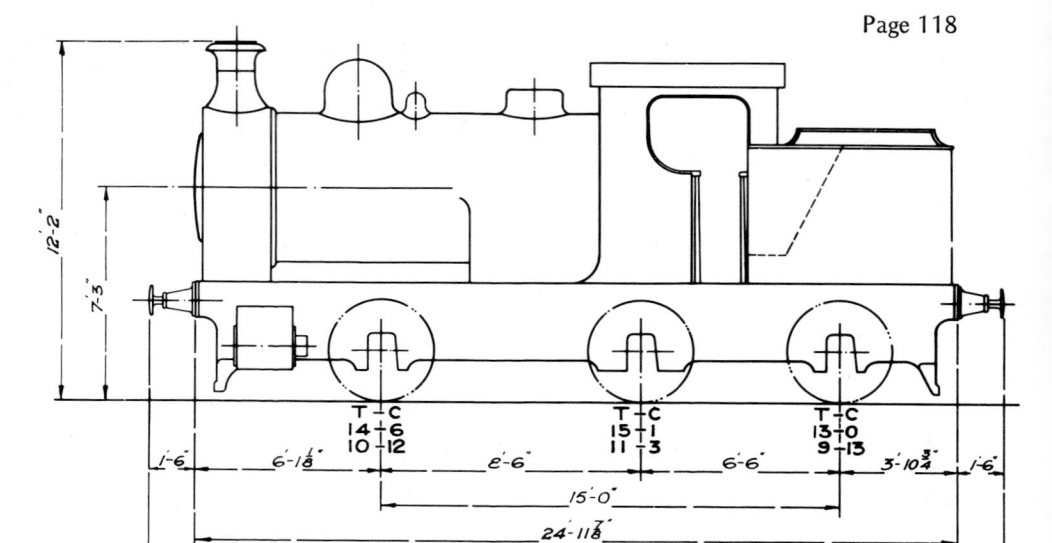

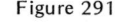

Figure 289

Diagram J seen in *Figure* 288, is the drawing which was issued by Swindon to cover the conversion of the Rhymney Railway 'L' class locomotives to the 'L1' configuration, although not one of the three engines survived to carry their new GWR numbers.

The last Rhymney engines to be illustrated in photograph and drawing are the two unusual Hudswell Clarke machines which started their lives on the R.R. in 1907 as the steam unit in Nos. 1 and 2 rail-motors. As built they were 4 wheel coupled, the wheels being 3′ 6″ diameter set at 8′ 6″ centres. Both units proved to be rough riders, and were altered to 0-4-2Ts by a rearward extension and the

fitting of a trailing pair of wheels of 2′ 9″ diameter to support same. Still not satisfactory, the engine unit from Car No. 2 was changed once more, being separated entirely from the carriage, fitted with a bunker, and the 2′ 9″ carrying wheels replaced by trailing drivers, thus making the unit into an 0-6-0T engine. Her sister was similarly rebuilt in 1919 and they were numbered 120 and 121 respectively. At the grouping Swindon allotted them Diagram A.66 (*Figure* 289) and renumbered them 661 and 662. Both were cut up in 1925. Our two photographs show in *Figure* 290 the left-hand side of No. 662, and in *Figure* 291 the right-hand side of No. 661.

Figure 290

Figure 291

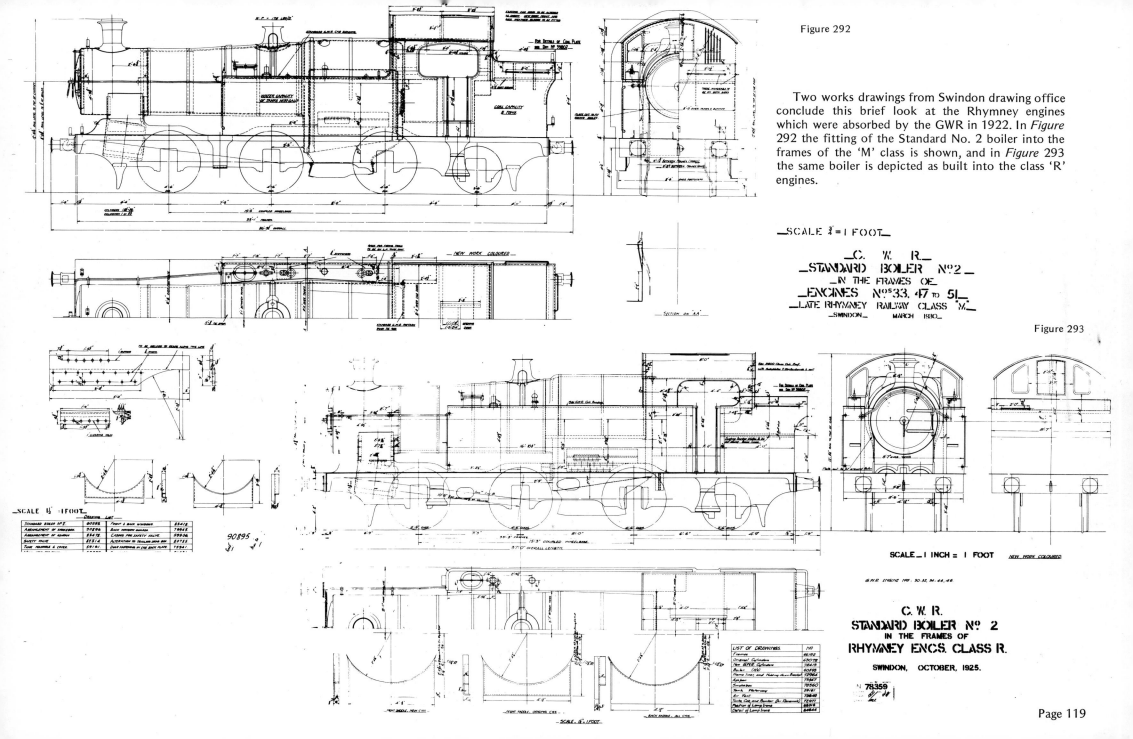

Figure 292

Two works drawings from Swindon drawing office conclude this brief look at the Rhymney engines which were absorbed by the GWR in 1922. In *Figure* 292 the fitting of the Standard No. 2 boiler into the frames of the 'M' class is shown, and in *Figure* 293 the same boiler is depicted as built into the class 'R' engines.

SCALE ¾ = 1 FOOT

G. W. R.
STANDARD BOILER Nº 2
IN THE FRAMES OF
ENGINES Nºs 33, 47 to 51
LATE RHYMNEY RAILWAY CLASS "M"
SWINDON   MARCH 1930

Figure 293

SECTION ON 'AA'

G. W. R.
STANDARD BOILER Nº 2
IN THE FRAMES OF
RHYMNEY ENGS. CLASS R.
SWINDON, OCTOBER, 1925.

SCALE — 1 INCH = 1 FOOT   NEW WORK COLOURED

Figure 294

Figure 294 shows one of the Rhymney Railway Company's 'K' class engines undergoing major repairs to the wheels and motion in Machen Shed. Alongside is a facsimile of the common seal of the company.

The TAFF VALE RAILWAY COMPANY

In 1922 when the South Wales Railway companies were absorbed into the Great Western Railway, the oldest, longest and most successful of the constituents was the Taff Vale Railway, handing over 275 locomotives in all to swell the GWR stock list. The Taff Vale had a close affinity with the GWR obtaining its act of incorporation in 1836, only months after the Great Western and sharing the same brilliant engineer, namely I. K. Brunel. The first line of route ran from Cardiff to Merthyr and opened in 1840. In 1841 a line was opened from Pontypridd into the Rhondda eventually reaching Treherbert in 1856. There were also many spur branches off the 'main' line, to Aberdare, Ynysybwl, and Llancaiach for instance and later into the Ely valley and others, when the Llantrisant and Taff Vale Junction Railway was absorbed in 1889. An extension was built to Cowbridge and finally on to Aberthaw. The T.V.R. promoted a dock company, and ran a branch from the Penarth Branch Junction at Radyr to connect with the Penarth Dock. Upon handing over to the GWR in 1922, the Taff Vale Railway owned approximately 112 miles of track (apart from dock sidings) and this even included 22 miles of four track route.

Taff Vale Number	GW Number	Type	GWR Diagram	Taff Vale Class	Taff Vale Number	GW Number	Type	GWR Diagram	Taff Vale Class
1	278	0-6-2T	A/2	O.4	39	286	0-6-2T	A/2 A26	O.4
2	279	"	A/2	O.4	40	588	"	A/13	U.1
3	438	"	A/4	A	41	455	"	A/10	O1
4	442	"	A/8	M	42	439	"	A/4	A
5	443	"	A/8	M	43	287	"	A/3	O.4
6	280	"	A/2	O.4	44	415	"	A/6	O.2
7	335	"	A/32	A	45	346	"	A/4	A
8	281	"	A/2	O.4	46	288	"	A/2	O.4
9	282	"	A/2	O.4	47	416	"	A/5	O.3
10	337	"	A/4	A	48	289	"	A/2	O.4
11	343	"	A/4	A	49	290	"	A/2	O.4
12	344	"	A/4	A	50	507	"	A/8	M
13	409	"	A/2	O.4	51	462	"	A/8	M
14	444	"	A/8	M	52	440	"	A/4	A
15	445	"	A/8	M	53	508	"	A/8	M
16	503	"	A/8	M	54	466	"	A/8	M
17	283	"	A/2	O.4	55	417	"	A/7	O.3
18	410	"	A/5	O.3	56	291	"	A/2	O.4
19	411	"	A/5	O.3	57	418	"	A/5	O.3
20	345	"	A/4	A	58	292	"	A26	O.4
21	446	"	A/9	O	59	293	"	A/3	O.4
22	505	"	A/8	M	60	471	"	A/10	O.1
23	587	"	A/12	U	61	472	"	A/10	O.1
24	506	"	A/8	M	62	473	"	A/10	O.1
25	447	"	A/9	O	63	474	"	A/10	O.1
26	448	"	A/9	O	64	475	"	A/10	O.1
27	449	"	A/10	O.1	65	476	"	A/10	O.1
28	450	"	A/10	O.1	66	419	"	A/6	O.2
29	451	"	A/10	O.1	67	294	"	A/3	O.4
30	602	"	A/13 A34	U.1	68	295	"	A/3	O.4
31	412	"	A/6	O.2	69	420	"	A/3	O.4
32	413	"	A/6	O.2	70	477	"	A/10	O.1
33	452	"	A/9	O	71	478	"	A/8	M
34	453	"	A/9	O	72	589	"	A/12	U
35	284	"	A/2	O.4	73	479	"	A/10	O.1
36	414	"	A/2	O.4	74	511	"	A/8	M
37	454	"	A/10	O.1	75	347	"	A/4	A
38	285	"	A/3	O.4	76	590	"	A/12	U

Taff Vale Number	GW Number	Type	GWR Diagram	Taff Vale Class
77	591	0-6-2T	A/12	U
78	480	”	A/10	O.1
79	592	”	A/13	U.1
80	348	”	A/4 A32	A
81	421	”	A/6	O.2
82	423	”	A/6	O.2
83	424	”	A/6	O.2
84	425	”	A/6	O.2
85	426	”	A/6	O.2
86	481	”	A/8	M
87	482	”	A/8	M
88	483	”	A/8	M
89	484	”	A/8 A33	M
90	349	”	A/4 A32	V&A
91	351	”	A/4 A32	V&A
92	427	”	A/5	O.3
93	428	”	A/5	O.3
94	296	”	A/3	O.4
95	297	”	A/2	O.4
96	429	”	A/5	O.3
97	298	”	A/2 A26	O.4
98	299	”	A/2 A26	O.4
99	786	0-6-0T	A/83	V
100	787	”	A/83	V
101	300	0-6-2T	A/2 A26	O.4
102	301	”	A/2 A26	O.4
103	430	”	A/5	O.3
104	302	”	A/2	O.4
105	236	”	A/2	O.4
106	485	”	A/11	N
107	486	”	A/11	N
108	310	”	A/2 A26	O.4
109	311	”	A/2	O.4
110	313	”	A/2	O.4
111	314	”	A/2	O.4
112	315	”	A/2 A26	O.4
113	317	”	A/2	O.4
114	318	”	A/2	O.4
115	319	”	A/2	O.4
116	320	”	A/2	O.4
117	431	”	A/5	O.3
118	321	”	A/2	O.4
119	324	”	A/2	O.4
120	441	”	A/4 A32	A
121	333	”	A/2 A26	O.4
122	352	”	A/4 A32	A
123	356	”	A/4 A32	A
124	357	”	A/4 A32	A
125	360	”	A/4 A32	A
126	432	”	A/5	O.3

Taff Vale Number	GW Number	Type	GWR Diagram	Taff Vale Class
127	361	0-6-2T	A/4	A
128	362	”	A/4	A
129	364	”	A/4 A32	A
130	365	”	A/4	A
131	433	”	A/5	O.3
132	366	”	A/4	A
133	367	”	A/4 A32	A
134	368	”	A/4 A32	A
135	370	”	A/4	A
136	371	”	A/4	A
137	434	”	A/5	O.3
138	372	”	A/4 A32	A
139	373	”	A/4 A32	”
140	374	”	A/4 A32	A
141	792	0-6-0T	A/84	H
142	793	”	A/84	H
143	794	”	A/84	H
144	375	0-6-2T	A/4	A
145	513	”	A/8	M
146	515	”	A/8	M
147	516	”	A/8	M
148	520	”	A/8	M
149	376	”	A/4	A
150	487	”	A/8	M
151	552	”	A/8	M
152	560	”	A/8	M
153	567	”	A/8	M
154	377	”	A/32	A
155	435	”	A/5	O.3
156	378	”	A/4	A
157	379	”	A/4	A
158	380	”	A/4	A
159	381	”	A/4	A
160	382	”	A/4	A
161	437	”	A/5	O.3
162	383	”	A/4	A
163	573	”	A/8	M
164	384	”	A/4	A
165	385	”	A/4	A
166	577	”	A/8	M
167	578	”	A/8	M
168	579	”	A/8	M
169	580	”	A/8	M
170	1301	4-4-2T	H	C
171	1302	”	H	C
172	1303	”	H	C
173	1305	”	H C	C
174	1306	”	H	C
175	1304	”	H	C
176	488	0-6-2T	A/8	M

Taff Vale Number	GW Number	Type	GWR Diagram	Taff Vale Class
177	489	0-6-2T	A/8	M
178	490	”	A/8	M
179	491	”	A/8	M
180	492	”	A/8	M
181	493	”	A/8	M
182	494	”	A/11	N
183	495	”	A/11	N
184	496	”	A/11	N
185	498	”	A/11	N
186	499	”	A/11	N
187	500	”	A/11	N
188	501	”	A/11	N
189	502	”	A/11	N
190	581	”	A/9	O
191	593	”	A/12	U
192	595	”	A/12	U
193	596	”	A/12	U
194	597	”	A/12	U
195	598	”	A/13	U.1
196	599	”	A/13	U.1
197	603	”	A/13	U.1
198	600	”	A/13	U.1
210	921	0-6-0	A/18	K
217	922	”	A/18	K
219	912	”	A/17	K
220	923	”	A/18	K
235	924	”	A/18	K
236	925	”	A/18	K
239	926	”	A/18	K
242	927	”	A/18	K
245	928	”	A/18	K
250	797	0-6-0T	A/86	D
252	929	0-6-0	A/18	K
253	913	”	A/17	L
259	914	”	A/17	L
261	915	”	A/18	K
264	795	0-6-0T	A/85	E
265	796	”	A/85	E
266	1343	0-4-0T	N	T
267	1342	”	M	S
270	798	0-6-0T	A/86	D
275	788	”	A/83	V
280	789	”	A/83	V
281	916	0-6-0	A/17	L
283	930	”	A/18	K
284	917	”	A/18	K
285	1133	4-4-0T	D	I
286	1184	”	D	I
287	999	”	D	I
288	918	0-6-0	A/17	L

Taff Vale Number	GW Number	Type	GWR Diagram	Taff Vale Class
290	790	0-6-0T	A/83	V
291	791	”	A/83	V
297	931	0-6-0	A/18	K
298	919	”	A/17	L
301	932	”	A/18	K
302	933	”	A/18	K
304	935	”	A/18	K
313	936	”	A/18	K
314	938	”	A/18	K
316	939	”	A/18	K
320	941	”	A/18	K
322	942	”	A/18	K
325	943	”	A/18	K
327	944	”	A/18	K
328	946	”	A/18	K
335	948	”	A/18	K
336	968	”	A/18	K
337	920	”	A/18	K
339	969	”	A/18	K
340	970	”	A/18	K
344	582	0-6-2T	A/8	M
349	583	”	A/8 A33	M
354	974	0-6-0	A/18	M
356	978	”	A/18	M
357	984	”	A/18	M
358	1000	”	A/18	M
359	1001	”	A/18	M
360	1002	”	A/18	M
362	584	0-6-2T	A/8 A33	M
364	585	”	A/8	M
365	586	”	A/8	M
400	386	”	A/4	A
401	387	”	A/4	A
402	388	”	A/4	A
403	389	”	A/4	A
404	390	”	A/4	A
405	391	”	A/4	A
406	393	”	A/4	A
407	394	”	A/4 A32	A
408	397	“	A/4	A
409	398	”	A/4	A
410	399	”	A/4 A32	A
411	401	”	A/4	A
412	402	”	A/4	A
413	403	”	A/4	A
414	404	”	A/4	A
415	406	”	A/4	A
416	408	”	A/4	A

Figure 295

Figure 296

The first Taff Vale absorbed engines to be illustrated are those of the 'N' class. This series consisted of ten 0-6-2T locomotives built by Messrs Kitsons in 1891, and were a development of the earlier 'M' series, having the same 4' 6" driving wheels set at 7' 5" and 6' 0" centres with trailing radial truck having 3' 8¼" diameter wheels. The T.V. numbering was from 182 to 191, but the last two were altered to No. 106 and 107. The whole class was rebuilt with new boilers by 1919 having a pressure of 150lbs. *Figure* 297 shows No. 183 in the Taff Vale days with the whistle mounted on the cab roof. At the grouping all ten were renumbered GW Nos. 494-6, 498 to 502 and 485-86, and No. 496 can be seen in *Figure* 296, with No. 502 illustrated at *Figure* 295. These two engines had been fitted with the GWR safety valve in place of the Ramsbottom style.

Figure 297

Figure 298

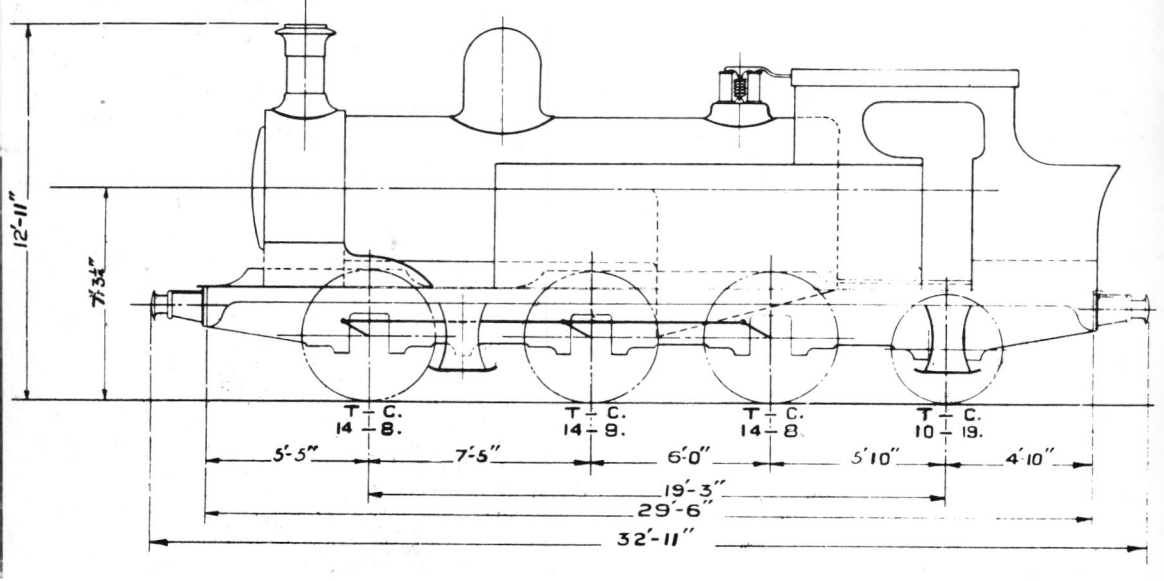

Figure 299

Figure 300

Another view of GW No. 502 (T.V. 189) is shown in *Figure* 298, giving a good front elevation, and in *Figure* 300 GW No. 499 (T.V. 186) illustrates the left-hand front view as the engine stands "dead" on one of the shed roads. The Diagram issued by Swindon for the 'N' class engines was A.11 and is shown in *Figure* 299. Nine of the series were scrapped at Swindon between 1928-30, but the tenth, No. 486, was offered for sale in 1934 and not finally cut up until 1936.

The 'O.2' class of Taff Vale engines was a series of nine locomotives built by Neilson Reid & Co. for mixed traffic duties. They were a compromise between the 'O1' and 'U1' series, being similar to the 'U1's but with the 4' 6½" wheels of the 'O1's. Delivered in 1899, they were numbered 85/82/84/32/83/81/31/66/44. At the grouping in 1922 the GWR renumbered the class 426/23/25/13/24/21/12/19/15 and prepared Diagram A.6 for the class (*Figure* 301). Very little rebuilding was done to these engines, with the exception of the fitting of GW type safety valves, all keeping their Taff boilers until withdrawal. One, No. 426 was sold, and lasted until the 1960s; *Figure* 303 shows this engine (T.V. No. 85) with her side rods off at Swindon prior to being sold, and No. 412 (T.V. No. 31) is seen at Cathays wearing her GWR boiler fittings (*Figure* 302). She was eventually cut up in 1928.

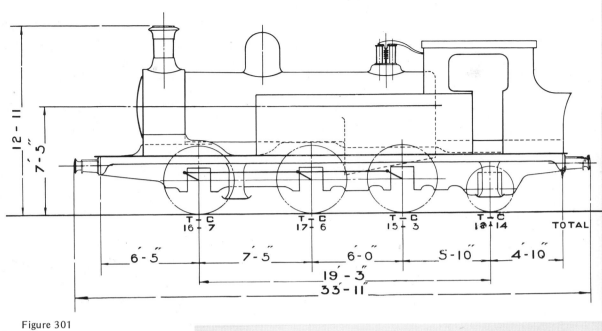

Figure 301

Figure 302

Figure 303

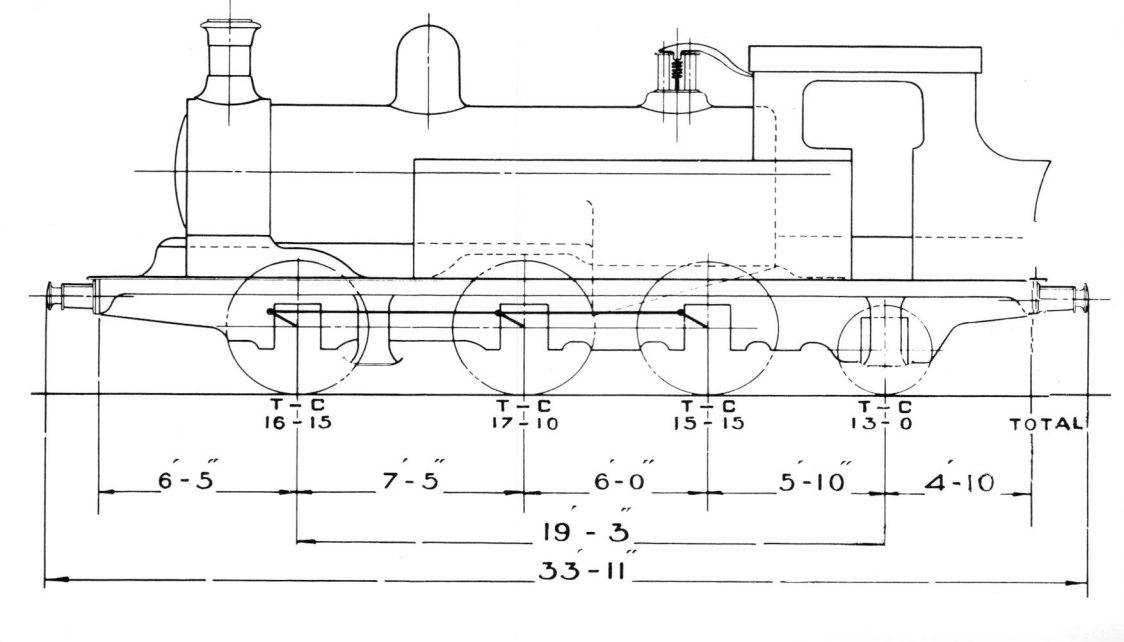

The 'O3' class of fifteen engines was built at three different dates by three different builders. In 1902 Hudswell Clarke & Co. constructed six, which were numbered 47/57/92/93/96/117. In 1904 Nos. 18/19/126 were built by Messrs Kitson & Co. and in 1905 Messrs Vulcan Foundry delivered Nos. 55/103/131/137/155/161. These fifteen were very similar to the 'O2' class but having slight differences in the pitch, firebox and grate area, and were used mainly on passenger train rosters. When introduced into GWR stock Swindon gave them Diagram A.5 (*Figure* 306) which it will be noted is identical with A.6 on the previous page, and of course they were renumbered, becoming GW 416/18/27/31/28/29/10/11/32/17/30/33/34/35/37. One engine, No. 55 (GW 417) was rebuilt with an O2 boiler, so had its own Diagram, Swindon A.7 (*Figure* 307).

No. 411 (T.V.19) is seen in *Figure* 304 at Cardiff Canton Shed in 1937 fitted with GW safety valve and bunker. *Figure* 305 shows No. 428 (T.V. 93) still retaining her Taff Vale fittings with the exception of the safety valve bonnet (note the whistles mounted just off the safety valve).

Figure 304

Figure 305

Figure 306

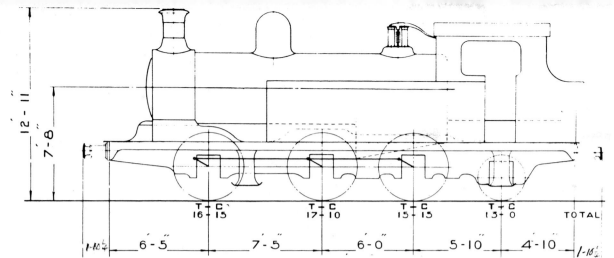

Figure 307

Nos. 410, 434 and 437 of the 'O3' class all had quite a major 'Western' refit, being rebuilt with GWR type side tanks, bunker and high roofed cab. *Figure* 308 shows No. 410 in this condition at Swindon in 1948, but still retaining her 'O3' Taff Vale boiler, and wearing an old 'O4' class chimney! Both this engine and No. 411 lasted until 1948, being withdrawn just before nationalisation.

Figure 308

Figure 309

Figure 310

Figure 311

A further look at the 'O3' class. No. 411 recorded by the camera of A. C. Sterndale standing in the sunshine at Swindon in 1948 (*Figures* 309 and 310). These pictures compare well with the right-hand broadside view with that of No. 410 in *Figure* 311; whilst No. 411 has the GWR bunker complete with lamp guard, she has retained the T.V. Railway boiler, cab and side tanks. No. 410, *left*, has been rebuilt with GWR type high domed roof cab, bunker and side tanks. This picture was taken at Cardiff Canton in 1937, where she spent many years as shed pilot.

In the lower picture (*Figure* 312) No. 430 (T.V. 103) is photographed in the works yard during February 1935. She also has the same 'Western' fittings as No. 411, and struggled on until May 1936 before being finally cut up.

Figure 312

Figure 313

Page 130

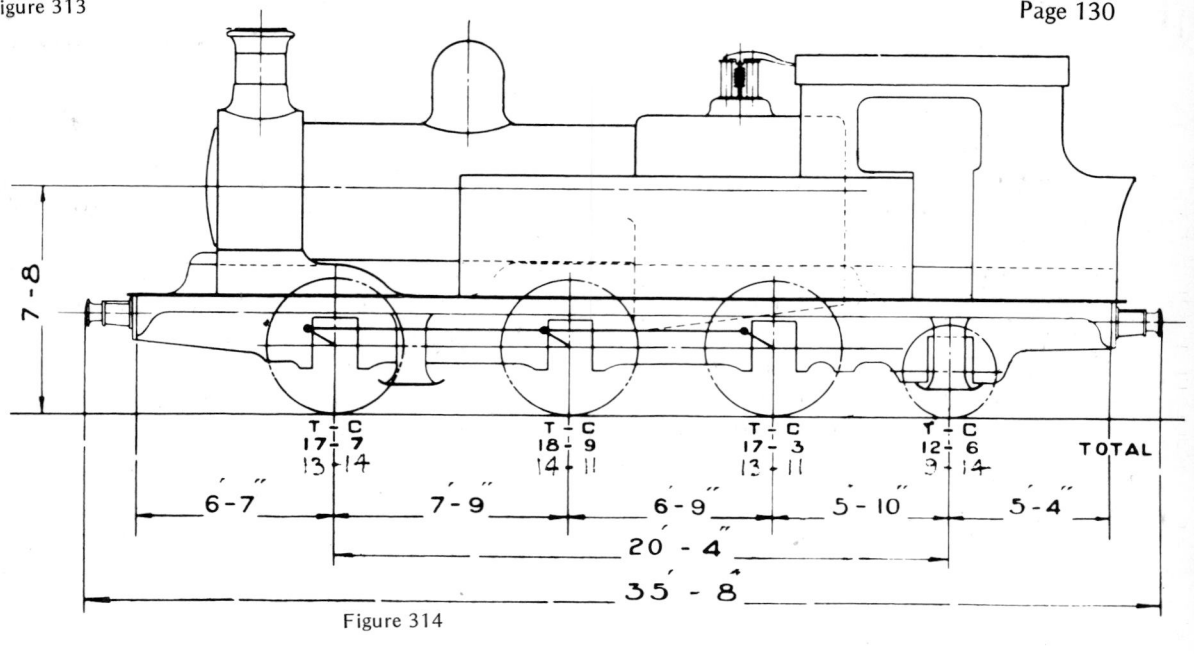

Figure 314

The next engines of the Taff Vale Railway to be considered are those of the 'O4' class. The series consisted of forty one engines all told, built between the years of 1907 and 1910. The first seven were constructed by Manning Wardle, the second batch of fourteen came from Beyer-Peacock in 1908 who also built ten more in 1910, and Vulcan Foundry made ten more in the same year of 1910, being mixed traffic engines, again of the 0-6-2T classification; there were slight differences in the various batches from the different builders, but they all had 4' 6½" wheels set at 7' 9" and 6' 9" centres with radial carrying wheels of 3' 1". As there were forty one numbers in this series, the reader is referred to pages 121-2 for both the complete list of Taff Vale numbers, and the GWR renumbering.

In *Figure* 313 No. 104 (GW No. 302) is seen inside the shed, and note that she has the short rear cab sheets at this time. No. 6 (GW No. 280) is pictured opposite the coal stage at Cardiff Canton in 1947 (*Figure* 315); this engine still has the smokebox 'wings'. She was the only one of the class to retain this feature until withdrawal.

Swindon issued Diagram A.2 for those of the 'O4' class built after and during 1908 known as 'the second batch' and this drawing features in *Figure* 314.

Figure 315

Figure 317

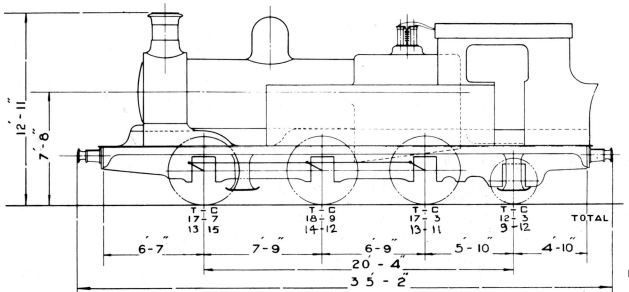

The 'first batch' of 'O4's, those built by Manning Wardle when taken over by the GWR were allotted Diagram A.3 seen in *Figure* 318. No. 283 (T.V. No. 17) is depicted in *Figure* 316 steaming up the valley near Treherbert with a train of coal from the mines in 1948. This engine was finally cut up at Caerphilly one year later. The other 'O4' locomotive to be illustrated on this page (*Figure* 317) is GW No. 289 (T.V. No. 48) — Note that this engine has been fitted with the GW type bunker and safety valve, but little else. She is pictured at Swindon in 1949, which was the year of her withdrawal.

Figure 318

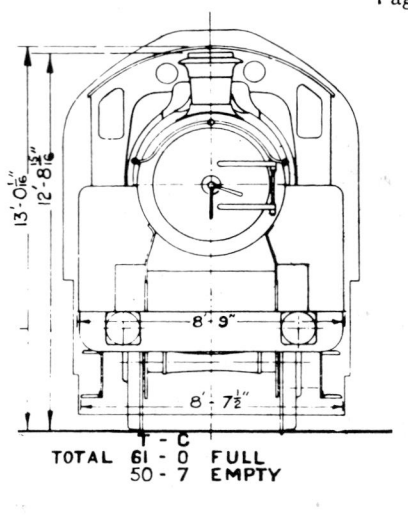

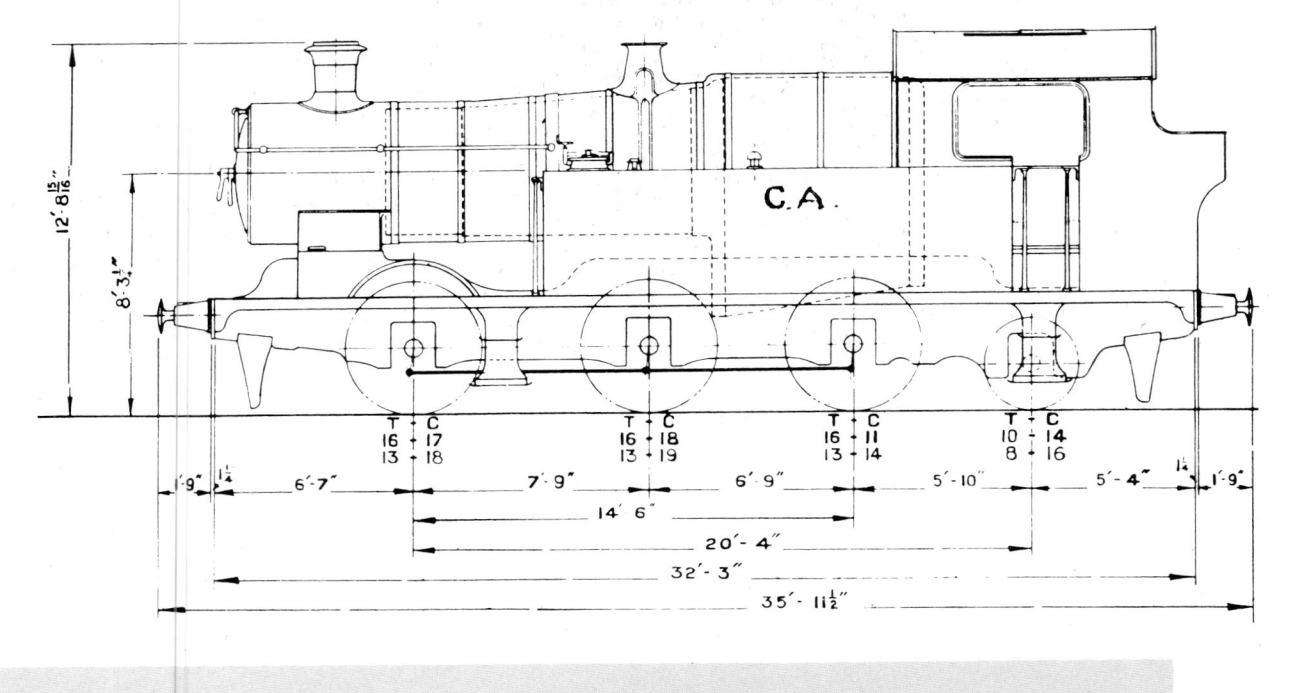

C.A.

12'-8 15/16"

8'-3 1/4"

T·C	T·C	T·C	T·C
16·17	16·18	16·11	10·14
13·18	13·19	13·14	8·16

1'9" 1 1/4"   6'-7"   7'-9"   6'-9"   5'-10"   5'-4" 1 1/4" 1'-9"

14'6"

20'-4"

32'-3"

35'-11 1/2"

13'-0 1/16"   12'-8 5/16"

8'-9"

8'-7 1/2"

TOTAL T·C
61-0   FULL
50-7   EMPTY

Figure 319

GREAT WESTERN 299

Thirty six out of the forty one 'O4' series of Taff Vale Railway engines were rebuilt eventually with the Swindon Standard No. 3 taper boiler, the work of so doing being spread over many years, starting in 1924 and No. 291 not being dealt with until 1946. For this transformation, Swindon issued Diagram A.26 seen in *Figure* 319, and the two official photographs in *Figures* 320 and 321 show No. 299 (T.V. No. 98) as she was turned out of the Swindon factory in 1924.

Figure 321

GREAT WESTERN 441

Figure 322

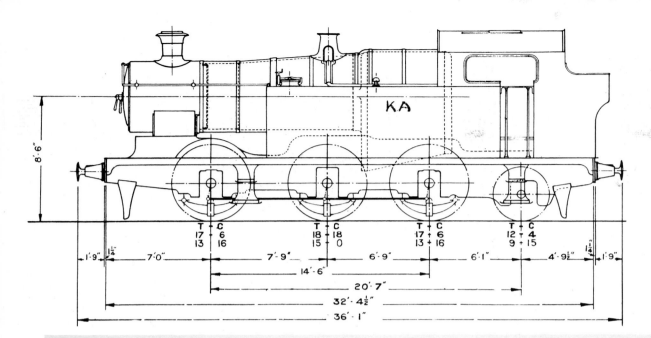

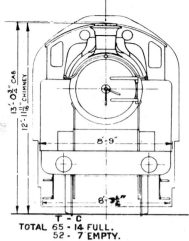

Figure 323

Made to the designs of Mr Cameron who succeeded Mr Hughes in 1912, the Taff Vale 'A' class locomotive was another 0-6-2T locomotive but with larger 5' 3" diameter driving wheels set at 7'9" and 6'9" centres. Designed primarily for passenger traffic, they had a short large diameter boiler of two rings, together with a Belpaire firebox, and the series of fifty eight engines were built between the years of 1914—1921 by three different locomotive builders, namely Hawthorn Leslie, North British Loco Co. and Vulcan Foundry.

The Taff Vale numbers were many and varied, and to save space the reader is again referred to pages 121-2 where both the T.V. numbers and the GW renumbering list is recorded.

No. 441 seen in both *Figure* 322 and *Figure* 324 was rebuilt at Swindon in 1923—24 being fitted with Standard No. 10 boiler, a 'Western' type bunker but still retaining her Taff Vale side tanks. The Diagram issued for the conversion was A.32 shown in *Figure* 323. No. 441 was used as a 'guinea pig', and proving successful, all the class were so rebuilt (with minor differences) over the years 1926—32.

Figure 324

Figure 325

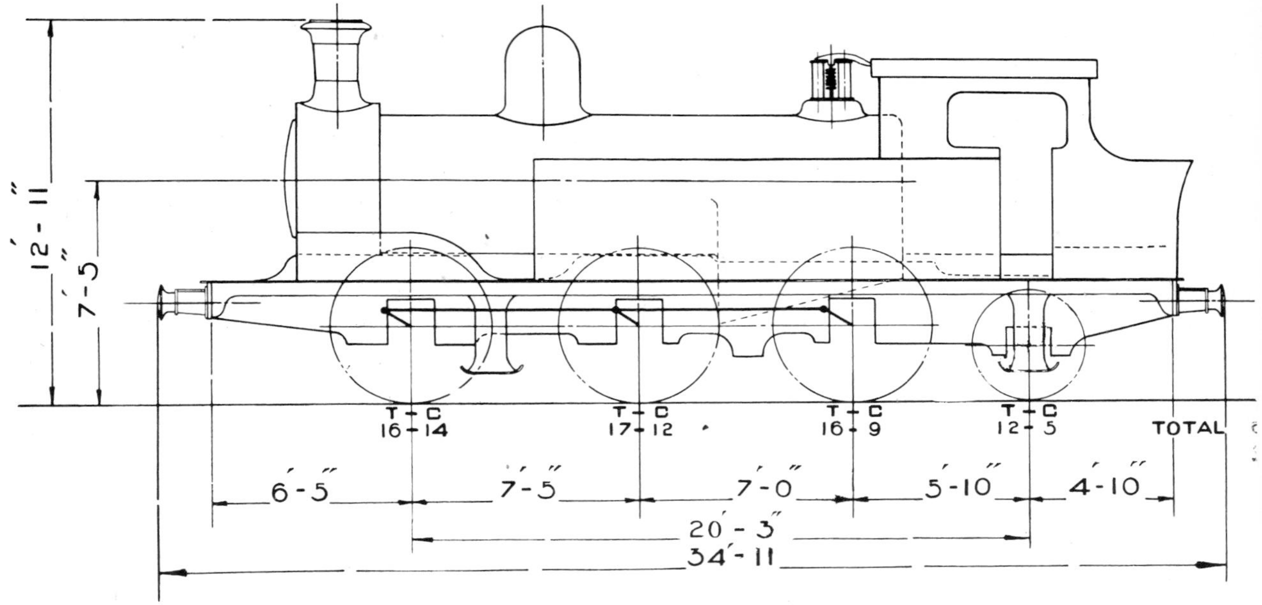

Figure 326

Figure 327

Figure 328

The 'U' class of engines were built to handle passenger traffic on the Taff Vale Railway in 1895. Having 5' 3" driving wheels and working at the slightly higher pressure of 160lbs, they also had bigger radial wheels than the 'U1' class, these being 3' 8¾" compared with 3' 1". Vulcan Foundry built this series of eight, and they were numbered 23/72/76/77/191-4. Fast popular engines, they worked the main line services until being superseded by the 'A' class mentioned on the previous page.

In 1922 Swindon allotted Diagram A.12 (*Figure* 326) and renumbered them GW 593/5/6/7/587/9/90/91. No. 593 herself is seen in *Figure* 328 in almost her Taff Vale condition, the only Swindon influence being the safety valve. The only 'U' class to be rebuilt with a Swindon No. 10 taper boiler was No. 587 (T.V. 23) seen in *Figure* 327, and No. 589 (T.V. 72) is illustrated in *Figure* 325.

Almost identical to the 'U' class, the 'U1' series differed in having the smaller trailing carrying wheels. Also built by Vulcan Foundry, this series of seven were delivered in 1896 and were numbered 30/40/79/195-8. In 1922 the GWR renumbered them 602/588/592/598/99/603/600 and issued Diagram A.13 (*Figure* 331).

In *Figure* 329 No. 195 is seen in Taff Vale days and livery, and it can be seen what handsome engines these were. In the bottom photograph No. 72 of the 'U' class is seen again showing the left-hand side of the locomotive, and conducting her lowly colliery shunting duties (*Figure* 330).

Figure 329

Figure 330

Figure 331

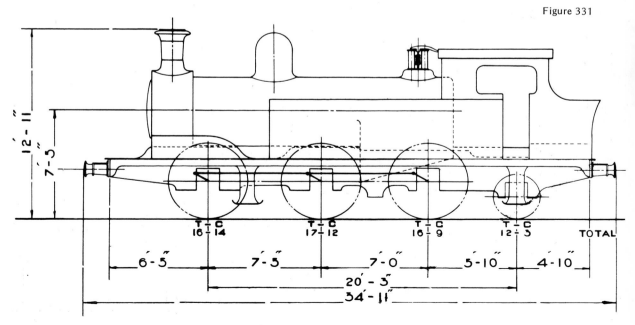

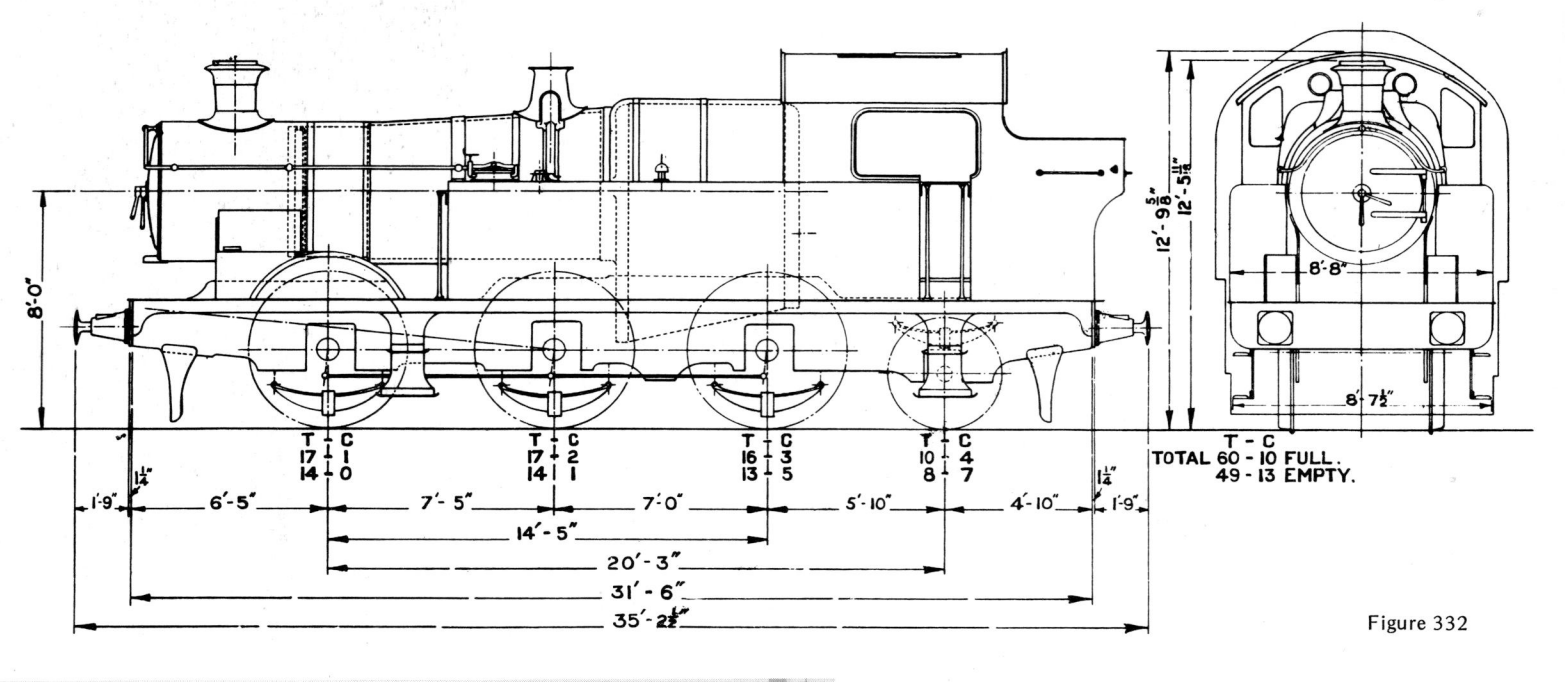

Figure 332

8'-0"

12'-9⅝"
12'-5 11/16"

8'-8"

8'-7½"

T - C
17 - 1   17 - 2   16 - 3   10 - 4
14 - 0   14 - 1   13 - 5   8 - 7

T - C
TOTAL 60 - 10 FULL.
49 - 13 EMPTY.

1'-9"   6'-5"   7'-5"   7'-0"   5'-10"   4'-10"   1'-9"

14'-5"

20'-3"

31'-6"

35'-2¼"

GREAT WESTERN 602

Figure 333

Diagram A.34 (*Figure* 332) was prepared at Swindon to cover the re-building of both No. 587 ('U' class) and No. 602 ('U1' class). The official photograph in *Figure* 333 shows No. 602 being turned on the shed turntable complete with attendant staff. Both these two rebuilds were withdrawn in 1931, the only example to outlive them being No. 589 (T.V. 72) seen in previous pages, which lasted until 1954 in private hands.

The 0-6-2T type of locomotive in South Wales owed their introduction to T. H. Riches who was Locomotive Superintendent to the Taff Vale Railway from 1873 to 1911. It was in 1884 that his design for the 'M' class was passed to Messrs Kitsons for construction, and Nos. 144 and 145 were built in December of that year. In the following six years 38 engines were completed by Kitsons, and three, Nos. 4/5/54, were erected by the Taff Vale themselves at Cardiff. A list of the numbers and renumbering by the GWR can be seen at the beginning of this chapter. During the years 1899 to 1907 twenty four of the 'M' class were rebuilt with new boilers and were identified by being dubbed 'M1's. On being handed over to the GWR in 1922 they were allotted Diagram A.8 (*Figure* 336) and of course were all renumbered. The two illustrations in *Figures* 334 and 335 show No. 583 (T.V. No. 349) and No. 584 (T.V. 362) after they had been rebuilt at Swindon with a Standard No. 11 boiler, a new bunker and had been fitted with gear to enable them to work with Auto trailers.

Figure 334

Figure 335

Figure 336

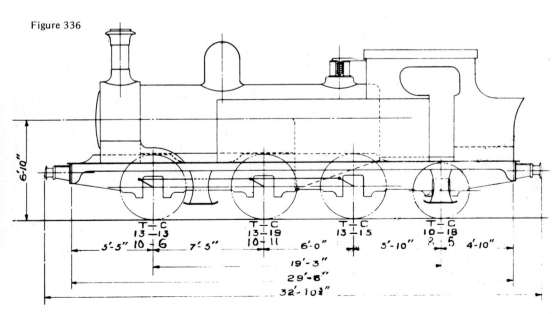

Figure 337

Figure 338

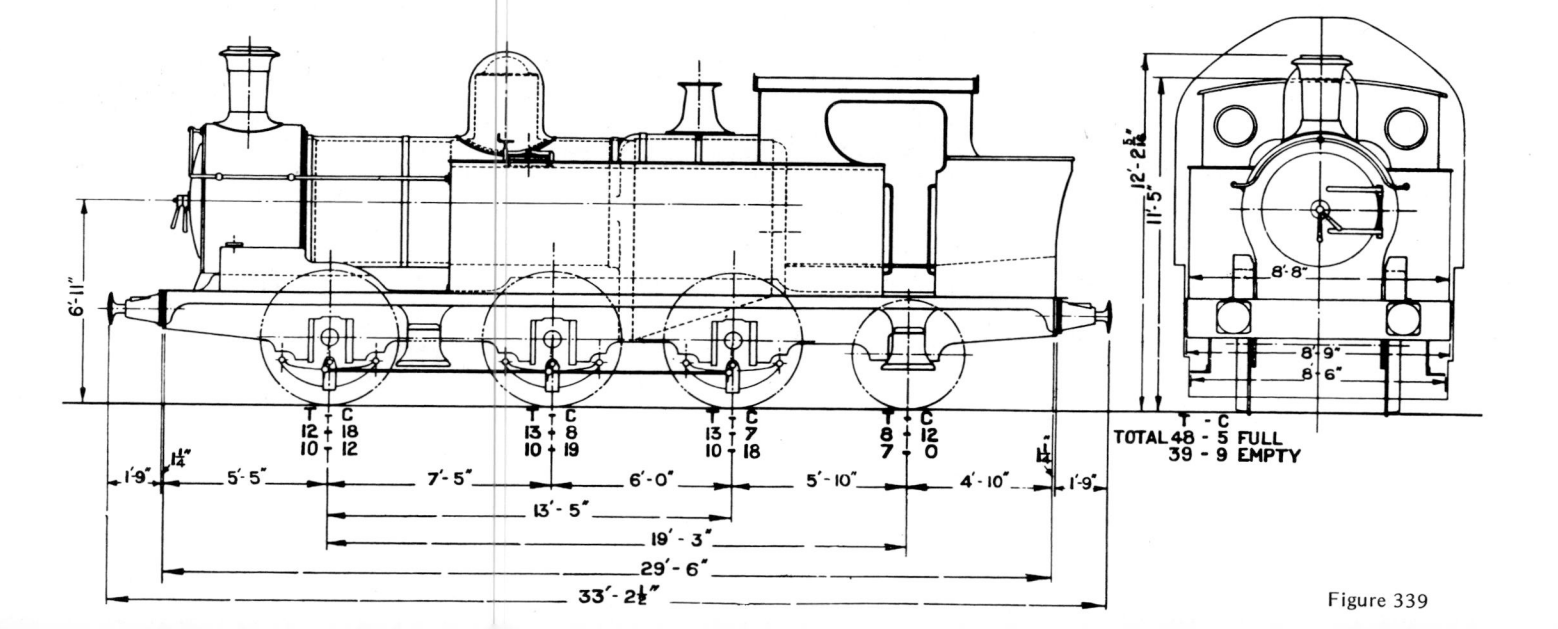

Figure 339

The 'M' and 'M1' engines which were rebuilt with Swindon boilers after the grouping, were issued with a new diagram, this being A.33 seen in *Figure* 339. Some of those converted had parallel chimneys and others had the tapered style. No. 573 (T.V. No. 163) shown in *Figure* 338 is one of the latter, and the auto-gear can be plainly seen on the front buffer beam. Another rebuilt 'M1' was No. 487 (T.V. No. 150) seen in *Figure* 337; this engine, built in 1885, lasted out until December 1934.

This page shows clearly the transformation that Swindon factory brought about in the rebuilding of the 'M' and 'M1' class of Taff Vale engines. In *Figure* 342 No. 482 is shown still with her own Taff boiler, tanks and bunker, the only GW concession being the safety valves mounted on the Taff Vale boiler. In contrast *Figures* 340 and 341 show No. 584 (T.V. No. 362) just out from Swindon works in 1925 resplendent in her 'Westernised' outline and livery. These two pictures show well the 4' 6" diameter driving wheels, and the large 3' 8¼" carrying wheels under the bunker.

Figure 340

Figure 341

Figure 342

Figure 343
Figure 344
Page 142

A small branch line on the Taff Vale Railway serving the Clydach Vale Colliery included the very steep Pwllyrhebog Incline. At the beginning of the climb the gradient was a fierce 1 in 13 for half a mile, which then eased to approximately 1 in 30 for the rest of ascent. The method of operating this incline was by means of engines propelling the empty wagons up the gradient assisted by a heavy wire rope attached to the locomotive, passing underneath the wagons around a pulley wheel at the summit, and thence underneath a descending train, which acted as a counterbalance, and helped to lift the ascending engine and empty wagons.

In 1884 Mr Riches had built three engines especially for working the Pwllyrhebog Incline. They were ordered from Kitsons and were delivered at the end of that year, being numbered 141-143. Unusual in several ways the engines had a tapered inner firebox and boiler, to allow plenty of water over the firebox crown when the engine was working on the incline, in addition a tall dome was mounted on the boiler back ring, directly over the firebox, this ensured a supply of fairly dry steam, and the safety valves were fitted to the top of this dome. These engines had quite large wheels for such work, but as they were rope assisted, power was of secondary importance to the need for clearance of the rope. Set at 7' 3" and 7' 9" centres the six coupled wheels were of 5' 3" diameter. In 1892 the trio formed the 'H' class. At the grouping the three were renumbered GW 792-94 and the Diagram

A.84 was issued to cover them (*Figure 345*). No. 792 (T.V. No. 141) is shown in *Figure 343* at her home shed of Treherbert, and in *Figure 344* No. 143 had been renumbered again by the date of this picture, 1951, having become No. 195.

The Great Western on taking over these engines, seemed to be content to leave well alone, as, apart from changing the safety valves at Caerphilly in 1928 the 'H' class remained virtually unchanged in their long lives, the last one, No. 193, being cut up in private hands in 1960.

In *Figure 346* No. 143 is seen at Treherbert shed wearing the intermediate GW No. 794. She became No. 195 in 1949 and was sold to the N.C.B. in 1951 and finished her days in 1957.

Taff Vale No. 142 which became GW 793, and eventually BR 194 was on loan at various times to the N.C.B., and did service on the Tar Plant at Caerphilly. She was finally sent to Swindon for scrapping in 1953, and the official photograph in *Figure 347* shows her outside the factory.

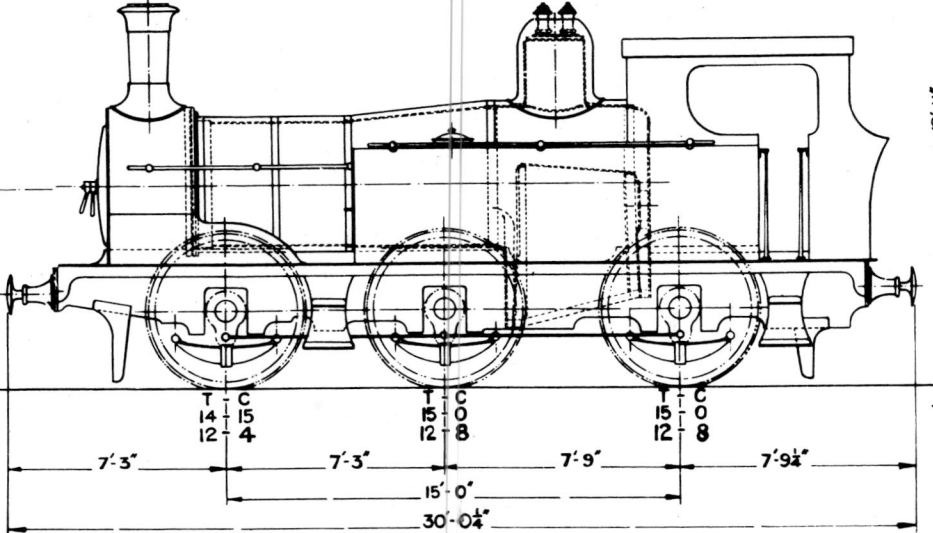
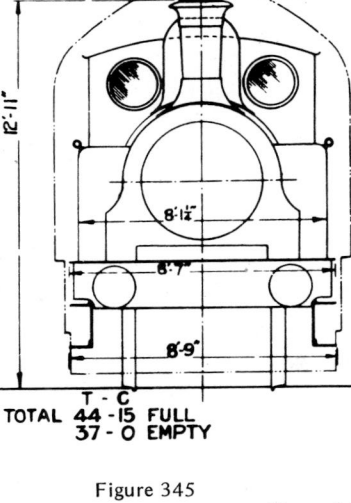
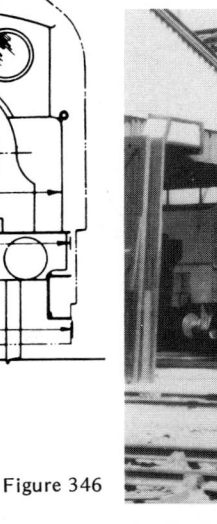

Figure 345

Figure 346

Figure 347

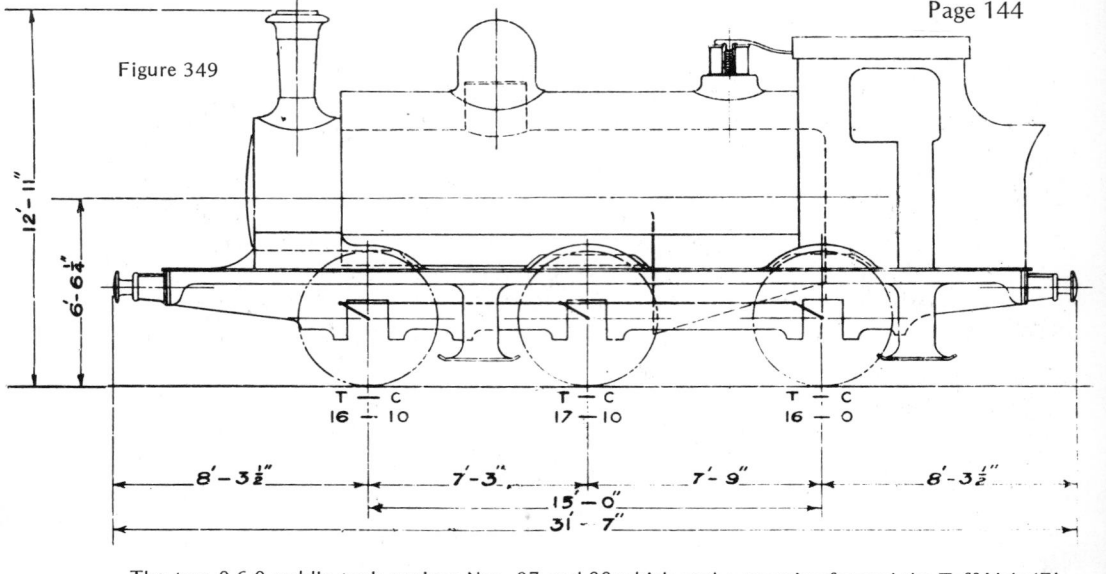

Figure 348
Figure 349
Page 144

The Taff Vale 'V' class consisted of six saddle tank engines of six wheels coupled, built by Kitsons in 1899 to replace earlier tanks of Metropolitan origin. They were numbered 75/80/90/91/99/100, and carried long saddle tanks which extended from the cab front to the rear of the smokebox. In *Figure 349* is the Diagram given to this small class of six engines, this was Swindon A.83 and like all other absorbed engines, upon entering the GWR they were renumbered, being given numbers 788-91/786/7. A small change was carried out at Cardiff in 1923-4, this was to cut a small bottom front section out of the saddle tank to improve the access to the motion. This can be seen in *Figure 348* where No. 791 was pictured by A. C. Sterndale in Hatfield Colliery sidings in 1950. Five out of the six 'V' class were sold into private hands, and the sixth, No. 790 was cut up at Swindon in 1928.

The two 0-6-0 saddle tank engines Nos. 87 and 88 which at the grouping formed the Taff Vale 'E' class, started life as tender engines. Four 0-6-0 locomotives were built by Sharp-Stewart in 1873 and were numbered 86-89. They had 4' 6½'' driving wheels set at 6' 9½'' and 8' 0'' centres and were coupled to four wheeled tenders which had a capacity of 1,600 gallons. All four were laid aside in 1891, and eventually they were converted to saddle tanks and renumbered 262-265. Only two survived into GWR days these being 264 and 265. They were renumbered again to GW 795-6 and allotted Diagram A.85 in *Figure 351*. No. 264 made the one-way journey to Swindon in 1923 and was quickly condemned, but her sister No. 265 received her number plates GW 796 and acted as pilot in Cardiff West Yard until being withdrawn in 1927. *Figure 350* shows this engine on the turntable at Cardiff Cathays in 1926.

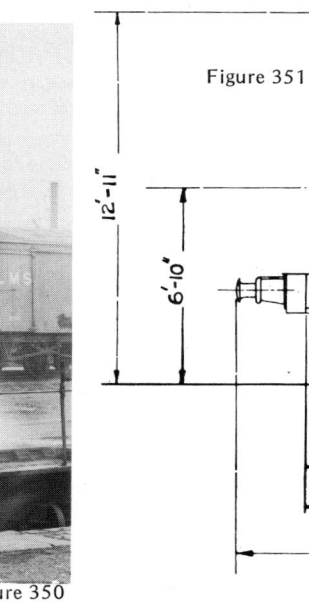

Figure 350

Figure 351

Figure 352

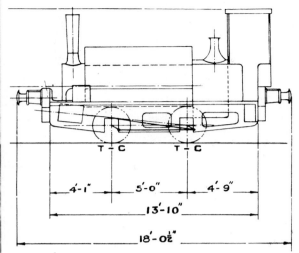

Figure 353

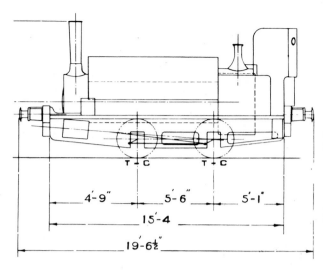

Figure 354

Figure 355

Figure 356

Two very small engines were ordered from Hudswell Clarke in 1876 to do shunting duties at the top of the Pwllyrhebog Incline; they were very tiny, only scaling 11½ tons, and with 4 coupled wheels of 2′ 6″ diameter set 5′ wheelbase. These two were numbered 106 and 107, and when classes were introduced on the Taff Vale No. 106 then renumbered 266 became the sole 'T' class, and No. 107 (renumbered 267) became the one only 'S' class. Both engines were shedded at Cathays and at the grouping were renumbered once again, No. 266 became GW 1343, and 267 was changed to 1342. Two separate diagrams were issued by Swindon, No. 1343 was allotted Diagram N (*Figure* 353) and No. 1342 took Diagram M (*Figure* 354), *Figure* 355 shows No 267 in Taff Vale days, and it is apparent the engine crews had to be slim to work on these little shunters! This engine is seen again in *Figure* 356, this time in GWR ownership and on shed at Cathays. The only photograph located of No. 1343 is seen in *Figure* 352 and it shows the difference in the two cab arrangements. These two did not survive long in 'Western' ownership. No. 1343 was cut up at West Yard Works in 1926, and No. 1342 went to Swindon in 1925 and stood "dead" on the Dump for twelve months before being cut up late in 1926.

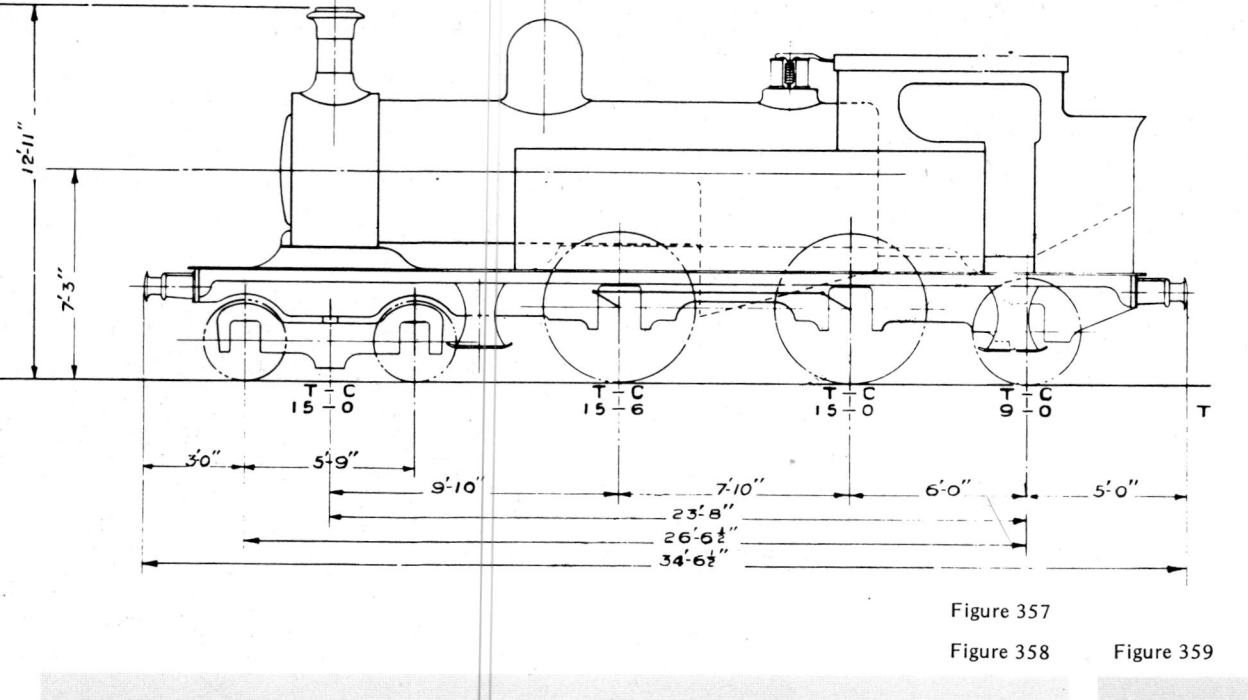

The Taff Vale liked to order their engines in threes, and an example of this was the placing of an order in 1888 for three inside cylinder 4-4-2T engines, built and designed for working passenger trains on the main line, and followed in 1891 by three similar locomotives to make up what eventually became class 'C'. All six were constructed by Vulcan Foundry and were numbered 170-5. The bogie wheels were 2' 9'' diameter with four coupled drivers of 5' 3'' diameter set at 7' 10'' centres, and the radial wheels under the bunker were of 3' 8¼'' diameter. No. 172 seen in *Figure 358* shows the engines as built, and in *Figure 359* the same locomotive is illustrated in GWR days fitted with the T.V. Railway system of overhead auto-gear. When the Great Western took them over they were given new numbers 1301-6 and allotted Diagram 'H' in *Figure 357*. For several years they continued working with trailer cars, but when the latter were converted to the GWR auto system, all six became redundant, and were cut up at Swindon between 1926-28.

Figure 357

Figure 358   Figure 359

The 'I' class was another series of three engines designed and built at Cardiff by Mr Riches in 1884 for working passenger services over the branch lines. When first constructed they were handsome little 4-4-0 tanks having lots of polished brass, which set off the sombre black livery with the red and yellow lining. They were numbered 67, 68 and 69 and had 5' 3" driving wheels set at 7' 10" centres. The four wheel leading bogie had wheels of 2' 9" diameter, set at 5' 9" centres and half covered with mud-guards. The superb illustration in *Figure 360* shows the engines as built and No. 67 in particular. Her sister No. 68, seen on next page in *Figure 361*, a little later in time, as the cab is now enclosed, and coal rails have been added to the bunker. Notice the very long oil feeder the bearded driver is holding to enable him to lubricate the inside bearings of the leading driving wheels. In 1907 these three engines were given a new lease of life, when it was decided that an engine and trailers was more effective than the Steam Rail Motors. The 'I' class were chosen for this job, and fitted with the rather "Heath Robinson" overhead gear stretching from chimney to cab, seen attached to No. 68 in *Figure 361*. Two years before they became auto-engines the three were renumbered 285-7, and the bottom illustration is of this period.

Figure 360

Figure 362

Page 148

Figure 361

The 'I' class fulfilled their auto-engine task so well, that instead of one trailer, often as many as four eight wheel carriages were attached to cope with the increased traffic, so much so, that in 1914-15, Nos. 285-7 were rebuilt with larger boilers, and it was in this condition that they were handed over into the GWR ownership. Swindon gave them Diagram D (*Figure* 363) and renumbered them again to 1133/1184/999. Four years later they were all withdrawn and scrapped in 1926. *Figure* 362 shows No. 286 in Taff Vale days. The only picture of the class in GWR days is that in *Figure* 364 in which No. 1133 is seen on shed. Notice the thicker chimney and smaller dome fitted after receiving the larger boilers, also the exhaust pipes on each side of the smokebox.

Figure 363

Figure 364

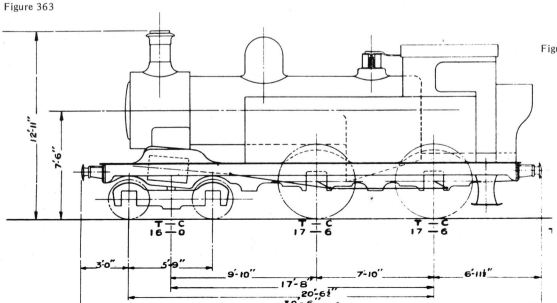

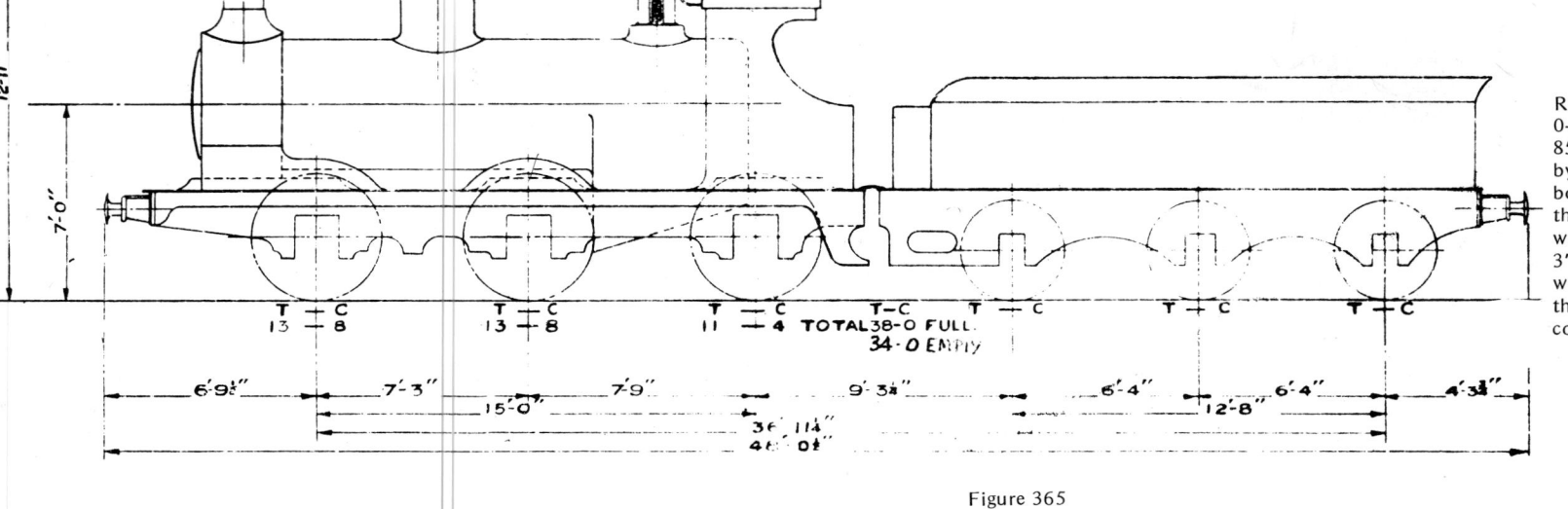

12'-11"

7'-0"

T — C
13 — 8

T — C
13 — 8

T — C
11 — 4   TOTAL 38-0 FULL.
34-0 EMPTY

T—C   T—C   T—C   T—C

6'-9½"   7'-3"   7'-9"   9'-3½"   6'-4"   6'-4"   4'-3½"

15'-0"

38'-11¼"
48'-0½"

The Taff Vale was, amongst all the absorbed South Wales Railways, the greatest user of tender engines, albeit all of the 0-6-0 configuration. By the year 1890 there were no less than 85 on the list, 12 of which had been built at Cardiff and 73 by Messrs Kitsons. They were all inside framed, with parallel boilers and six coupled drivers of 4' 6" (later 4' 6½" with thicker tyres) set at 7' 3" and 7' 9" centres. All the tenders were, strangely, outside framed with six carrying wheels of 3' 8¼" diameter, could carry 1½ tons of coal, and had a water capacity of 1,850 gallons. The numbers were so many that once again the reader is referred to the initial pages for a complete list.

Figure 365

Figure 366

In 1892 a stronger boiler was fitted to No. 105 which later was given the classification 'K', the other 85 engines being formed into class 'L'. Over the ensuing years many of these 0-6-0 goods engines were rebuilt with the modified boiler, and so all those changed from 'L's to 'K's. At the grouping 43 had been scrapped, and only six 'L' class (which had by then received M1 boilers) and thirty six 'K' class remained to be passed across to the GWR, although one 'K' class No. 333 never actually ran under Great Western administration, being scrapped at Cardiff in 1922. Swindon allotted Diagram A.18 for the 'L' class, and this is seen in *Figure* 365. *Figures* 366 and 367 show Nos. 155 and 10 as new, or nearly new, and a comparison is possible with No. 337 (GW No. 920) as seen in *Figure* 368 during GWR days.

Figure 368

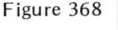

Figure 367

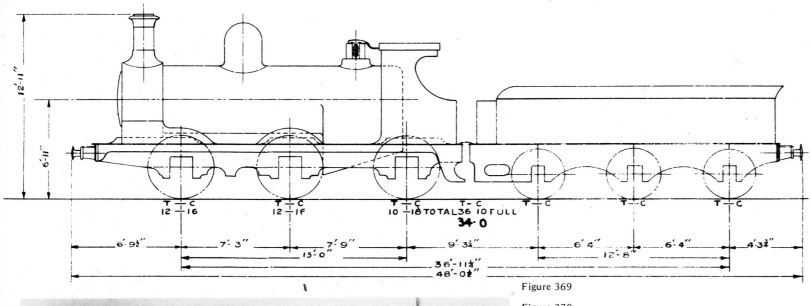

12'-11"

6'-11"

T—C
12—16

T—C
12—16

T—C
10—18 TOTAL 36 10 FULL
34·0

T—C

T—C

T—C

6'-9½"

7'-3"

7'-9"

9'-3¼"

6'-4"

6'-4"

4'-3¾"

15'-0"

12'-8"

36'-11½"

48'-0½"

Figure 369

Figure 370

For the rebuilt 'K' class, the GWR Diagram A.17 was issued (*Figure* 369). Again a comparison can be drawn on this page between before and after absorption. No. 284 seen at Roath Branch Junction in 1923 (*Figure* 371) still is in the Taff Vale condition, whereas in *Figures* 370 and 372, No. GW 919 (which was originally No. 98, afterwards 298) is seen at Swindon in 1932 on the sales list; in fact she was the very last in the class to go. It might be of interest to mention here, that only one engine out of the 41 passed across to the GWR received any major attention at Swindon. This was No. 284 seen in *Figure* 371. She was re-numbered GW 917, rebuilt with the boiler from 'K' class No. 357, given a GW smokebox and boiler fittings, and returned to work in 1924. However she did not last long, being scrapped at Caerphilly in 1927.

Figure 372

Figure 371

The
BRECON & MERTHYR RAILWAY

The Brecon & Merthyr Railway opened its first section in 1863, this being the single line running south from Brecon, down to Pant. Later in 1863, the B & M absorbed the Rumney Railway which ran from Bassaleg to Rhymney, and also had powers to run over the Monmouthshire Railway and Canal Company to Newport. The second section from Pant to Deri Junction was completed; and a short piece of the Rhymney Railway from Deri Jct. to Bargoed was used to connect up with the southern section and in 1868 a through service was commenced from Brecon to Newport. A branch was opened to Merthyr in August of the same year, and another branch was completed in 1869, from Pant to Dowlais. A third short line had been built in 1864, and the building of the Machen loop in 1891 practically doubled the access to Caerphilly. When the full distance of 47 miles from Brecon to Newport became available, Machen was chosen as the workshops for the B & M, and locomotive sheds were situated at Bassaleg, Brecon, Rhymney, Talyllyn and Dowlais.

The Brecon & Merthyr engines were painted a shade of brick red with black panels lined with yellow, and the dome and safety valve seats were polished brass.

In 1922 the Brecon & Merthyr handed over to the GWR 47 locomotives, a list of which appears hereunder.

B. & M. No.	GWR No.	Type	Builder	GWR Diagram	
1	2177	0-6-0T	Fowler	A105	
2	2178	"	"	"	
3	2179	"	"	"	
4	2180	"	"	"	
5	2181	"	Stephenson	"	
6	2182	"	"	"	
7	2183	"	"	"	B14
8	2184	"	"	"	B20
9	1402	2-4-0T	"	S	
10	1412	"	"	"	
11	1460	"	"	"	
12	1452	"	"	"	
13	2185	0-6-0T	Fowler	A105	
14	2186	"	"	"	B14
15	2187	"	Stephenson	"	
16	2188	"	"	"	B14
17	2190	"	Sharp Stewart	A106	B26
18	2191	"	"	"	"
19	1674	0-6-2T	Vulcan	A18	
20	1677	"	"	"	
22	2169	0-6-0T	Kitson	A103	
23	1692	0-6-2T	Vulcan	A18	
24	2170	0-6-0T	Kitson	A103	
25	1458	2-4-0T	Stephenson	S	
26	1833	0-6-2T	Vulcan	A18	
27	2171	0-6-0T	Nasmyth Wilson	A103	
28	2172	"	"	"	B15
29	2173	"	"	"	"
32	1685	"	G.W.R.	D	A47
33	1693	"	"	"	A29
34	1694	"	"	"	A47
35	2161	"	Kerr, Stuart	A102	B13
36	11	0-6-2T	Stephenson	A15	A22
37	21	"	"	"	
38	332	"	"	"	A22
39	504	"	"	"	
40	698	"	"	"	
41	888	"	"	"	
42	1084	"	"	"	
43	1113	"	"	"	
44	1391	4-4-2T	Beyer Peacock	I	
45	1372	0-6-2T	Stephenson	A17	
46	1373	"	"	"	
47	1374	"	"	"	
48	1375	"	"	"	
49	1668	"	"	"	
50	1670	"	"	"	

Figure 373

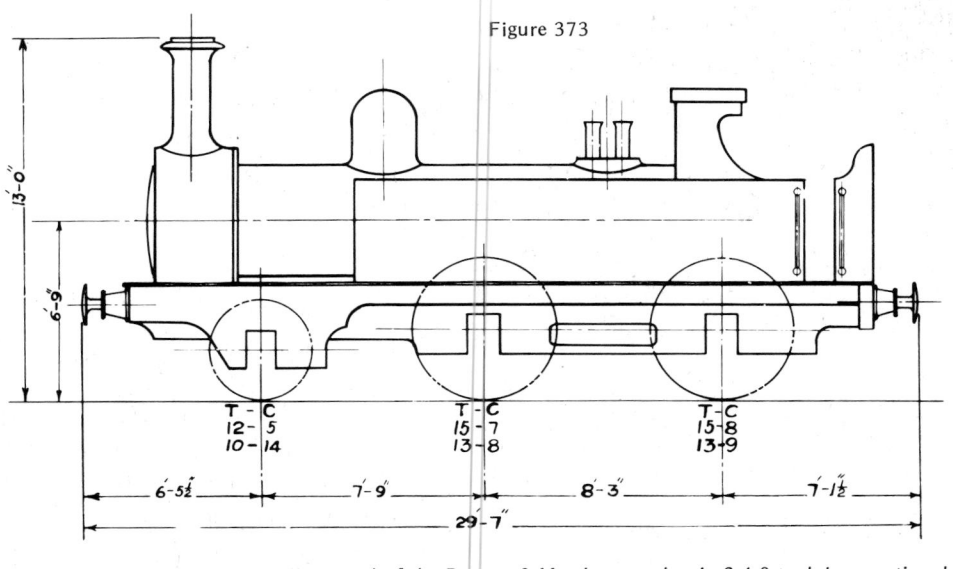

Figure 373

Figure 375

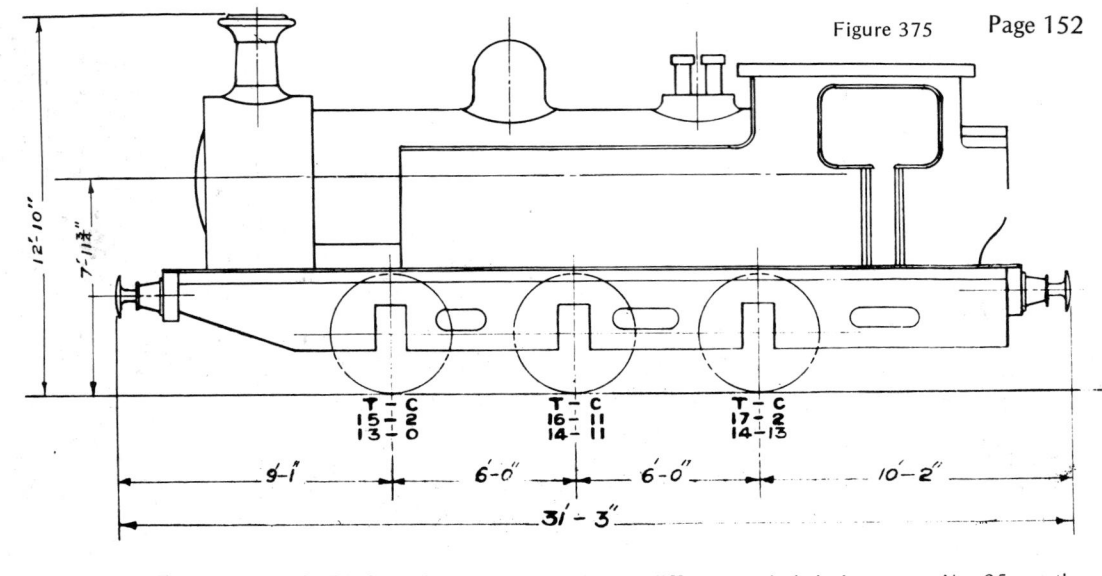

Figure 375

The first engines to be illustrated of the Brecon & Merthyr are the six 2-4-0 tank locomotives built by R. Stephenson for the working of the main line from 1888 onwards. This order came about by the loan of a GWR Metro tank in 1888, which proved so successful that this type was immediately decided upon. Nos. 9 and 10 were delivered in 1888, Nos. 11 and 12 in 1889, No. 25 was completed at Machen in 1898, and finally No. 21 in 1904. As can be seen from the photographs, these engines were very similar to the Swindon 'small Metros', having 4 coupled wheels of 5′ diameter set at 8′ 3″ centres. The leading carrying wheels were of 3′ 6″ diameter carried in outside bearings. The first five of the engines were allotted GWR numbers being 1402/12/60/52/58 (No. 21 going to Swindon minus its boiler and being scrapped forthwith) but only No. 11 actually carried the GW No. 1460. The Diagram issued by Swindon was 'S' as seen in *Figure* 373, and No. 11 is shown in *Figure* 374 in the B. & M. livery. The delightful shot on the lower page is of No. 9 at the head of her little train in 1905, starting off uphill from Machen station (*Figure* 377). Note the bracket signal with the arm lowered for the Brecon line, the other arm controlling the branch to Caerphilly.

Figures 375 and 376 show the same engine, but at different periods in its career. No. 35 was the last locomotive added to the Brecon & Merthyr Railway in 1920. She was built by Messrs Kerr Stuart of Stoke on Trent in 1917, and was one of ten ordered by the government for the Inland Waterways & Docks Division at Portsmouth. After hostilities ceased in 1919 the engines were offered for sale, and the B. & M. purchased what was No. 605 and renumbered her No. 35. Upon the 1922 grouping the GWR issued Diagram A.102 to cover this one small 0-6-0 side tank with the 4′ diameter wheels, and of course renumbered it yet again, this time to 2161. The engine made the trip to Swindon in 1922 and was fitted with various GW fittings, but strangely, she kept her Ross pop safety valves, contrary to usual practice. A new Diagram was prepared, which also covered two similar engines which had been bought by the Alexandra Dock Railway Co. This was Diagram B.13 seen in *Figure* 376. No. 2161 worked on until 1929 when she was sold to Ashington Coal Co. which was taken into the National Coal Board eventually, and the little Kerr Stuart was finally cut up in 1951.

Figure 374

Figure 374

Figure 376

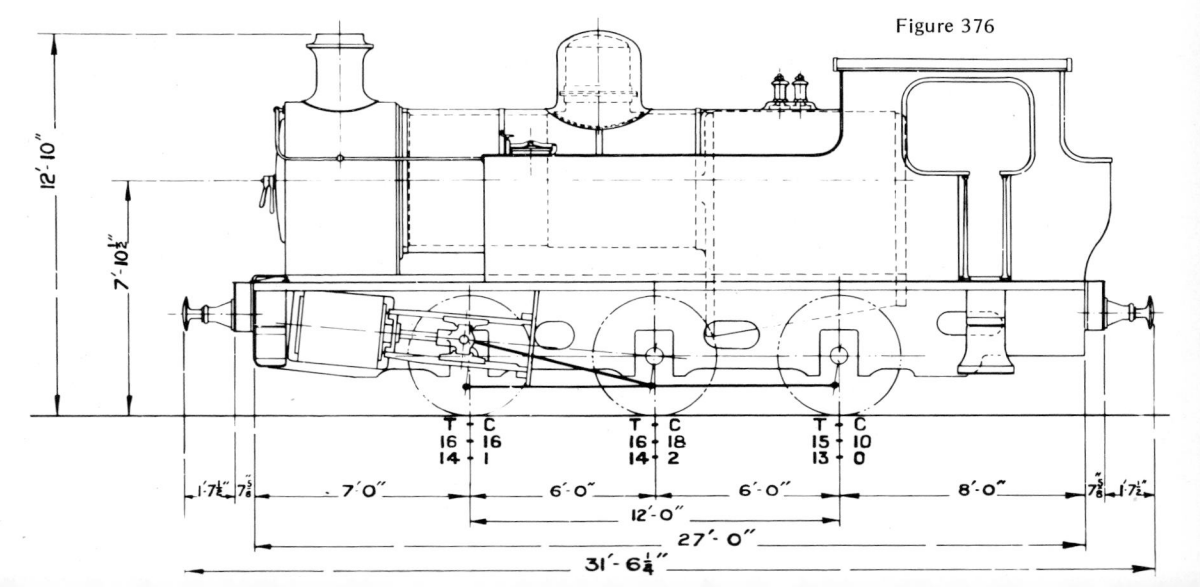

Figure 376

Figure 377

Messrs Kitson & Co. received an order for two outside framed saddle tanks in 1896 for working the Brecon & Merthyr goods traffic. Six wheel coupled with 4' 7½" diameter wheels they had full length saddle tanks, with an enclosed cab. The first two were numbered 22 and 24, and in 1900 three similar engines were ordered from Messrs Nasmyth Wilson & Co. These were numbered 27, 28 and 29 and upon being taken into GWR stock their numbers were changed to 2169-73, and the Diagram drawn for this class of five was A.103 seen in *Figure* 380. Three of the series, Nos. 28, 29 and 22, passed through Swindon factory in 1922-23 and were rebuilt with '2301' saturated boilers, Belpaire fireboxes, pannier tanks, and GW type cab and bunker. In this condition they appeared as in *Figure* 378 where No. 2169 features, and the Diagram issued to cover this transformation was B.15 seen in *Figure* 379. Nos. 2170 and 2171 received minor refits, but always remained on Diagram A.103. All five were scrapped between 1927 and 1932.

Figure 378

Figure 379

Figure 380

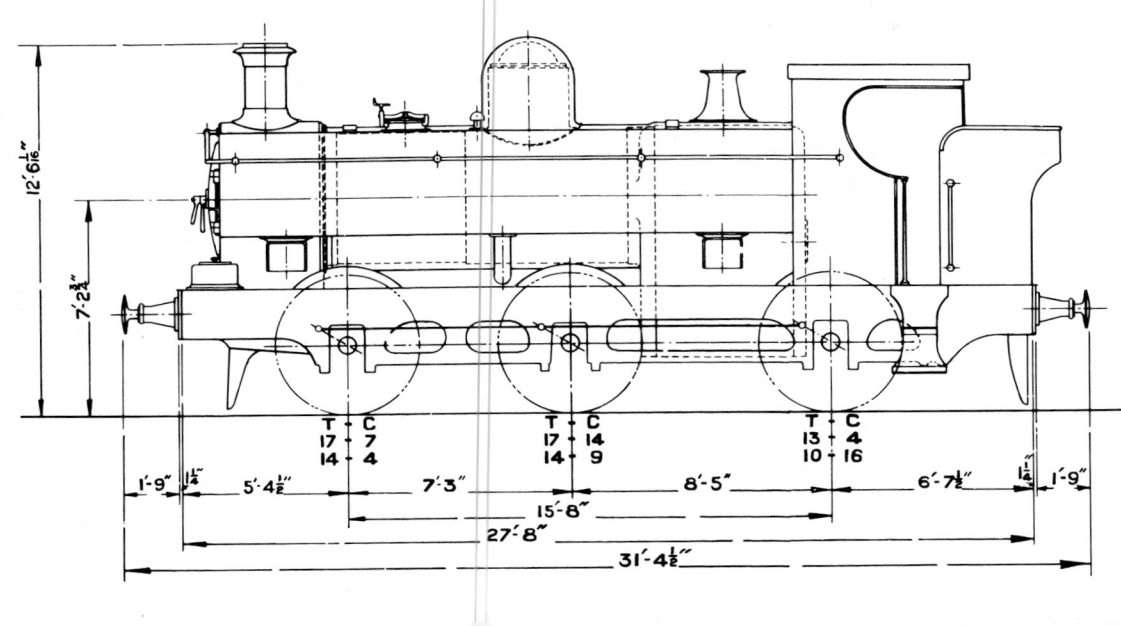

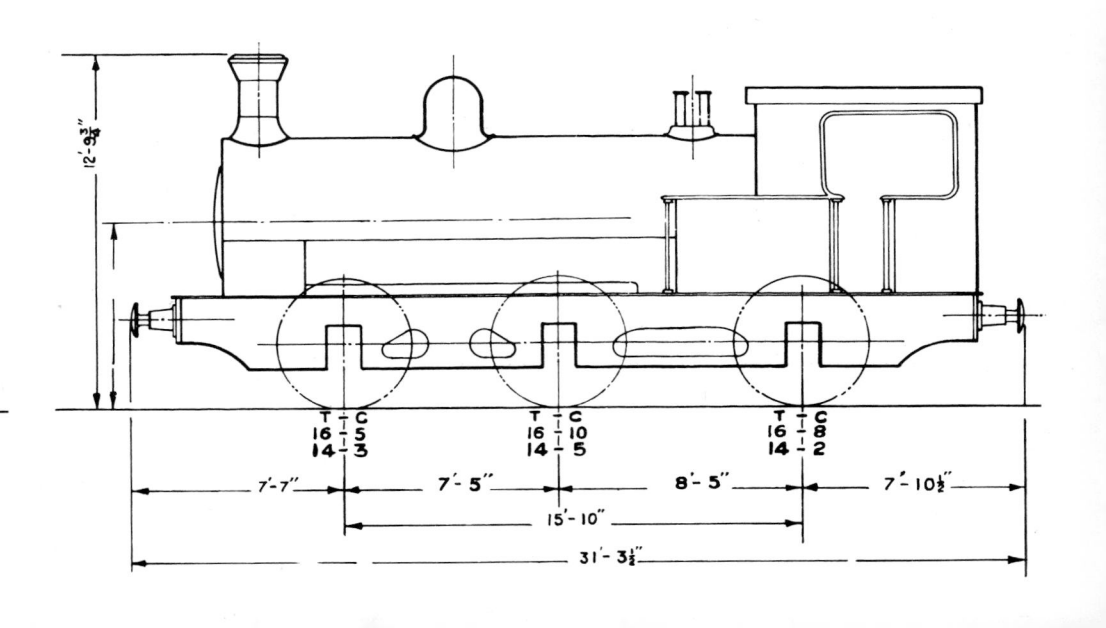

Figure 381

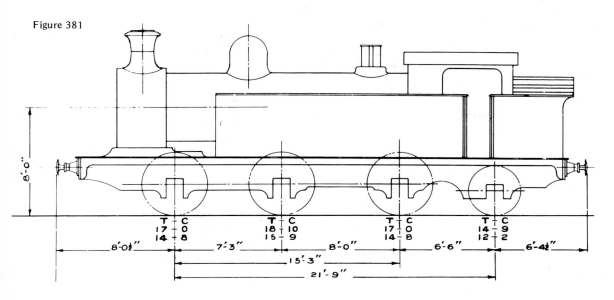

The first modern side tanks purchased by the Brecon & Merthyr were four big 0-6-2 side tanks, built by Messrs Stephenson's to the designs of the Rhymney Railway. They only differed from the Rhymney 'R' class, in that these engines had round topped fireboxes in place of the Belpaires of the R.R. They were delivered in 1909-10 and numbered 36-39. Proving successful, four more were ordered in 1913 and Stephenson's delivered them in 1914. Swindon allotted Diagram A.15 to these engines, *Figure* 381, and two of the class can be seen in the two illustrations. No. 40 in *Figure* 382 is shown with GW type chimney and safety valve, and with the sandboxes mounted above the running plate. *Figure* 383 depicts No. 42 (GW 1084) almost as built, except for safety valve, number plates and lettering, at Newport Pill in 1947.

Figure 382

Figure 383

Figure 384

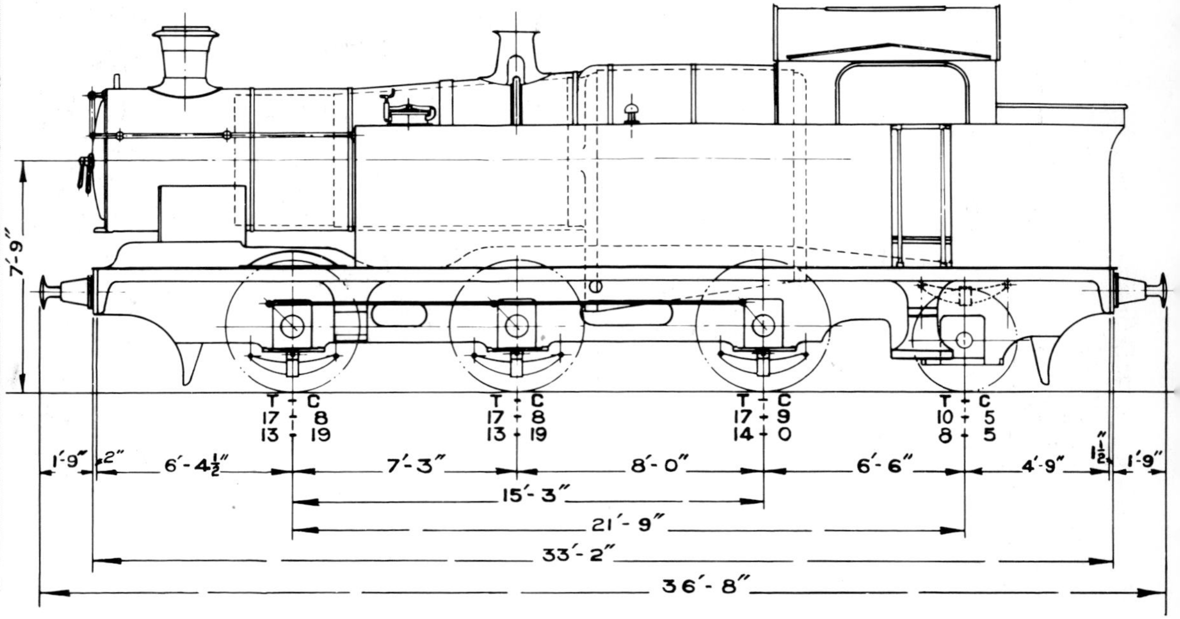

Figure 385

Figure 386

In 1922, four of the Brecon & Merthyr Stephenson engines of the '36' class made the journey to Swindon factory, and Nos. 41, 42 and 43 (GW Nos. 888, 1084 and 1113) were fitted with GW type bunker, smokebox, chimney and fittings. No. 38 and No. 36 (GW Nos. 332 and 11) however were rebuilt with a Standard No. 2 taper boiler, No. 11 also getting new side tanks. No. 37 (GW No. 21) was similarly dealt with in 1929, and at Caerphilly Works in 1941, No. 41 (GW 888) was also converted. The Diagram issued for this transformation was Swindon A.22 (*Figure* 385). Our lower illustration, *Figure* 386, shows No. 11 just as she was turned out of the factory in 1924, whereas in *Figure* 384, No. 38 is seen at Swindon in 1950 just before being scrapped. In 1946 four of this class were renumbered once again, Nos. 21/698/888/1113 becoming 422/5/6/8.

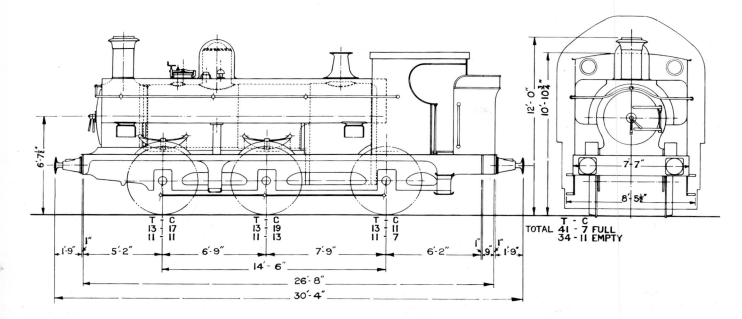

Two small saddle tanks, built by Sharp-Stewart & Co. in 1881 were supplied to the Brecon & Merthyr to help work the passenger services on the main line. As can be seen in our *Figure* 389, they were neat little engines, having full length saddle tanks, open cab, and with 6 wheels coupled of 4' 7½" diameter set at 6' 9" and 7' 9" centres. Originally they were numbered 11 and 17, but in 1889 No. 11 was renumbered to 18. At the grouping Swindon gave them Diagram 106 (*Figure* 388) and they had the distinction of being the oldest B. & M. engines taken over by the GWR. Like so many other absorbed engines, these two went to Swindon in 1922, and several years later, were renumbered 2190 and 2191, and given pannier tanks, bunkers, chimneys and other GW fittings and returned to service looking to all intents and purposes a 'Western' pannier tank. The new Diagram given for the rebuilds was B.26 seen in *Figure* 387, and No. 2190 is seen wearing a spark-arresting chimney on the next page in *Figure* 390.

Figure 387

Figure 388

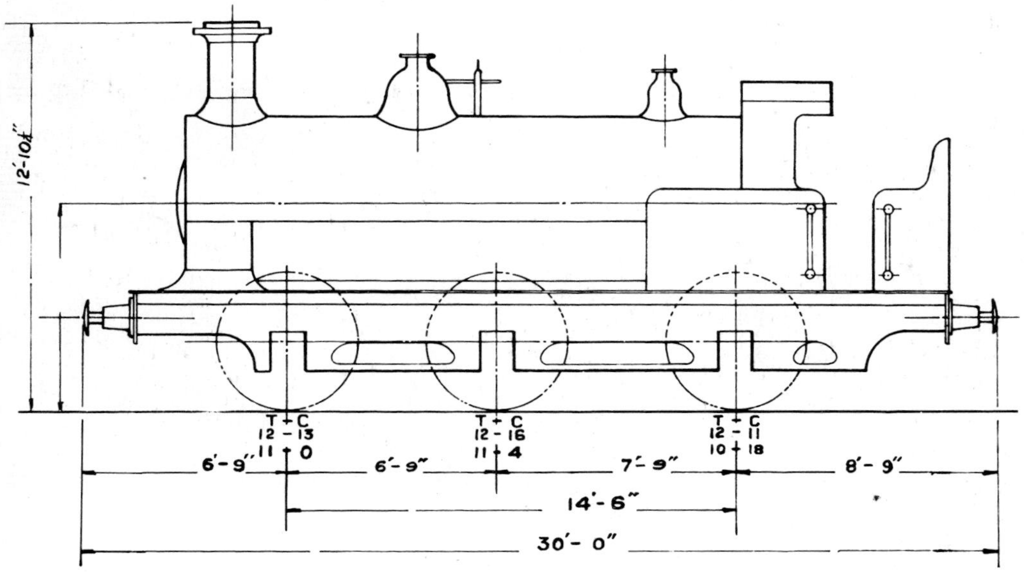

Figure 389

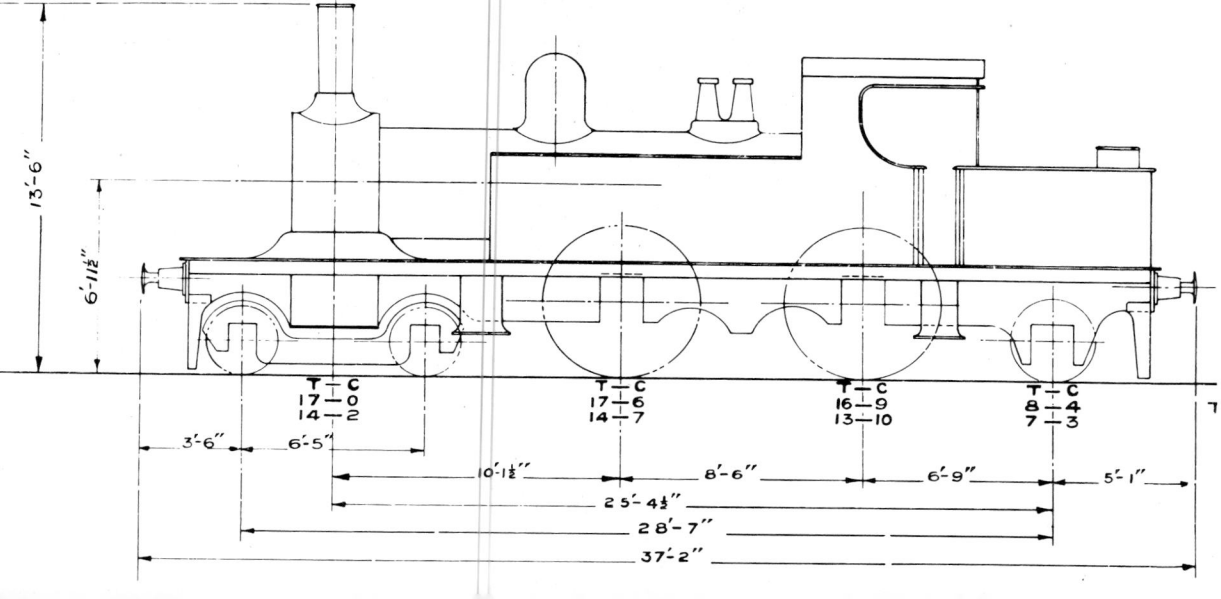

Figure 390

Figure 391

No. 44 was a lone example of the 4-4-2 tank engine class running on the B. & M. No. 44 was purchased by Mr Dunbar, the Locomotive Superintendent, in 1914. She was built for the L.S.W.R. to W. Adams designs in 1879 by Beyer Peacock & Co. to the 4-4-0T outside cylinder form. Altered to the 4-4-2T configuration in 1883, she was sold to the Bute Works Supply Co. who in 1903 passed her on to the Brecon & Merthyr Railway. The engine had driving wheels of 5′ 6″ diameter set at 8′ 6″ centres, with a bogie having solid wheels of 2′ 6″ diameter. Although overhauled early in 1922, the trip to Swindon proved to be her last, as although she was allotted GW No. 1391 and given Diagram I (*Figure* 391) the authorities at the factory condemned her, and she never carried the new number.

Figure 392

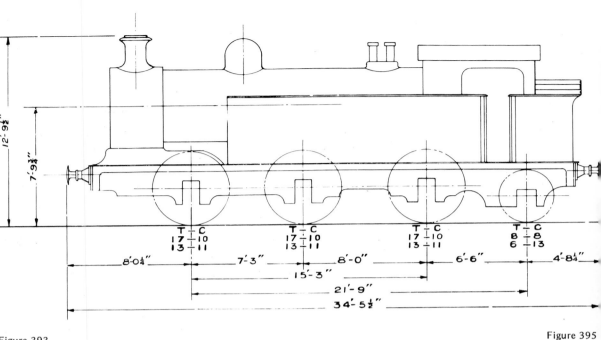

Figure 393

Figure 394

Figure 395

The '45' class of the Brecon & Merthyr, was a class of six engines, purchased originally for working the passenger traffic of the B. & M. The class was built by Messrs Stephenson & Co. in two lots, three in 1915 being Nos. 45-47 and three more after the War in 1921, numbered 48-50. In design this series of six locomotives were similar to the 'P' class of the Rhymney Railway. Of 0-6-2T type, the driving wheels were 5' 0" diameter set at 7' 3" and 8' 0", with trailing wheels of 3' 6" diameter. In 1922 Swindon gave the class Diagram A.17 seen in *Figure* 395 and renumbered the six to 1372-5/1668/70. As these engines were reasonably young, they were not immediately rebuilt, apart from being refitted with the usual GW fittings. One of the class, No. 50, further renumbered 436 is seen in *Figure* 393 at Nine Mile Point in 1952 when in BR ownership, and the lower illustration shows the same engine in a leafy scene at Risca, also in 1952.

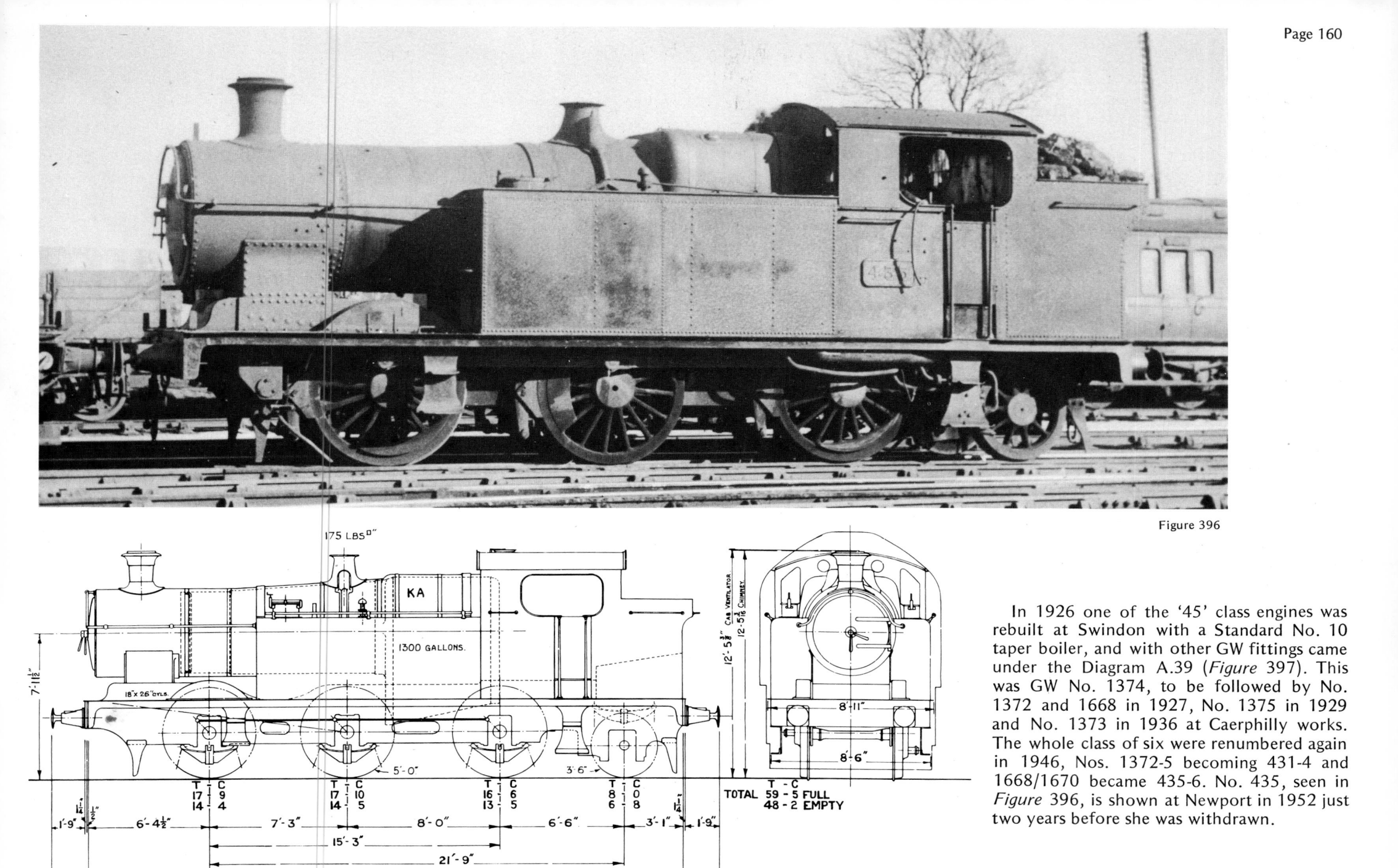

Figure 396

175 LBS□″

KA

1300 GALLONS.

18″x 26″ CYLS.

7′-11½″

5′-0″

3′-6″

1′-9″

1½″ 1½″

6′-4½″

7′-3″

8′-0″

6′-6″

3′-1″

1′-9″

15′-3″

21′-9″

31′-2½″

34′-11½″

TRACTIVE EFFORT 20885 LBS.

T	C	T	C	T	C	T	C
17	9	17	10	16	6	8	0
14	4	14	5	13	5	6	8

12′-5⅝″ CAB VENTILATOR

12′-5⅝″ CHIMNEY

8′-11″

8′-6″

T - C
TOTAL 59 - 5 FULL
48 - 2 EMPTY

Figure 397

In 1926 one of the '45' class engines was rebuilt at Swindon with a Standard No. 10 taper boiler, and with other GW fittings came under the Diagram A.39 (*Figure* 397). This was GW No. 1374, to be followed by No. 1372 and 1668 in 1927, No. 1375 in 1929 and No. 1373 in 1936 at Caerphilly works. The whole class of six were renumbered again in 1946, Nos. 1372-5 becoming 431-4 and 1668/1670 became 435-6. No. 435, seen in *Figure* 396, is shown at Newport in 1952 just two years before she was withdrawn.

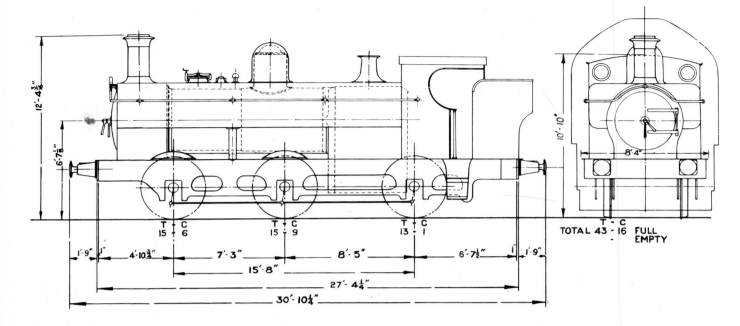

The largest class (in number) of locomotives the Brecon & Merthyr ever possessed was a series of twelve outside framed 0-6-0 saddle tanks, six built by Stephenson in 1884, and a further six by John Fowler of Leeds in 1885-6. The first six were numbered 6/7/8/5/15/16, followed by Nos. 1/2/3/4/13/14. Each had a saddle tank which reached from the cab to the rear of the smokebox and a strange little bunker shaped with a high back plate, and six coupled wheels of 4' 2'' diameter. On passing over to the GWR they were renumbered 2177-88 and took the Diagram A.105 (*Figure* 399). Only one of the class was rebuilt with a Swindon boiler, this was No. 2184 which received a 'Metro' boiler and returned to the B. & M. in 1924. The Diagram issued for this was that in *Figure* 398, namely B.20.

The illustration in *Figure* 400 is of No. 7 (GW No. 2183) when she was on the sales list at Swindon in 1932. The only engine of the series actually sold out of the Great Western was No. 2186 which was used by several collieries until cut up in 1944.

Figure 398

Figure 399

Figure 400

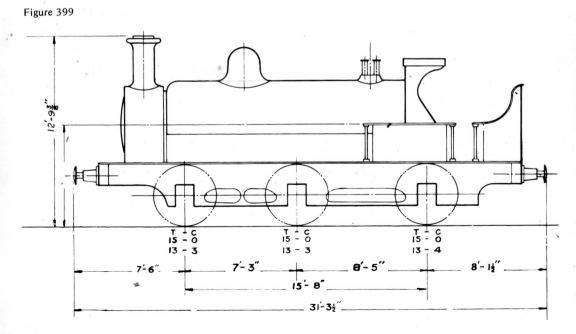

Figure 401

Another photograph of No. 7 (GW No. 2183) is seen above in *Figure* 401. This picture was taken in 1935 at Swindon, when the engine was placed on the Sales List, but found no buyers. Note the slender coupling rods, and also the whistles mounted on the rear of the safety valve.

The Diagram B.14 seen in *Figure* 402 was that issued to cover the rebuilding of Nos. 16 and 14 (GW Nos. 2188/2186). No. 2188 kept its own boiler, was re-tubed, and received GW smokebox and boiler fittings, but No. 2186 went one stage further and reappeared with pannier tanks, GW cab and bunker. As mentioned before, this engine was the only one of the series to be sold, and lasted out until 1944.

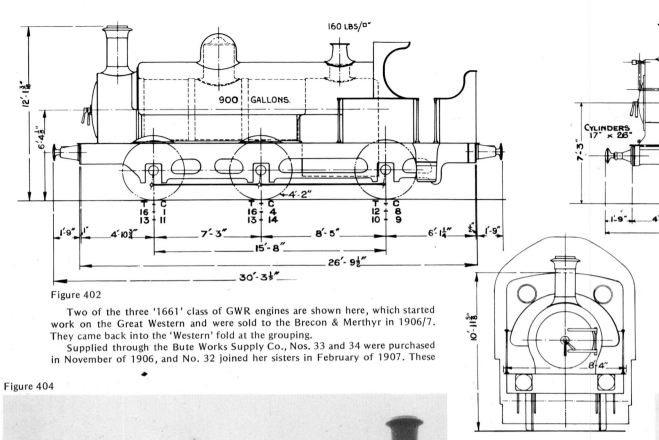

900 GALLONS.

160 LBS/□"

Figure 402

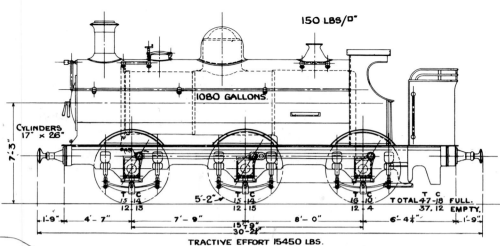

150 LBS/□"

1080 GALLONS

CYLINDERS 17" × 26"

TOTAL 47-18 FULL.
37.12 EMPTY.

TRACTIVE EFFORT 15450 LBS.

Figure 403

Two of the three '1661' class of GWR engines are shown here, which started work on the Great Western and were sold to the Brecon & Merthyr in 1906/7. They came back into the 'Western' fold at the grouping.

Supplied through the Bute Works Supply Co., Nos. 33 and 34 were purchased in November of 1906, and No. 32 joined her sisters in February of 1907. These engines had been built at Swindon in 1886/7 and served most of their B. & M. time on the Rhymney branch. On returning to the Great Western in 1922, they took numbers 1685/93/94, and although returning to their Diagrams D, seen in *Figure* 403 with the original saddle tanks, they were soon rebuilt with the pannier tanks, as seen in *Figure* 404 showing No. 32 (GW 1685) and *Figure* 405 illustrating No. 33 (GW No. 1693).

Figure 404

Figure 405

Figure 406

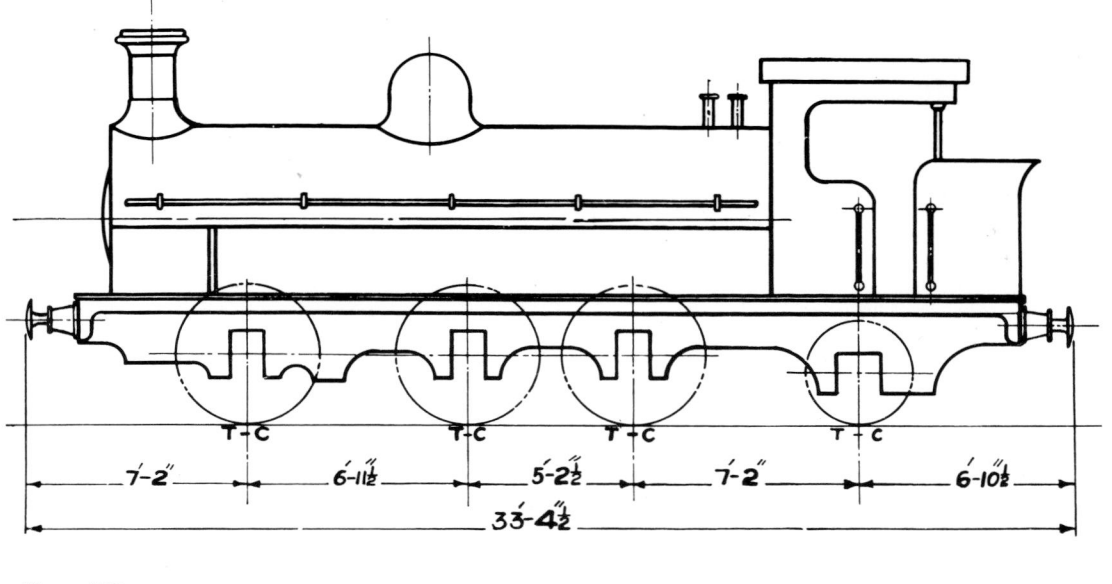

Figure 407

The last class to be illustrated for the Brecon & Merthyr Railway is the 0-6-2T long saddle tanked type made by Vulcan Foundry. Two were ordered in 1893 and were numbered 23 and 26, and twelve years later, two more were supplied in 1905, and these took the numbers 19 and 20. These engines had the usual 4' 7½'' driving wheels, set at 6' 11½'' and 5' 2½'' centres, with trailing carrying wheels of 3' 6'' diameter. The cabs of the first two had a roof, but no rear plate, being supported at the rear by two pillars, see Diagram A.18 *Figure* 407, but the second pair had totally enclosed cabs. The GWR renumbered them 1692/1833/1677 and 1674, but the latter never actually carried the plates. No. 20 (GW 1677) seen in *Figure* 406 lasted the longest of all, being withdrawn in 1928, and perhaps it is worth mentioning that all four spent most of their working life on the Brecon section. Nos. 23 and 26 had their moment of glory in 1896, when they were used for the Royal Train.

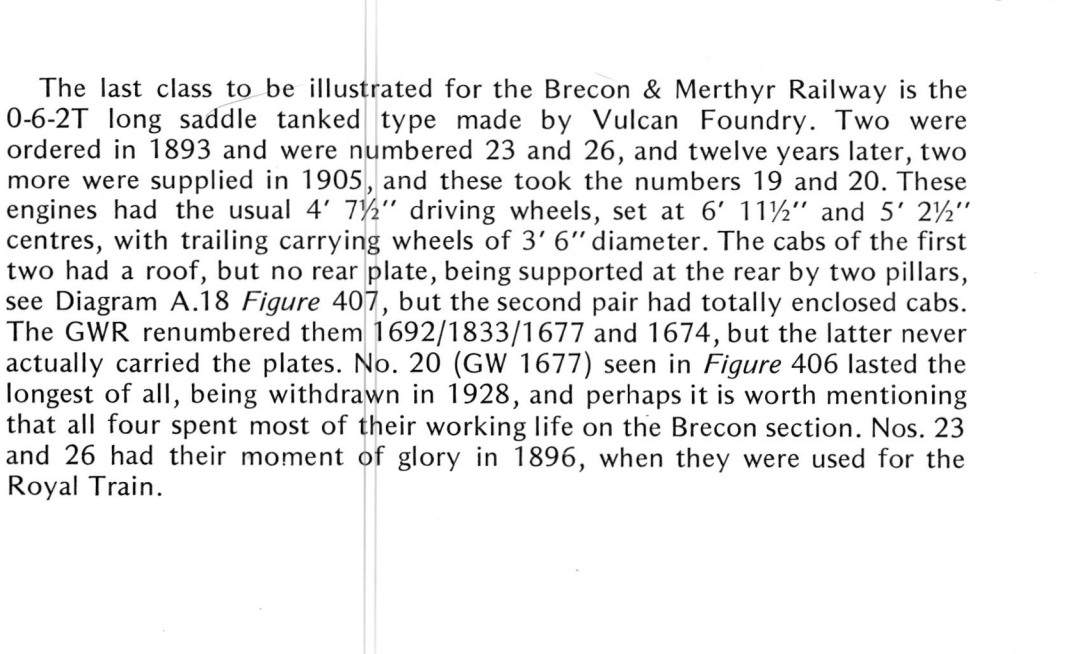

The
SWANSEA HARBOUR TRUST

The Swansea Harbour Trust came into being by an Act of Parliament in 1854 for the purpose of loading and unloading cargoes at the Docks in Swansea. Many contractors came and went, until by the year 1900, the Trustees decided to work the Harbour themselves with their own stud of steam locomotives. In 1905 the Trust owned six small shunting engines and with the death of C. Rowlands in 1910, who had been operating on behalf of the Midland & L.N.W. Railway, a further batch of shunting locomotives came into the S.H.T. ownership.

At the grouping and absorption into the GWR fourteen small engines were handed over, and a table of numbers is appended hereunder:—

S.H.T. No.	GWR No.	Type	Maker	Diagram	Withdrawn
3	150	0-4-0T	Hudswell Clarke		1929
5	701	,,	A. Barclay		1958
7	886	,,	Peckett		1928
8	926	,,	,,		1929 (sold)
9	930	,,	,,		1927
10	933	,,	,,		1927 (sold)
11	929	,,	,,		1952
12	968	,,	,,		1960
13	974	,,	Hawthorn Leslie	Q	1960
14	943	,,	Hudswell Clarke	X	1959
15	1085	0-6-0T	Peckett	B.33	1951
16	1086	,,	,,	B.33	1951
17	937	,,	,,		1926
18	1098	0-4-0T	,,		1959

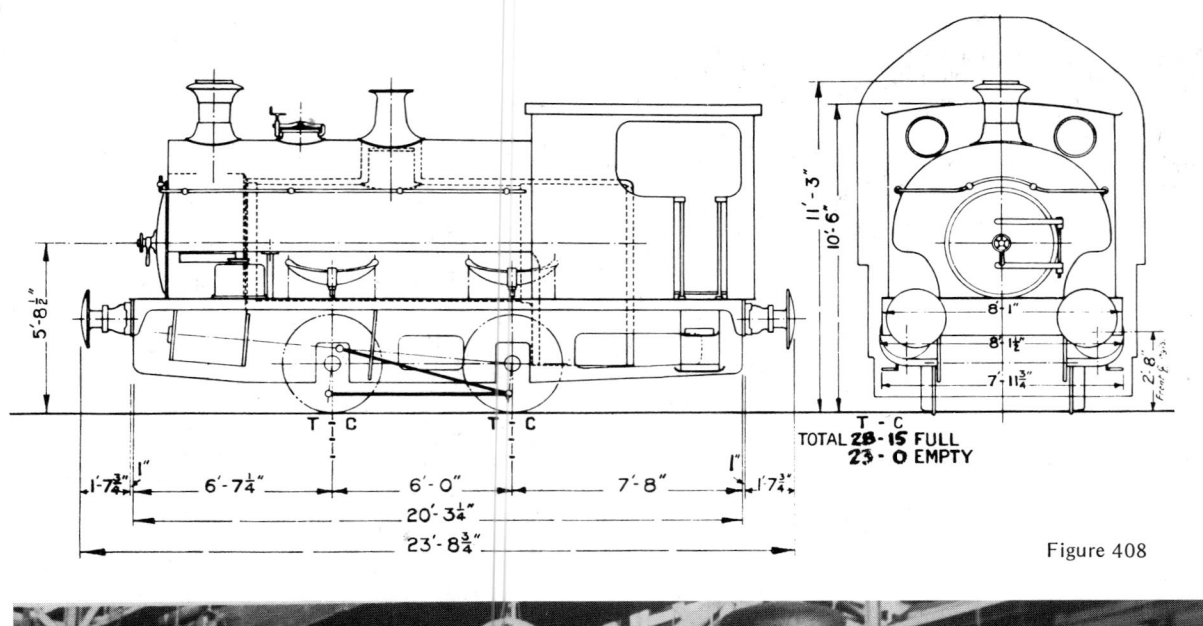

Figure 408

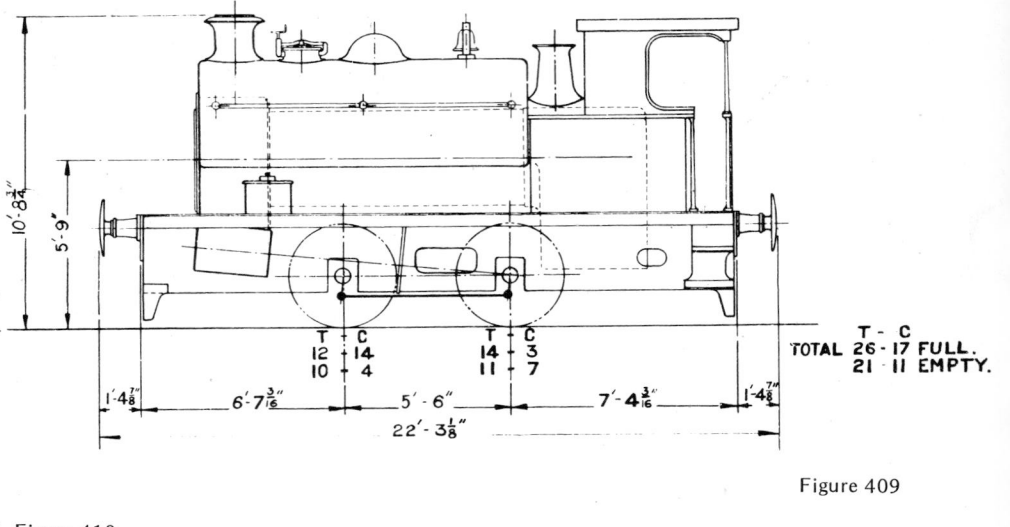

Figure 409

Figure 410

The Diagram shown in *Figure* 409 is the Swindon Q which was allotted to No. 13 (GW No. 974) the only Hawthorn Leslie engine to work for the S.H.T. She had 4 coupled wheels of 3' 6" diameter on a 5' 6" wheelbase, and the full weight came out at 26 tons 17 cwts. New in 1909 she was repaired at Swindon in 1924, but like all the others was not rebuilt in any drastic way, lasting out not only into BR days, as No. 1144, but on until scrapped in 1960.

The other 0-4-0T engine of the S.H.T. to receive a Swindon Diagram was the Hudswell Clarke No. 14 (GW No. 943) and Diagram X (*Figure* 408) was drawn for her.

She had wheels of 3' 4" diameter on a 6' wheelbase, with a weight of 28 tons 15 cwts. This little engine was overhauled at Swindon in 1926, but with the exception of being fitted with a GW safety valve, was otherwise unaltered. She, like No. 13, went into BR days (as 1142) and lasted until 1960.

Figure 410 shows No. 1143, one of the Peckett 0-4-0T engines. Before the 1948 numbering she was GW No. 968, and originally S.H.T. No. 12. The picture was taken in Danygraig Shed in 1949, just after she received her new numbering.

Three of the small 0-4-0T engines of the Swansea Harbour Trust are seen on this page. At the top in *Figure* 411 we have one of the first three locomotives which the Trust purchased in 1905. This is No. 3, a Hudswell Clarke which became GW No. 150. She lasted until 1929, and in that time the only Great Western items the engine acquired were the chimney and the lettering on the saddle tank. *Figure* 413 shows another locomotive from that first series of six, this was No. 5, one of three by Andrew Barclay; she became GW No. 701. Neither No. 3 nor No. 5 ever had a diagram drawn for them, even though the latter carried on working until 1958. In fact *Figure* 412 depicts this same little engine in 1951 after a thorough overhaul and further renumbering and in the livery of British Railways.

Figure 411

Figure 412

Figure 413

Figure 416

Figure 414

Figure 415

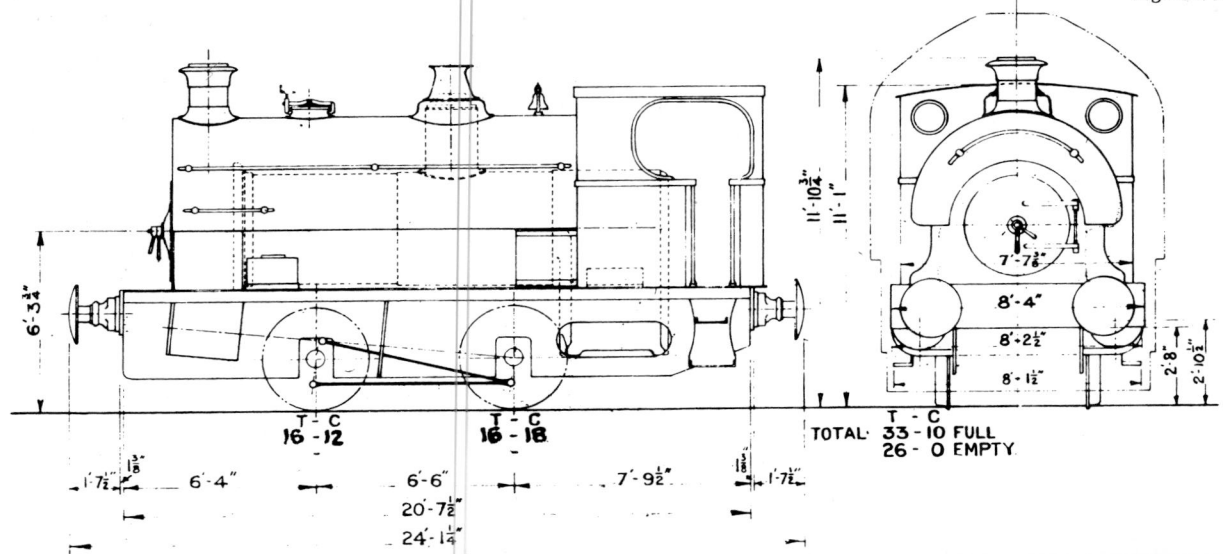

The two 4 wheeled saddle tanks illustrated here are both Pecketts, and shared the same Diagram at the grouping, namely Swindon Y (*Figure* 415). However, No. 779 in *Figure* 414 belonged to Powlesland and Mason, and No. 11 in *Figure* 416 was on the S.H.T. strength. These Pecketts and others like them, when in GWR hands seemed to have a little class of their own, and many were fitted with that compromise of a dome and safety valve, which can be seen in these pictures.

GREAT WESTERN

1086

W5535

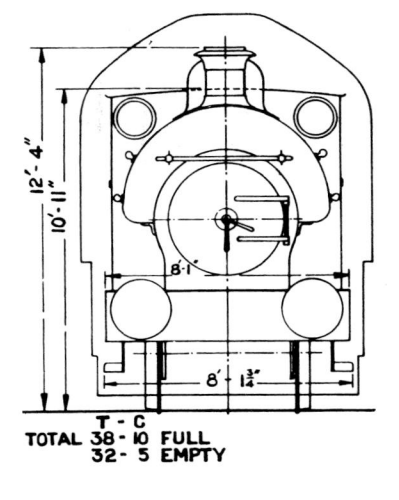

Figure 418

The biggest engines owned by the Swansea Harbour Trust, were the three 0-6-0 saddle tanks, bought from Pecketts in the years 1912/13/15. Their six coupled wheels were 3' 10'' diameter, set at 5' 6'' and 6' 3'' centres, they were pressed for 160 lbs, and scaled 40 tons. The S.H.T. Nos. were 15/16 and 17. All three passed to the GWR and their numbers were changed to 1085/6 and 937. The trio went through Swindon factory in 1926, the first two coming out again, but No. 937 was condemned and scrapped. Nos. 1085/6 were given Swindon Diagram B.33 (*Figure* 419) and in 1948 took the BR numbers 1146/47.

Figure 417 shows GW No. 1086 just fresh out of the factory in 1926 proudly carrying the 'Great Western' on the saddle tank sides *(on previous page)*.

On this page (*Figure* 418) the same engine is seen at Danygraig in 1949 when she was No. 1147 of British Railways. Note that she has still retained her docks bell, fixed at the top front of the cab. Both lasted until 1951.

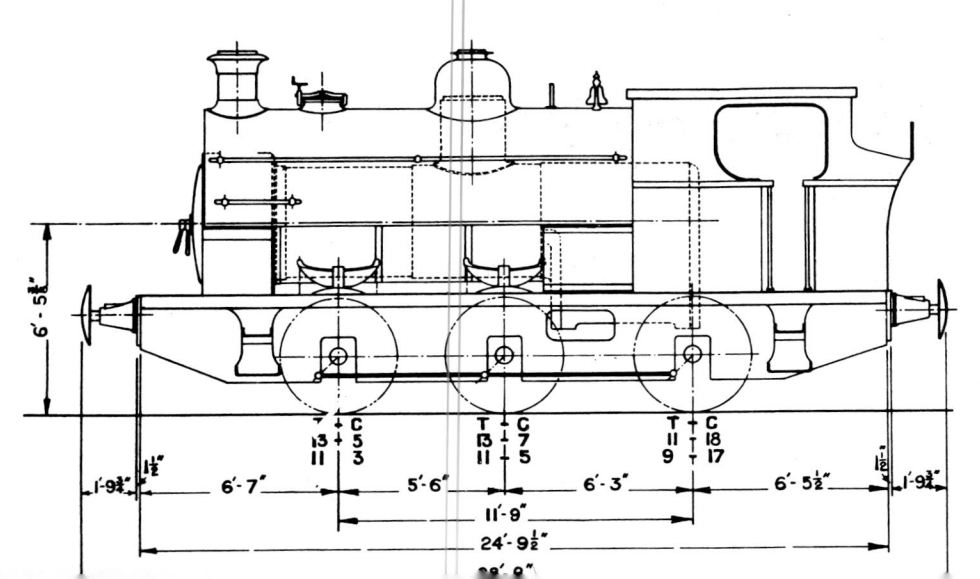

Figure 419

The

MIDLAND & SOUTH WESTERN

JUNCTION RAILWAY

The Midland & South Western Junction Railway was the fusion of two earlier Companies in 1884. The first, the Swindon, Marlborough and Andover Railway which opened in 1881 connected Marlborough with Swindon at first, then the southern part, Andover to Grafton was opened in 1882, and in 1883 the link between Grafton and Marlborough meant that through running was possible between Swindon and Andover. The second line was the Swindon and Cheltenham Extension Railway, which was opened in 1883 from Cirencester to Rushby Platt. These two small companies then joined forces, to form the Midland & South Western Junction Railway in 1884, and it was not until 1891 that the M. & S.W.J. was opened through to Andoversford Junction where, with running powers granted over the GWR, it was possible to reach Cheltenham. This meant that the M.S.W. Jct. Railway was a useful north-south link in the rail network where it was feasible for either the Midland Railway, the Great Western Railway or the London & South Western Railway to secure connections from Gloucester — Cheltenham direct to Southampton. At the grouping the M. & S.W. Jct. Railway handed over 29 locomotives of a very diverse nature, and a list of these engines appears opposite:—

M. & S.W. Jct. No.	GW No.	Type	Maker	GWR Diagram
1	1119	4-4-0	N. B. Loco	A.35/38
2	1120	”	”	A.35/38
3	1121	”	”	A.35/37
4	1122	”	”	A.35/37
5	1123	”	”	A.35/38
6	1124	”	”	A.35/37
7	1125	”	”	A.35/38
8	1126	”	”	A.35/38
9	1127	”	Dubs	
10	1334	2-4-0	”	A.7/9
11	1335	”	”	A.7/9
12	1336	”	”	A.7/9
13	825	0-6-0T	”	B.16
14	843	”	”	B.16
15	23	0-4-4T	Beyer Peacock	F/G
16	24	2-6-0	”	N/O
17	25	4-4-4T	Sharp-Stewart	A
18	27	”	”	A/B
19	1003	0-6-0	Beyer Peacock	A.19/24
20	1004	”	”	A.19/24
21	1005	”	”	A.19/24
22	1006	”	”	A.19/24
23	1007	”	”	A.19/24
24	1008	”	”	A.19
25	1009	”	”	A.19/24
26	1010	”	”	A.19/24
27	1011	”	”	A.19/24
28	1013	”	”	A.19
31	1128	4-4-0	N. B. Loco	A.35/37

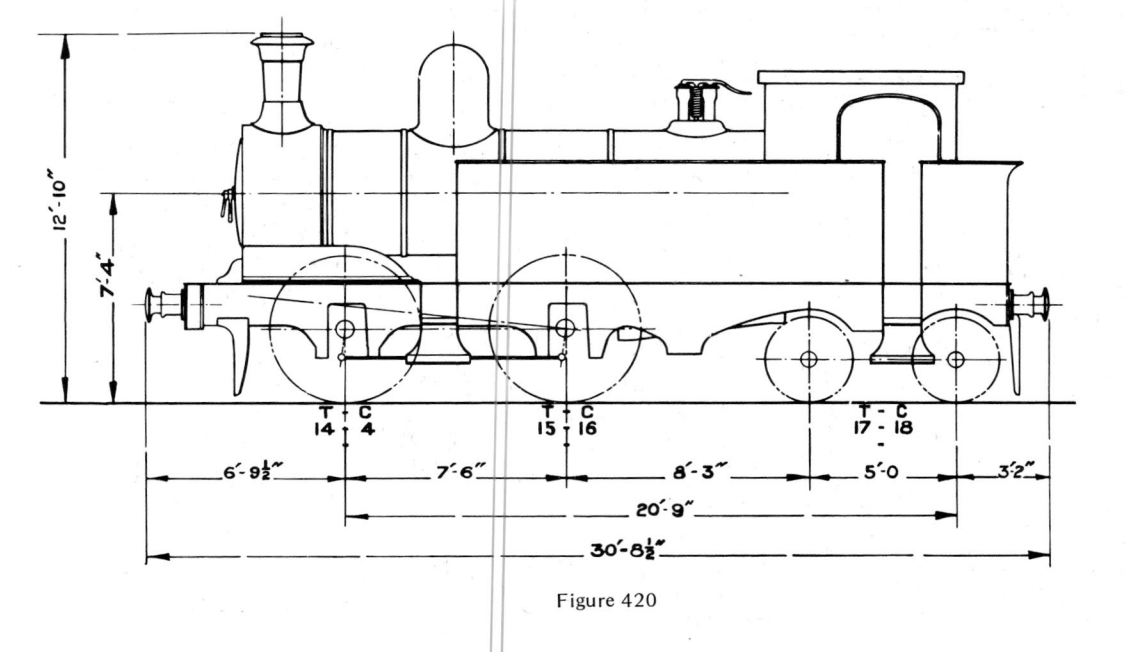

Figure 420

Figure 422

Figure 421

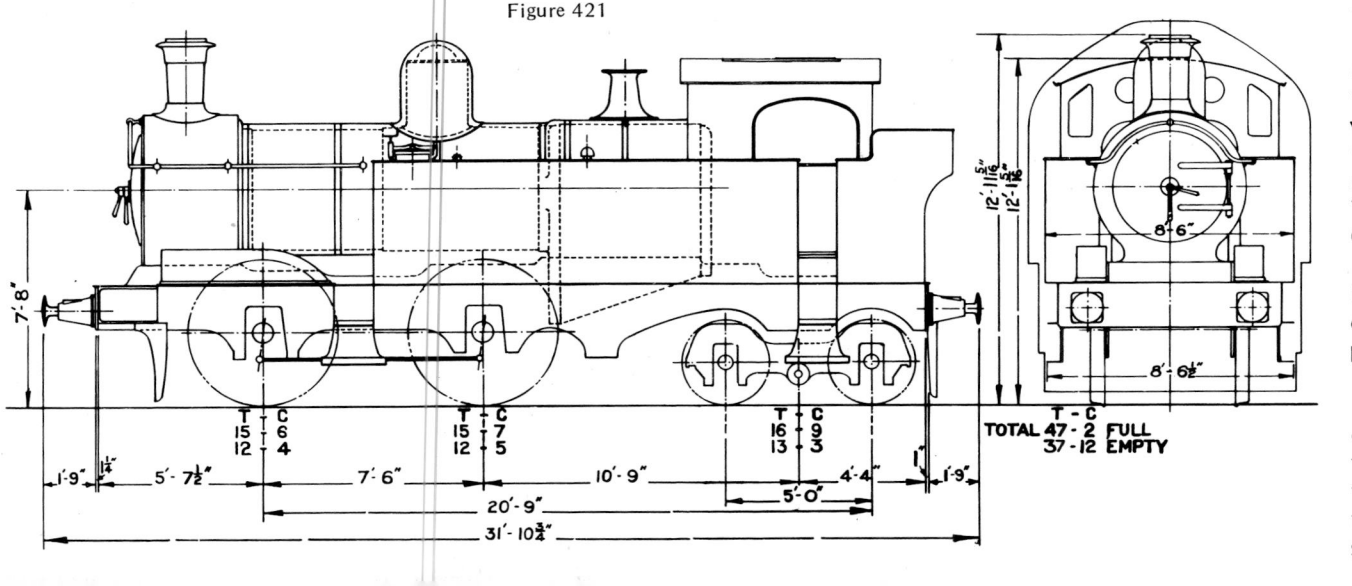

There was only one 0-4-4T engine on the M. & S.W. Jct. Railway at the grouping. This was No. 15 which was a Beyer Peacock product of 1895, with four coupled wheels of 5' 2" diameter set at 7' 6" centres, and a trailing bogie under the cab having 3' 0" diameter wheels on a 5' wheelbase. The engine duly passed to the GWR and became No. 23 and was given Diagram F by Swindon drawing office, *Figure* 420. When at work for the M. & S.W. Jct. she was usually employed on the central section of the line from Swindon to either Cirencester or Marlborough. The picture in *Figure* 422 shows No. 15 running round her train at Cirencester.

In 1925 No. 15 was rebuilt at Swindon with a Standard No. 11 boiler with Belpaire firebox, and usual GWR fittings, such as chimney, dome, safety valve, whistles and drawgear, and a new Diagram was prepared, being 'G' as seen in *Figure* 421.

The official photograph (*Figure* 423) shows No. 15 as GW 23, just out of factory in 1925. The usual style of the GWR "Studio" was followed, namely the full broadside shot. After a few more years working on her old rosters, she eventually finished her days in 1930, on the shuttle service between Swindon Junction and Swindon Town stations.

Figure 423

Figure 424

Figure 425

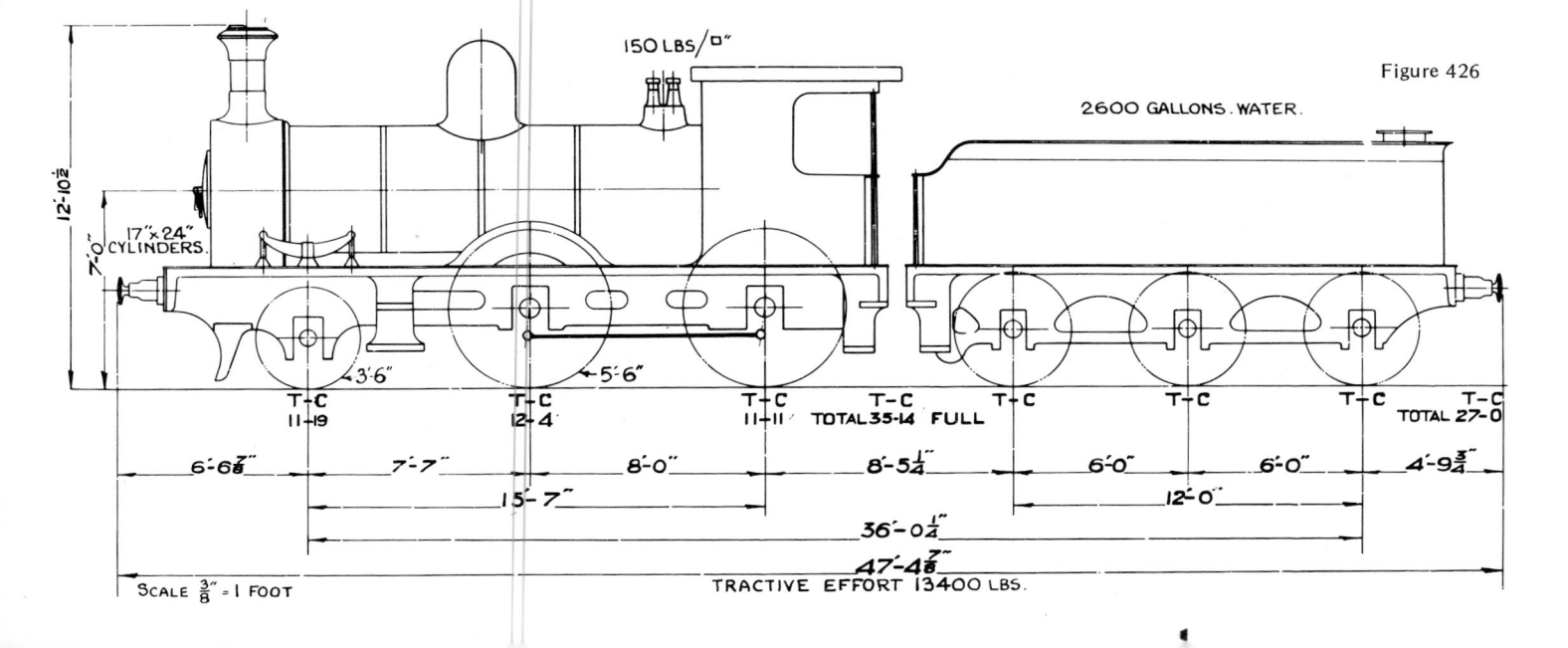

Figure 426

150 LBS/□"

2600 GALLONS. WATER.

12'-10½"

17"×24"
CYLINDERS.

3'-6"   ←5'-6"

T-C   T-C   T-C   T-C   T-C   T-C   T-C   T-C
11-19   12-4   11-11   TOTAL 35-14 FULL   TOTAL 27-0

6'-6⅞"   7'-7"   8'-0"   8'-5¼"   6'-0"   6'-0"   4'-9¾"

15'-7"   12'-0"

36'-0¼"

47'-4⅞"

SCALE ⅜" = 1 FOOT   TRACTIVE EFFORT 13400 LBS.

Being a long struggling cross-country line, the M. & S.W. Jct. had more tender engines than the tank variety, and three of these, built by Dubs in 1894, were the 2-4-0 engines numbered 10-12. As can be seen from the illustrations, these locomotives were inside cylindered, four coupled, having driving wheels of 5' 6" diameter, with the leading carrying wheels of 3' 6". Their duties were concerned with the passenger trains on the through line, and also were responsible for the Mail trains which ran once a week, starting at Southampton when the trans-atlantic liners docked.

At the grouping, these three 2-4-0 engines were given Swindon Diagram A.7 (*Figure* 426), and the two illustrations show No. 12 in *Figure* 424 in immaculate condition and No. 11 in *Figure* 425 as a cab view.

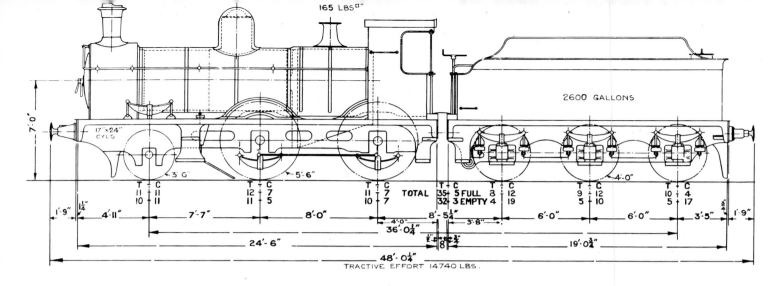

165 LBS□"

17"x24" CYLS

7'-0"

3'-6"

5'-6"

4'-0"

2600 GALLONS

T C	T C	T C	T C	T C	T C	T C	T C
11 11	12 7	11 7	TOTAL 35 5	8 12	9 12	10 4	
10 11	11 5	10 7	32 3	4 19	5 10	5 17	

FULL
EMPTY

1'-9" 1¼"
4'-11"   7'-7"   8'-0"   4'-0"   8'-5¼" 3'-8"   6'-0"   6'-0"   3'-5"   1'-9"

36'-0¼"
24'-6"   19'-0¾"
48'-0¼"
TRACTIVE EFFORT 14,740 LBS.

Figure 427

In Great Western ownership No. 10 became GW 1334, No. 11 became GW 1335 and No. 12 took the new number 1336. In 1924 all three were rebuilt with Standard No. 11 boilers and GW fittings, and their tenders received coal side sheets to increase their capacity, and as such were issued with Diagram A.9 (*Figure* 427).

For many years these engines worked the Lambourn branch, and I remember them both at Reading and Didcot Sheds. They lived on into British Railways days and 1334/5 went in 1952, whilst 1336 hung on until 1954. In *Figure* 428 No. 1335 is seen at Newbury in 1952 portrayed by the camera of my friend A. C. Sterndale who also captured No. 1336 at Reading Shed in 1952 (*Figure* 429). These two photographs show both sides of the class very nicely and to the advantage of would-be modellers.

Figure 428

Figure 429

Figure 430

Figure 431

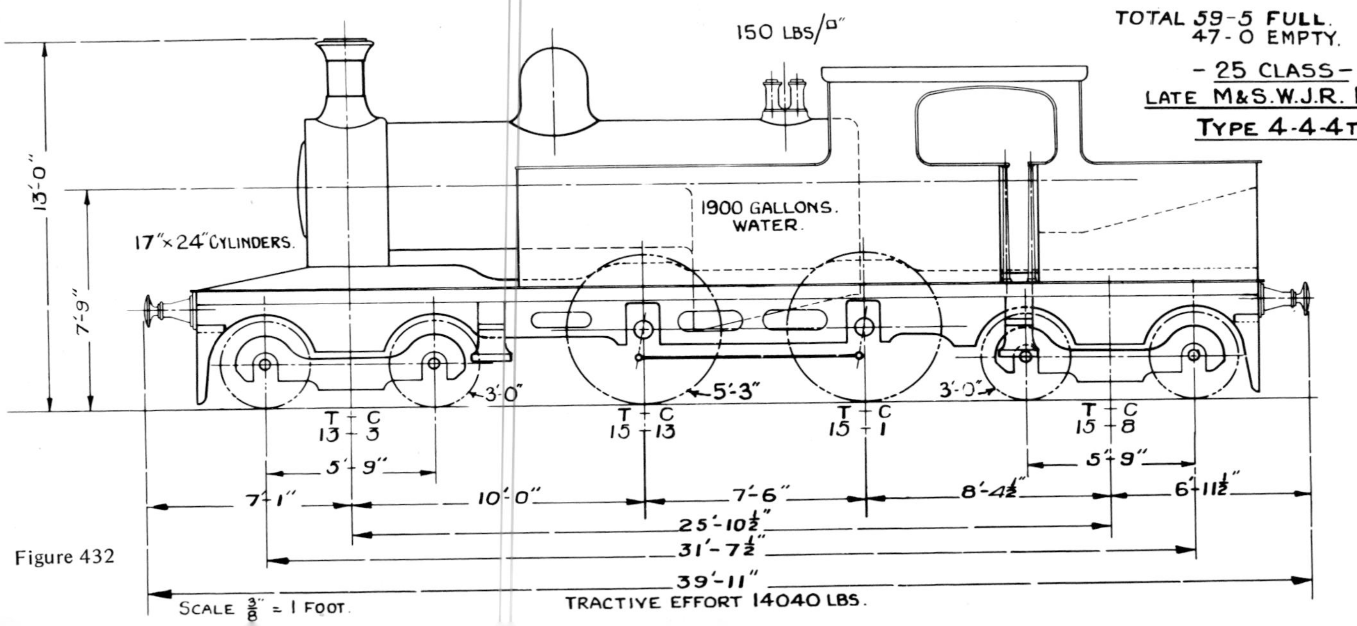

GREAT WESTERN 27

TOTAL 59·5 FULL.
47·0 EMPTY.

- 25 CLASS -
LATE M&S.W.J.R. 17
TYPE 4-4-4T.

150 LBS/◻"

13'-0"

7'-9"

17"×24"CYLINDERS.

1900 GALLONS.
WATER.

3'-0"   5'-3"   3'-0"

T C   T C   T C   T C
13 3   15 13   15 1   15 8

5'-9"   5'-9"

7'-1"   10'-0"   7'-6"   8'-4½"   6'-11½"

25'-10½"

31'-7½"

39'-11"

Figure 432

SCALE ⅜" = 1 FOOT.   TRACTIVE EFFORT 14040 LBS.

The year 1897 saw two very handsome Sharp-Stewart engines delivered to the M. & S.W. Jct. These were Nos. 17 and 18, big 4-4-4Ts with 5'3" coupled wheels set at 7' 6" centres and a four wheel bogie at each end of the locomotive having 3' 0" diameter wheels set at 5' 9" wheelbases. When new these two were shedded at Cheltenham and worked up to Swindon. In 1922 the GWR issued Diagram A for the class (*Figure* 432) as these were the only engines of the classification ever to work on the Great Western. *Figure* 431 shows No. 25 as she was reconditioned in 1924/5, being fitted with GW boiler fittings but retaining her own boiler. No. 18 (GW 27) on the other hand, received the full treatment, and was rebuilt with a Standard No. 10 boiler, GW fittings, and a new high arched cab, and was turned out in 1925 in the condition seen in *Figure* 430.

The Swindon Diagram B was allotted to this one engine No. 18 (GW 27) and can be seen in *Figure* 434 (*overleaf*). I have always admired this rebuild, and had ideas for making a 4mm model, but like many schemes of mice and men, it has not yet material-ised. This 4-4-4 tank engine after being 'Westernised' did not rejoin her sister on the M. & S.W. Jct. metals, but was directed to the Kidderminster area, where she worked on local trains, until finally withdrawn in the Autumn of 1929. The large official photo-graph in *Figure* 433 shows No. 27 at Swindon in 1925 in the usual head-three-quarters position.

Figure 433

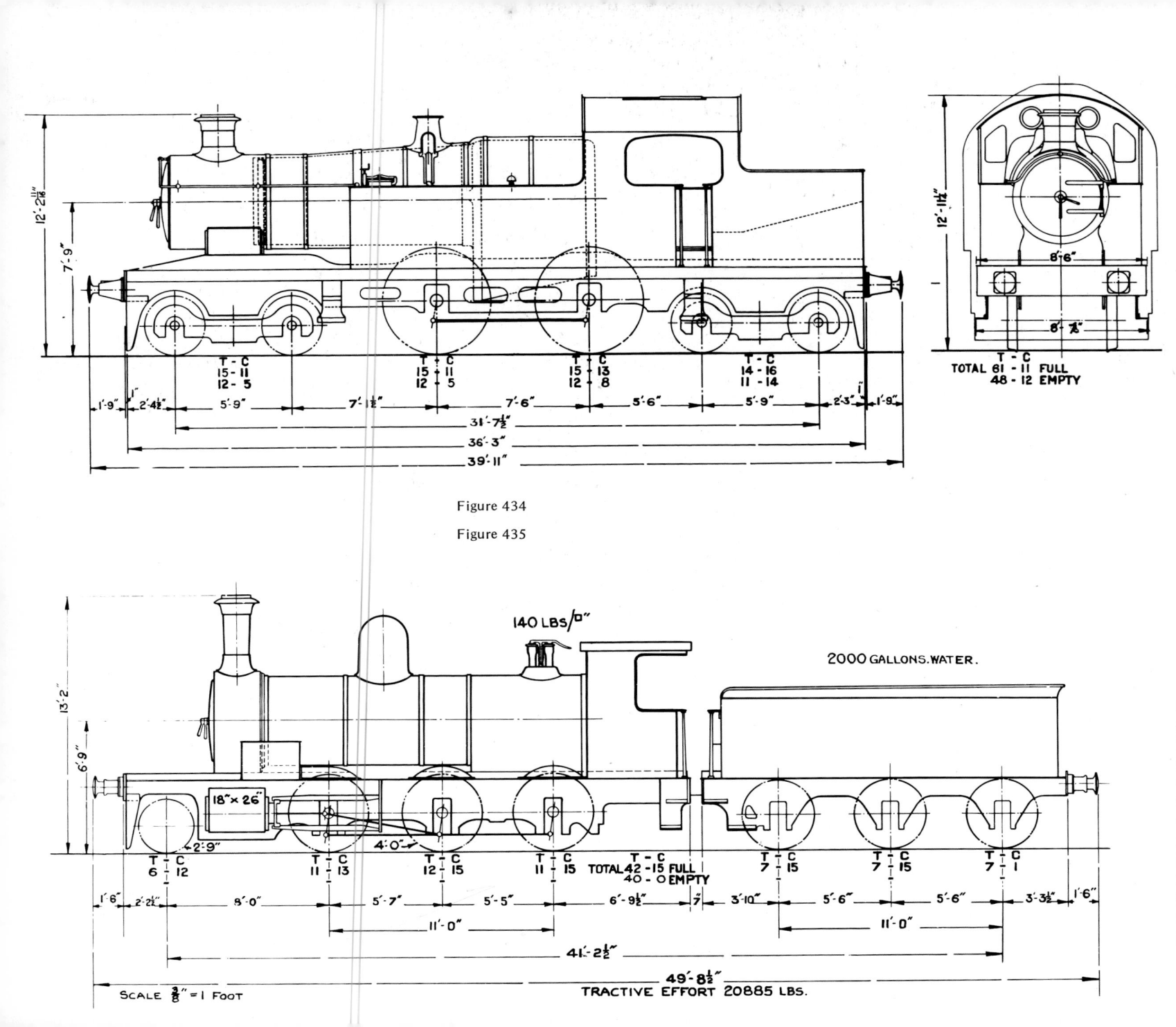

Figure 434

Figure 435

12'-2⅛"
7'-9"

T - C
15 - 11
12 - 5

T - C
15 - 11
12 - 5

T - C
15 - 13
12 - 8

T - C
14 - 16
11 - 14

1'-9" 2'-4½" 5'-9" 7'-1½" 7'-6" 5'-6" 5'-9" 2'-3" 1'-9"

31'-7½"
36'-3"
39'-11"

12'-1½"

8'-6"

6'-7½"

T - C
TOTAL 61 - 11 FULL
48 - 12 EMPTY

140 LBS/□"

2000 GALLONS. WATER.

13'-2"
6'-9"

18"×26"

2'-9"

T - C
6 - 12

T - C
11 - 13

T - C
12 - 15

T - C
11 - 15

TOTAL 42 -15 FULL
40 - 0 EMPTY

T - C
7 - 15

T - C
7 - 15

T - C
7 - 1

1'-6" 2'-2½" 8'-0" 5'-7" 5'-5" 6'-9½" 7" 3'-10" 5'-6" 5'-6" 3'-3½" 1'-6"
4'-0"
11'-0"
11'-0"
41'-2½"
49'-8½"

SCALE ⅜" = 1 FOOT
TRACTIVE EFFORT 20885 LBS.

Two more Beyer Peacock engines joined the M. & S.W. Jct. stud in 1895. They were numbered 14 and 15, and were 2-6-0 tender engines which had been built originally for a South American buyer, whose contract lapsed. These engines had quite a foreign appearance with parallel boiler, large overhanging cab and outside cylinders set horizontal and low on the frames. The six coupled wheels were of 4' 0" diameter set at 5' 7" and 5' 5" centres, with a loading pony truck having wheels of 2' 9" diameter. No. 14 does not really concern this work, as she was not handed over to the GWR, being sold to various collieries until scrapped in 1943. No. 16 did pass over to the Great Western in 1922, and was recorded on Diagram N (*Figure* 435) and the six wheeled tender (which was identical to that of No. 14) held 3 tons of coal and had a water capacity of 2,000 gallons.

No. 16, like all other absorbed engines was renumbered at the grouping, and became No. 24. She passed through the factory in 1925 and emerged with a Standard No. 9 boiler, a GWR style cab and boiler fittings. The old tender was replaced by a Standard 2,500 gallon pattern, and in this condition, she was trundled to the east end of 'A' shop to enable the official photographs to be taken. *Figure* 436 on the lower page gives the three-quarter view, and in *Figure* 437 (*overleaf*) is shown the full broadside angle. At the time of course, a new Diagram was prepared being Swindon 2-6-0 'O' as seen in *Figure* 438 (*overleaf*). When new the two Beyer Peacock engines were used on through goods traffic, and No. 24 finished her days working local goods between Stoke Gifford and Swindon, and was condemned in 1930.

Figure 436

Figure 437

Figure 438

The only 0-6-0 tank engines passed over to the Great Western by the M. & S.W. Jct. Railway were Nos. 13 and 14. Built by Messrs Dubs in 1894 number 14 was at first given the number 4 and carried this until 1914 when she became 14. No. 13 on the other hand started out with that number, and *Figure* 439 shows the engine in these early days. As can be seen, they had flush topped boilers with stove-pipe chimney, a closed cab, with side tanks of 1,000 gallons capacity. Wheels were of 4' 7" diameter set at 7' 3" and 8' 1" and the weight came out at 44 tons in working order. In 1922 the two engines were shown on Diagram B.16 (*Figure* 440) and became GW Nos. 825 and 843. With the exception of having cast-iron chimney with flared top and capuchon, these two did not receive any alterations at Great Western hands, and were both withdrawn in mid-1926.

Figure 439

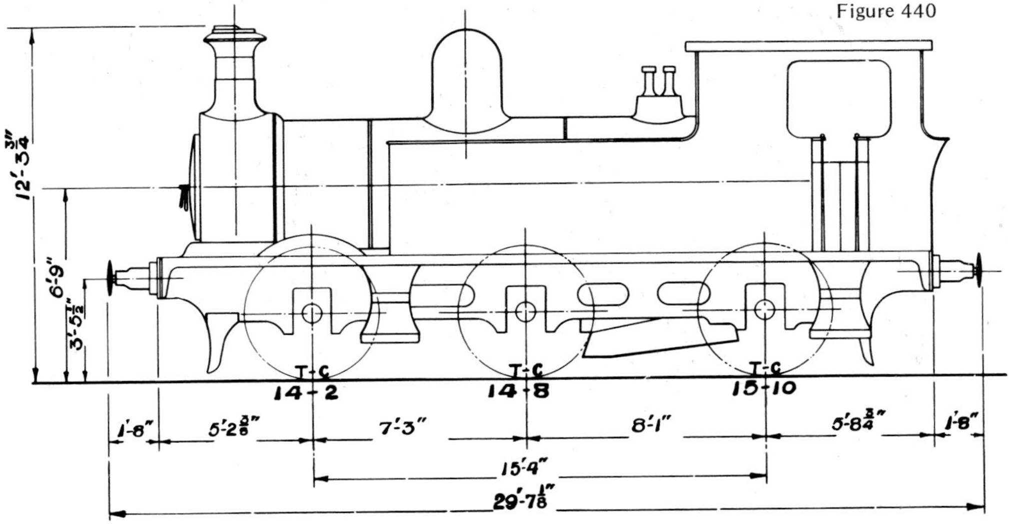

Figure 441

Figure 440

Figure 442

Figure 443

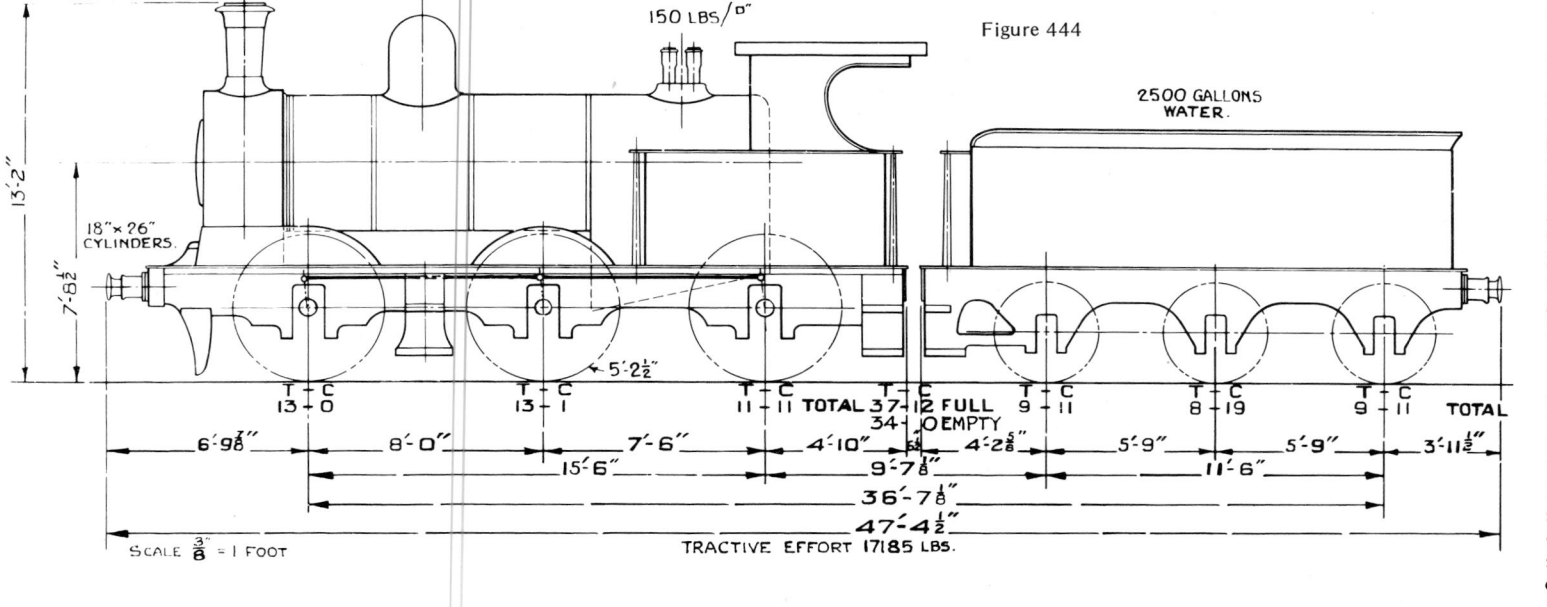

150 LBS/□"

Figure 444

2500 GALLONS
WATER.

18"× 26"
CYLINDERS.

13'-2"

7'-8½"

5'-2½"

T+C
13 - 0

T+C
13 - 1

T+C
11 - 11 TOTAL 37-12 FULL
34- 0 EMPTY

T+C
9 - 11

T+C
8 - 19

T+C
9 - 11   TOTAL

6'-9⅞"

8'-0"

7'-6"

4'-10"

4'-2⅝"

5'-9"

5'-9"

3'-11½"

15'-6"

9'-7⅞"

11'-6"

36'-7⅛"

47'-4½"

SCALE ⅜" = 1 FOOT

TRACTIVE EFFORT 17185 LBS.

Beyer Peacock & Co. were the builders of the ten 0-6-0 tender engines which formed the backbone of the motive power destined to handle the goods traffic on the M. & S. W. Jct. which built up between the military camps at Ludgershall and Southampton Docks. Six of these engines, Nos. 19-24, were handed over in 1899, and four more very similar arrived in 1902 taking the numbers 25-28. *Figure 442* shows one of the class, No. 24, as built in 1899 in works grey and still having the square cab panels, which were later removed. Driving wheels were 5' 2½'' diameter and wheel-bases were 8' 0'' and 7' 6''. The first Diagram allotted to the class was A.19 seen in *Figure 444*, and this also shows the square panels which were so disliked by the crews. *Figure 443* shows No. 28 in GWR days when she had been renumbered 1013. In this picture can be seen the different style of cab side sheets, and note that coal rails have been added to the tender, to increase its capacity.

In 1922 all ten were passed across to the GWR and were renumbered 1003-11 and 1013, and between the years of 1925-1927 each and every one was rebuilt with a Standard No. 10 boiler and a Swindon cab, and the tenders were fitted with side plates in place of coal rails. Swindon issued a new Diagram to suit the transformation, this being 0-6-0 A.24 seen in *Figure 445*, and as was usual, one of the class was chosen to act as a model for record purposes; No. 1005 is shown in full broadside, outside the Works in 1925, fresh out of the factory (*Figure 446*).

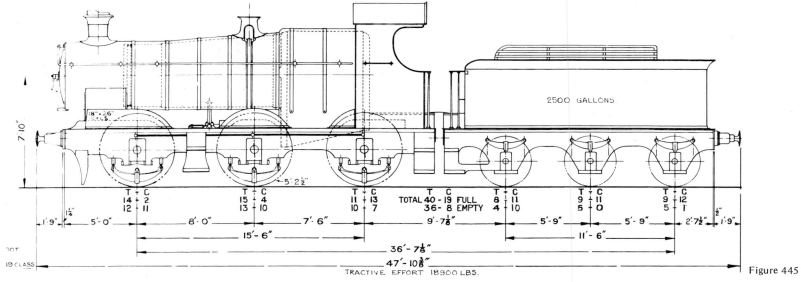

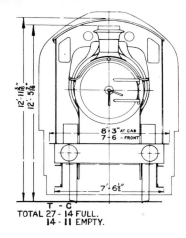

8'·3" AT CAB
7'·6" FRONT

TOTAL 27·14 FULL.
14·11 EMPTY.

1003 CLASS
TYPE 0·6·0

18"×26"
CYLS.

7'·10"

2500 GALLONS

T·C
14·2
12·11

T·C
15·4
13·10

T·C
11·13
10·7

T·C
TOTAL 40·19 FULL
36·8 EMPTY

T·C
8·11
4·10

T·C
9·11
5·0

T·C
9·12
5·1

1'·9"   5'·0"   8'·0"   7'·6"   9'·7⅛"   5'·9"   5'·9"   2'·7½" 1'·9"

15'·6"

11'·6"

36'·7⅛"

47'·10⅜"

TRACTIVE EFFORT 18900 LBS.

19 CLASS

Figure 445

Figure 446

Figure 447

Figure 448

Figure 449

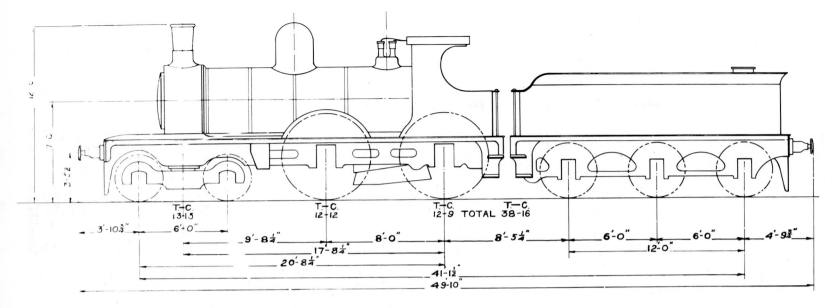

These handy little 0-6-0 tender engines, although originally designed to handle the through goods traffic on the M. & S.W. Jct. eventually in Great Western days were given passenger services to run, and I've had many smart trips down to Marlborough from Swindon Town with these engines in charge of three eight wheel carriages. In *Figure 448* No. 1008 is seen on Swindon Shed, and in *Figure 447* No. 1005 is seen in the usual GW three quarter picture. Three of the class, Nos. 1008, 1011 and 1013 were transferred to the Bristol Division in 1936 where they worked for several months before being withdrawn. The last engine to be withdrawn was No. 1005, illustrated in both official pictures, she hung on until March of 1938. One small note – how very similar these rebuilt engines were to Mr Collett's 2251 class.

Figure 450

Figure 451

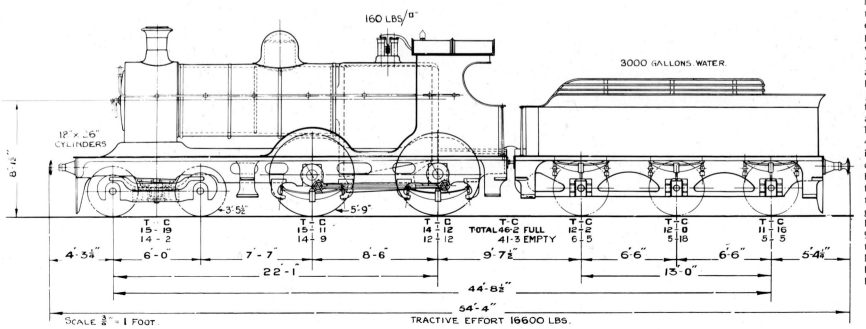

The final batch of locomotives belonging to the M. & S.W. Jct. Railway, which were absorbed into the Great Western, were the large 4-4-0 tender engines, designed and built for operating the passenger services on this cross-country line. There were nine eventually in the class, (discounting No. 9, a Dubs built 4-4-0 which was scrapped in 1924) and they were all constructed by the North British Locomotive Co. Their delivery to the M. & S.W. Jct. was extended over several years, No. 1 which features in *Figure 449* was built in 1905, Nos. 2 and 3 followed in 1909, No. 6 in 1910, No. 7 in 1911, Nos. 5 and 8 in 1912 and finally in 1914 Nos. 4 and 31. They were fine large engines, having inside cylinders, four coupled wheels of 5' 9'', covered with big wide splashers, plus a leading bogie having 3' 5½'' wheels. Belpaire boilers were fitted, and deep roomy cabs, and a high capacity tender was attached, capable of carrying 3,000 gallons. *Figure 450* on this page is Swindon Diagram A.36 the drawing prepared for engine No. 9, the one and only Dubs 4-4-0 which was mentioned previously, but did not last to carry her GW No. of 1127. The drawing prepared for the North British engines at the grouping was Swindon Diagram A.35 as in *Figure 451*.

Figure 452

The whole class of nine 4-4-0 engines were renumbered on the GWR becoming 1119-26 and 1128 and several had an unusual arrangement of two domes mounted on the boiler, the leading one being the usual steam dome, and the rear fitting being a combination of top feed and Ross pop safety valve. No. 1, later renumbered 1119, was also fitted out with this double dome system in 1924, and *Figures* 454 and 455 illustrate both sides of this engine at this period. Some of the class had superheaters added to the old M. & S.W. Jct. boilers, and in this condition were given Swindon Diagram A.38 seen in *Figure* 453 on the lower page. GW Nos. 1119, 1122 and 1125 were three so fitted, and lasted out until the mid 1930s.

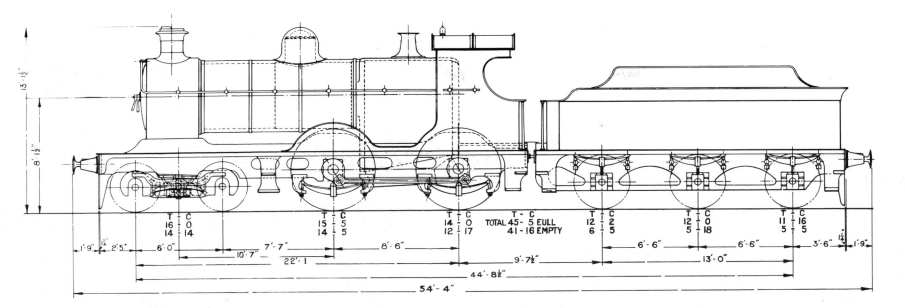

T — C
16 — 0
14 — 14

T — C
15 — 5
14 — 14

T — C
14 — 0
12 — 17

TOTAL 45 — 5 FULL
41 — 16 EMPTY

T — C
12 — 2
6 — 5

T — C
12 — 0
5 — 18

T — C
11 — 16
5 — 5

1'·9" 1'¼" 2'·5" 6'·0" 10'·7" 7'·7" 8'·6" 6'·6" 6'·6" 3'·6" 1¼" 1'·9"

22'·1 9'·7½" 13'·0"

44'·8½"

54'·4"

13'·1½"

8'·1½"

12'·5⅛"

8'·3"

8'·7"

TOTAL 35 — 18 FULL
17 — 8 EMPTY

Figure 453

Figure 454   Figure 455

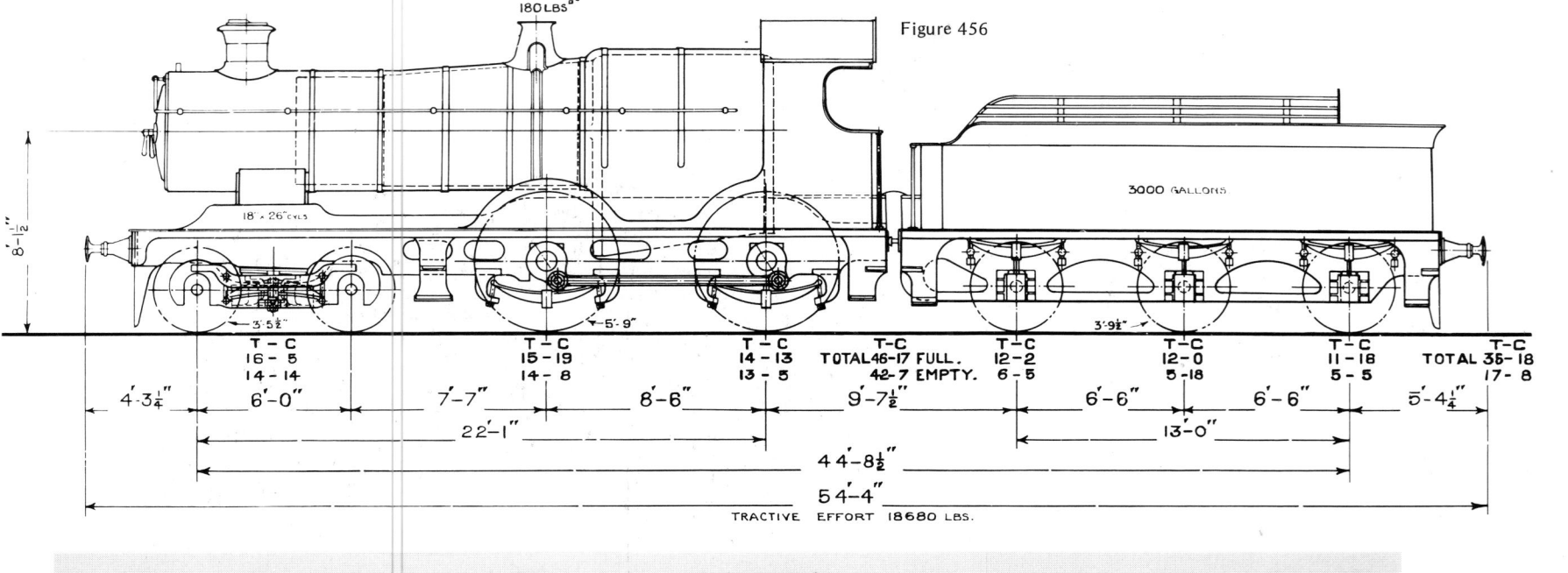

180 LBS"

Figure 456

18"×26" CYLS

3000 GALLONS

8'-1½"

3-5½   5-9   T~C
T~C   14-8   T~C   T~C   13-5   T~C   TOTAL 46-17 FULL.   T~C   3-9½   T~C   T~C   T~C   TOTAL 35-18
16-5   15-19   14-13   42-7 EMPTY.   12-2   12-0   11-18   17-8
14-14   14-8   13-5   6-5   5-18   5-5

4'-3¼"   6'-0"   7'-7"   8'-6"   9'-7½"   6'-6"   6'-6"   5'-4¼"

22'-1"   13'-0"

44'-8½"

54'-4"

TRACTIVE EFFORT 18680 LBS.

Six of the 4-4-0 M. & S.W. Jct. engines were rebuilt in Swindon factory with Standard No. 2 taper boilers, a new cab, and had their driving controls changed over from the left-hand side to the more "Westernised" style of right-hand drive. Diagram A.37 was issued for this rebuild (*Figure* 456) and the engines so converted were GW Nos. 1120/1/3/4/6/8. *Figure* 457 shows the official broadside shot of No. 1121 just out of works, with a tender having coal rails, and in *Figure* 458 No. 1124 shows the right-hand side of the class, but with side plates on her tender.

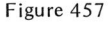

Figure 457

Figure 458

The PORT TALBOT RAILWAY & DOCKS COMPANY

The Port Talbot Railway & Docks came into being in 1894 to take over and work the docks and harbours at Port Talbot, situated in Swansea Bay. Like so many similar undertakings in the South Wales area, the prime motive was the movement and shipment of coal from the collieries to the docks. Unlike the Swansea Harbour Trust, the Port Talbot Railway also opened lines of rail up the valleys direct to the mining areas, in the Llynvi and Garw coalfields. In 1897 a line was opened from Port Talbot to Lletty Brongu via Maesteg, and in the following year, a branch was extended to meet the GWR at Pontyrhyll Junction, and another extension was opened to the eastward, making connection with the Great Western again at Pyle and Cefn Junction. Other small branches linked up with the South Wales Mineral Railways and the Rhondda and Swansea Bay line, and reached out to both Blaenavon and Whitworth. One of these branch lines, the one towards Cefn Junction, is now under the management of British Rail, still carrying heavy traffic due to the setting up of Margam Steelworks near Port Talbot.

The engines handed over to the Great Western at the amalgamation were 22 in total and were as under:—

P.T. Number	GWR No.	Type	Maker	Diagram
3	815	0-6-0T	Stephenson	A.90
8	183	0-6-2T	,,	W.
9	184	,,	,,	W.A35
10	185	,,	,,	W.
11	186	,,	,,	W.
12	187	,,	,,	W.A35
13	188	,,	,,	W.A35
14	189	,,	,,	W.
15	816	0-6-0T	,,	A.90
17	1358	0-8-2T	Sharp-Stewart	A.
18	1359	,,	,,	A.
19	1360	,,	,,	A.
20	1378	,,	Cooke Loco.	B.
21	1379	,,	,,	B.
22	808	0-6-0T	Hudswell Clarke	A.89
23	809	,,	,,	A.89
24	811	,,	,,	A.89
25	812	,,	,,	A.89
26	813	,,	,,	A.89
27	814	,,	,,	A.89
36	1326	2-4-2T	Sharp-Stewart	S.
37	1189	2-4-0T	,,	N.

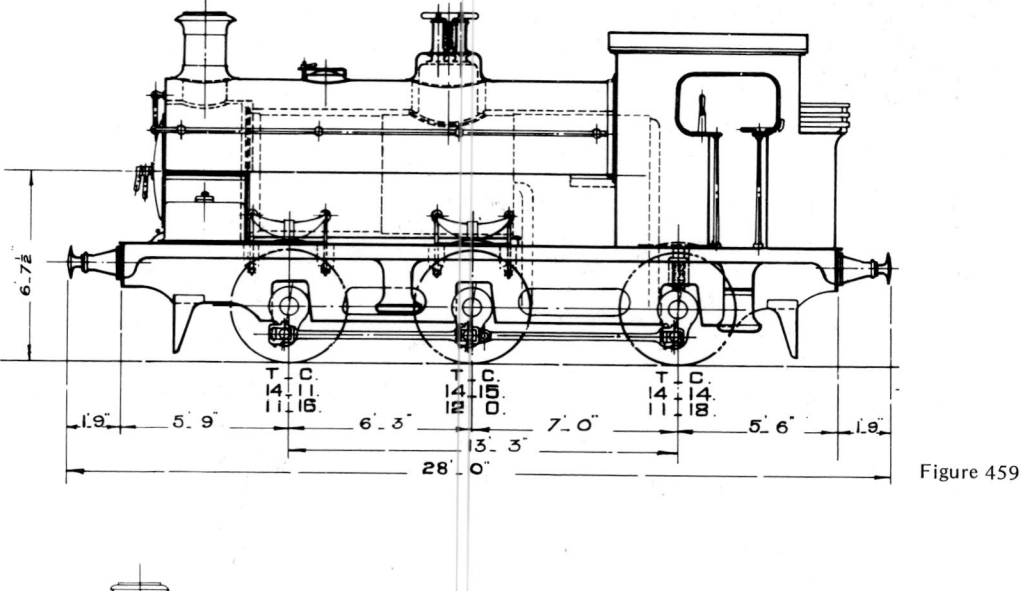

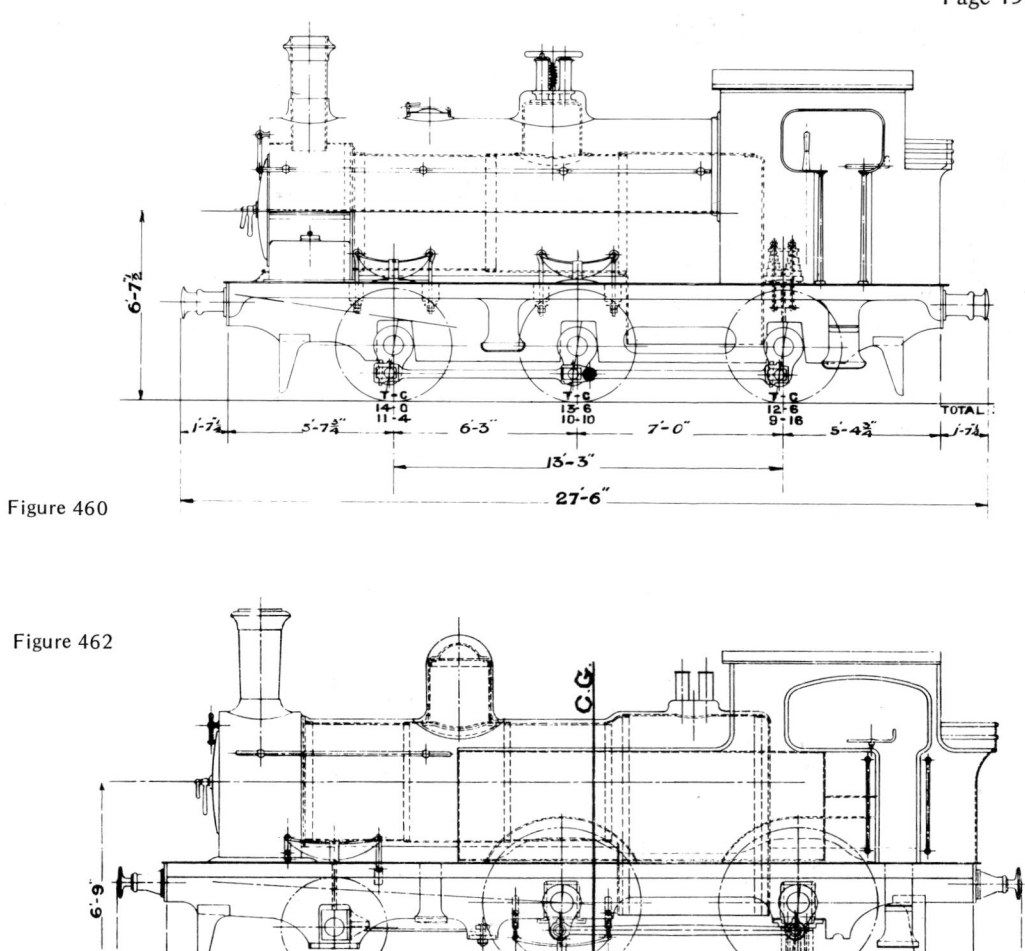

Figure 459   Figure 460

Figure 461   Figure 462

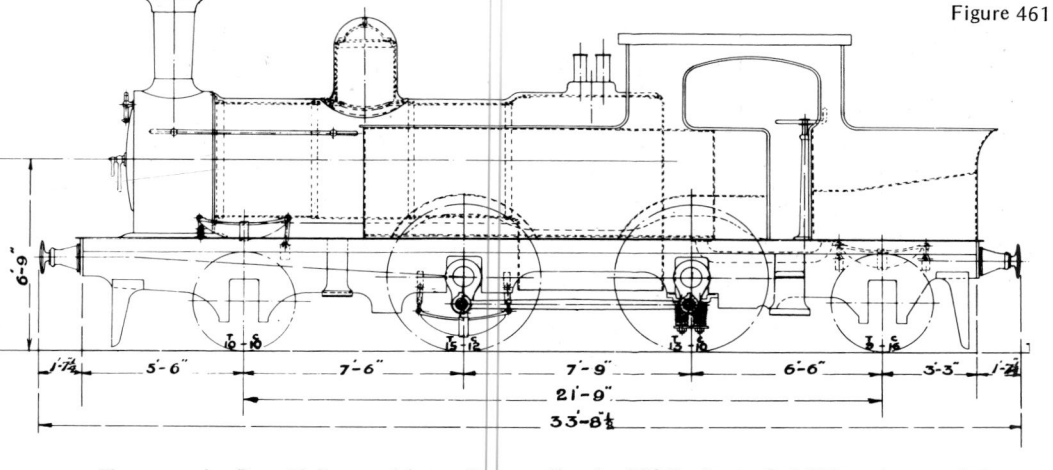

To open the Port Talbot — Lletty Brongu line in 1897, eleven 0-6-2T engines and three 0-6-0T small saddle tanks were ordered from Messrs Stephenson and were delivered in 1898. The three smaller locomotives were numbered 2, 3 and 15 and had six coupled wheels of 4' diameter set at 6'3" and 7'0" centres. The safety valves were of the Ramsbottom pattern, and mounted on top of the steam dome. Swindon allotted them Diagram A.90 as in *Figure 459*, but only Nos. 3 and 15 survived to come under GWR ownership. Six other small tank engines, very similar in design to these first three, were those built by Hudswell Clarke in 1901, and given P.T. Nos. 22-27. On passing to the GWR they were renumbered 808/9/11-14 and given Diagram A.89 seen in *Figure 460*. Also in 1898 the Port Talbot Railway purchased from the Barry Railway two locomotives No. 37 and No. 52 which had been built as 2-4-0 tanks by Sharp-Stewart in 1890. On

coming to the P.T. Railway No. 52 was renumbered 36 and had been rebuilt to a 2-4-2T form (see chapter on Barry Railway). On being absorbed, the engine was renumbered once again to GW No. 1326 and Diagram P (*Figure 461*) was issued. No. 37, seen in *Figure 462* as Diagram M was renumbered GW 1189 and spent her last years at Swindon as station pilot, being scrapped in 1926.

Figure 463 illustrates engine No. 36, referred to above, and shows her just as taken over from the Barry Railway. In the bottom photograph (*Figure* 465) the same locomotive is seen as renumbered 1326. Her sister engine, No. 37, is shown in *Figure* 464, as GW 1189, and in the original 2-4-0T condition.

Figure 463

Figure 464

Figure 465

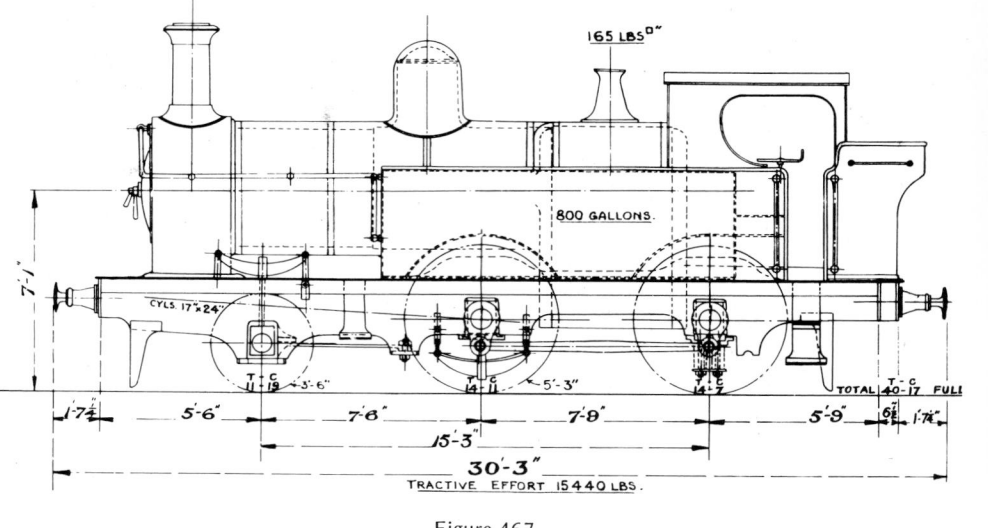

Figure 467

Figure 466

Figure 468

Two photographs showing the pair of Stephenson 0-6-0 saddle tanks which survived into GWR days and beyond as colliery engines into the 1950s. In the lower picture No. 3 is seen as GW No. 815 in 'Western' days, having received a short parallel chimney, a new safety valve, and a GWR type bunker. This little engine was eventually sold to Stephenson's of Darlington, who rebuilt her, and passed her on to Seeton Burn Coal Co. who in turn sent her to Hartley Main Colliery, where she worked until condemned in 1952. The other delightful study by A. C. Sterndale, is of No. 15 (GW No. 816) taken at Big Arch, Pontypool in 1951 when she was in the ownership of Partridge Jones Paton Ltd. of Abersychan. Three years later she was scrapped at Tredegar Shops. *Figure 467* is Swindon Diagram M which was of No. 1189 (shown on previous page) after slight modifications.

Referring back to the eleven Stephenson 0-6-2T engines purchased in 1898, only seven came over into the GWR in 1922, as Nos. 4 and 7 had been sold to the R. & S.B. in 1901, and Nos. 5 and 6 went to the Neath & Brecon in 1903. This left Nos. 8-14 in the class at the grouping. Shown on Swindon Diagram W (*Figure 469*) they were fitted with three ring boilers with a round topped firebox and had 4' 6" diameter coupled wheels, with a trailing truck under the bunker, with wheels of 3' 6" diameter. Renumbered in 1922 they became GW Nos. 183-9. Two of the class were rebuilt in 1925 with Standard No. 10 boilers and fittings, together with the high roofed cab and buffing-gear, and Swindon Diagram A.35 was drawn to suit (*Figure 472*).

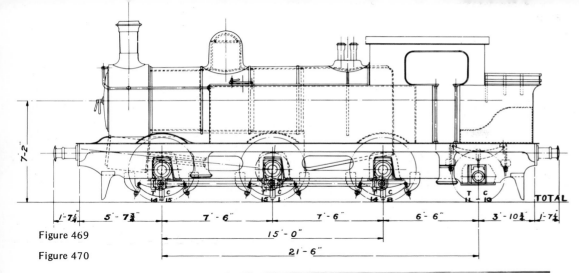

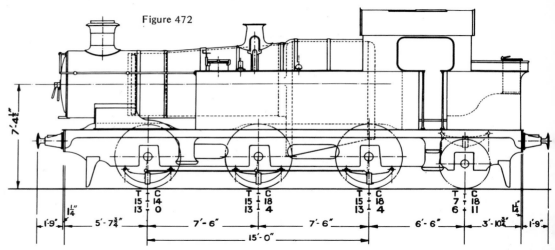

Figure 472

Figure 469

Figure 470

The two official photographs of No. 188 (*Figures* 471 and 473), one broadside and one three-quarter view (*on next page*), just as the engine was turned out of Swindon factory. This locomotive and her sister No. 184 were the only two of the Port Talbot 'Stephenson' 0-6-2Ts to be so rebuilt.

Figure 471

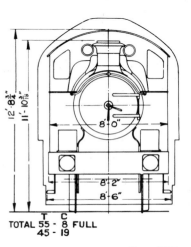

GREAT WESTERN 188

Figure 473

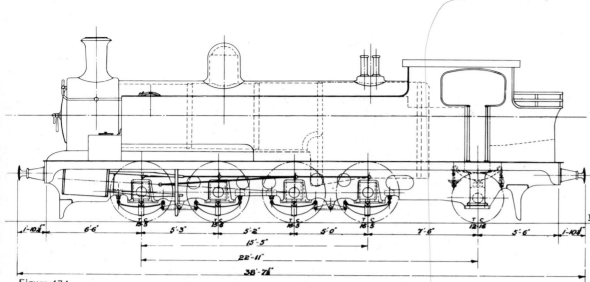

Figure 474

Figure 475

The biggest engines to work on the Port Talbot Railway were the massive 0-8-2T locomotives. There were five in all, three built by Sharp-Stewart's in 1901, and the first two built in America by the Cooke Locomotive Co. of Paterson, New Jersey in 1899. The British engines were numbered 17-19, and had outside cylinders driving the eight coupled wheels of 4' 3" diameter, with trailing wheels of 3' 6". Water capacity in the side tanks was 2,000 gallons, and 2½ tons of coal could be accommodated in the bunker. The working weight of these big tanks was almost 76 tons, and Swindon gave them the Diagram A seen in *Figure* 474. Nos. 17-19 became GW Nos. 1358-60 in 1922 and having already received Great Western modifications in 1908-9, further work was carried out on them, giving them Swindon style bunkers and smokeboxes. No. 1360 was scrapped in 1926, 1359 in 1935, and No. 1358 lasted until 1948.

The two American engines were shipped over from the States dismantled and were erected in the Barry workshops in 1899. As can be seen in Swindon Diagram B at *Figure* 476, these engines had a three ring boiler, the centre ring having a pronounced taper. The eight driving wheels were of 4' 4" diameter, with the two centre pairs being flangeless and set so close together as to have only 1" clearance. Port Talbot numbered them 20-21 and another Swindon Diagram B was issued as at *Figure* 477. An official picture is overleaf of engine No. 20 (*Figure* 478).

Figure 476

Figure 477

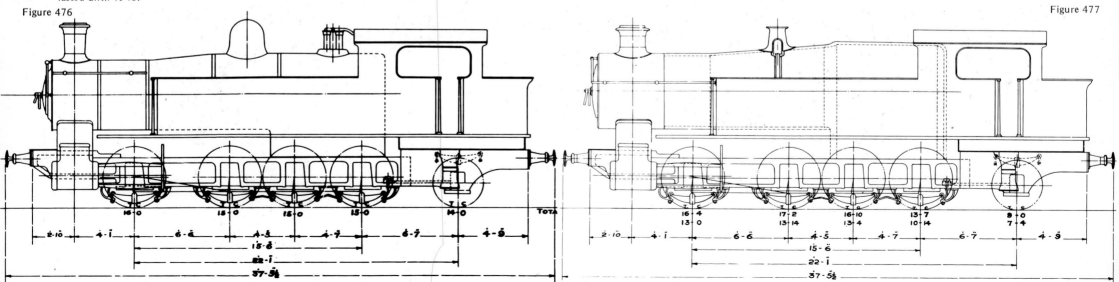

Figure 478

The BURRY PORT & GWENDRAETH VALLEY RAILWAY COMPANY

The Burry Port & Gwendraeth Valley Railway was formed in 1865-66 from the culmination of canal, harbour and tramway works dating back to 1765. Being the farthest westward of the South Wales Mineral lines, the route of the little line followed the course of the old Kymers Canal. Starting at Burry Port on the coast to the west of Llanelly it ran on up the valley to the terminus at Cwm Mawr. A small branch to Kidwelly was opened in 1873 and in 1891 a connection with the Llanelly & Mynydd Mawr Railway was made at Sandy Gate Junction.

Until 1909 the B.P. & G.V. Railway handled goods and mineral traffic only, but on the 30th June 1909 a Light Railway order was granted, and a passenger service on a small scale was commenced, first from Burry Port to Pontyberem, and in 1913 on up the Gwendraeth Valley to Cwm Mawr. In 1922 on being absorbed into the Great Western Railway fifteen engines were handed over, and these are listed hereunder:—

B.P. & G V. No.	GWR No.	Type	Builder	Name	Diagram
1	2192	0-6-0T	Chapman & F.	Ashburnham	A113
2	2162	”	Hudswell Clarke	Pontyberem	A109
3	2193	”	Chapman & F.	Burry Port	B10
4	2194	”	Avonside Engine	Kidwelly	A114/B22
5	2195	”	Avonside Engine	Cwm Mawr	B22
6	2196	”	Avonside Engine	Gwendraeth	A111
7	2176	”	Avonside Engine	Pembrey	A112
8	2197	”	Hudswell Clarke	Pioneer	B11/44
9	2163	”	Hudswell Clarke		A110
10	2198	”	Hudswell Clarke		B12
11	2164	”	Hudswell Clarke		A109
12	2165	“	Hudswell Clarke		A109
13	2166	”	Hudswell Clarke		A109
14	2167	”	Hudswell Clarke		A109
15	2168	”	Hudswell Clarke		A109

Figure 479

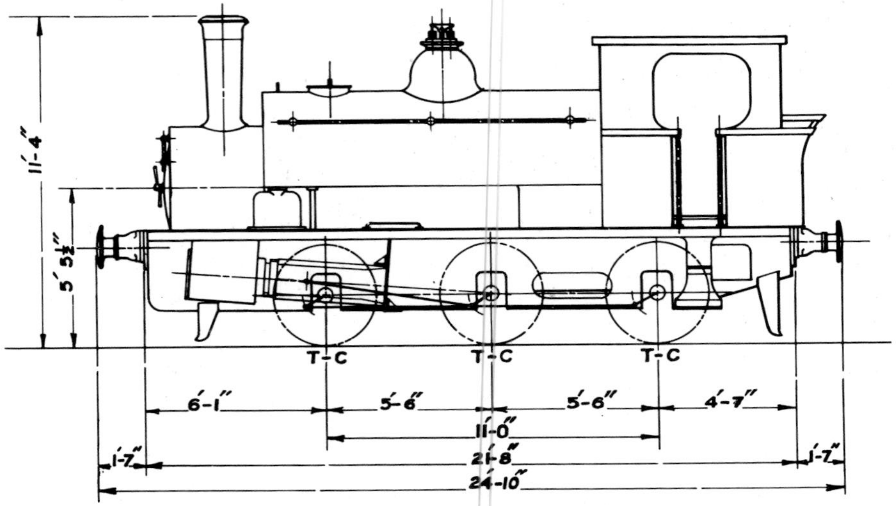

Figure 480

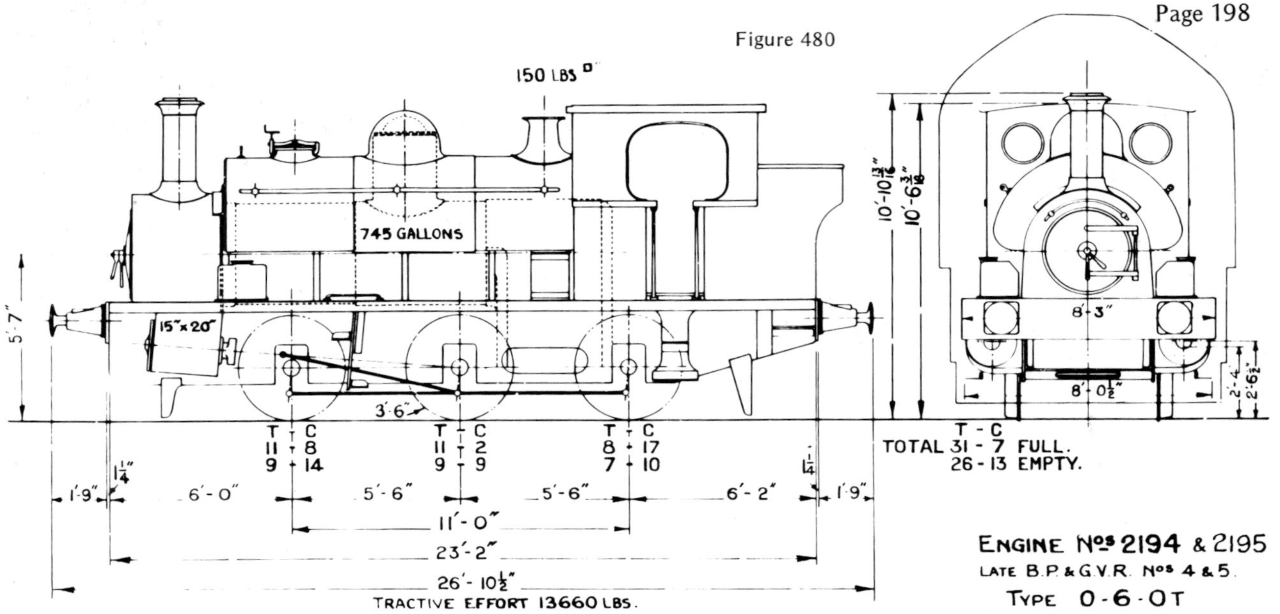

150 LBS

11'-4"

5'-5½"

T-C   T-C   T-C

6'-1"   5'-6"   5'-6"   4'-7"

11'-0"

21'-8"

24'-10"

1'-7"   1'-7"

745 GALLONS

15"x 20"

5'-7"

3'-6"

T - C   T - C   T - C   T - C
11 · 8   11 · 2   8 · 17
9 · 14   9 · 9   7 · 10

1'-9"   1'4"   6'-0"   5'-6"   5'-6"   6'-2"   1'-9"

11'-0"

23'-2"

26'-10½"

TRACTIVE EFFORT 13660 LBS.

10'-10½"
10'-6¾"

8'-3"

8'-0½"

2'-4"
2'-6½"

TOTAL 31 - 7 FULL.
26 - 13 EMPTY.

ENGINE Nos 2194 & 2195
LATE B.P. & G.V.R. Nos 4 & 5.
TYPE O-6-O T

Figure 481

Perhaps one of the best known engines of the Burry Port & Gwendraeth Valley Railway was *Kidwelly*, one of seven new engines purchased for the Company between 1900 and 1907. She was built by Avonside Engine Co. of Bristol and delivered in 1903. All seven were saddle tanks with 3' 8" diameter wheels set at 5' 6" and 5' 6" centres.

They had inclined outside cylinders and although very similar to each other, nevertheless every one was slightly different. The Great Western in 1922 gave them all new numbers, Nos. 1 to 7 becoming 2192-96, 2176 and 2162 and *Kidwelly* and *Cwm Mawr* were allotted Diagram A.114 seen in *Figure* 479. In 1923 No. 4 (GW No. 2194) went to Swindon and was rebuilt with GWR boiler fittings and coal bunker, and her boiler was brought up to 'Western' standards. She returned to work in 1926, and was given Diagram B.22 (*Figure* 480) to cover the conversion; her duties now took her to Weymouth, where, fitted with a bell, she hauled the Channel Boat Trains from the station to the Quay and back. This is where I first saw her from my carriage window en route to Jersey. Leaving the Dorset coast in 1940, she had a short spell at Cathays, and finally ended her days at Taunton, where Tony Sterndale took the lovely picture in 1952, just twelve months before withdrawal.

Another engine named *Kidwelly* is shown in *Figure* 482, this was No. 1 of the Gwendraeth Valley Railway, built in 1905 by Hudswell Clarke; she was renamed *Velindre* and passed over to the GWR at the grouping and became No. 26. No diagram was issued and the little engine ended its days at Neath Shed in 1927.

Figure 483 shows B.P. & G.V. Railway No. 3, one of the Chapman & Furneaux built engines of 1901. She was named *Burry Port* and on entering Great Western stock, became No. 2193. This engine had six coupled wheels of 3' 6" diameter, and the wheelbase was 5' 8" and 6' 5". The GWR gave her boiler fittings and she lasted out until 1952.

No. 2194 *Kidwelly* is seen in broadside left-hand view in *Figure* 484, this being taken in 1952 at Taunton. No. 2195, originally named *Cwm Mawr* is seen at Swindon in 1951 (*Figure* 485). She spent some time at Weymouth in company with *Kidwelly*, and also saw service at Bristol.

Figure 482

Figure 483

Figure 484

Figure 485

Figure 486

Figure 487

Figure 488

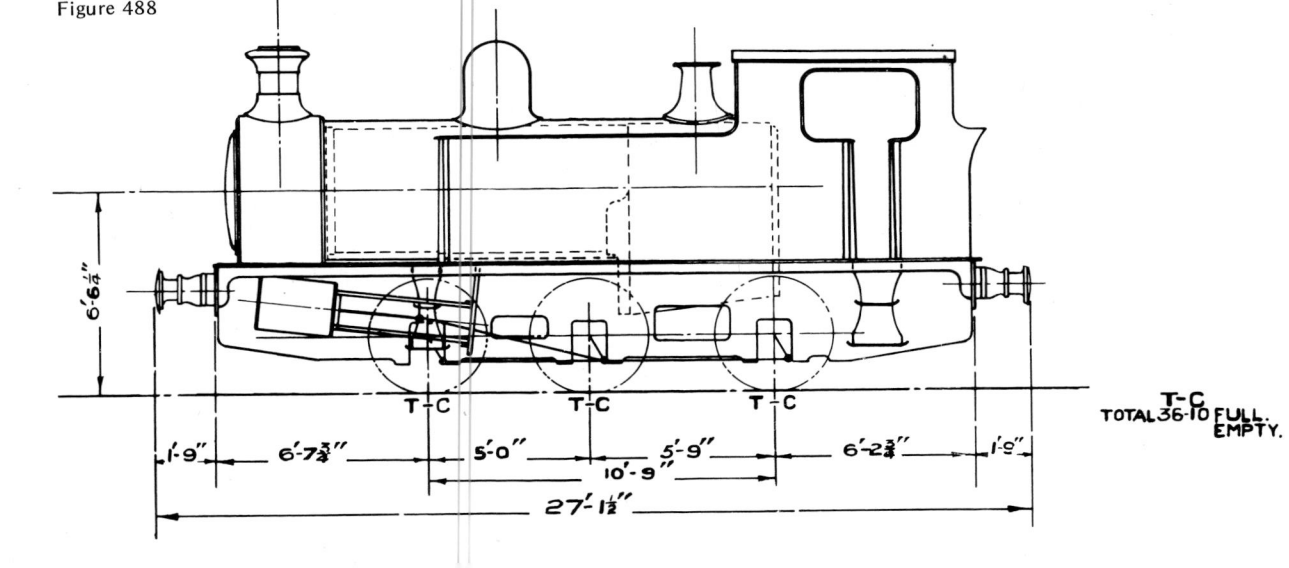

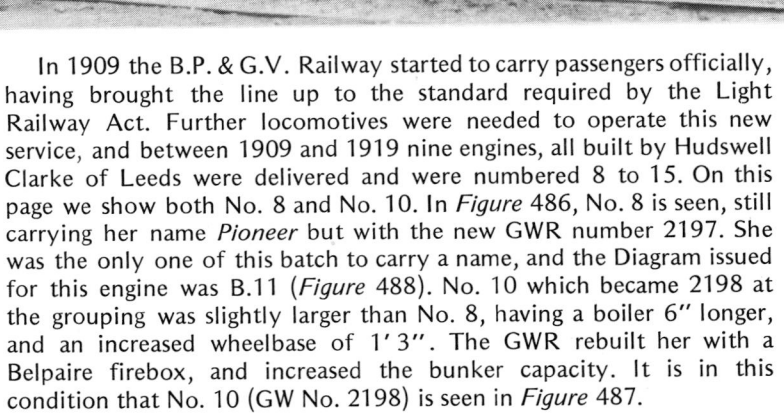

In 1909 the B.P. & G.V. Railway started to carry passengers officially, having brought the line up to the standard required by the Light Railway Act. Further locomotives were needed to operate this new service, and between 1909 and 1919 nine engines, all built by Hudswell Clarke of Leeds were delivered and were numbered 8 to 15. On this page we show both No. 8 and No. 10. In *Figure* 486, No. 8 is seen, still carrying her name *Pioneer* but with the new GWR number 2197. She was the only one of this batch to carry a name, and the Diagram issued for this engine was B.11 (*Figure* 488). No. 10 which became 2198 at the grouping was slightly larger than No. 8, having a boiler 6″ longer, and an increased wheelbase of 1′ 3″. The GWR rebuilt her with a Belpaire firebox, and increased the bunker capacity. It is in this condition that No. 10 (GW No. 2198) is seen in *Figure* 487.

The diagrams shown below refer to engine No. 10 (GW No. 2198). *Figure* 489 is Swindon Diagram B.40 which was drawn for the rebuilt condition of the locomotive, and *Figure* 491 is Diagram B.12 allotted to No. 10 before the 'Western' alterations. The photograph in *Figure* 492 is of No. 13 which became GW No. 2166, she was one of five which had the longer wheelbase of 13′ 7″, the others were 11-12/14-15.

The other drawing (*Figure* 490) is of engine No. 6 *Gwendraeth*, one of the Avonside Engine Co. products. She was given this Diagram A.111, but did not go to Swindon after the grouping, being repaired at Messrs Kitsons during 1925 instead.

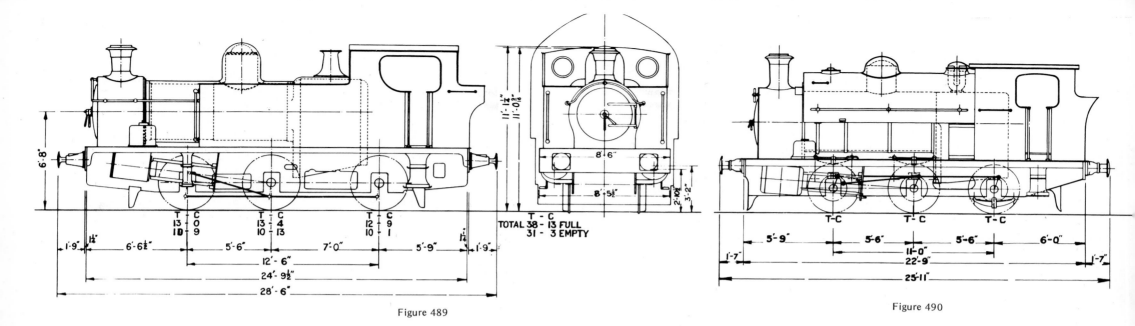

11'-1¼"
11'-0⅞"

6'-8"

8'-6"

8'-5½"

2'-0¾"
3'-2"

T-C
13
10 ― 9
T-C
13
10 ― 4
13
T-C
12
10 ― 9
91

T-C
TOTAL 38 - 13 FULL
31 - 3 EMPTY

1'-9" 1¼" 6'-6½" 5'-6" 7'-0" 5'-9" 1¼ 1'-9"

12'-6"

24'-9½"

28'-6"

Figure 489

T-C T-C T-C

5'-9" 5'-6" 5'-6" 6'-0"

1'-7" 11'-0" 1'-7"

22'-9"

25'-11"

Figure 490

Figure 492

Figure 491

6'-6¾"

T-C
11 ― 9
T-C
14 ― 18
T-C
11 ― 4

1'-9" 6'-4" 5'-9" 7'-0" 5'-11" 1'-9"

12'-9"

28'-6"

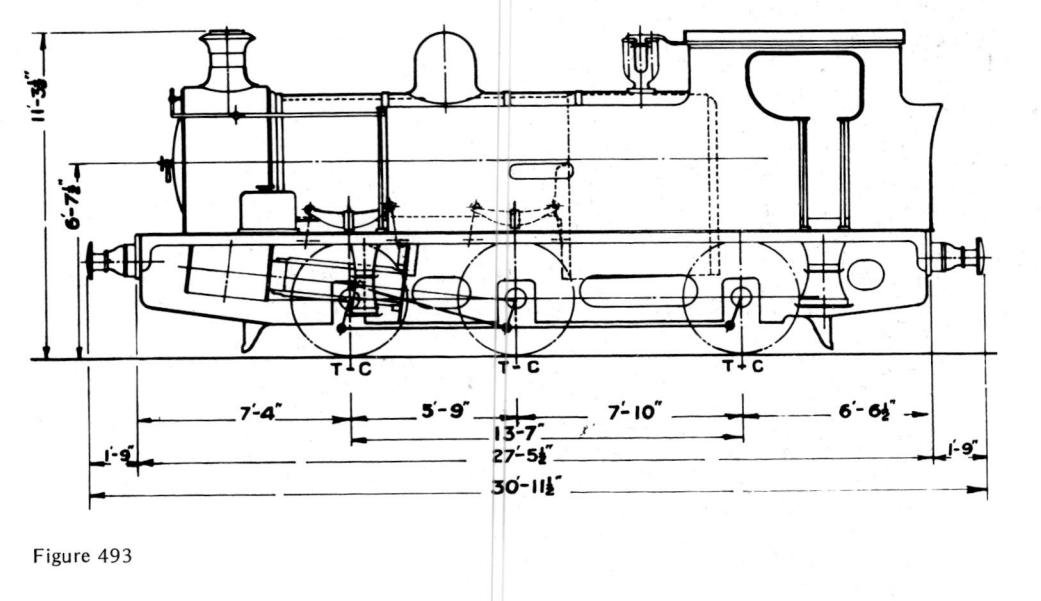

Figure 493

Figure 494

Figure 495

Figure 496

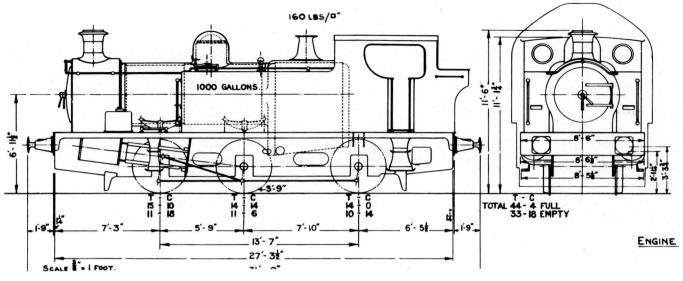

160 LBS/◻"

1000 GALLONS

11'-6"
11'-1½"

8'-6"
8'-6¼"
8'-5¾"

2'-1½"
3'-3½"

6'-11½"

T C
15 10
11 18

T C
14 14
11 6

T C
14 10
10 14

T C
TOTAL 44- 4 FULL
33-18 EMPTY

-3'-9"

1'-9"
¼"

7'-3"

5'-9"

7'-10"

6'-5½"

1'-9"

13'-7"

27'-3½"

SCALE ⅛" = 1 FOOT.

ENGINE

Figure 497

Figure 498

Swindon Diagram A.109 was the drawing allotted to the engines Nos. 2 and 11-15 of the B.P. & G.V. Railway, and shows the extra long wheelbase of these six locomotives, *Figure* 493.

Figures 494 and 495 show No. 9 (GW No. 2163) at two different periods of her working life; in the upper illustration she still has her own safety valve, chimney and small bunker, and in the other picture she has been fitted with a new chimney, GWR safety valve and enlarged bunker. Also note that the number plate has been moved from the side tanks to the centre of the bunker.

In *Figure* 496 we show No. 12 (GW No. 2165) which has received a modified Standard No. 11 boiler and fittings, together with an enlarged bunker. This engine lasted until 1955 before being withdrawn.

Figure 497 depicts the Swindon Diagram B.44 which was drawn for the rebuilding of those engines previously shown on A.109 seen on the adjoining page. It will be seen that a Belpaire firebox has been fitted, plus an enlarged bunker. *Figure* 499 shows Diagram A.110 which was drawn for B.P. & G.V. No. 9 only, the engine shown in the pictures on the upper page. GW No. 2166 standing in the sunshine at Danygraig in the lower photograph (*Figure* 498), was originally B.P. & G.V. No. 13, and as previously mentioned was the only engine of the series to be repaired at Messrs Kitsons in Leeds. Note that she kept her original bunker until 1955 when she was withdrawn.

Figure 499

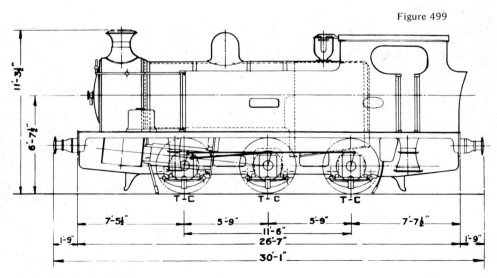

11'-3¼"

6'-7¼"

T C   T C   T C

7'-5¼"

5'-9"

5'-9"

7'-7½"

1'-9"

11'-6"

26'-7"

30'-1"

1'-9"

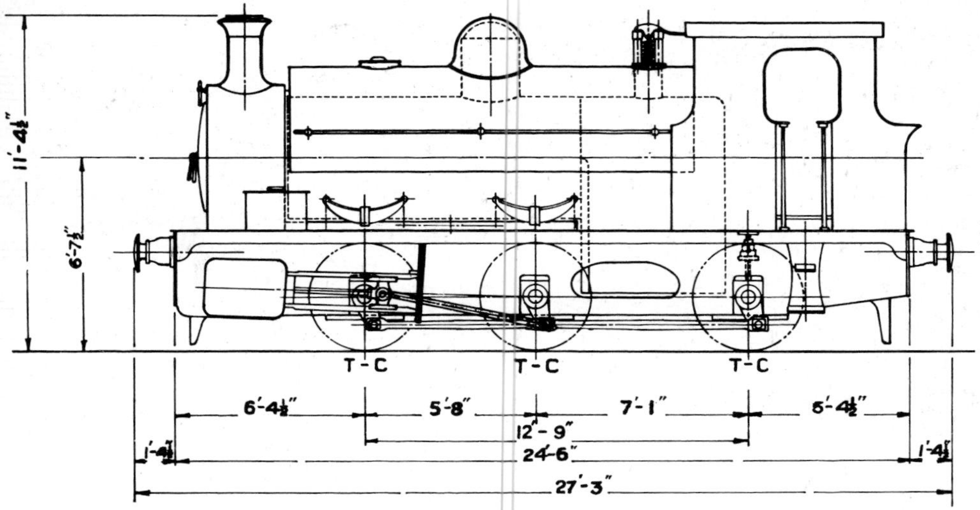

Figure 500

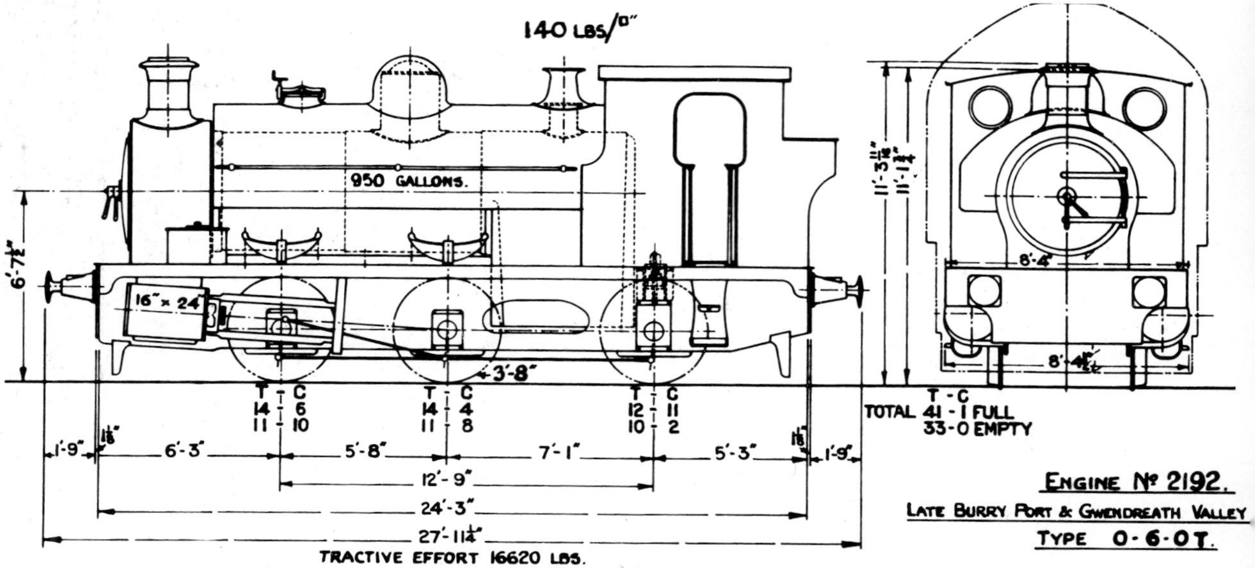

140 LBS/□"

950 GALLONS.

16" x 24"

3'-8"

TRACTIVE EFFORT 16620 LBS.

Engine Nº 2192.

Late Burry Port & Gwendreath Valley

TYPE O·6·OT.

TOTAL 41·1 FULL
33·0 EMPTY

Figure 501

Burry Port and Gwendraeth Valley No. 1 was named *Ashburnham* after the Company's Chairman, the Earl of Ashburnham. She was built in 1900 by Chapman & Furneaux and had six coupled wheels of 3' 8" diameter. At the grouping she was renumbered 2192, and given Diagram A.113 seen in *Figure* 500. Later she was altered in respect of tube heating surface, given GWR boiler fittings and Diagram B.49 was issued, *Figure* 501.

The photograph in *Figure* 502 is also of No. 1 (GW No. 2192) but at the end of her working life in the condemned siding at Swindon during 1951. The sister engine of No. 1 was No. 3, made by the same builders and delivered in 1901. She was renumbered 2193, and carried her name *Burry Port* until withdrawal in 1952. The photograph in *Figure* 503 was taken during 1949 inside Llanelly Shed.

Figure 503

Figure 502

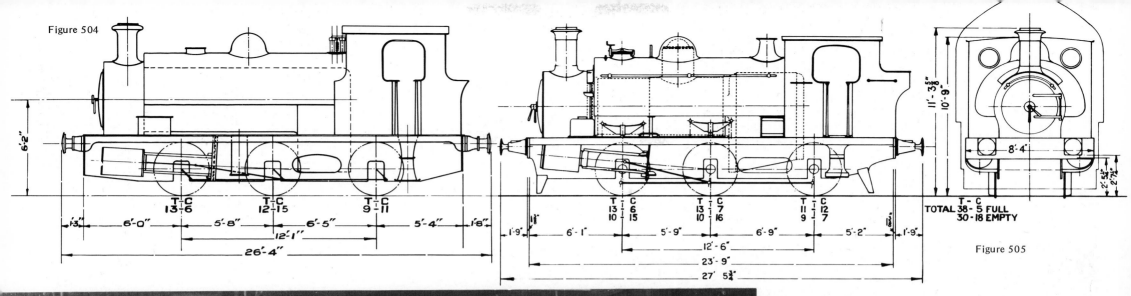

Figure 504

Figure 505

TOTAL 38 - 5 FULL
30 - 18 EMPTY

Figure 506

Burry Port GW No. 2193 was given Diagram B.10 by Swindon drawing office, and this is shown in *Figure 504*. Another photograph of No. 1 *Ashburnham* is shown here, taken inside Neath Shed in 1950; some enterprising cleaner had polished her GW number plate which shows up the '2192' well. B.P. & G.V. No. 7 was named *Pembrey,* and in GWR hands, took the new number 2176, and went through the factory in 1923. Before being rebuilt she was given Diagram A.112 (*Figure* 508 on next page) and after 'Western' treatment, was allotted Diagram B.39 seen here in *Figure 505*.

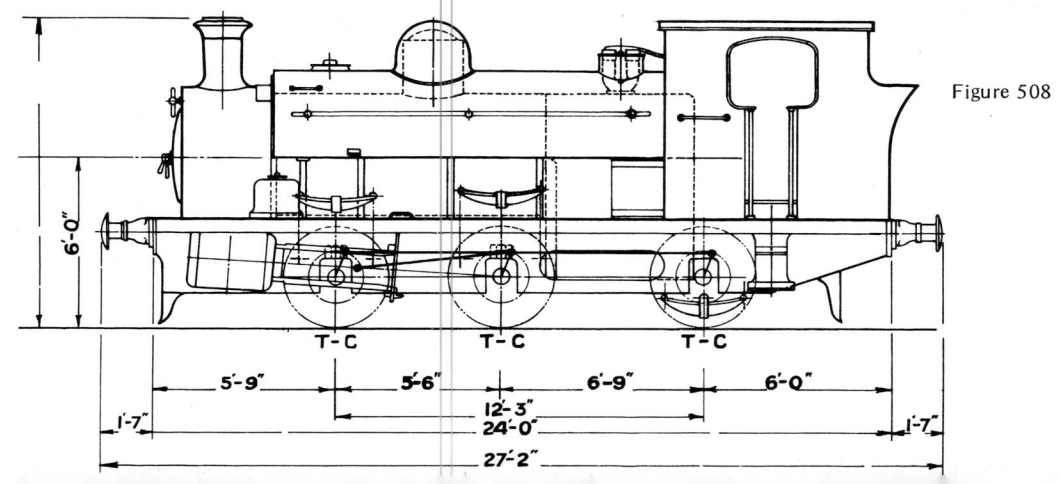

Figure 507

Figure 508

No. 5 which eventually became GW No. 2195, is shown in *Figure* 507 at Swindon Works Yard in 1949. This little tank was originally named *Cwm Mawr*, but lost her name plates in 1939. The Diagram is A.112 which was No. 7 mentioned on the previous page before refitting. The enlarged picture of No. 2195 in *Figure* 509 was taken inside Swindon Stock Shed in 1939. This shows the GWR type bunker to advantage.

6'-0"

T-C   T-C   T-C

5'-9"   5'-6"   6'-9"   6'-0"

1'-7"   12'-3"   1'-7"

24'-0"

27'-2"

Figure 509

Figure 510

Finally in this complex look at the stud of 0-6-0 saddle tanks belonging first to the B.P. & G.V. and then to the Great Western Railway, it is shown what delightful little locomotives they became when receiving the 'treatment' at Swindon factory. These two photographs are the official record of No. 2195 immediately after being wheeled out of the paint shop in 1926, before joining *Kidwelly* on the Dock duties at Weymouth.

Figure 511

The
RHONDDA & SWANSEA BAY
RAILWAY COMPANY

Another Railway promoted to serve the Welsh coalfields and in particular to move the coal from the Rhondda Valley to the docks at Port Talbot, Briton Ferry and Swansea. The Act was obtained in 1882, with extension to Swansea Docks in the following year, although it was 1899 before the terminus at Swansea Riverside was opened. The first section from Aberavon to Cymmer was opened in 1885, and nearly five years later an end-on link up with the Taff Vale Railway at Treherbert with running powers gave access to the mining valleys. A swing bridge over the River Neath enabled Danygraig to be reached in 1894, which in effect put Swansea Docks within the grasp of the R. & S.B. Railway. In 1895 Neath was also brought into the system by means of a short branch which gave a track mileage, including the dock lines, of approximately 29 miles.

When the R. & S.B. was absorbed into the Great Western in 1922 the locomotive stud consisted of 37 locomotives which are classified hereunder:—

R. & S.B. No.	GWR No.	Type	Maker	Diagram
1	799	0-6-0T	Beyer Peacock	A.88
2	1660	,,	GWR	
3	801	,,	Beyer Peacock	A.88
4	181	0-6-2T	Kitson	V.
5	802	0-6-0T	Beyer Peacock	A.88
6	805	,,	,,	A.88
7	806	,,	,,	A.88
8	168	0-6-2T	Kitson	R.
9	169	,,	,,	R.
10	170	,,	,,	R.
11	171	,,	,,	R.
12	172	,,	,,	R.
13	173	,,	,,	R.
14	174	,,	,,	R.
15	175	,,	,,	R.
16	176	,,	,,	R.
17	1307	2-4-2T	,,	K.
18	1309	,,	,,	K.
19	1310	,,	,,	L.
20	177	0-6-2T	,,	S.
21	178	,,	,,	T.
22	179	,,	,,	S.
23	180	,,	Stephenson	U.
24	182	,,	,,	U.
25	164	,,	Kitson	P.
26	165	,,	,,	P.
27	166	,,	,,	P.
28	167	,,	,,	P.
29	637	0-6-0T	GWR	
30	1834	,,	,,	
31	1652	,,	,,	
32	728	,,	,,	
33	2756	,,	,,	
34	1167	,,	,,	
35	1756	,,	,,	
36	1710	,,	,,	
37	1825	,,	,,	

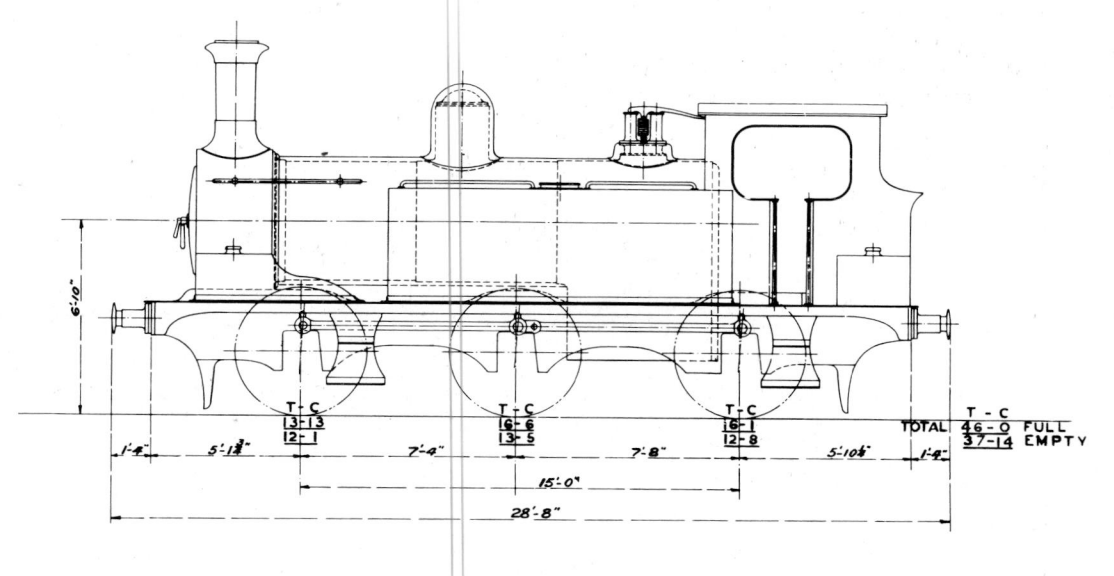

Figure 512

Figure 514

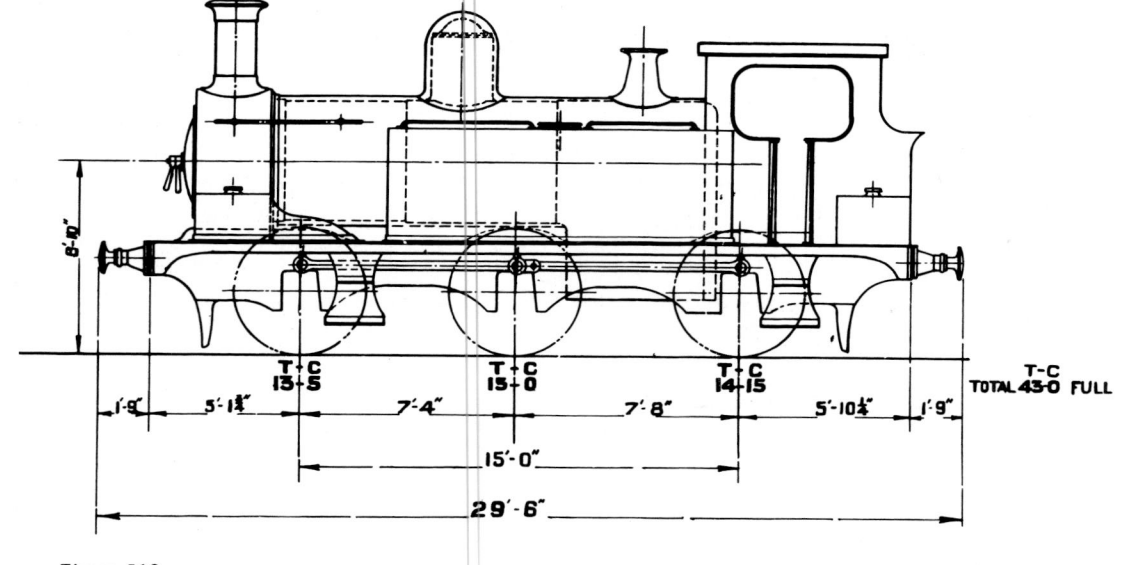

Figure 513

Beyer Peacock and Messrs Kitson & Co. were the favoured engine builders for the Rhondda & Swansea Bay Railway, and apart from two early engines which are no concern of this work, Messrs Beyer Peacock produced the first series of five between 1885 and 1889. They were numbered 1/3/5-7 and were six coupled side tank engines, having wheels of 4' 6'' diameter set at 7' 4'' and 7' 8'' centres. They were neat little machines, with round topped boilers, and covered cabs, and a tiny bunker holding 32 cwt of coal. On being handed over to the GWR Diagram A.87 was issued to cover, as seen in *Figure 512*. All five were renumbered to Nos. 799/801/802/ 805/806 and were eventually rebuilt with GW boilers and mountings. Various modifications were made to all of the class, some having top feed and others square topped water tanks.

The new Diagram allotted was A.88 shown in *Figure 513*. No. 5 is seen in *Figure 514* at Port Talbot Shed in 1929. Note the Great Western boiler, bunker, side tanks, smokebox and fittings.

Three of the Beyer Peacock 0-6-0Ts in Great Western days, and showing the slight differences between engines. In *Figure* 515, No. 3 is seen, as GW No. 801. Note that although she has the GWR boiler and smokebox, and a sloping back bunker, she had kept the R. & S.B. round topped side tanks. No. 805 in *Figure* 516 was R. & S.B. No. 6; she has been rebuilt with new boiler, smokebox, fittings, square top tank and bunker, almost pure 'Western'. Note that several were equipped with an additional rear sand box mounted on the running plate alongside the coal bunker. Old No. 7 (GW No. 806) seen in *Figure* 517, showing the left-hand side of the series, has been similarly rebuilt to No. 3, but does not have the facility of the extra sandbox.

Figure 515

Figure 516

Figure 517

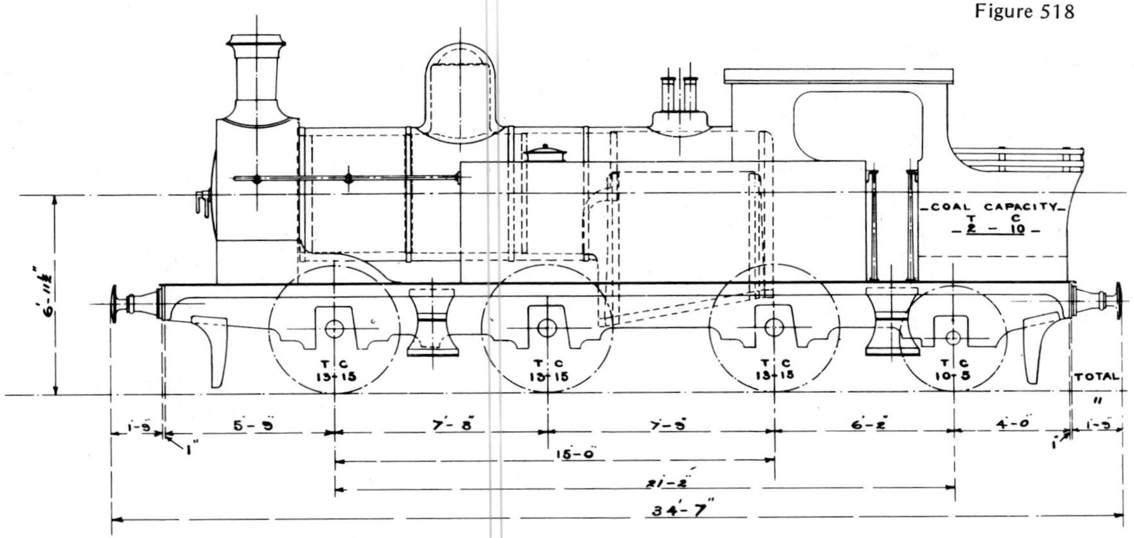

Figure 518

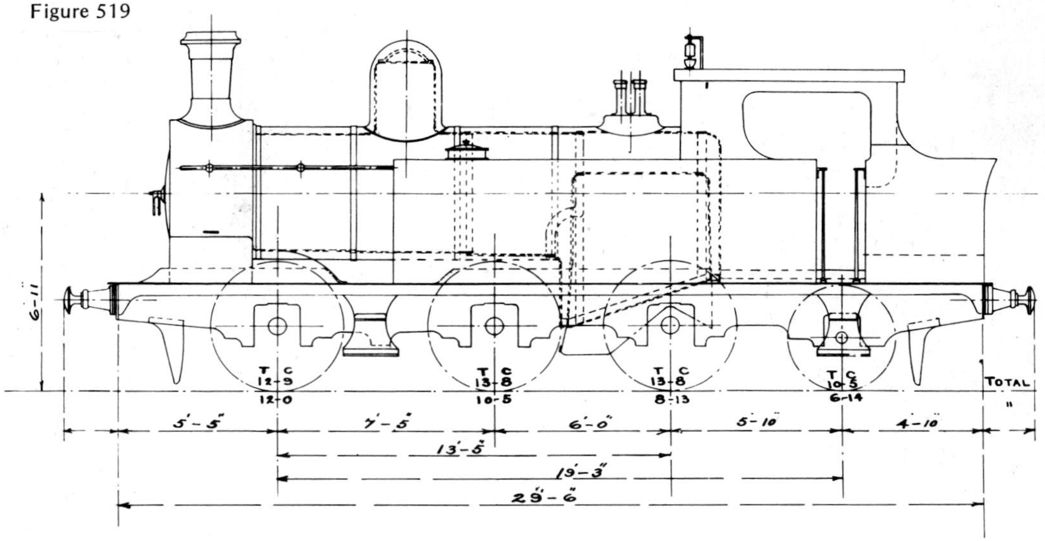

Figure 519

COAL CAPACITY
T C
2 - 10

The R. & S.B. Railway had nineteen 0-6-2T class engines at the grouping, and all but two were made by Messrs Kitson of Leeds. The first to be ordered and delivered was No. 4 which was added to the stock in 1885. The six coupled wheels were again 4' 6'' diameter set at 7' 5'' and 6' 0'' centres, and the trailing radial truck had 3' 8¼'' diameter wheels. A large bunker was fitted, having a capacity of 2½ tons, and the round topped tanks held 1,500 gallons.

In 1922 No. 4 was renumbered 181 and Swindon issued Diagram V seen in *Figure 518*. Proving successful, twelve more similar 0-6-2T locomotives were ordered from Messrs Kitsons between 1889 and 1899, and were given R. & S.B. numbers 8-16 and 20-22. On being absorbed, Swindon gave this series the Diagram Q shown in *Figure 519*. No. 9 (GW No. 169) is depicted in *Figure 520*, as rebuilt with Swindon boiler and mountings.

Figure 520

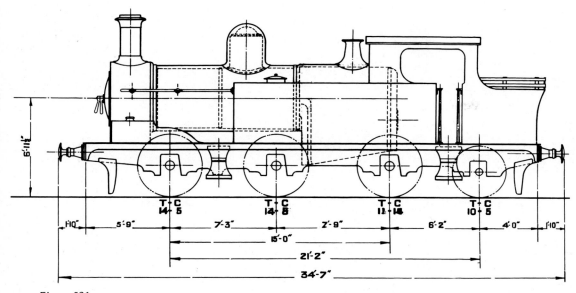

Figure 521

Many of the Kitson 0-6-2T engines were taken in hand by the GWR before the grouping, and even before 1910 new boilers had been fitted to all the class, with the exception of No. 13. In this condition, the engines were depicted on Swindon Diagram R (*Figure 521*) which showed them having the GW Appendix Group 102 round topped firebox boilers. The diagram in *Figure 522* shows the class fitted with taper boiler and Belpaire firebox. The photograph in *Figure 523* is of No. 12 (GW No. 172) in Great Western ownership at Danygraig. Note that the boiler has been fitted with top feed.

Figure 523

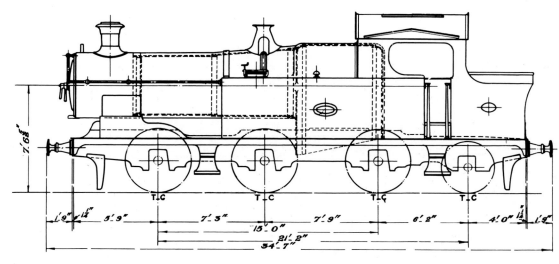

Figure 522

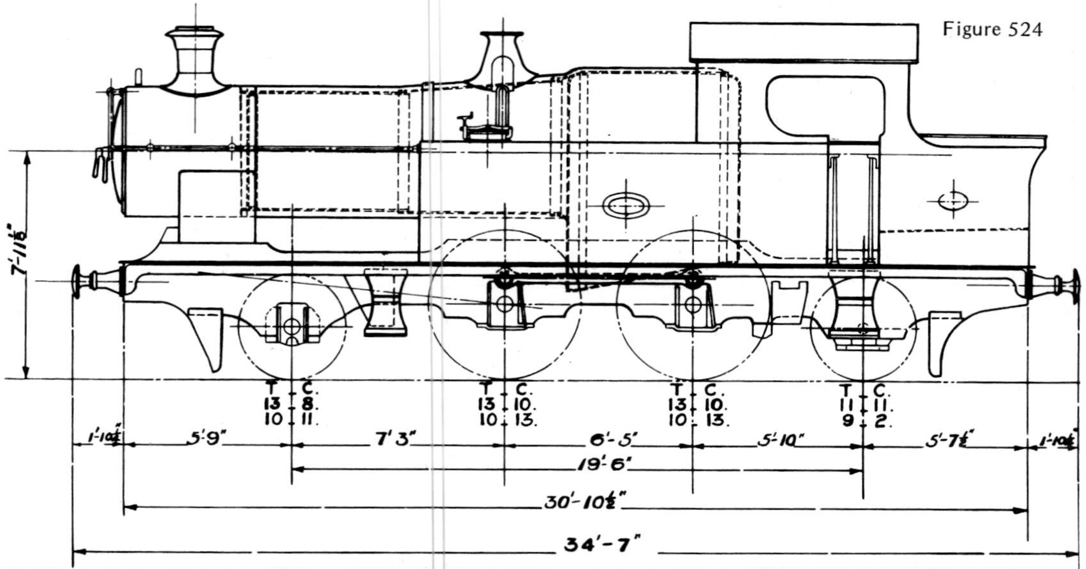

Figure 524

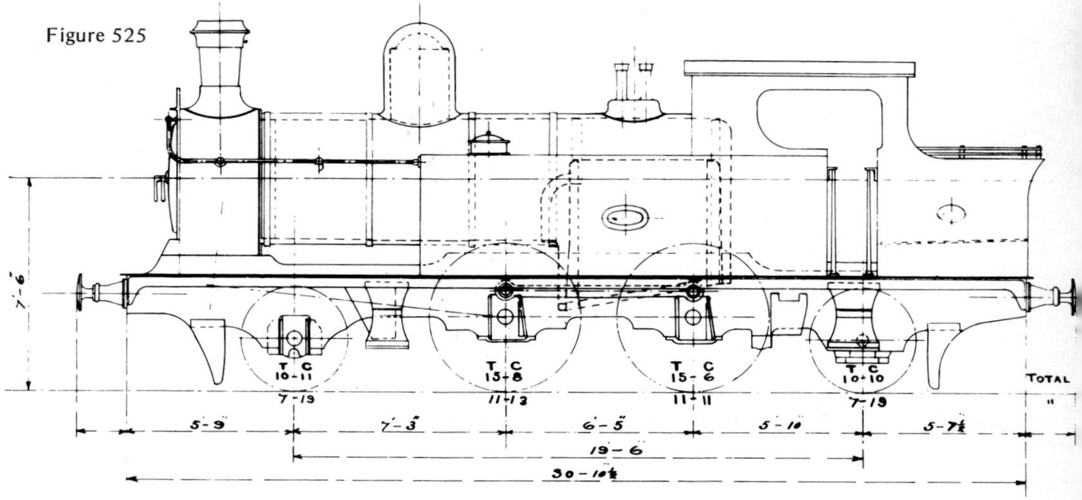

Figure 525

Figure 526

To handle the passenger services on the R. & S.B. line, three 2-4-2 side tank locomotives were ordered from Kitsons and delivered to stock in mid-1895. In general design from the running plate upwards, they closely resembled the 0-6-2Ts mentioned previously, but below they were quite different, having four coupled wheels of 5' 3" diameter set at a close wheelbase of 6' 5". The leading carrying wheels were 3' 8¼" set 7' 3" ahead of the driving wheels, and the trailing wheels were of the same size but at 5' 3" from the driving trailing wheels. Swindon gave them Diagram J (*Figure 525*), and their original numbers 17, 18 and 19 were changed in 1922 to 1307/9/10. In 1921 No. 19 was rebuilt at Swindon with a No. 5 boiler and a high roof cab and returned to work as shown in the official photograph in *Figure 526*. To suit this rebuild, Diagram L was drawn and allotted as seen in *Figure 524*.

Figure 527

Figure 528

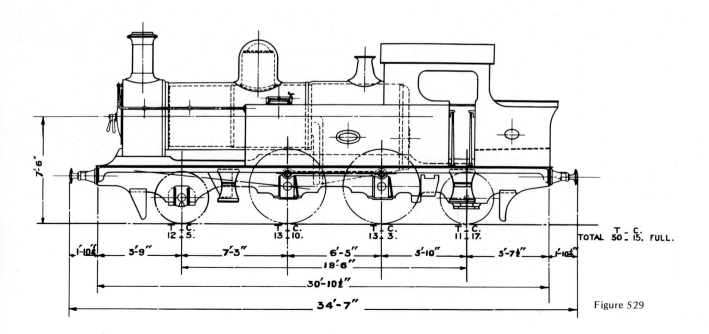

Figure 529

Nos. 17 and 18 received the same type of boiler rebuilding as issued to the 0-6-2Ts, and this was accomplished several years before the grouping. Fitted with the '102' flush topped boiler, they came under Diagram K as in *Figure* 529. No. 18 herself is seen in *Figure* 528 as GW No. 1309, and for a direct comparison, the 0-6-2T No. 9 (GW No. 169) is shown in *Figure* 527.

Figure 530

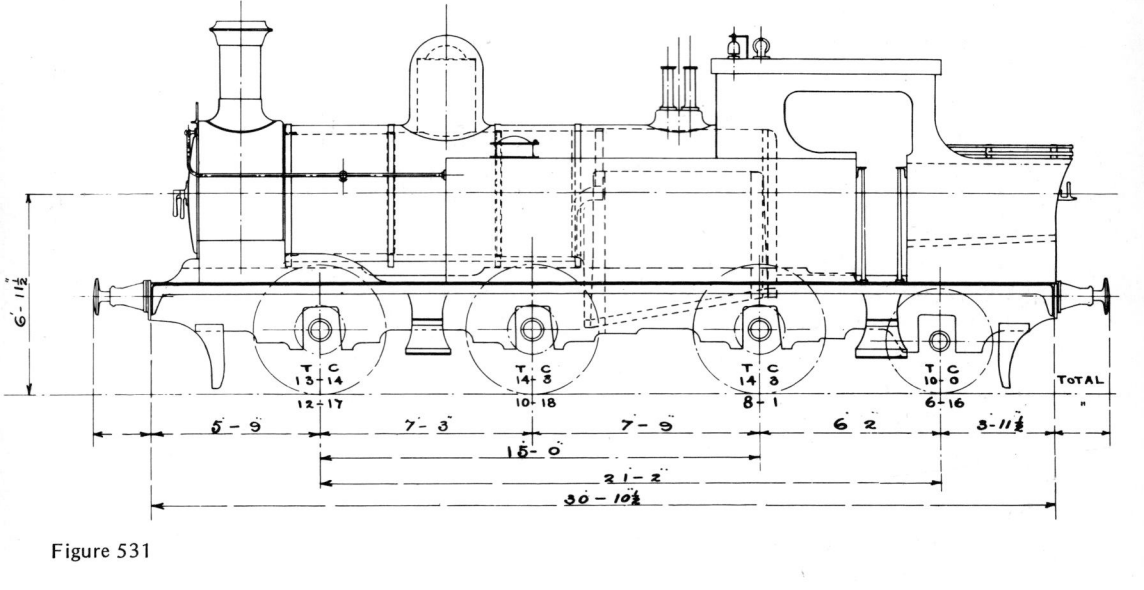

Figure 531

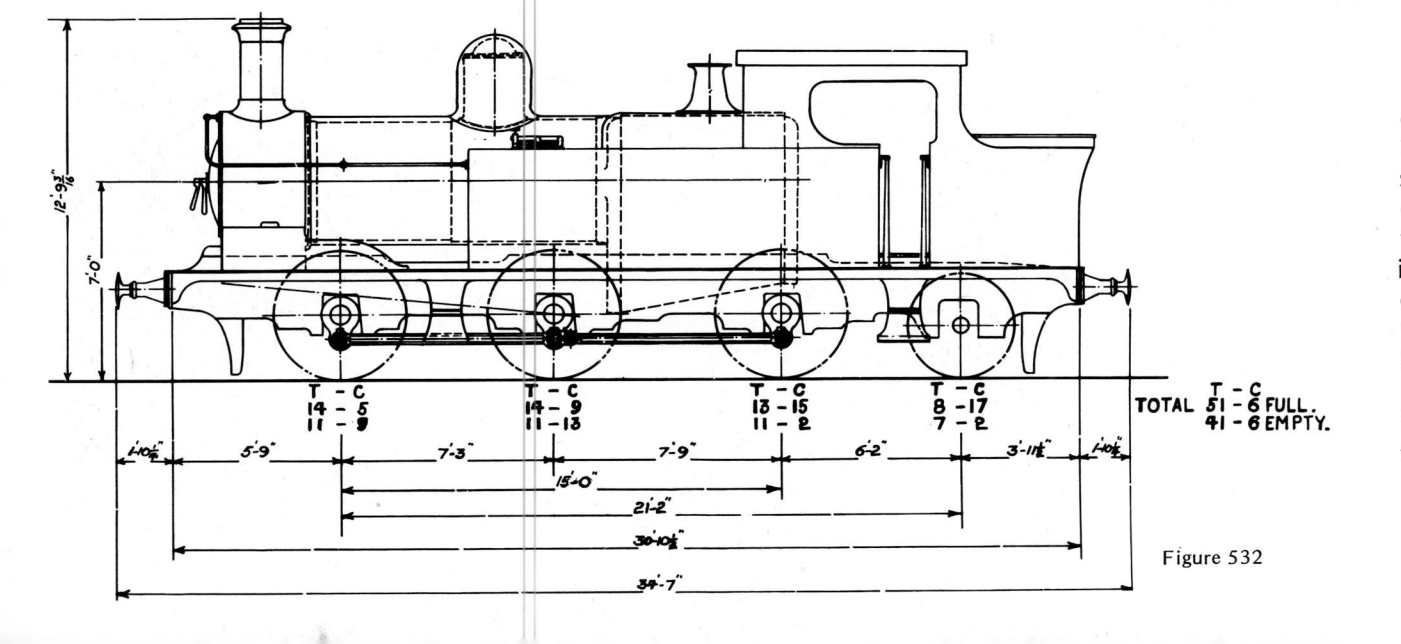

Figure 532

Three more 0-6-2T engines, built by Messrs Kitson, were delivered to the R. & S.B. in 1899. They were numbered 20, 21 and 22, and differed only slightly from Nos. 8-16 of the same design. In fact the fireboxes were 6" longer, the boilers one inch larger in diameter, and there were 12 additional tubes. Swindon gave these three later engines Diagram S seen in *Figure* 531 and they took the Nos. 177, 178 and 179. One of the trio, No. 21, seen in *Figure* 530 was rebuilt in 1911 with a Swindon Belpaire firebox and boiler, another similar boiler being fitted later, in 1916; in this condition she had a Diagram to herself, which was 0-6-2T 'T' seen in *Figure* 532. No. 20 was the first to be withdrawn, in 1935, followed by the other two one year later.

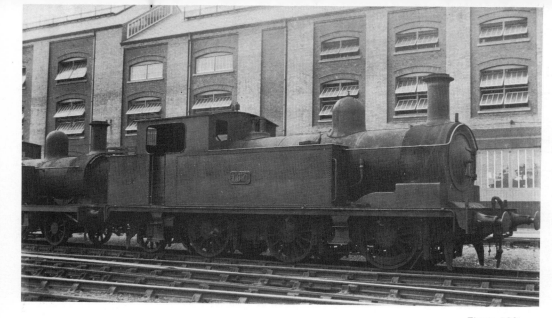

Figure 533

Figure 534

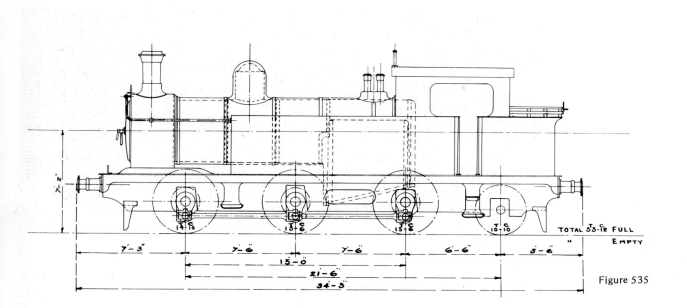

Figure 535

Nos. 23 and 24 of the R. & S.B. engines, were purchased from the Port Talbot Railway in 1901. Built by Stephenson & Co. in 1897/8 they were two of a series of eleven carrying P. T. Railway numbers 4-14. These two Nos. 4 and 7 were loaned to the R. & S.B. and must have proved themselves, as they were bought outright in October of 1901. Of 0-6-2T classification, the six coupled wheels were 4' 6" diameter, with trailing truck wheels of 3' 6" diameter. Upon being absorbed into the GWR, they were renumbered 180 and 182, and given Diagram U (*Figure* 535). They did not receive any Swindon treatment, No. 180 being repaired by the Avonside Engine Co. in 1925 and both being taken out of service in 1928/9. *Figure* 533 shows No. 180 at Swindon at this time.

The last engines built for the Company were also 0-6-2Ts, and Kitson & Co. were the chosen builders. They were numbered 25-28 and were much bigger engines than the other R. & S.B. tanks. *Figure* 534 shows No. 25, after being renumbered 164 and reconditioned at Swindon.

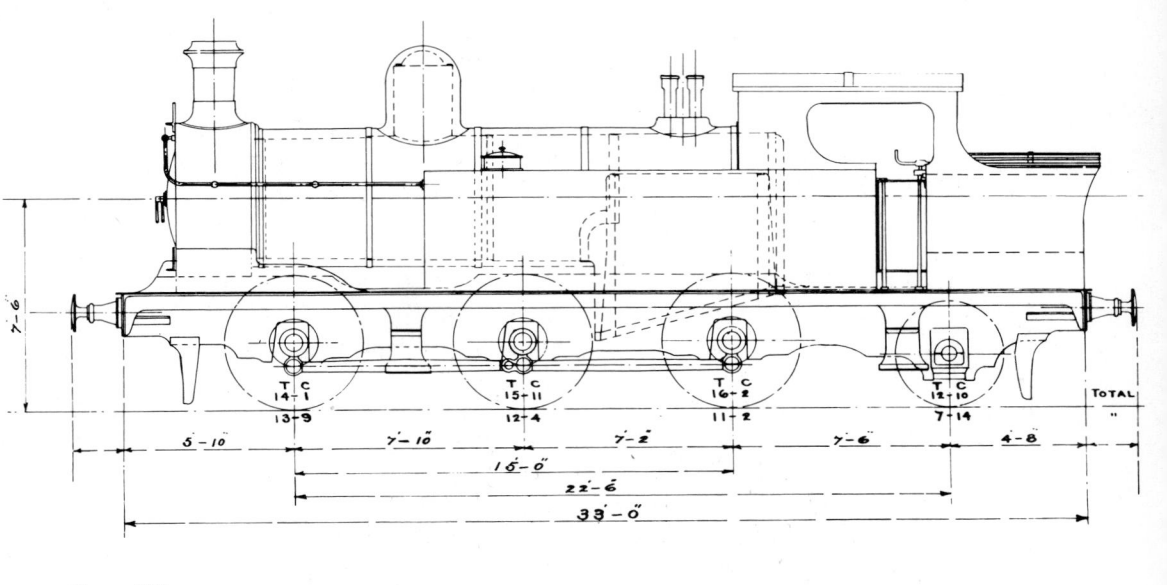

Figure 536   Figure 537

Figure 538

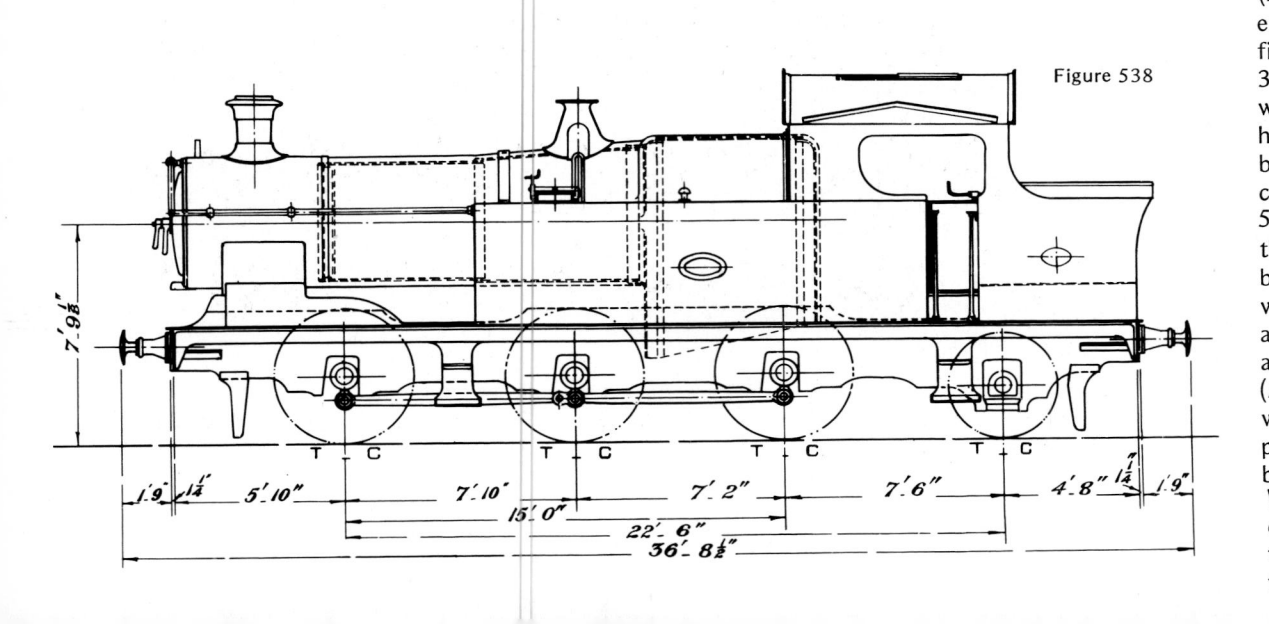

Figure 539

Diagram P was drawn at Swindon (*Figure* 537) to cover the four Kitson engines Nos. 25-28 and shows they were fitted with 4' 9" coupled wheels, with 3' 9" radial trailing trucks. The total wheelbase was 22' 6", and side tanks had a capacity of 1,825 gallons, with bunkers capable of holding 2½ tons of coal. Weight in working condition was 58 tons 4 cwt., six tons heavier than the earlier Kitson 0-6-2Ts. Renumbered by the GWR to 164-167 their boilers were brought up to Swindon standards, and three were fitted with top feed apparatus. A Diagram was prepared (*Figure* 538) showing the class fitted with a Standard No. 5 boiler, but this project was not carried through, all being withdrawn by September of 1936. Wherever possible, facsimiles of the old companies' seals have been added to the chapters, and *Figure* 539 is that of the Rhondda & Swansea Bay Railway.

The SOUTH WALES MINERAL RAILWAY COMPANY

AND

The LLANELLY & MYNYDD MAWR RAILWAY COMPANY

The South Wales Mineral Railway was a small line of nearly 13 miles, running from Briton Ferry, through Cymmer to Glyncorrwg Colliery. In 1908 together with the Port Talbot Railway, the S.W.M. Railway was taken over by the GWR although like the P.T. Railway, keeping nominally independent until 1922 when it became an official subsidiary of the Great Western Railway Company.

The Llanelly and Mynydd Mawr Railway was a small private concern, working under the direction of a railway contractor, one John Waddell of Edinburgh, who undertook to rebuild the railway on the site of an old tramway of 1806, supply the rolling stock and work the line for a share of the receipts. In 1875 the L. & M.M. Railway was authorised, but it was not until 1883, that the line was opened. The twelve miles of track started at Llanelly and followed the old tramway route up to Cross Hands. At the grouping, eight locomotives were added to the GWR stock in 1923, and were distinctive in all being named, and without numbers. The list is as hereunder:—

Name	GW No.	Type	Builder	GW Diagram	Withdrawn
George Waddell	312	0-6-0T	A. Barclay	B.45	1934
Tarndune	339	”	Hudswell Clarke	B.37	1943
Hilda	359	”	”	B.34	1954
Victory	704	”	Manning Wardle		1943
Ravelston	803	”	Hudswell Clarke	B.38	1951
Merkland	937	”	”		1923
Great Mountain	944	”	Avonside Engine		1928
Seymour Clarke	969	”	Fox Walker		1925

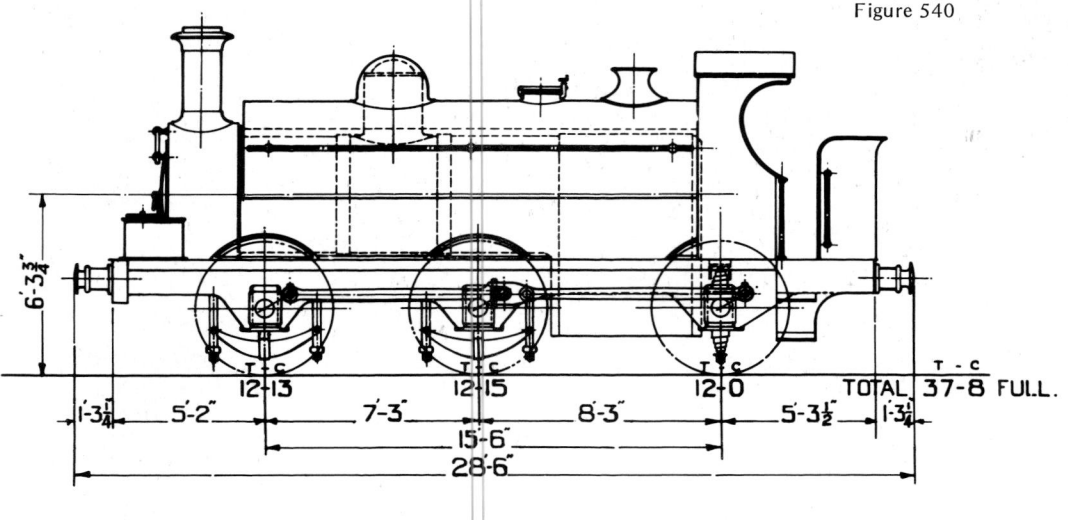

Figure 540

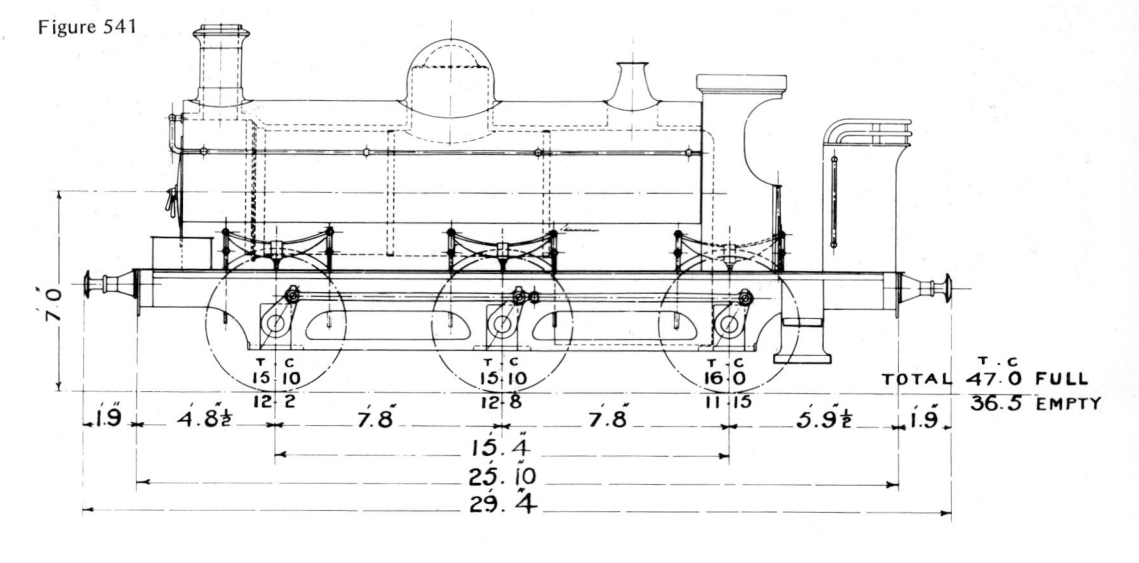

Figure 541

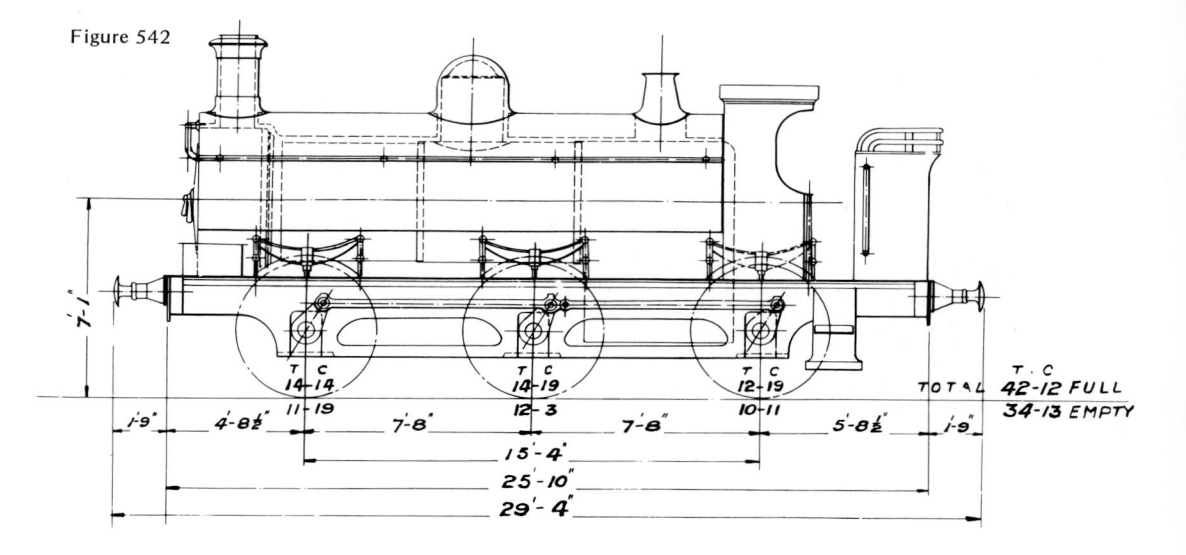

Figure 542

Naturally on such a small undertaking as the S.W.M. Railway there was only a small stock of engines, and apart from the earliest, which do not concern this work, all came from the GWR, only to return to the fold at the grouping. When the S.W.M. Railway was converted from broad gauge to standard gauge in 1872, the Great Western supplied the Company with three '645' class saddle tanks, brand new from Wolverhampton. These became Nos. 1, 2 and 3, and in 1873 another engine of the same series joined the first three and became No. 4. Although Nos. 1 and 3 were withdrawn in 1910, and Nos. 2 and 4 went into the ownership of Glyncorrwg Colliery in 1908, they are mentioned here, because No. 4 was still reported at the colliery as late as 1926, four years after the grouping. The diagram in *Figure 540* shows the design and wheelbases of No. 4, which was standard to all four. The engines handed over in 1922 were five in all, numbered 6/7/5/3/1. Nos. 6 and 7 became GW Nos. 817 and 818 and were originally South Devon saddle tanks built to broad gauge standards by the Avonside Engine Co. in 1873.

Both engines went through Swindon Works in 1910 when No. 7 was refitted with a Metro boiler, and No. 6 acquired a new boiler with a Belpaire firebox. Two Diagrams were issued, No. 7 was given A.92 as in *Figure 541*, and by some error No. 6 was allotted A.91 shown in *Figure 542*, but this must be incorrect, as it does not show the Belpaire firebox.

Figure 543

S.W.M. Railway engine No. 7 which became GW No. 818 was rebuilt again in 1924, with a Belpaire firebox boiler, and having pannier tanks replacing the old saddle tanks. The photographs on this page show both No. 817, in *Figure* 543 with the saddle tanks just before being scrapped in 1926, and two views of No. 818 as rebuilt in 1924. She lasted in this condition until 1932. The other three engines handed over in 1922 were already pure Great Western types and therefore need no illustrating. They were S.W.M. Nos. 5, 3 and 1 of the '1501' class, originally numbered 1546, 1806 and 1811. They reverted to their old 'Western' numbers upon returning to the fold.

Figure 544   Figure 545   Page 221

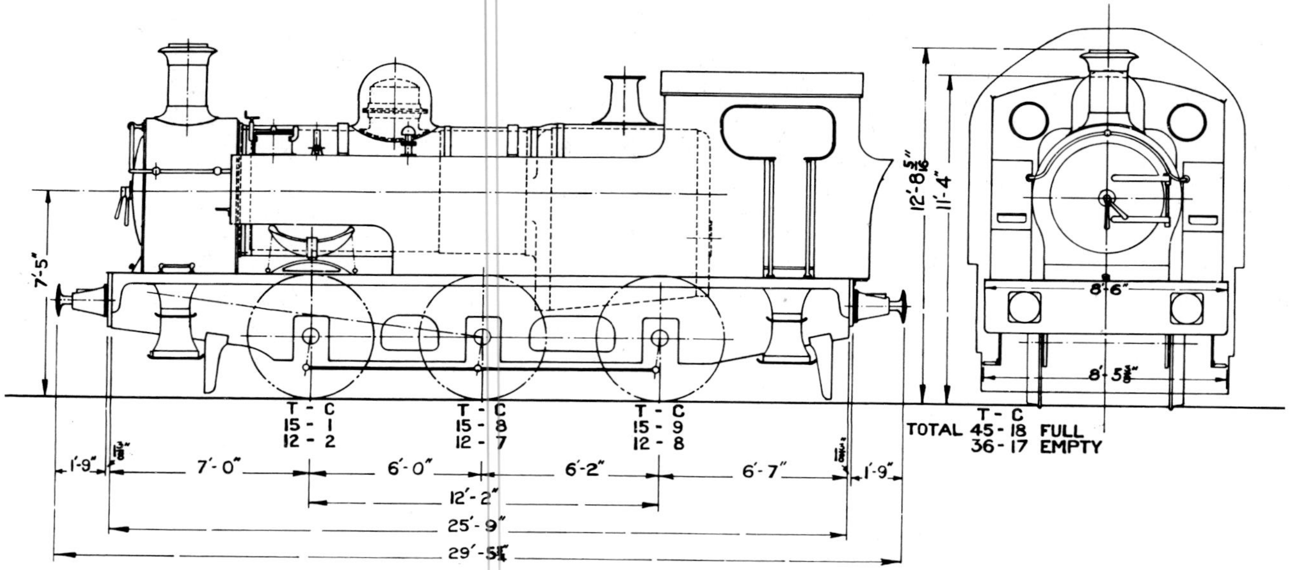

Figure 546

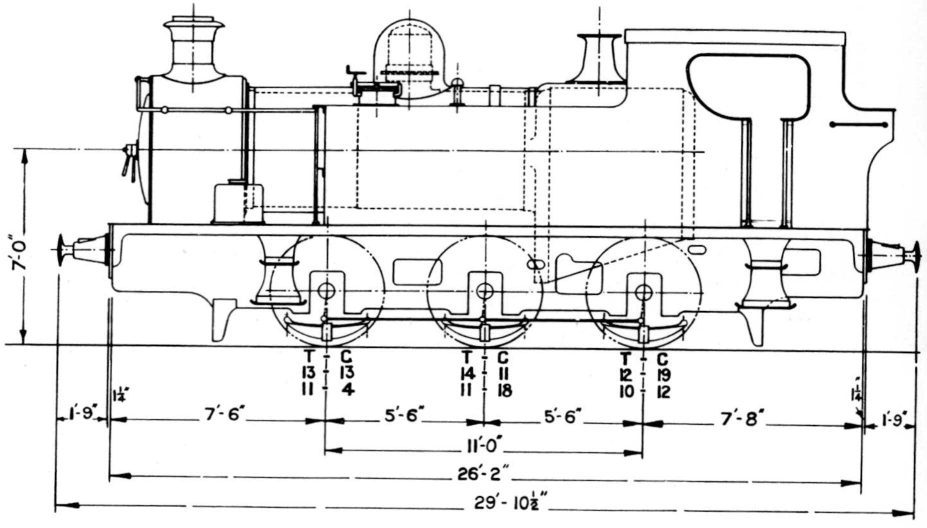

12'-8 5/16"
11'-4"

8'-6"

7'-5"

8'-5 3/8"

T - C
15 - 1
12 - 2

T - C
15 - 8
12 - 7

T - C
15 - 9
12 - 8

T - C
TOTAL 45 - 18 FULL
36 - 17 EMPTY

1'-9"   7'-0"   6'-0"   6'-2"   6'-7"   1'-9"

12'-2"

25'-9"

29'-5 1/4"

Figure 547

7'-0"

T   C
13   13
11   4

T   C
14   11
11   18

T   C
12   12
10   12

1'-9"   1 1/4"   7'-6"   5'-6"   5'-6"   7'-8"   1'-9"   1 1/4"

11'-0"

26'-2"

29'-10 1/2"

12'-8 1/2"
11'-6 5/8"

8'-4"
8'-6"

7'-4 1/4"

8'-4"

T - C
14 - 10
11 - 14

T - C
15 - 10
12 - 11

T - C
15 - 11
12 - 12

T - C
TOTAL 45 - 11 FULL
36 - 17 EMPTY

1'-9"   1"   6'-9"   6'-3"   5'-9"   7'-1"   1"   1'-9"

12'-0"

25'-10"

29'-6"

Figure 548

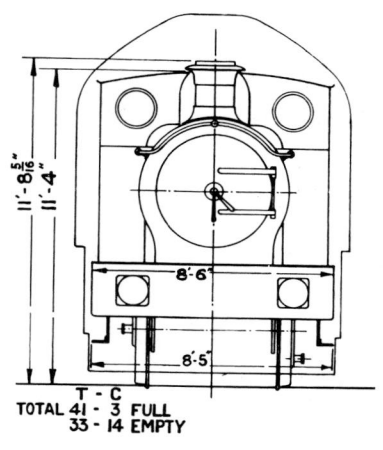

11'-8 5/16"
11'-4"

8'-6"

8'-5"

T - C
TOTAL 41 - 3 FULL
33 - 14 EMPTY

The next pages refer to the eight engines previously owned by the L. & M.M. Railway.

Upon being absorbed by the GWR all eight were allotted their new numbers, but *Merkland* and *Seymour Clarke* never actually carried the plates. *Merkland* although only built in 1912, was sent to Swindon in 1923 and was condemned immediately; *Seymour Clarke* on the other hand was constructed in 1875 by Fox Walker, worked on Tyneside until 1885, was transferred to the L. & M.M. and rebuilt by Avonsides in 1903. Making the one-way trip to Swindon in 1923, it was finally condemned in 1925.

Tarndune, one of the Hudswell Clarke engines, was a twin of *Merkland* but unlike her short-lived sister, she was refitted with new boiler and Belpaire firebox, a GWR smokebox, chimney and safety valve, numbered 339, had the nameplates removed, and was allotted Diagram B.37 (*Figure 546*). *Ravelston*, another Hudswell Clarke side tank was also sent to Swindon in 1923 and emerged in 1927 as No. 803 with a renovated boiler, Belpaire firebox, GW smokebox and safety valve, plus an extended bunker, and was given Diagram B.38 seen in *Figure 547*. *George Waddell* the Andrew Barclay engine of 1907 was similarly treated, and had Diagram B.45 (*Figure 548*) drawn for her, and was given No. 312. This engine worked on at Llanelly until 1934 finally being sold in 1935 to Broomhill Collieries, not being scrapped until 1961.

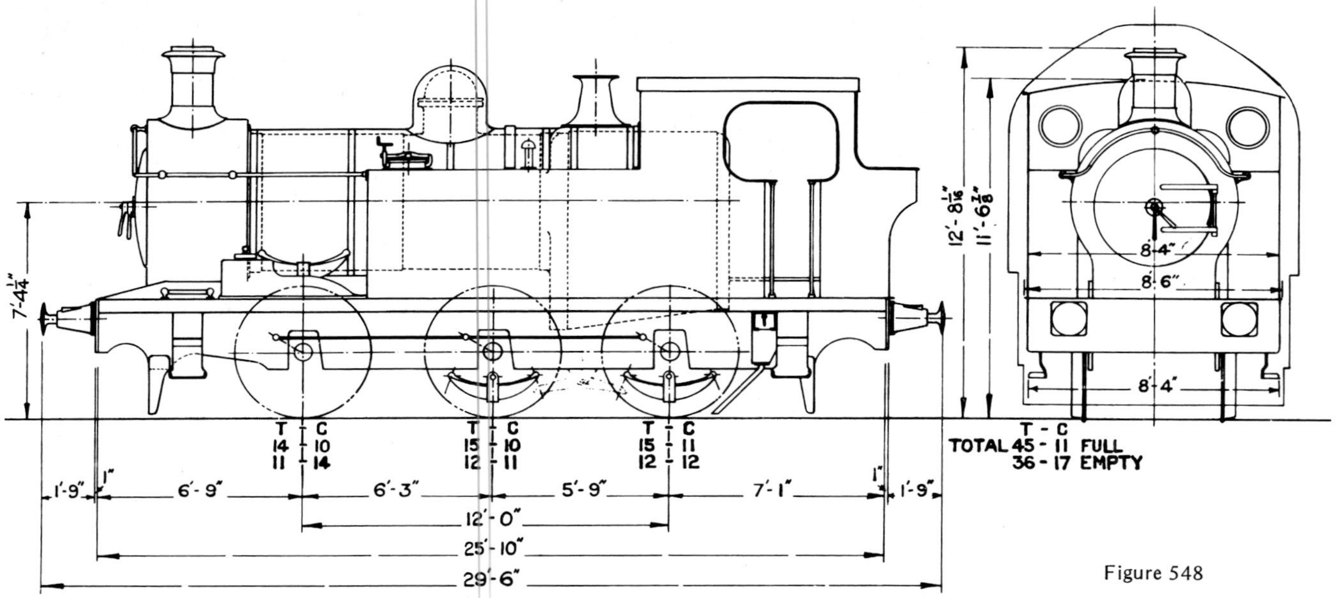

Figure 549   Figure 550

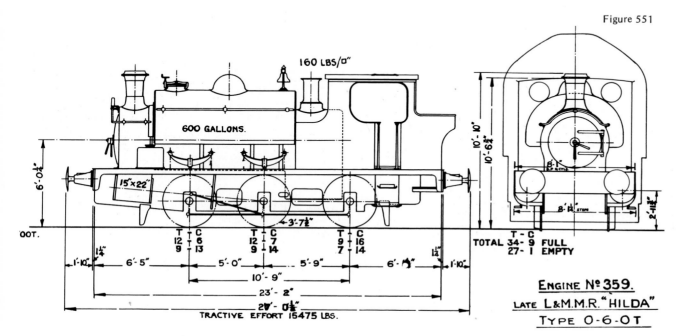

Figure 551

160 LBS/□″

600 GALLONS.

15″×22″

ENGINE Nº 359.

LATE L&M.M.R. "HILDA"

TYPE O-6-OT

TRACTIVE EFFORT 15475 LBS.

A like fate awaited *Great Mountain*, staying on her home ground until 1928 when eventually being sold to Hatfield Main Collieries she worked on as *Hatfield No. 4* until 1964 at least.

But perhaps the most well known of the L. & M.M. engines was the Hudswell Clarke saddle tank, given the name *Hilda*. Built in 1917, she passed through the Works in 1926, with a minimum of rebuilding, having an extension of sorts to her bunker, and the inevitable safety valve bonnet, and unlike her sisters keeping her name plates as well as becoming GW No. 359. In passing out she was given Diagram B.34 (*Figure* 551) and returned to Swansea Docks where she acquired the warning bell mounted on the tank top. The two pictures in *Figures* 549 and 550 show No. 359 in both right-hand and left-hand three quarter views.

Figure 552

Figures 552 and 553 show two enlargements of *Hilda* taken at Danygraig shed in 1948, just prior to the fitting of BR smokebox number plates. The little engine lasted out until 1954 before being withdrawn. Perhaps a few dimensions would be of interest. The six coupled wheels were of 3' 7½" diameter, set at 5' 0" and 5' 9" centres. The boiler was 8' 10" x 3' 11" and 3' 10", and the firebox had an area of 74 square feet. The water tank held 600 gallons, and the working weight was 34½ tons.

Figure 553

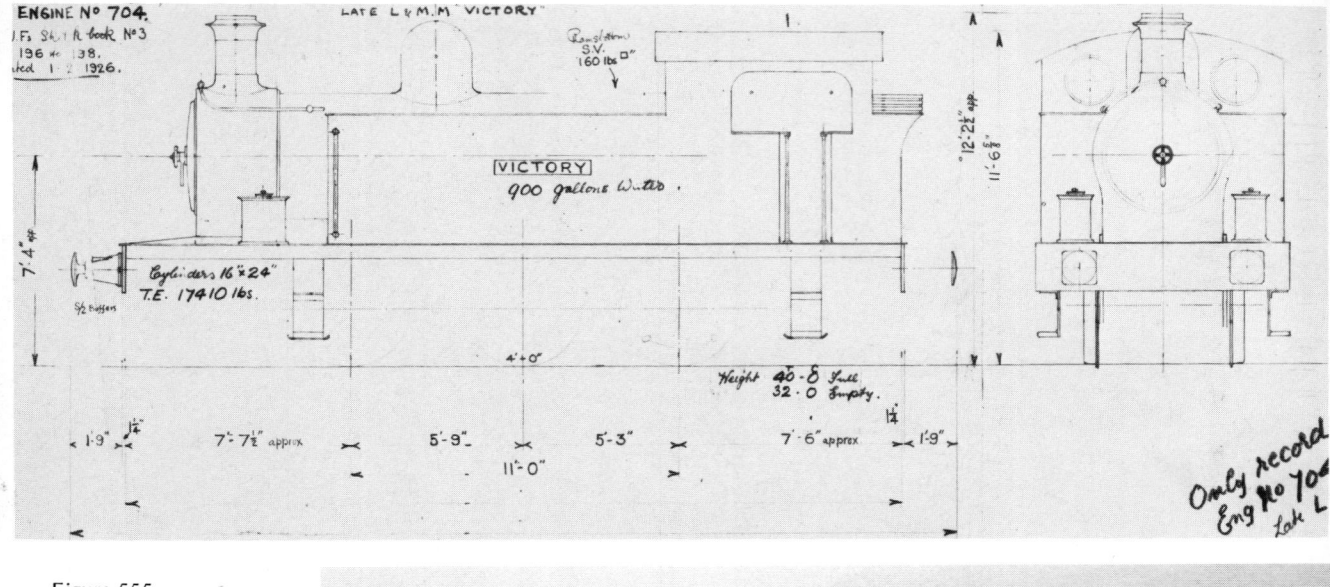

Figure 554   Figure 555

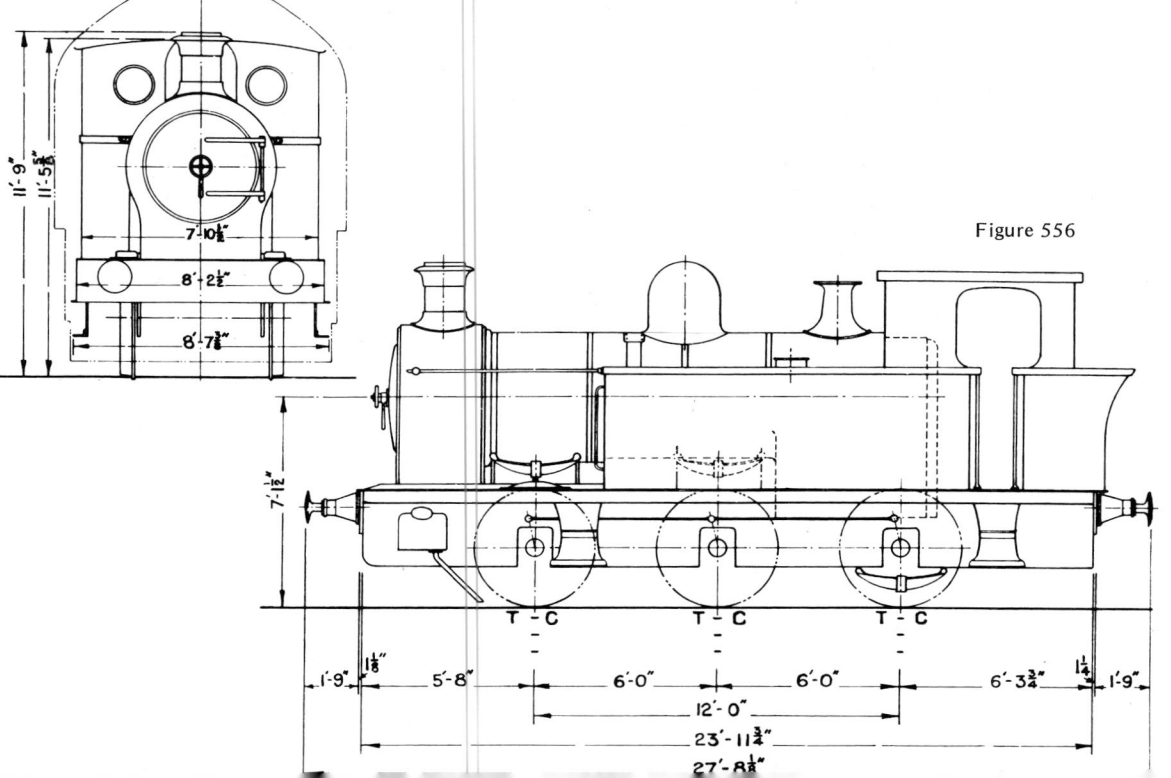

Figure 556

Figure 557

GW No. 944 seen in *Figure 554*, was the L. & M.M. engine *Great Mountain* mentioned before, built by Avonside Engine Co. and delivered in 1902. Her wheels were 4′ 0″ diameter set at 6′ 0″ and 6′ 0″ centres, and her side tanks held 900 gallons. The GWR issued Diagram B.50 for this engine, seen in *Figure 556* and gave her a short parallel chimney and an enlarged bunker.

The last L. & M.M. engine to be illustrated is *Victory*, built in 1920 by Manning Wardle & Co. The GWR took her name plates off, and numbered her 704 (*Figure 557*). No Diagram was ever issued for this locomotive, but I did make this copy from the Swindon Diagram book, and it is reproduced just as it was found (*Figure 555*). No. 704 was eventually scrapped at Caerphilly in 1943.

The NEATH & BRECON RAILWAY COMPANY

The Neath & Brecon Railway, obviously, ran from Neath, through Crynant, Onllwyn, Colbren Junction, Craig-y-nos, Cray, Sennybridge, Aberbran and Cradoc to Brecon. The opening date through to Brecon was 1867, a small branch ran from Colbren Junction to Ynys-y-Geinon Junction, where through trains to Swansea could be routed, with the sanction of the Swansea Vale Railway. In 1874 the Midland Railway took over the S.V. Railway and had an agreement with the Neath & Brecon to work their line. This arrangement meant that the N. & B. engines were confined to the Neath — Colbren Junction section until 1903.

The GWR absorbed the Neath & Brecon in 1922, but the newly constituted London, Midland & Scottish Railway continued to work the services until 1930 after which date, the Great Western finally assumed control. At the grouping the Neath & Brecon had 15 locomotives to pass on to the GWR, and they are set out hereunder:—

N. & B. No.	GWR No.	Type	GW Diagram	Maker	Withdrawn
1	2199	0-6-0T	A.107/B.18	Avonside E.	1931
2	2189	”	A.108	”	1931
3	1882	”	E./A.25	GWR	1946
5	1392	4-4-0T	G.	Yorkshire E.	1926
6	1400	2-4-0T	R.	Sharp-Stewart	1926
7	2174	0-6-0T	A.104	Nasmyth Wilson	1927
8	2175	”	A.104	”	1933
9	1327	0-6-2T	W.	Stephenson	1929
10	1371	”	W./A.35	”	1929
11	1114	”	A.16	”	1930
12	1117	”	A.16	”	1930
13	1277	”	A.16	”	1929
14	1563	0-6-0T	B./A.22	GWR	1931
15	1591	”	B.	”	(cut up) 1922
16	1715	”	E./A.25	”	1949

Figure 558

Figure 559

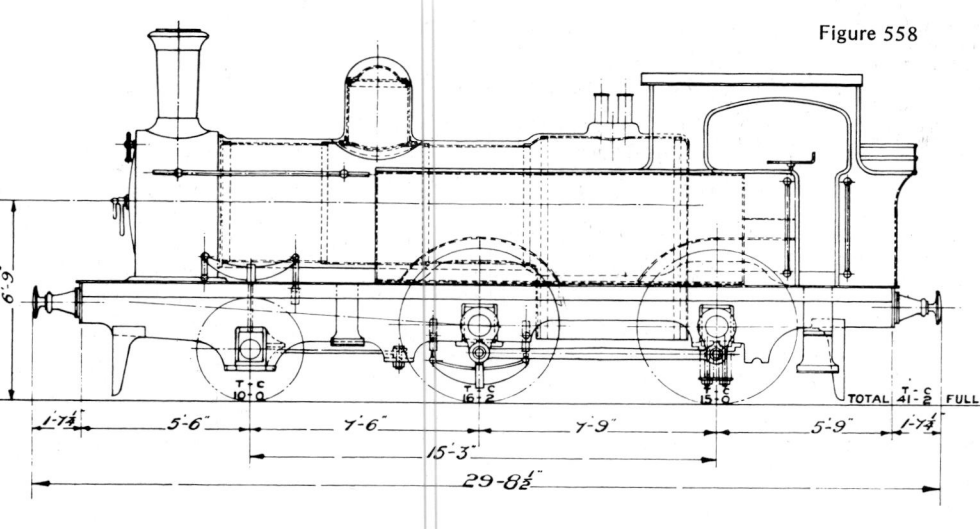

In 1872 the Avonside Engine Co. supplied the Neath & Brecon Railway with two 0-6-0 saddle tank engines which proved themselves so well, that four more similar were ordered, so that by 1874 there were six in the small class. They were originally numbered 5 to 10. Three years later Nos. 7 and 8 were purchased by the Brecon and Merthyr, and Nos. 5, 6, 9

and 10 became N. & B. Nos. 1-4. No. 3 was cut up by the GWR in 1909, and No. 4 was sold in 1916, which left two engines only to be absorbed in 1922, numbers 1 and 2. Swindon prepared Diagram A.107 for No. 1, seen in *Figure* 560, and renumbered this engine to 2199. No. 2 became GW No. 2189 and both the photograph in *Figure* 559 and the Diagram A.108 in *Figure* 561, show this locomotive, after rebuilding in 1921.

Figure 560

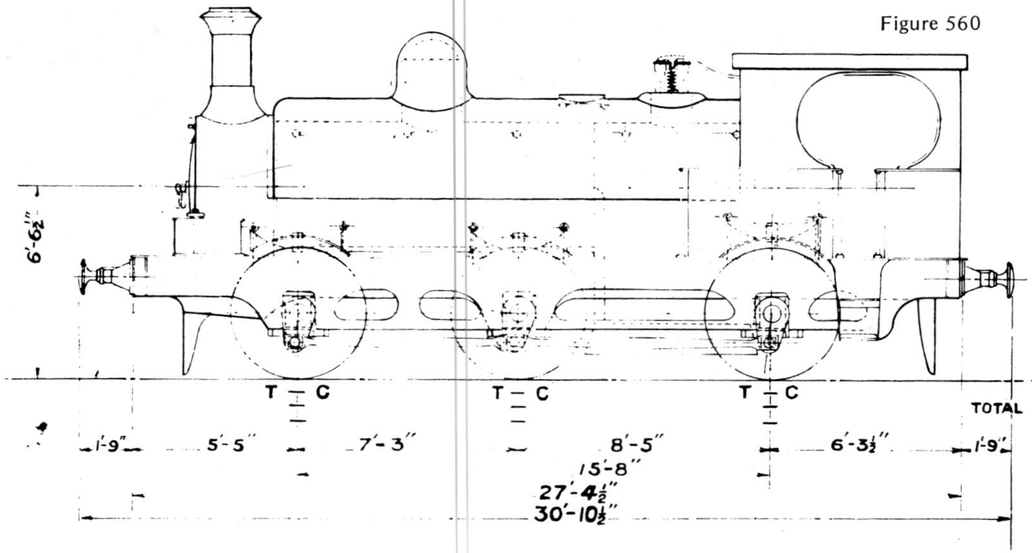

Figure 561

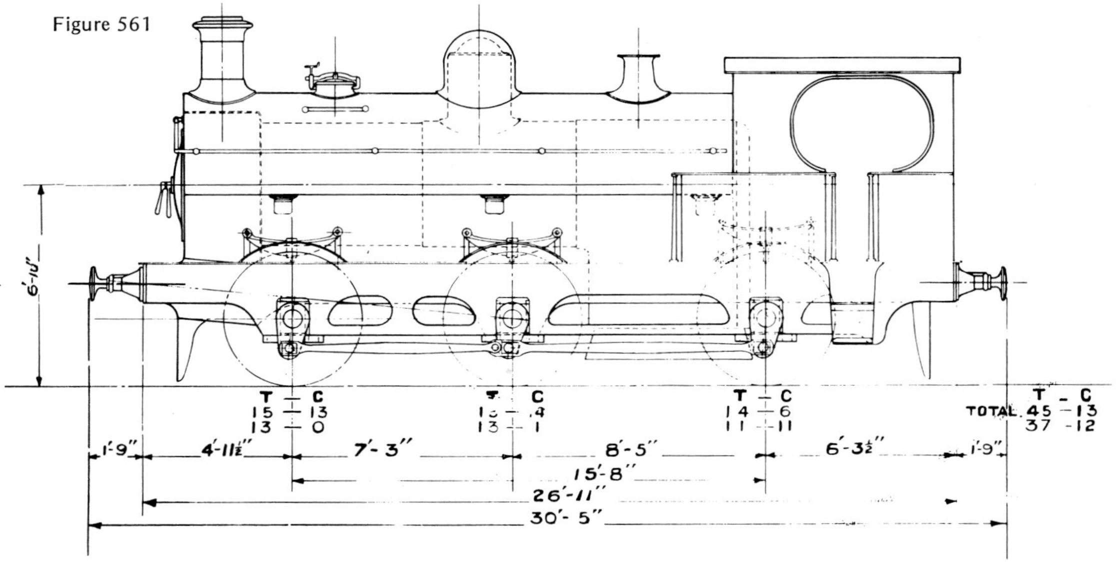

Figure 562

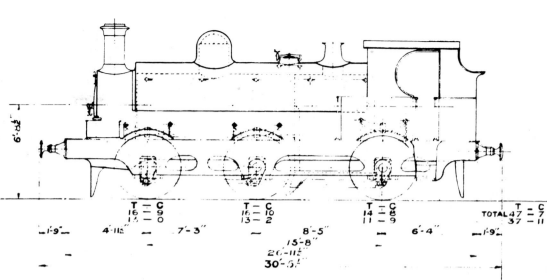

Figure 563

Figure 564

No. 1 which became GW No. 2199 is seen in *Figure* 562 as rebuilt at Swindon in 1924, and offered for sale at Swindon in 1932. She was bought by R. Frazer & Sons, who passed her on to Broomhill Collieries, Northumberland. *Figure 564* shows the engine at these collieries in 1949, six years before being condemned and cut up. The GWR drawing office issued Diagram B.18 for this rebuild, and although a poor copy, it is shown in *Figure* 563. Both Nos. 1 and 2 had 4′ 7″ coupled wheels set at 7′ 3″ and 8′ 5″ centres.

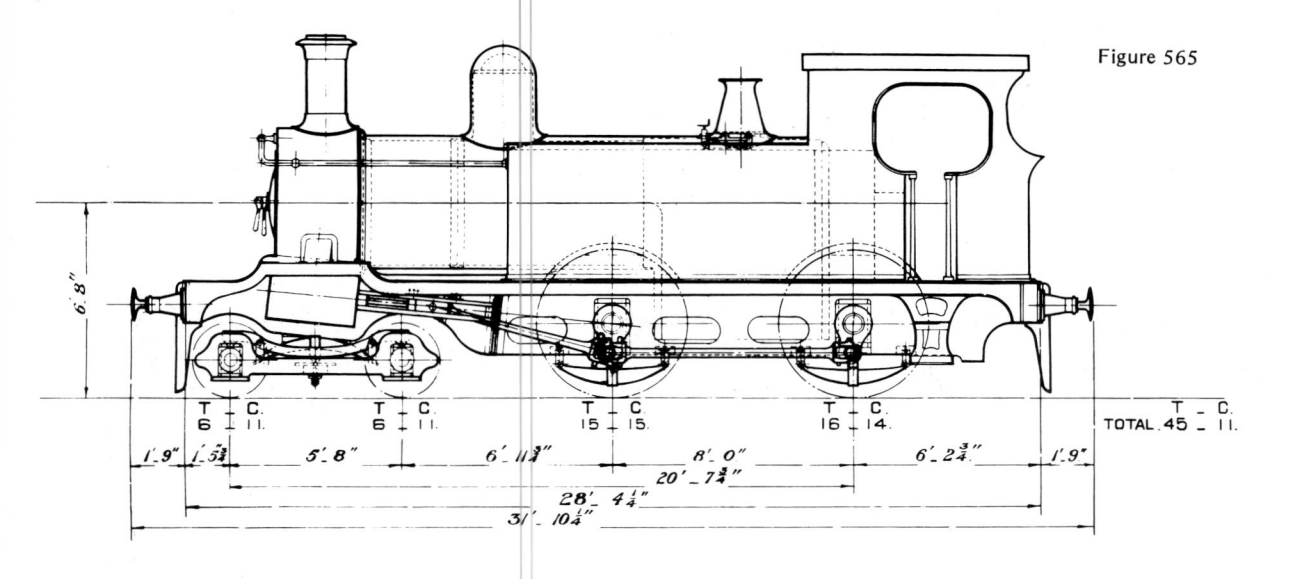

Figure 565

There was only one engine of the 4-4-0T classification handed over to the GWR by the Neath & Brecon. This was originally No. 4, and was built by the Yorkshire Engine Co. in 1871. A very handsome little engine with polished brass, and copper-topped chimney, the photograph in *Figure 567* shows the engine as new, with taper chimney and open cab. The driving wheels were 5' 0" diameter at 8' centres, and the leading bogie had four wheels of 2' 8" diameter. In 1884 the engine was renumbered 5 and rebuilt with a closed cab and new boiler over the ensuing fourteen years (*Figure 566*).

In 1921 No. 5 came out of Swindon factory after a major overhaul. Several modifications were made, such as GWR safety valves and parallel chimney, and the Diagram G (*Figure 565*) was issued to cover. Number plates were fixed to the tank sides, which proclaimed her as GW No. 1392, and as such, she worked on until 1926.

Figure 566   Figure 567

Figure 568

The Directors of the Neath & Brecon having seen with interest the success of the small passenger engines of the Barry Railway, the class 'C' 2-4-0Ts, decided to order one for themselves. Messrs Sharp-Stewart delivered the engine in 1893 and it received the number 6 (*Figure* 568) and was rostered to work the passenger traffic together with No. 5 previously described. The little Sharp-Stewart was built with 5' 3" driving wheels set at a wheelbase of 7' 9", and the leading axle had wheels of 3' 6" diameter. A new boiler similar to the original, was made at Swindon in 1908 for this engine, and a GWR smokebox and chimney were fitted at the same time. At the grouping Swindon gave the engine Diagram R seen in *Figure* 558 on *page* 228. The photograph above shows the locomotive during her Neath & Brecon days. When she entered into Great Western stock, she was renumbered 1400. In 1926 she was placed on the Sales List, but no offers were forthcoming and she was cut up late in 1928.

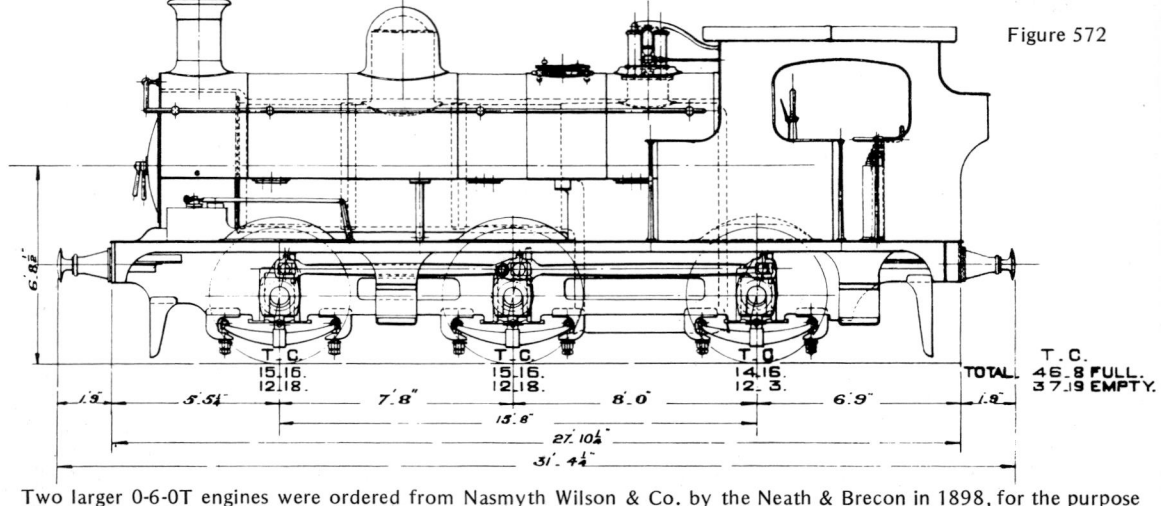

Figure 572

Figure 569

Figure 570

Two larger 0-6-0T engines were ordered from Nasmyth Wilson & Co. by the Neath & Brecon in 1898, for the purpose of handling the increasing coal traffic. They were saddle tanks and received the numbers 7 & 8. Driving wheels were 4' 7'' diameter and the wheelbases were 7' 8'' and 8' 0'', giving a total of 15' 8''. Water capacity of the tanks was 990 gallons and the working weight came out at 46½ tons. Both engines were rebuilt by the GWR before the Grouping and given Diagram A.104 (*Figure 572*). No. 7 became GW No. 2174 and No. 8 was renumbered 2175. The upper illustration (*Figure 569*) shows No. 8 in Neath & Brecon ownership, and the centre picture shows the same engine at Swindon, where she acted as works pilot after being withdrawn in 1933, carrying the Swindon plates No. 2175.

The last engines built for the Neath & Brecon, were three 0-6-2T locomotives, constructed by Stephenson's in 1904. The design was almost the same as the 'M' class series, which Stephenson's built for the Rhymney Railway. The Neath & Brecon trio were numbered 11, 12 and 13, and had six coupled wheels of 4' 6'' diameter at 7' 3'' and 8' 0'' centres, with a trailing truck having 3' 6'' diameter wheels with large capacity water tanks capable of holding 1,600 gallons. No. 13 was repaired at Swindon in 1917, and the Diagram issued for the class A.16 (*Figure 573*) shows the series in this condition. *Figure 571* gives an idea of the size of these large tanks, with No. 11 seen in Neath & Brecon days. In 1922 the three engines were given the GW Nos. 1114, 1117 and 1277. No. 1114 received a GW type smokebox and parallel chimney in 1921, and No. 1277 was refitted with a 'Western' type bunker.

All three were withdrawn in 1929-30.

Figure 571

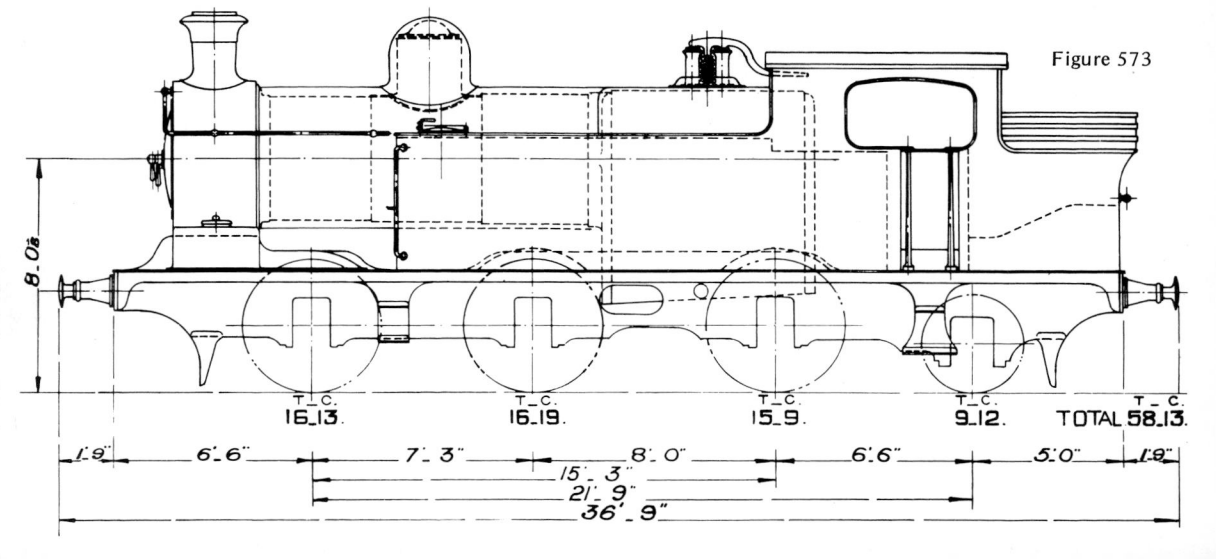

Figure 573

The
VALE OF RHEIDOL
LIGHT RAILWAY COMPANY

One of the many narrow gauge railways of Wales, the Vale of Rheidol line had its headquarters at Aberystwyth and following the valley of the Yswyth, climbed, slowly at first, and then steeply towards the end of the 11¾ miles to a terminus at Devil's Bridge. Operating commenced in 1902 but passenger traffic did not start until the last two weeks of that year. This small light railway was amalgamated with the Cambrian Railway ten years later, in July of 1913 in fact, and after another decade had passed, the ownership changed again, and the GWR took over the management. Strange to relate, that in this year of writing (1977) the locomotives of the Vale of Rheidol are the only steam railway engines to be owned and maintained by British Rail, as seen in *Figure 574* (overleaf).

Figure 574

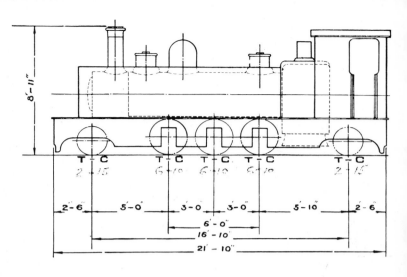

Figure 577

As a private company, the V. of R. owned three locomotives. One small 2-4-0T built by Bagnall's of Stafford and sold to the Talybont Quarries, found its way on to the Rheidol stock in 1903. She became No. 3 and was named *Rheidol*. At the grouping she was renumbered GW 1198, but was withdrawn in 1924. A Diagram was issued for this engine and was lettered Q and can be seen in *Figure* 579.

The other two engines were much larger, and were of the 2-6-2T classification. Built specially for the 1' 11½" gauge, by Messrs Davies and Metcalfe of Manchester, they were used to open the line in 1902, and were painted deep ochre. On being taken into Cambrian stock they were repainted green with black and white lining. No. 1 was named *Edward VII* and No. 2 *Prince of Wales*. In 1922 Swindon issued Diagram X to cover these two narrow gauge engines (*Figure* 576) and renumbered them GW 1212 and GW 1213. The two illustrations on this page show No. 1213 in *Figure* 575, still as built with Stephenson valve gear and boiler fittings, and in *Figure* 577 No. 1212 as fitted with GWR fittings in 1923, but still with the Stephenson gear in place.

Figure 578

Page 236

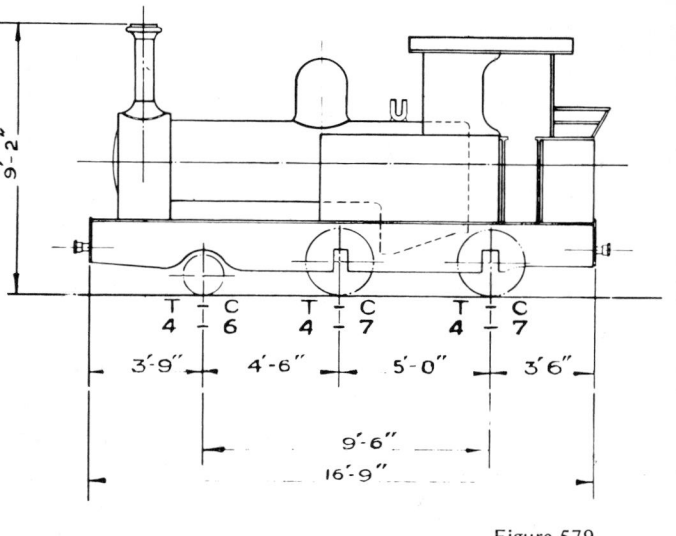

Figure 579

Figure 580

No. 1213 (old No. 2), was taken into Swindon factory in 1923 and returned to service in 1924, with a new boiler and fittings, larger cylinders, and Walschaerts gear in place of the original Stephenson's. Swindon decided to add to the Vale of Rheidol stock by building two new engines at the factory, to practically the Davies and Metcalfe design, and in 1923 Nos. 7 & 8 were produced. When British Railways assumed ownership, No. 7 was named *Owain Glyndŵr*, No. 8 became *Llywelyn*, and old No. 1213 was renumbered once more and joined the GWR pair in becoming No. 9, keeping her original name *Prince of Wales*. *Figure* 578 shows this engine in BR days at Devil's Bridge station in August of 1959 so numbered and named. Although not strictly fitting into this work, an official photograph of GWR No. 8 is shown in *Figure* 580, which shows clearly how closely Swindon followed the original D & M design.

The WELSHPOOL & LLANFAIR LIGHT RAILWAY COMPANY

Another small narrow gauge line, absorbed into the Great Western Railway in 1922, was the nine miles of 2' 6" track which ran from Welshpool to Llanfair Caereinion. This light railway was worked by the Cambrian Railway for a large percentage of the revenue, but not actually owned by the C.R. There were two engines only, both built by Beyer-Peacock Co. in 1902. They were No. 1 named *The Earl*, and No. 2 called *The Countess* seen in *Figure* 581 (overleaf).

Figure 581

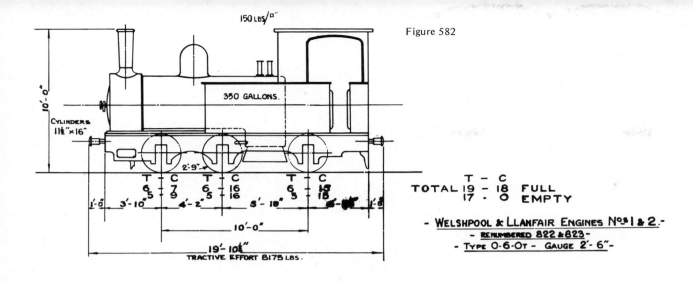

Figure 582

350 GALLONS.

150 LBS/□"

CYLINDERS
11½"×16"

10'-0"

2'-9"

T — C   T — C   T — C
6   7   6   16   6   15
5   9   5   16   5   15

1'-6"   3'-10"   4'-2"   5'-10"   6'-8½"   1'-6"

10'-0"

19'-10½"
TRACTIVE EFFORT 8175 LBS.

T — C
TOTAL 19 — 18 FULL
        17 — 0 EMPTY

- WELSHPOOL & LLANFAIR ENGINES Nos 1 & 2 -
- RENUMBERED 822 & 823 -
- TYPE 0-6-0T - GAUGE 2'-6" -

Upon being absorbed into the Great Western Railway Co. at the grouping No. 1 was renumbered GW 822, and No. 2 became GW 823, but both engines kept their names, although *The Countess* was abbreviated to *Countess*.

As usual Swindon drawing office followed the Cambrian Diagram closely and produced A.95 for these two engines as seen in *Figure 582* and the photograph of *The Countess* shows the engine in the 'as built' condition (*Figure 584*). Both Nos. 822 and 823 were rebuilt in 1930 being given new boilers, boiler fittings and tap feed, a new Diagram B.54 (*Figure 583*) being issued to show the new modifications.

No. 823 (seen overleaf in *Figure 584*) is shown at Llanfair Caereinion during 1952. Four years later both engines were put into store at Oswestry, and it is pleasant to report that these two 0-6-0T narrow gauge engines are once more in action with their new owners, the Welshpool and Llanfair Light Railway Preservation Society.

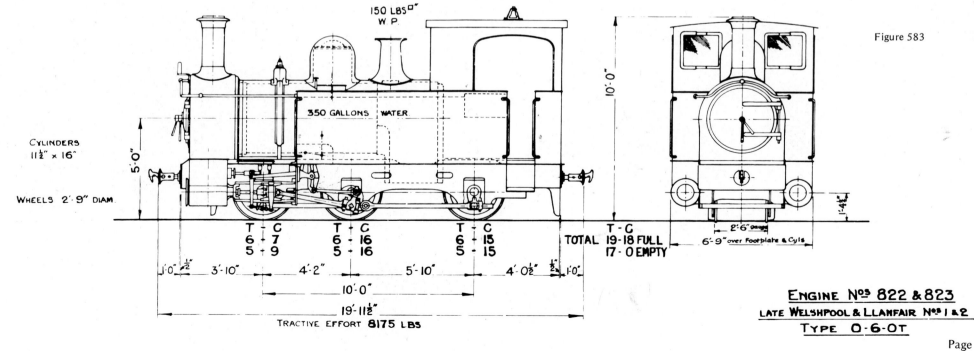

Figure 583

150 LBS□"
W.P.

350 GALLONS WATER

CYLINDERS
11½" × 16"

5'-0"

WHEELS 2'-9" DIAM.

10'-0"

T — C   T — C   T — C   T — C
6   7   6   16   6   15   TOTAL 19-18 FULL
5   9   5   16   5   15   17 - 0 EMPTY

1'-0" ½" 3'-10"   4'-2"   5'-10"   4'-0½" ½" 1'-0"

10'-0"

19'-11½"
TRACTIVE EFFORT 8175 LBS

2'-6" Gauge
6'-9" over Footplate & Cyls

1'-4½"

ENGINE Nos 822 & 823
LATE WELSHPOOL & LLANFAIR Nos 1 & 2
TYPE 0-6-0T

Page 239

THE COUNTESS

Figure 584

The CLEOBURY MORTIMER & DITTON PRIORS LIGHT RAILWAY COMPANY

A small Shropshire line of standard gauge, which, like the Welshpool only had two engines, was the Cleobury Mortimer & Ditton Priors. Opened in 1908, to work granite down from the Abdon Clee quarries to the GWR Leominster — Kidderminster branch at Cleobury Mortimer, the system consisted of twelve miles of route, with stopping places at Cleobury Town, Detton Ford, Prescott, Stottesdon, Aston Botterell, Burwarton, Cleobury North and the terminus at Ditton Priors.

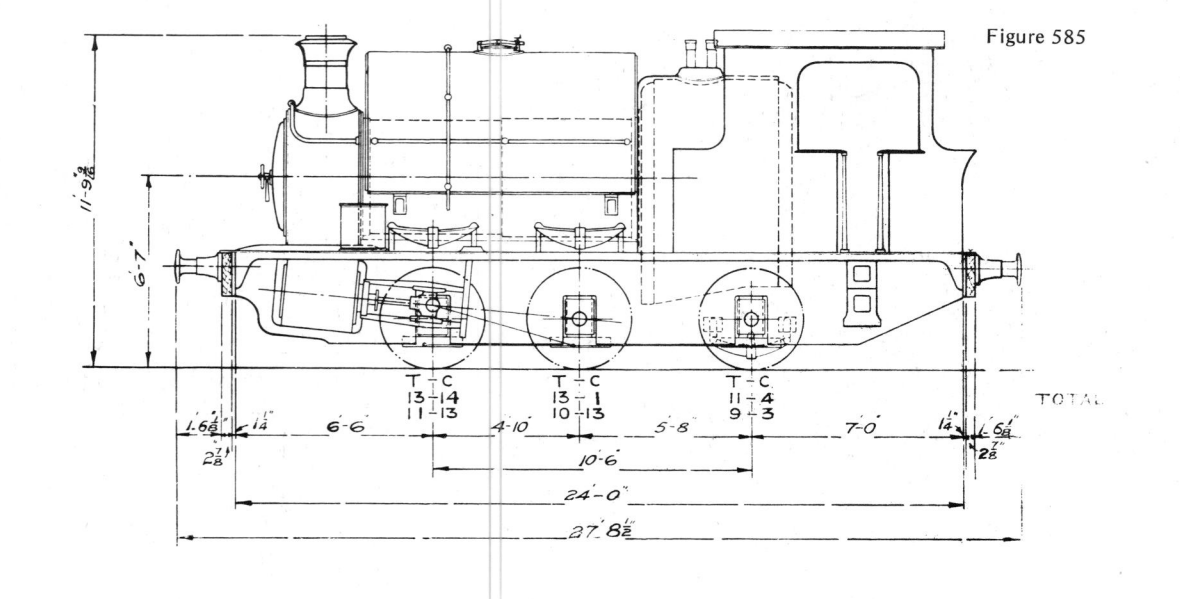

Figure 585

Both locomotives were 0-6-0T saddle tanks, by Manning Wardle & Co. with six coupled wheels of 3' 6" diameter, outside cylinders, and short saddle tanks resting on the centre section of the boiler. Whilst with their parent company they carried no numbers, but were named *Burwarton* and *Cleobury* respectively. When taken into the Great Western fold in 1922, *Cleobury* became GW No. 28, and *Burwarton* received the number 29. A Diagram was drawn for them and was enumerated A.101 (*Figure* 585). The photograph in *Figure 588* shows *Cleobury* after receiving attention at the GWR's shops, having repairs and alterations to boiler and firebox, a parallel chimney and an extension added to the bunker.

The sister engine *Burwarton* No. 29 was sent to Swindon works in 1924 and was completely transformed, emerging with a GW type domed boiler, with Belpaire firebox, a new enclosed cab, with a coal bunker in the 'Western' style and contours, and full length pannier tanks having a capacity of 850 gallons. Diagram B.30 was drawn and issued for the rebuild, and can be seen in *Figure 587*. It was deemed necessary to remove her nameplates at this time which always seemed a pity, and *Figure 586* shows No. 29 in the 1930's before she was fitted with a spark arresting chimney. *Cleobury* GW No. 28 also passed through the factory in 1931, and was rebuilt in the same way as her sister No. 29 and both engines continued on at the C.M. & D.P. L. Rly. until 1938 when the passenger service was discontinued. No. 29 was used at Hereford, Gloucester and Worcester, returning to Kidderminster in 1951 three years before withdrawal. No. 28 was on loan to a colliery at Wrexham and finally spent her last days at Dock Street, Newport, being withdrawn in 1953. *Figure 589* on page 244 is an excellent study by A.C. Sterndale of No. 28 outside the Drawing Office at Swindon in 1951, before going to the N.C.B. at Hafod.

Figure 587

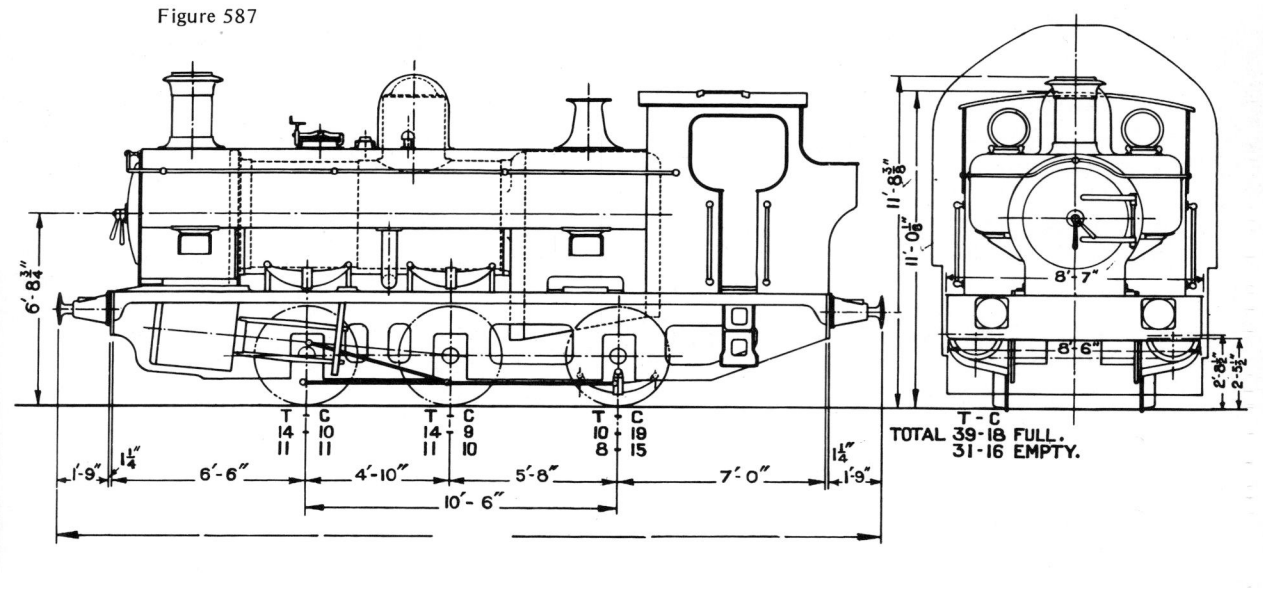

Figure 586

Figure 588

Figure 589

The WESTON, CLEVEDON & PORTISHEAD LIGHT RAILWAY COMPANY

The Great Western Railway served the Bristol Channel resorts of Weston-super-Mare, Clevedon and Portishead but never linked directly these three towns. The legacy of the old Bristol & Exeter Railway, meant that Weston was on a loop line from Uphill Jn. to Worle Jn., Clevedon was on a short branch from Yatton, and Portishead served from Bristol, via St. Annes Park Jn. In 1885 a new company was formed to achieve this direct linkage, and so the 'Weston-super-Mare, Clevedon, and Portishead (Steam—Tramways) Company' came into being.

This grandiose title was shortened in 1899 to 'Weston, Clevedon & Portishead Railway Co.' and the whole 14¼ miles, from Weston to Portishead Docks was opened in 1907. Unlike the foregoing railways which were absorbed into the GWR in 1922/3, the W.C. & P. L. Rly. was always independent, and was quite successful in the conveying of passengers between the three towns, especially during the summer months. The whole line was closed at the time of the retreat from Dunkirk in 1940, and as the Great Western was at that time one of the principal creditors, the company was entitled to some of the assets, which meant taking over the locomotives No. 2 and No. 4.

These engines were a couple of Stroudley 'Terriers' built in 1875 and 1877 at Brighton for the L.B.S.C. Rly. No. 2 was originally L.B.S.C. No. 43 *Gipsy Hill*, and No. 4 was L.B.S.C. No. 53 *Ashtead*. In 1899 and 1902, they were renumbered to 653 and 643, and rebuilt to A1X class in 1912/19. The Weston, Clevedon & Portishead purchased 643 in 1926, and 653 (later 2653) in 1937. Only No. 2 was named by the W.C. & P. L. Rly. becoming *Portishead*.

The GWR upon accepting these two 'Terriers', renumbered them 5 and 6 and they were overhauled in 1942, emerging in Great Western colours with the yellow roundel on the tank sides. Shedded at St. Philip's Marsh, Bristol they saw service on the Harbour lines, but No. 6 was withdrawn in 1948. No. 5 moved to Taunton, and on to Newton Abbot, before being confined to the stock shed in Swindon in 1950, being finally cut up in 1954. *Figure* 592 (on the next page) shows No. 5 at this late date outside 'A' erecting shop at Swindon, and the Diagram B.76 which was allotted to these two L.B.S.C. engines is shown in *Figure* 590. Although not taken on to GWR stock, one other engine of the W.C.P.L.Rly is shown on this page (*Figure* 591); this is No. 5 by Manning Wardle, seen coupled to one of the large bogie cars.

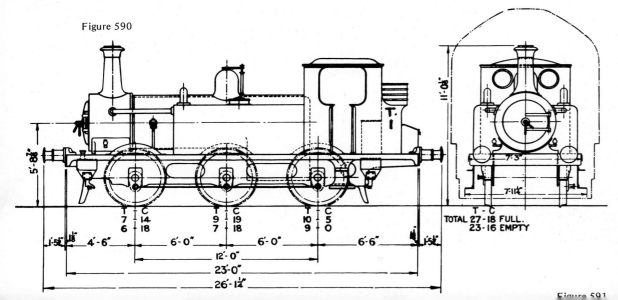

Figure 590

Figure 591

Figure 592

The
WANTAGE TRAMWAY

The Wantage Tramway was never absorbed by the Great Western Railway, but as one of the small engines was purchased by the GWR for preservation, this is surely excuse enough to include No. 5's photograph in this work. Wantage town itself was 2½ miles from the Great Western main line, and the nearest station on the Paddington-Swindon route, was Wantage Road, which explains why the Wantage Tramway came into being in 1875, to convey passengers and merchandise from the Great Western station, to the town of Wantage itself. At first, horse drawn vehicles were used, but steam traction became established until at one time as many as five steam engines of various types and ancestries were stabled at Wantage.

The two most satisfactory of these were No. 5 and No. 7. Taking No. 7 first, she was an 0-4-0 saddle tank built by Manning Wardle, new in 1888, bought from Manchester Ship Canal in 1893, and was the last engine to work on the Tramway, lifting the track in 1946. No. 5 *Shannon* seen in *Figure* 593 (on the next page) is now 120 years old, having been built by George England in 1857 for the Sandy and Patton Railway in Bedfordshire. This little line closed in 1862 and the engine passed to the Bedford and Cambridge Railway Contractor, one Joseph Firbank. From there she eventually found her way on to the LNWR, and was at work on the Cromford & High Peak line in 1863. Bought by the Wantage Tramway in 1878, she arrived in 1882 and remained there until being bought by the Great Western for £100 in 1946. She was restored and set up on a dais at Wantage Road Station. When the Station was closed, the little well tank passed to the Museum at Clapham, who put her in store, and in 1969, she was loaned to the Great Western Society at Didcot, who overhauled her, and ran her in steam at the 150th anniversary of steam passenger railways at Shildon in 1975.

Figure 593

WAR DEPARTMENT R.O.D's

Other engines which were absorbed into the GWR must include the Robinson designed 2-8-0 freight locomotives of the War Department after the First World War. Five hundred and seventeen of these engines were built between 1917 and 1919 by many locomotive builders all over the Kingdom, and their prime function was for service with the Railway Operating Division of the Royal Engineers in France during hostilities. Many of those built, did not get to the continent, but all those that did, eventually were returned to Britain, and the War Department began offering the engines for sale to any would-be buyers.

The GWR bought 20 in 1919 and these were as new, having only been built in that year. They were numbered 3000-19. A further eighty-four were hired, and having seen service in France, were not in very good order. These later engines were returned in 1921/2 and it was not until 1925 that the Great Western purchased 80 of these engines at £1,500 each and allotted them the numbers 3020-99. After a short while in service all this later batch of eighty, were gathered at Swindon Dump, and it was decided that 30 of the best should be 'Westernized' and numbered 3020-49. All the remainder were to be painted black, numbered 3050-99 and returned to traffic, whence they should be used until unfit, and then promptly scrapped. So it will be seen that the R.O.D. engines which lasted longest, and were maintained to a reasonable degree, were the numbers 3000-19 and 3020-49, many lasting into British Railways ownership. Included are photographs and a diagram representing this class.

Figure 594

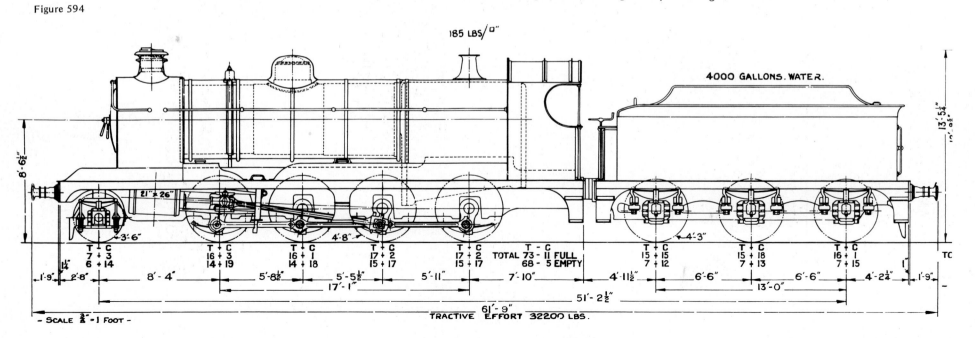

Figure 595

Page 250

Figure 596

Figure 597

The CORRIS RAILWAY COMPANY

The Corris Railway of 1858 was a small narrow gauge line, which ran from Machynlleth in the Dovey Valley to Upper Corris and on to Aberlleefeni, where slate was quarried in abundance. Together with the small branch spurs into the quarries, the mileage was just in excess of 12 miles. Eventually taken over by Imperial Tramways of Bristol in 1878, who started a passenger service five years later, the railway prospered until the owners instituted a road omnibus service into the Corris area.

The GWR took over the Corris Railway in 1929, at the same time as the Crosville Motor Co. took over the bus services of the district, and in 1931, all passenger services on the little line were withdrawn. The two engines which concern this work are Nos. 3 and 4. No. 3 was built in 1878 by the Falcon Engine & Car Co. with two similar engines as an 0-4-0T. Rebuilt in 1900 to 0-4-2T form, she was rebuilt yet again in 1926. Her sisters, Nos. 1 and 2 were condemned and a new 0-4-2T locomotive was purchased from Messrs Kerr-Stuart, which became No. 4. Swindon gave No. 4 Diagram O, and No. 3 received Diagram N (*Figures 598 and 599*).

In 1948, severe flooding of the River Dovey affected the bridge over the river, and left the two engines cut off from the Corris, down in the yard at Machynlleth, and it was there that Tom Rolt, Bill Trinder and myself discovered them, and eventually purchased them from Swindon for use on the Talyllyn Railway . . . but thereby hangs another tale!

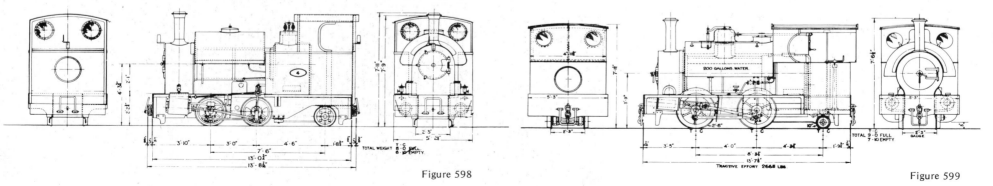

Figure 598

Figure 599

Figure 600

Figure 600 shows No. 4, and No. 3 is seen in Figure 601, both at Maespoeth shed, which was the small housing for the engines approximately halfway between Corris and Machynlleth.

Figure 601

POWLESLAND & MASON

Figure 602

This small business was not a railway company as such, it was a firm that had its own locomotives, which it used for hauling traffic about the Swansea Harbour Trust lines, on behalf of the Great Western Railway. As carting agents, the concern was started in 1865, by a Mr. Powlesland, who was joined ten years later, by a Mr. Mason, and these worthy gentlemen gave their names to the business.

Dealing exclusively in shuttling about the Swansea Docks, only diminutive steam engines were used, and it was not until 1924 that the collection of 9 locomotives were finally taken over by the GWR.

P.M. No.	GWR No.	Type	Diagram	Builder	Date	Withdrawn
3	696	0-4-0T		Peckett	1913	1952
4	779	"		Peckett	1916	1963
5	795	"	V	Brush Elec.	1903	Sold
6	921	"	U	Brush Elec.	1906	Sold
7	925	"	R	Avonside	1874	1929
11	927	"		Peckett	1907	1928
12	935	"		Peckett	1912	1961
14	928	"		Barclay	1912	1927
Dorothy	942	"	W	Hawthorn L.	1903	1955

At the top of the page in *Figure* 602, is P & M No. 12, one of the Peckett built tanks, of which the firm had four. This engine was built in 1912, and another sister engine was No. 4 in *Figure* 603, built in 1916. The third Peckett was No. 11, the oldest of the four, constructed in 1907. No. 3, the last of the quartet, was dated 1913. All four were renumbered by the GWR as can be seen in the table above, and Swindon issued Diagram Y which covered the S.H.T. Pecketts also.

Figure 603

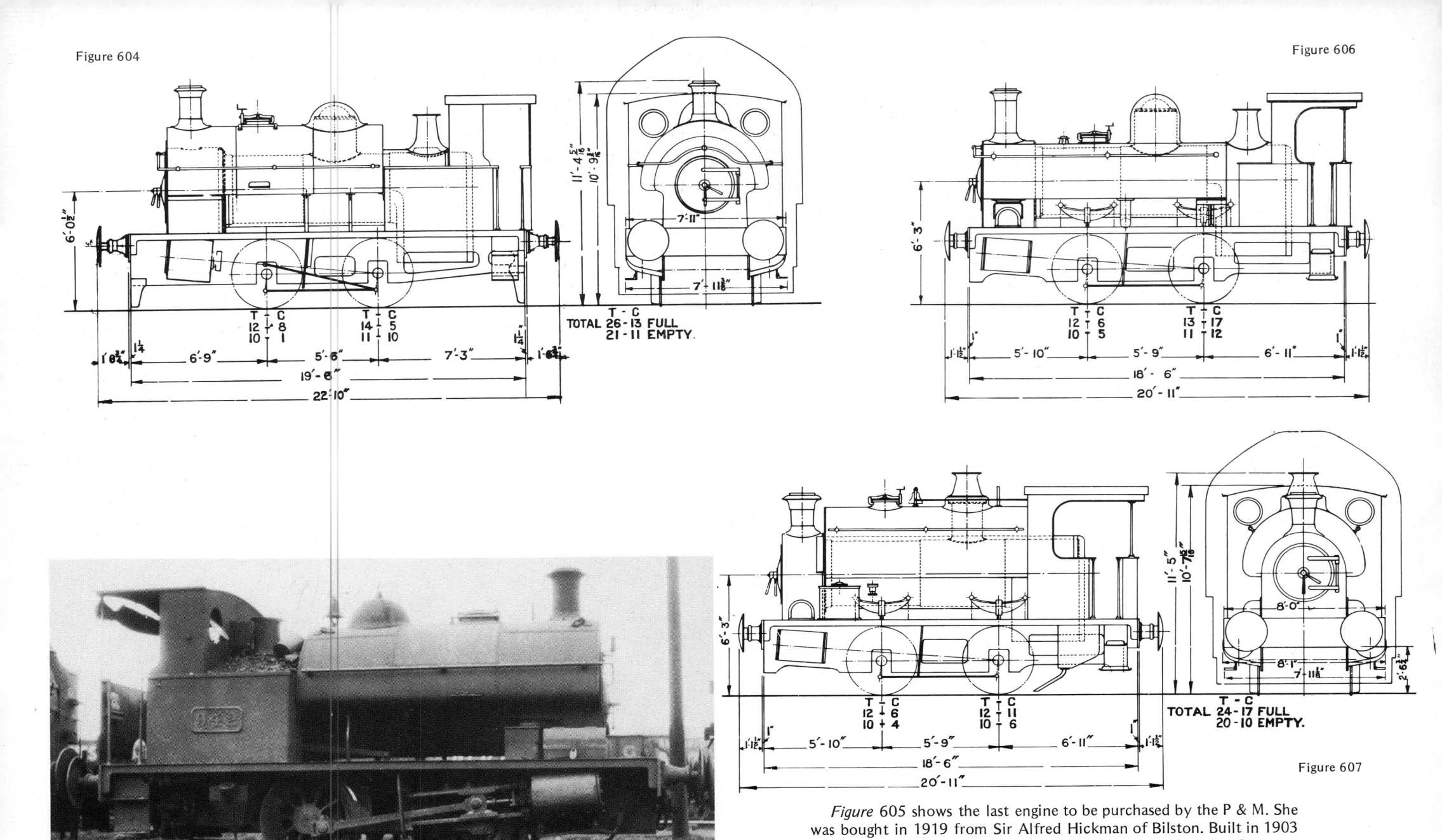

Figure 604

Figure 606

11' - 4 5/16"
10' - 9 1/2"
6' - 0 1/2"
7' - 11"
7' - 11 3/8"
T - C
TOTAL 26-13 FULL
21-11 EMPTY.
T - C
12 8
10 1
T - C
14 5
11 10
1 1/4
1 6 1/2
6' - 9"
5' - 6"
7' - 3"
1 1/4
19' - 6"
22' - 10"

6' - 3"
T - C
12 6
10 5
T - C
13 17
11 12
1"
1 - 1 1/2
5' - 10"
5' - 9"
6' - 11"
1 - 1 1/2
18' - 6"
20' - 11"

Figure 605

6' - 3"
T - C
12 6
10 4
T - C
12 11
10 6
1"
1 - 1 1/2
5' - 10"
5' - 9"
6' - 11"
1"
1 - 1 1/2
18' - 6"
20' - 11"

11' - 5"
10' - 7 1/16"
8' - 0"
8' - 0"
7' - 11 3/8"
2' - 6 1/2"
T - C
TOTAL 24-17 FULL
20-10 EMPTY.

Figure 607

Figure 605 shows the last engine to be purchased by the P & M. She was bought in 1919 from Sir Alfred Hickman of Bilston. Built in 1903 she worked at Spring Vale Furnaces until being transferred to Swansea. The Great Western fitted one of their own boiler mountings and numbered her 942, took away her name, and allotted Diagram W (*Figure* 604) to this little Hawthorn Leslie.

On this page is illustrated one of the two small engines which were built by Brush Electric Engineering Co. of Loughborough. They were Nos. 5 and 6 and the GWR renumbered them 795 and 921 respectively. No. 6 which was given Diagram U (*Figure* 607) remained very much as built after 1924, the exception being the combined dome and safety valve bonnet. On the other hand No. 5 (GW 795) was rebuilt at Swindon in 1926 with a "1376" class boiler, fittings and pannier tanks and the photograph in *Figure* 608 shows the result of this transformation. The Diagram V was issued to cover this rebuild and this is shown in *Figure* 606.

Figure 608

Figure 609

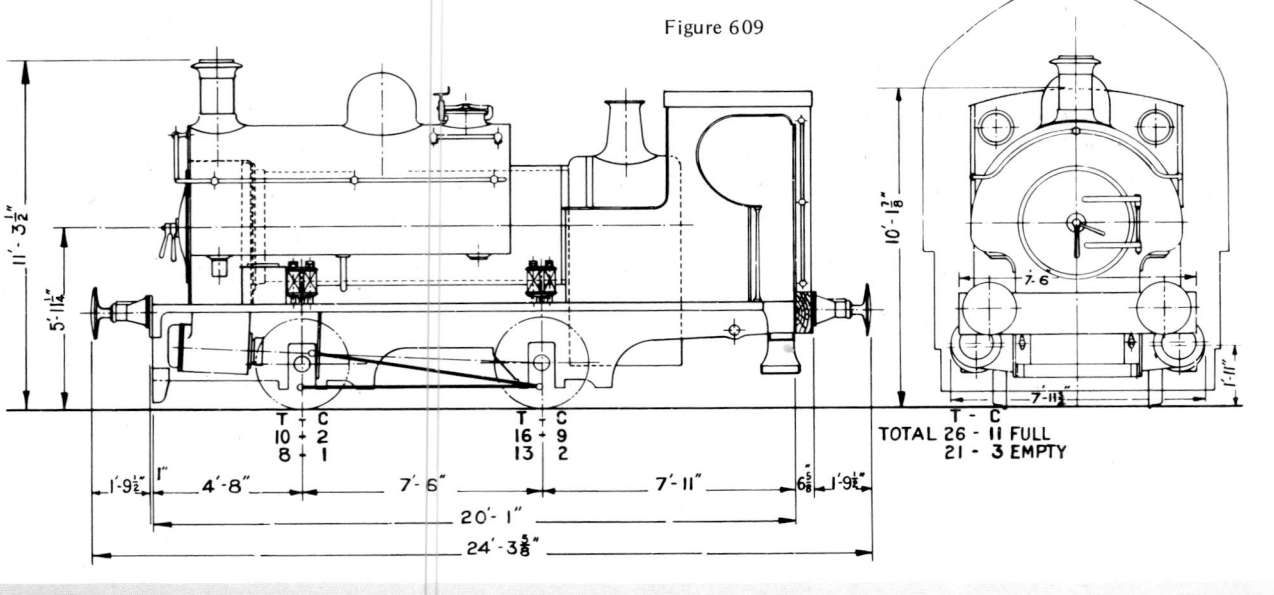

11' - 3½"

5' 11½"

T C
10 2
8   1

T C
16 9
13 2

1'-9½"
1"
4'-8"
7'-6"
7'-11"
6⅝"
1'-9¼"

20'-1"

24'-3⅝"

10' - 7⅞"

7-6

7-11½

1'-11"

TOTAL 26 - 11 FULL
21 - 3 EMPTY

The last P & M engine to be illustrated is No. 7, the oldest locomotive on the stock. She was one of four engines built in 1874 by the Avonside Engine Co. for the South Devon Railway. Starting life as broad gauge engines they came to the GWR in 1876 and were altered to the standard gauge. No. 7 was purchased by Powlesland & Mason and in 1924 became GW 925. She passed through the reconditioning test, and was turned out as shown in the official photograph in *Figure* 610, and to link up with this refit Diagram R was drawn (*Figure* 609).

Figure 610

GREAT WESTERN

925

ENGINES ON LOAN TO THE GREAT WESTERN RAILWAY

During the War years of 1939-45 the Great Western transferred 108 goods engines to the military authorities for use on foreign soil. These were the '2301' class 0-6-0 Dean Goods and many found their way all over the world, one or two even being reported in China! This exodus naturally left the GWR very short of freight locomotives, and to alleviate this desperate situation, arrangements were made to borrow engines from the other three main railway companies, LMS, SR and LNER.

The LNER for instance, passed over 40 0-6-0 goods tender engines of the J 25 type, class P.1, see *Figure* 611 for the diagram. The numbers were as under. . .

29 — 257 — 536 — 1725 — 1963 — 1964 — 1967 — 1969 — 1970 — 1973 — 1981 — 1982 — 1983 — 1986 — 1989 — 1992 — 1994 — 2000 — 2040 — 2043 — 2047 — 2051 — 2053 — 2058 — 2059 — 2061 — 2065 — 2069 — 2071 — 2072 — 2073 — 2075 — 2076 — 2126 — 2134 — 2135 — 2136 — 2138 — 2141 — 2142, and all these engines were handed back to the LNER by November 1946.

From the LMS another 40 similar engines were sent on loan, these were the Johnson Class 2 built for the Midland Railway between 1875-1902 and fitted with the LMS G6 boilers. Their numbers were . . . . 3023 — 3027 — 3038 — 3039 — 3047 — 3048 — 3071 — 3078 — 3081 — 3085 — 3090 — 3094 — 3096 — 3103 — 3108 — 3109 — 3113 — 3119 — 3121 — 3126 — 3127 — 3196 — 3372 — 3473 — 3485 — 3492 — 3516 — 3517 — 3526 — 3536 — 3543 — 3545 — 3564 — 3603 — 3616 — 3688 — 3689 — 3696 — 3725 — 3729. All 40 were passed back to the LMSR by November 1945, might I say, with a sigh of relief, as these machines were only capable of the very lightest of duties; I had personal experience of their failings.

From the Southern Railway, only 12 engines were loaned. Four S.15 class, one H.15, five N.15/X, and two 4-4-2T's class 13.

Numbers and types are as follows:

S.15. Nos. 496 — 497 — 498 — 499. Returned August 1943.
N.15/X Nos. 2327 — 2328 — 2329 — 2331 — 2332. Returned August 1943.
H.15 No. 478, returned June 1942 and Class 13 Nos. 2089 — 2091, returned July 1943.

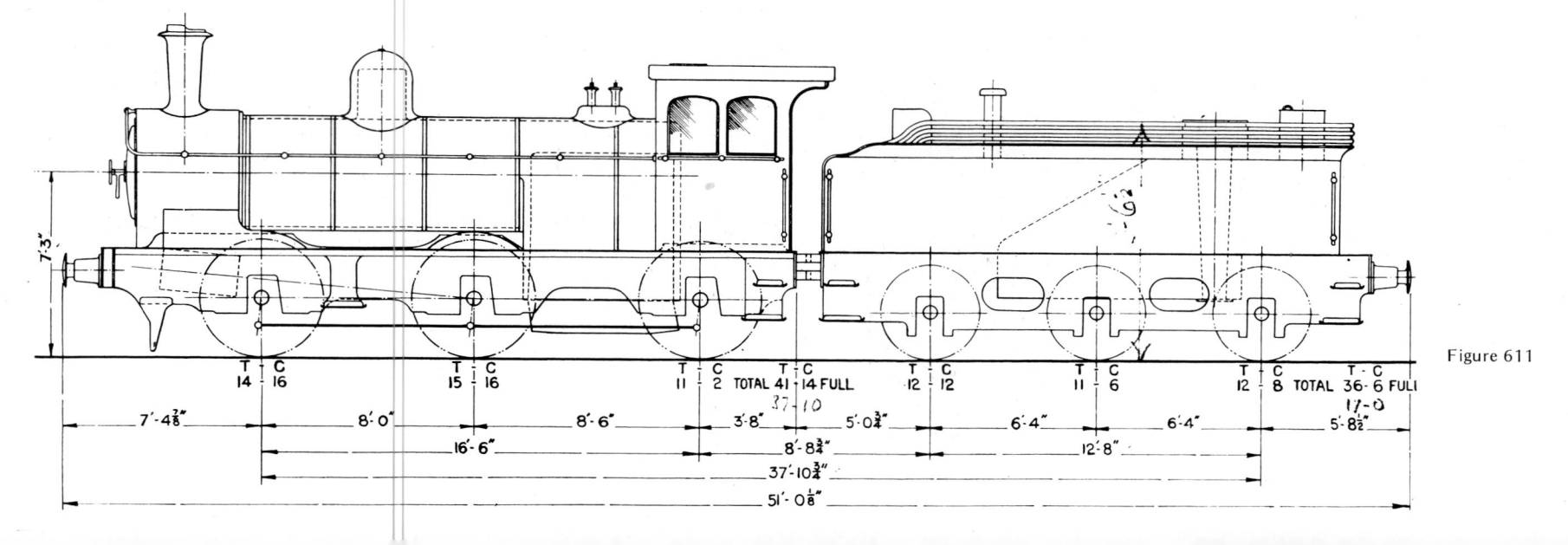

Figure 611

The next relief to the acute locomotive shortage came when the LMSR loaned to the Great Western 25 of the superb Stanier 2-8-0 freight engines in November of 1940. These were numbers: 8226 — 8237 — 8238 — 8239-44 — 8252-3 — 8257 — 8261 — 8286-96 and 8300. However all these had to be returned to the parent company by September 1941, and in 1943 Swindon together with other locomotive works, were given instructions to commence building the Stanier 2-8-0s. In all, 80 engines of the class were built at Swindon and numbered from 8400 to 8479. All except four were handed to the LMS as from November 1946. See *Figure* 613 for diagram and *Figure* 612 for photograph of first engine turned out of the GWR factory.

Figure 612

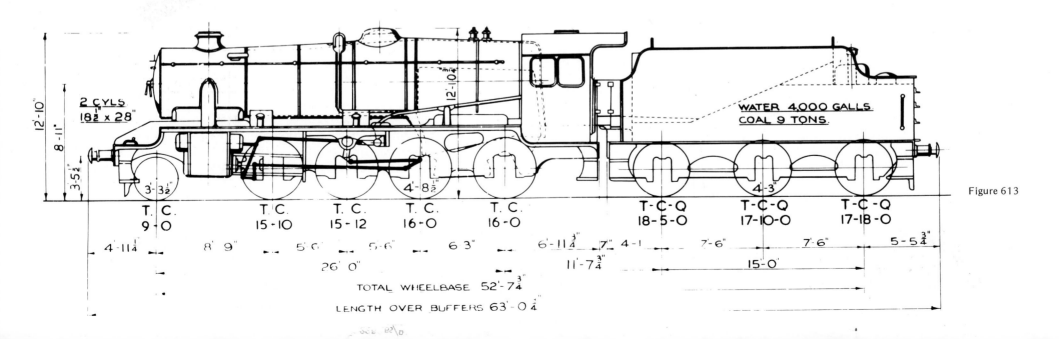

Figure 613

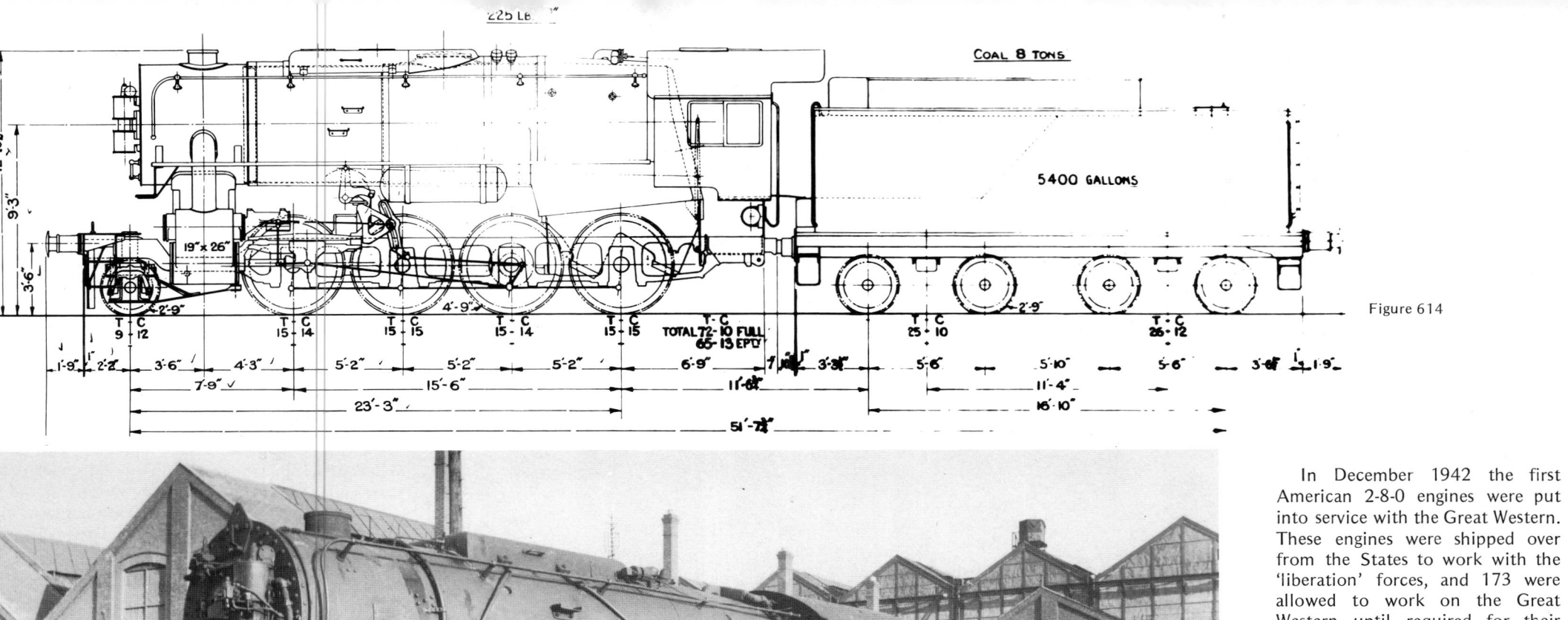

225 LB.

COAL 8 TONS

5400 GALLONS

12'-10⅛"

9'-3"

3'-6"

19" X 26"

Figure 614

T·C
9-12

T·C
15-14

T·C
15-15

T·C
15-14

T·C
15-15

T·C TOTAL 72-10 FULL
65-13 EPTY

T·C
25-10

T·C
26-12

1-9" 2'-2" 3'-6" 4'-3" 5'-2" 5'-2" 5'-2" 6'-9" 3'-3" 5'-6" 5'-10" 5'-6" 3'-6" 1'-9"

2'-9" 4'-9½" 2'-9"

7'-9" 15'-6" 11'-6½" 11'-4"

23'-3" 16'-10"

51'-7½"

In December 1942 the first American 2-8-0 engines were put into service with the Great Western. These engines were shipped over from the States to work with the 'liberation' forces, and 173 were allowed to work on the Great Western until required for their military service on the Continent. The numbers were as follows:—
1601-24, 1628, 1632, 1639, 1641-49, 1651, 1654-6, 1658-65, 1681-84, 1687-89, 1749, 1757, 1835-6, 1841, 1877, 1880, 1881, 1883-4, 1891-99, 1900-2, 1909-10, 1913-5, 2096, 2098, 2100, 2102-3, 2109-10, 2112, 2116, 2118, 2121, 2129-45, 2147-51, 2159, 2164-5, 2167, 2267, 2269-70, 2279, 2280, 2290, 2294, 2312-15, 2318-19, 2323-4, 2326-27, 2338-39, 2349-54, 2357-60, 2368-69, 2375, 2377, 2403-5, 2407-8, 2410, 2422-24, 2430-35, 2438-43, 2448, 2450. The official diagram and photograph are shown in *Figures* 614 and 615.

Figure 615

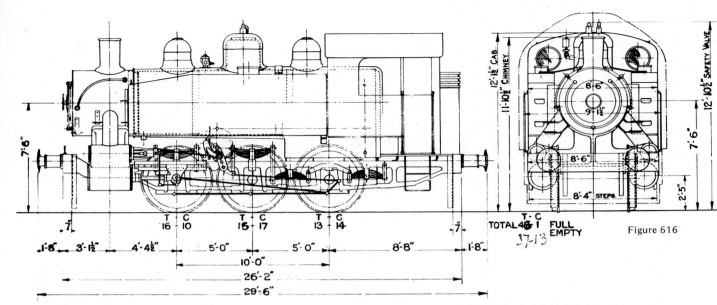

T-C
16 · 10

T-C
15 · 17

T-C
13 · 14

TOTAL 46 · 1
37·13

FULL
EMPTY

Figure 616

As well as the 2-8-0 freight engines, the GWR took into stock 22 of the U.S.A. 0-6-0T shunting tank engines in July 1944. The Diagram issued was B.77 (*Figure* 616) and the photograph shows No. 4384 at Cardiff Docks. The twenty individual numbers were 1307, 1945-6, 1948, 1976, 1979, 1981, 1983, 1985, 1987, 4381, 4383-4, 4388-9, 4390, 4392-3, 4395, 4397, 4399 and 4401. I have no knowledge of these engines actually being steamed on the Great Western as they were all returned to the American authorities by September of the same year, 1944, although I did see some at work in Southampton Docks.

Figure 617

Finally, after the War, in September of 1946, the GWR was loaned 81 of the magnificent Ministry of Supply 'Austerity' 2-8-0 heavy freight locomotives. The Diagram for this engine was Q and can be seen in *Figure* 618, and the official photograph is seen in *Figure* 619.

The numbers were as follows:— 70801, 70808, 70836, 70843, 70876, 77000, 77001, 77005, 77012, 77014-5, 77026, 77028, 77040, 77049, 77053, 77058, 77064, 77077, 77079, 77097, 77099, 77102, 77106, 77115-6, 77123, 77130, 77142, 77151, 77161, 77165, 77184, 77196, 77200, 77202-3, 77210, 77214, 77234, 77241, 77247, 77255, 77257, 77288-9, 77291, 77294, 77297, 77310, 77325-6, 77368, 77378, 77380, 77388, 77393, 77407-8, 77421, 77429, 77423, 77489, 77508, 78510, 78512, 78521-2, 78542-3, 78604, 78632, 78671, 78695, 78711, 78714, 78717, 78719, 79219, 79224-6, 79232, 79234-5, 79261, 79274, 79278, 79301, 79303, 79309.

All these engines went over into British Railways ownership at the Nationalization on 1st January 1948.

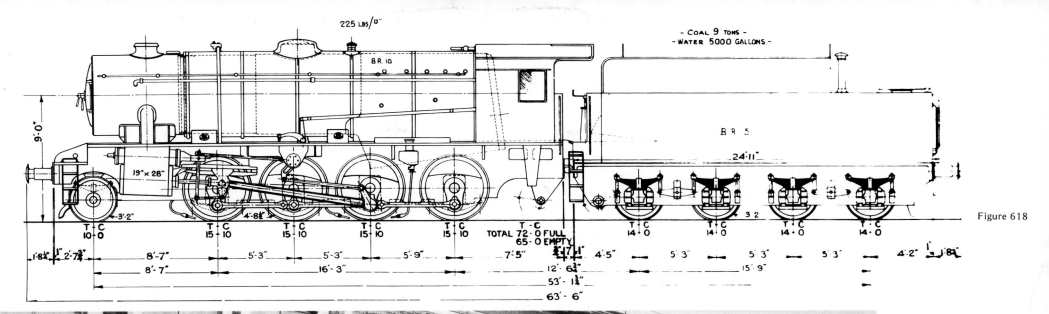

225 LBS/▫"

B.R. 10

- COAL 9 TONS -
- WATER 5000 GALLONS -

B.R. 5

24·11"

9'-0"

19" × 28"

Figure 618

3'-2"

4'-8½"

T·C
10·0

T·C
15·10

T·C
15·10

T·C
15·10

T·C
15·10

T·C
TOTAL 72·0 FULL
65·0 EMPTY

T·C
14·0

T·C
14·0

3 2

T·C
14·0

T·C
14·0

1'-8½" 2-7¾"   8'-7"   5'-3"   5'-3"   5'-9"   7'-5"   4·5"   5·3"   5·3"   5·3"   4·2" 8½"

8'-7"   16'-3"   12'-6¾"   15'-9"

53'-1¼"

63'-6"

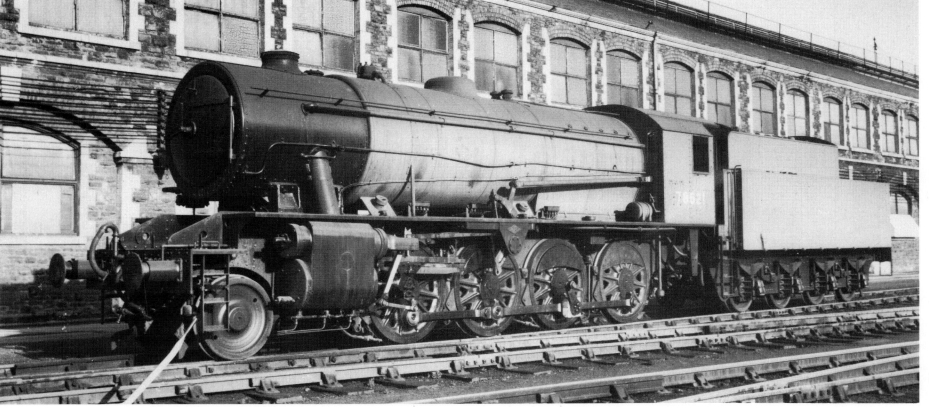

Figure 619

Page 261

SOUTH WALES PARLIAMENTARY SESSIONS MAPS

Any railway map of South Wales, which purports to show all the many and various companies lines and branches, is of necessity, very complicated and bewildering.

Wanting to show the geographical parts of the country where these 'absorbed' engines actually belonged and worked, I searched around for a suitable map of the area, but always came up against the complexity disadvantage. However, during my researches, I located several interesting pictures of the 'Parliamentary Sessions' maps, and, as this little work deals mainly with the period when the Great Western Railway was considering absorption, what better than to utilise these final pages with illustrations of these authentic documents.

No explanation or description is necessary, as each one is headed or titled, and as they are each historic documents in their own right, I hope they will prove of interest to the 'Absorbed' reader!

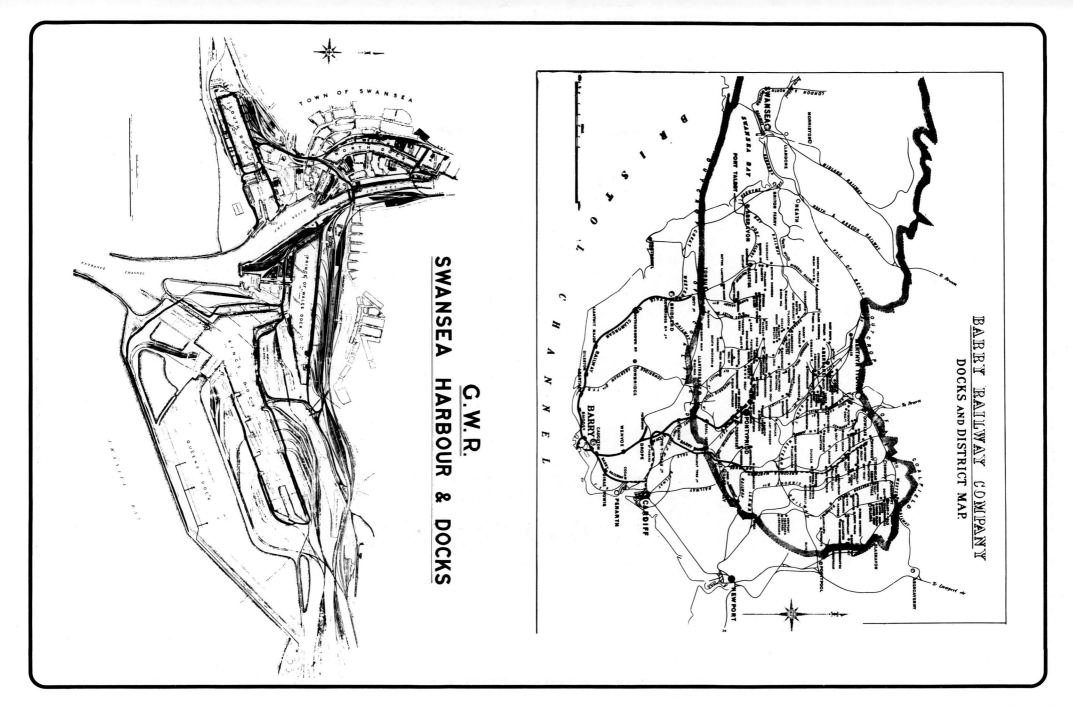

G.W.R.

SWANSEA HARBOUR & DOCKS

BARRY RAILWAY COMPANY

DOCKS AND DISTRICT MAP

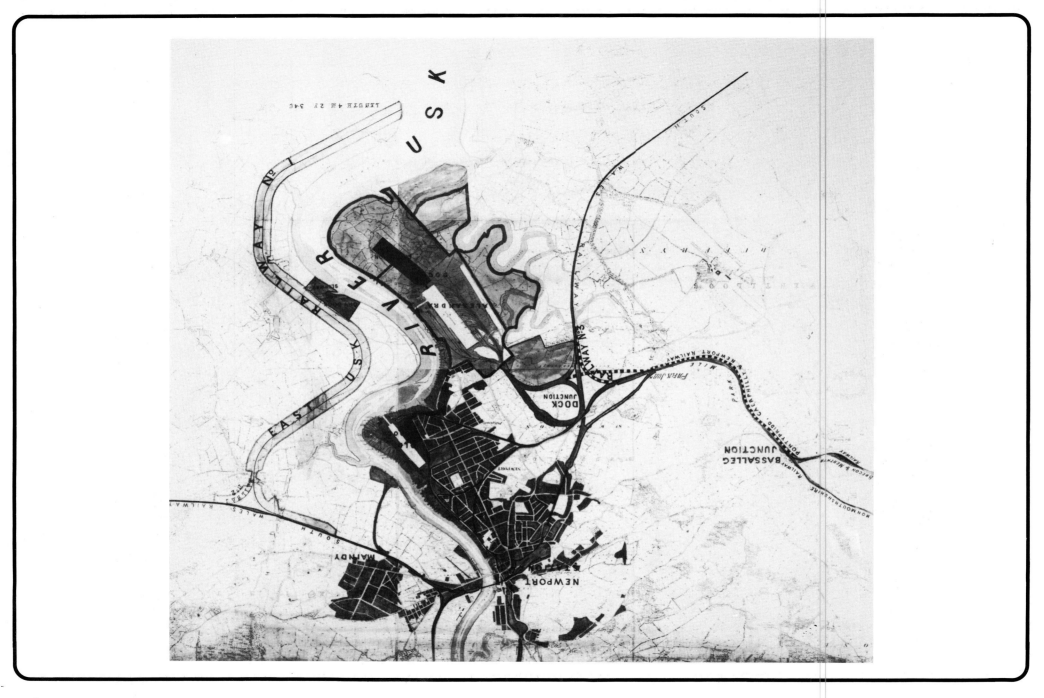

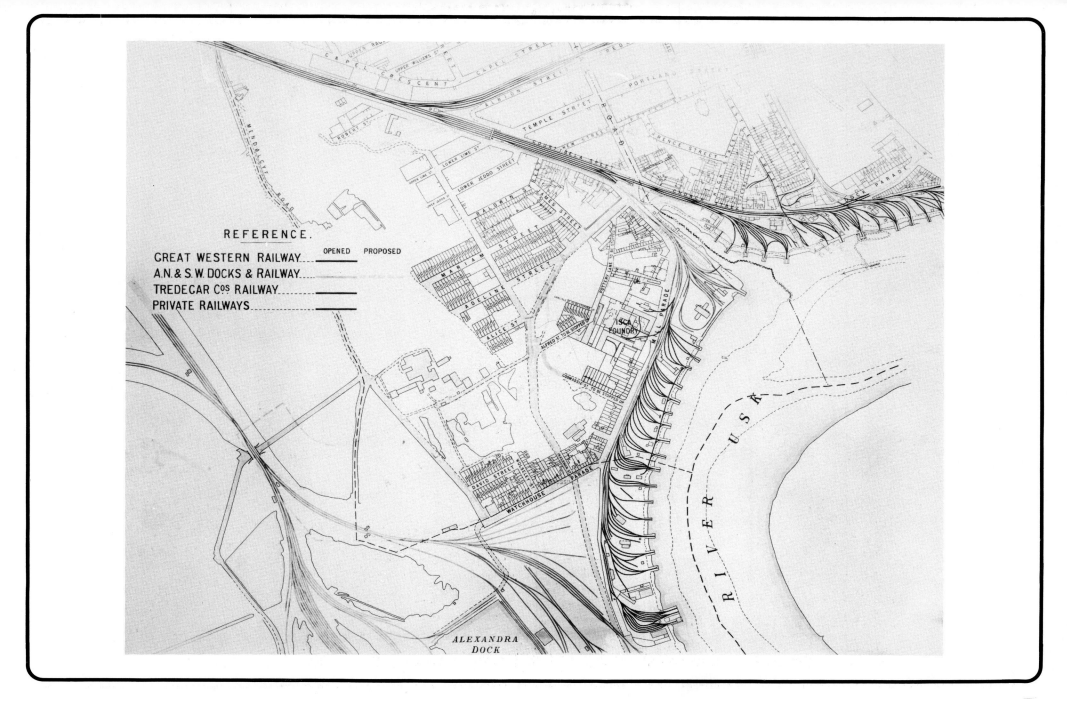

REFERENCE.

	OPENED	PROPOSED
GREAT WESTERN RAILWAY		
A.N.& S.W. DOCKS & RAILWAY		
TREDEGAR Cᵒˢ RAILWAY		
PRIVATE RAILWAYS		

GREAT WESTERN RAILWAY.
SESSION 1882.

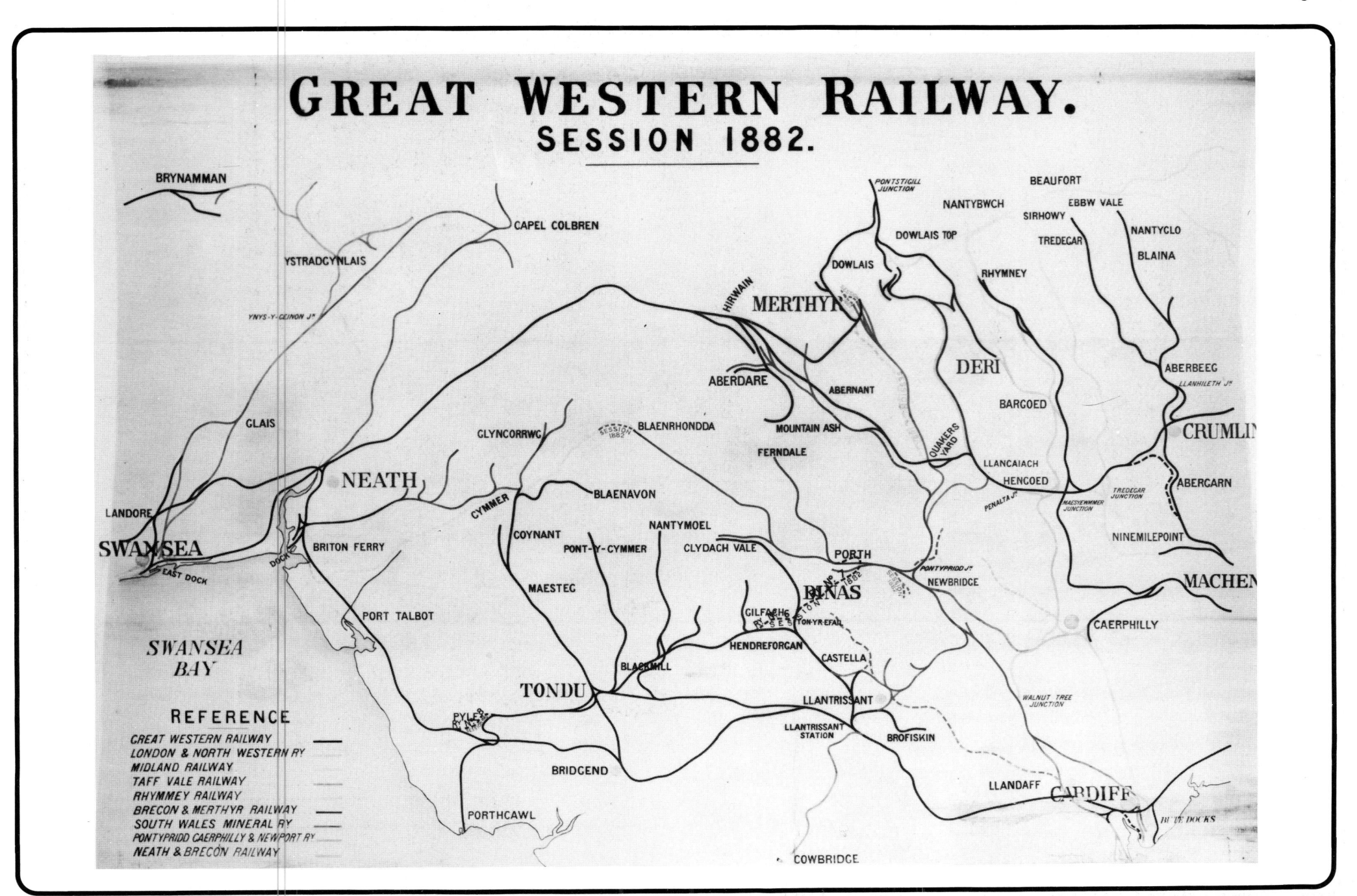

REFERENCE

GREAT WESTERN RAILWAY	—
LONDON & NORTH WESTERN RY	
MIDLAND RAILWAY	
TAFF VALE RAILWAY	
RHYMMEY RAILWAY	
BRECON & MERTHYR RAILWAY	—
SOUTH WALES MINERAL RY	
PONTYPRIDD CAERPHILLY & NEWPORT RY	
NEATH & BRECON RAILWAY	

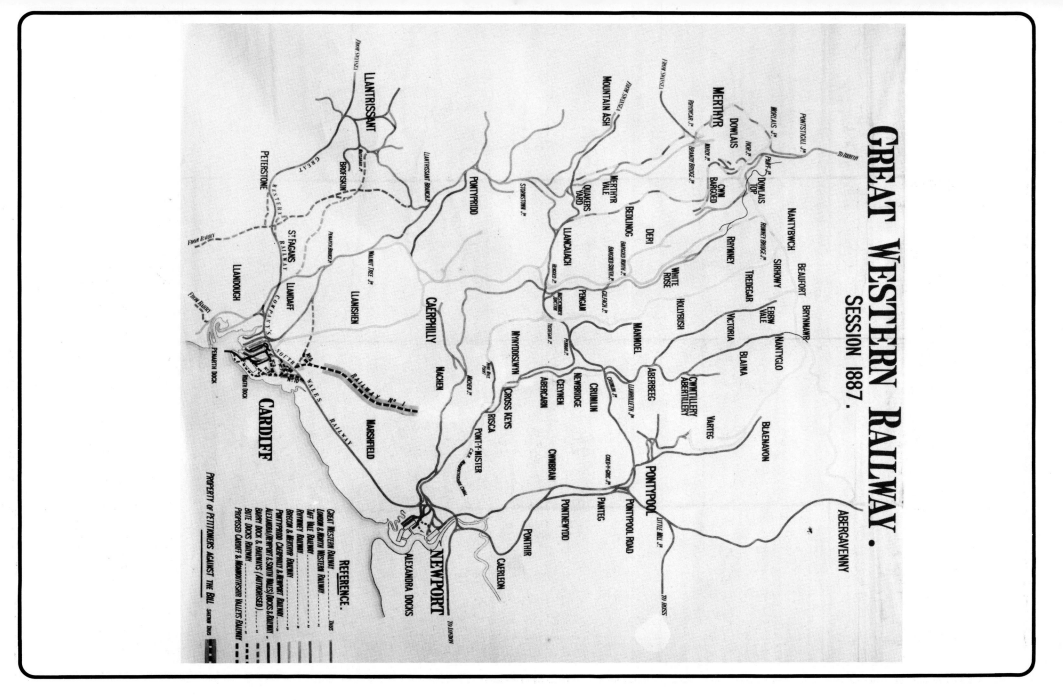

GREAT WESTERN RAILWAY.

SESSION 1887.

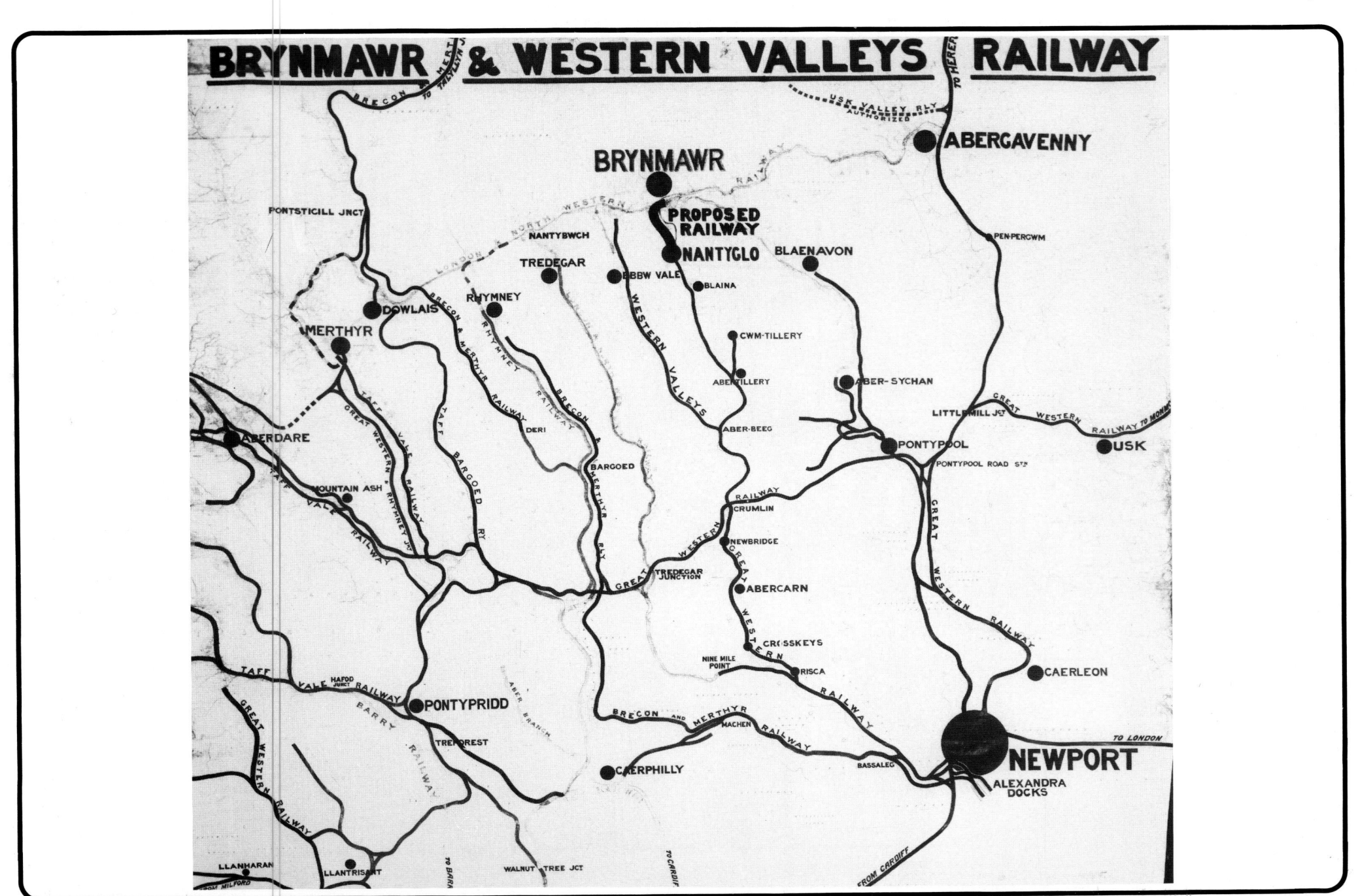

BRYNMAWR & WESTERN VALLEYS RAILWAY

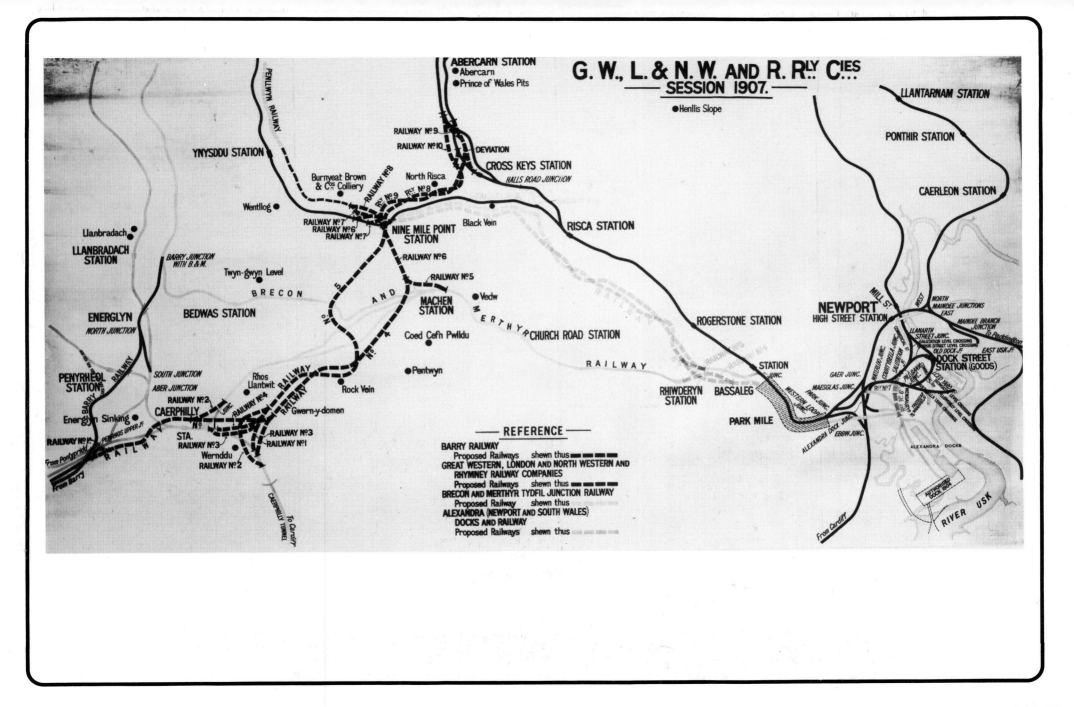

G. W., L. & N. W. AND R. R.LY C.IES

SESSION 1907.

● Henllis Slope

REFERENCE

BARRY RAILWAY
  Proposed Railways   shewn thus ▄▄ ▄▄ ▄▄ ▄▄
GREAT WESTERN, LONDON AND NORTH WESTERN AND
RHYMNEY RAILWAY COMPANIES
  Proposed Railways   shewn thus ▄▄ ▄▄ ▄▄ ▄▄
BRECON AND MERTHYR TYDFIL JUNCTION RAILWAY
  Proposed Railway   shewn thus ▄▄ ▄▄ ▄▄
ALEXANDRA (NEWPORT AND SOUTH WALES)
DOCKS AND RAILWAY
  Proposed Railways   shewn thus ▄▄ ▄▄ ▄▄

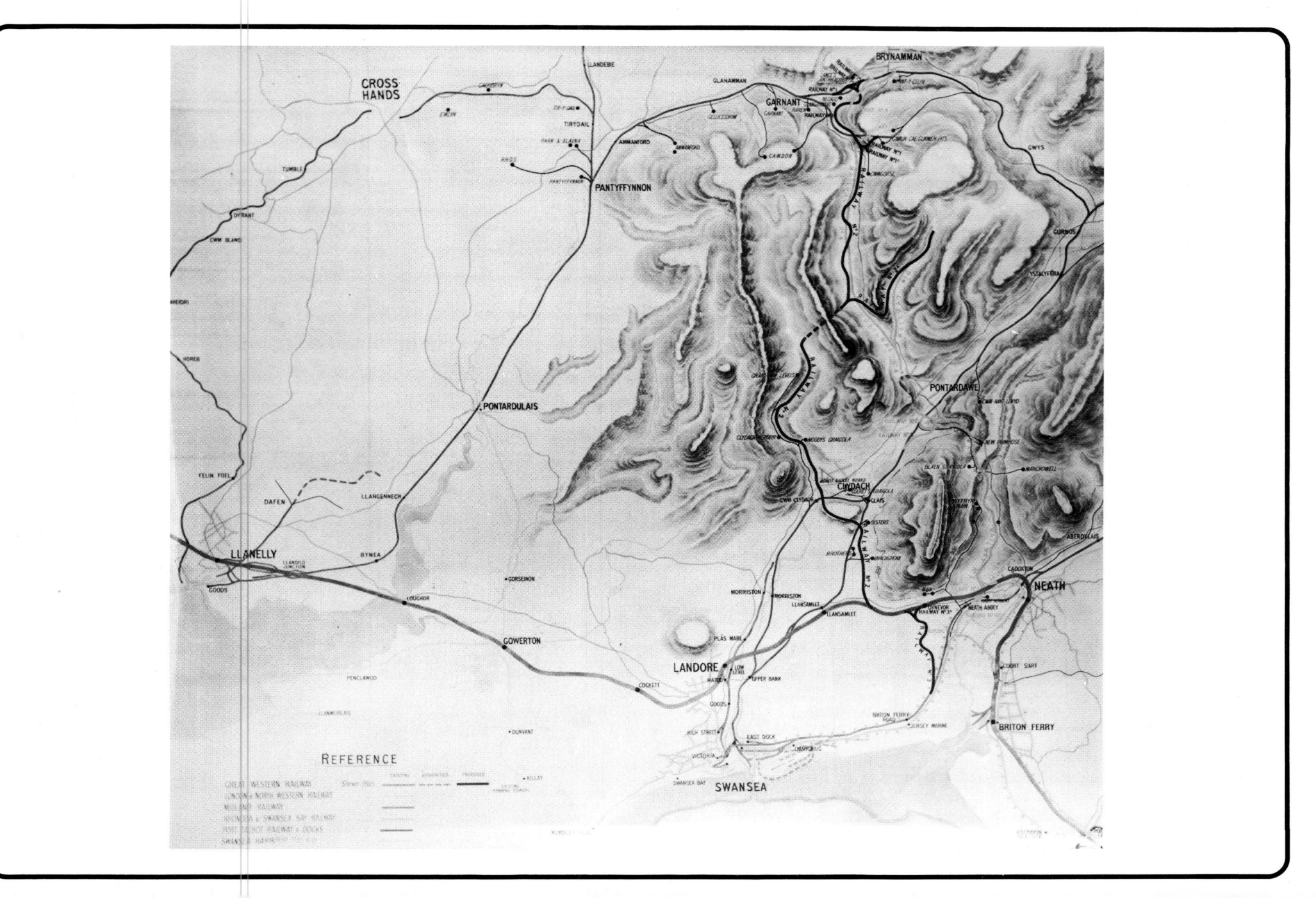

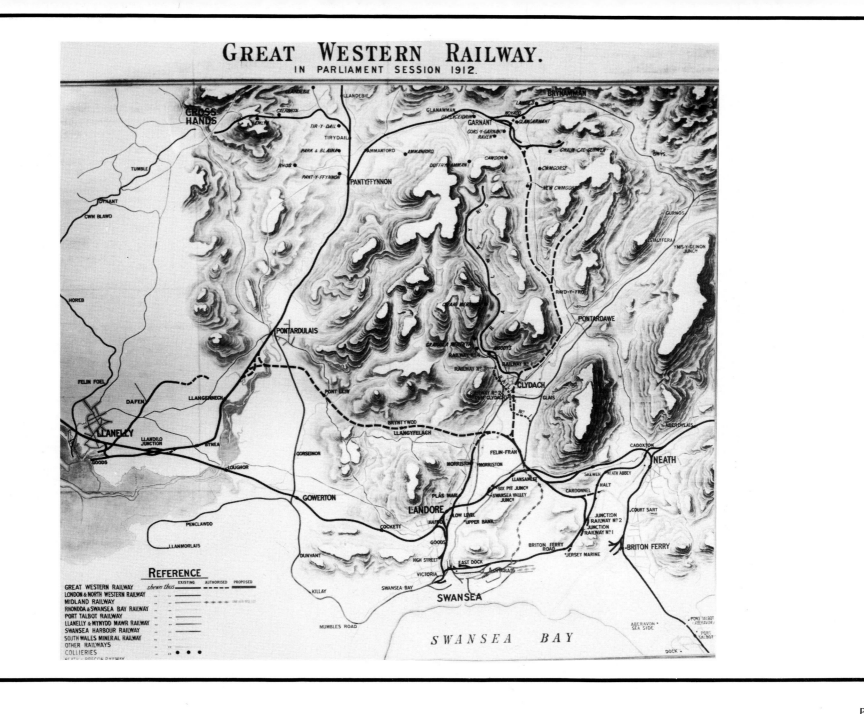

GREAT WESTERN RAILWAY.
IN PARLIAMENT SESSION 1912.

SWANSEA BAY

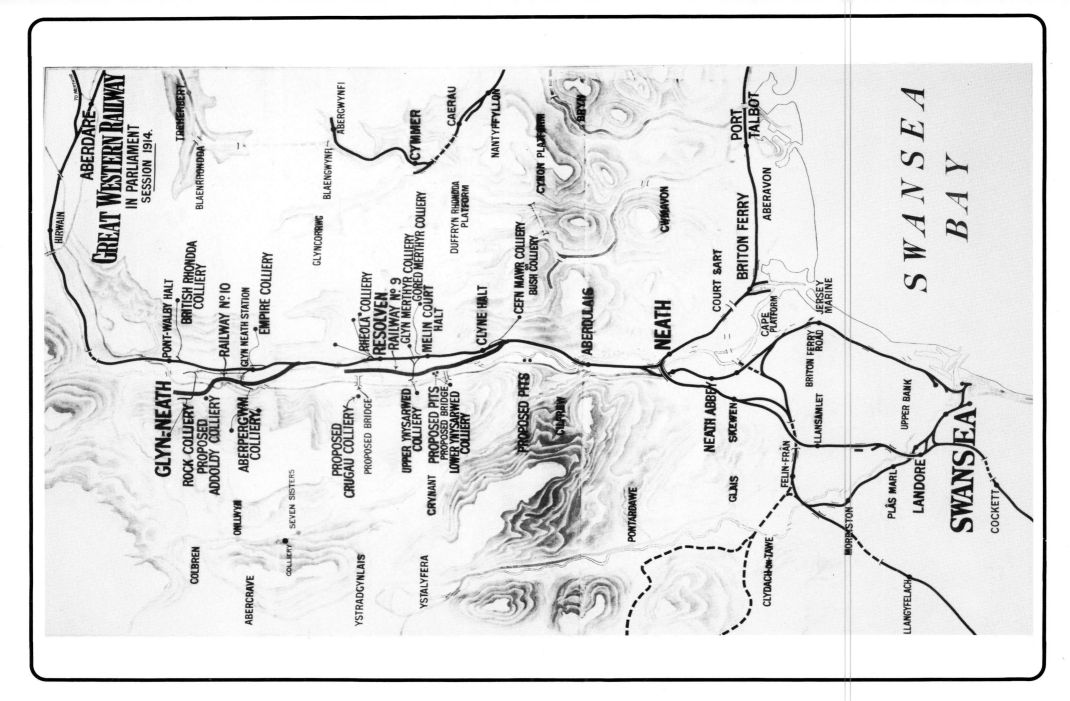

ABERDARE–

GREAT WESTERN RAILWAY

IN PARLIAMENT
SESSION 1914.

TO MERTHYR

HIRWAIN

TREHERBERT

BLAENRHONDDA

ABERGWYNFI

BLAENGWYNFI

CYMMER

CAERAU

BRYN

GLYNCORRWG

NANTYFFYLLON

PONT-WALBY HALT

BRITISH RHONDDA COLLIERY

RAILWAY No. 10

GLYN NEATH STATION

EMPIRE COLLIERY

DUFFRYN RHONDDA PLATFORM

CYMON PLATFORM

CWMAVON

GLYN-NEATH

ROCK COLLIERY

PROPOSED ADDOLDY COLLIERY

ABERPERGWM COLLIERY

RHEOLA COLLIERY

RESOLVEN

RAILWAY No. 9

GLYN MERTHYR COLLIERY

GORED MERTHYR COLLIERY

MELIN COURT HALT

CLYNE HALT

CEFN MAWR COLLIERY OR BUSH COLLIERY

ABERDULAIS

NEATH

COURT SART

BRITON FERRY

ABERAVON

PORT TALBOT

PROPOSED BRIDGE

PROPOSED CRUGAU COLLIERY

UPPER YNYSARWED COLLIERY

PROPOSED PITS

PROPOSED BRIDGE

LOWER YNYSARWED COLLIERY

PROPOSED PITS

CRYNANT

CILFREW

NEATH ABBEY

CAPE PLATFORM

JERSEY MARINE

BRITON FERRY ROAD

COLBREN

ONLLWYN

SEVEN SISTERS

COLLIERY

YSTRADGYNLAIS

ABERCRAVE

YSTALYFERA

PONTARDAWE

GLAIS

SKEWEN

FELIN-FRÂN

LLANSAMLET

UPPER BANK

SWANSEA BAY

CLYDACH-ON-TAWE

MORRISTON

PLÂS MARL

LANDORE

SWANSEA

COCKETT

LLANGYFELACH

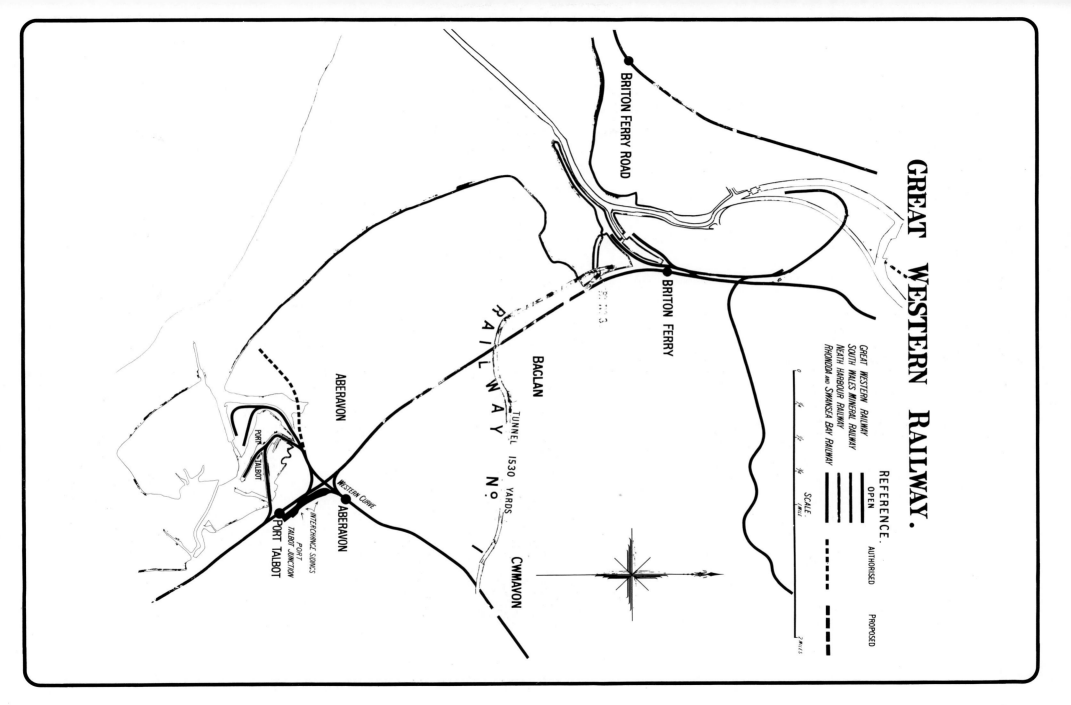

GREAT WESTERN RAILWAY.

BRITON FERRY ROAD

BRITON FERRY

BAGLAN

Tunnel 1530 YARDS

RAILWAY No.3

RAILWAY No.2

CWMAVON

ABERAVON

PORT TALBOT

ABERAVON

WESTERN CURVE

INTERCHANGE SIDINGS

PORT TALBOT JUNCTION

PORT TALBOT

REFERENCE.

	OPEN	AUTHORISED	PROPOSED
GREAT WESTERN RAILWAY			
SOUTH WALES MINERAL RAILWAY			
NEATH HARBOUR RAILWAY			
RHONDDA AND SWANSEA BAY RAILWAY			

SCALE.
0   ¼   ½   ¾   1 MILE   2 MILES

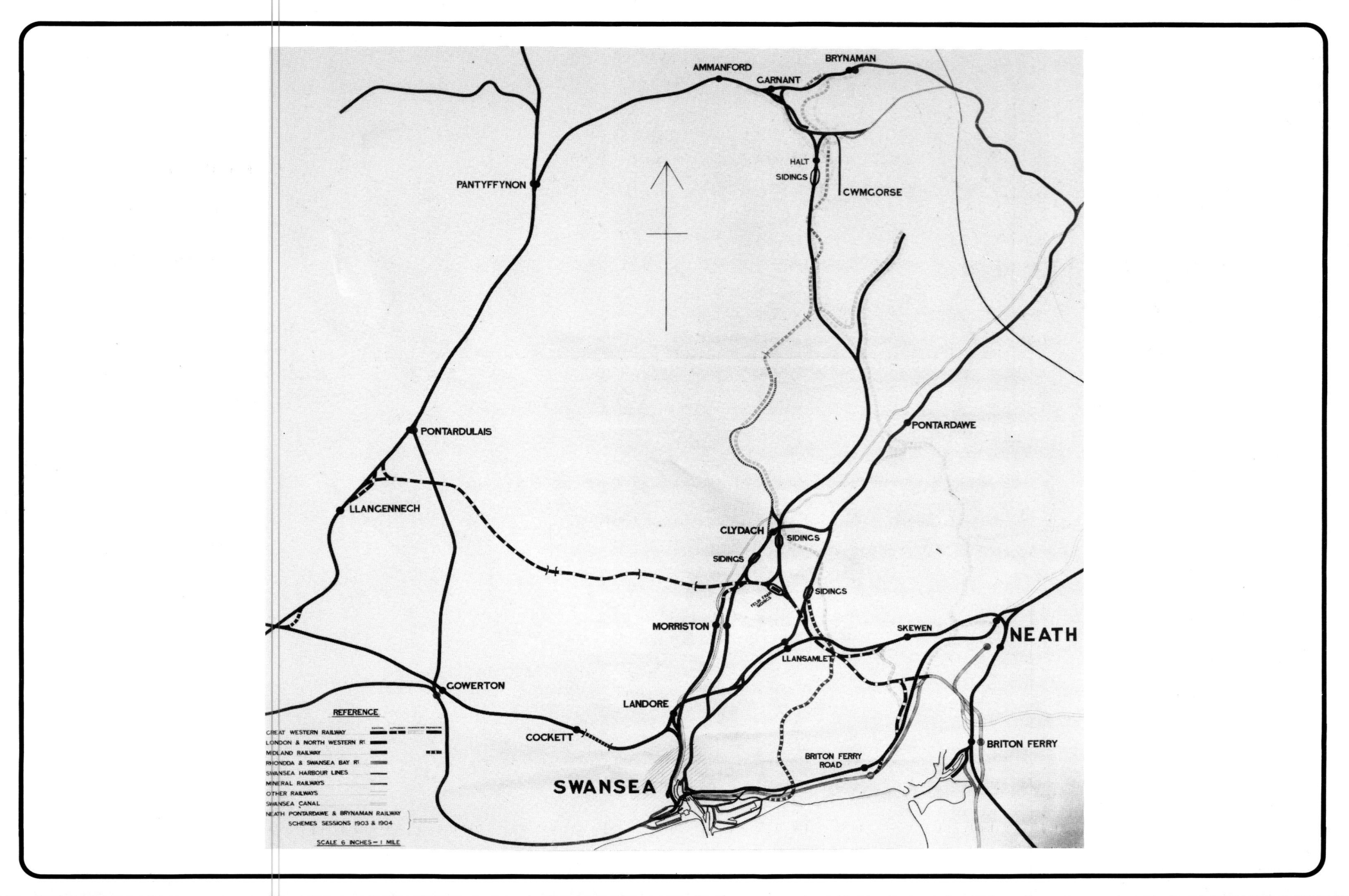

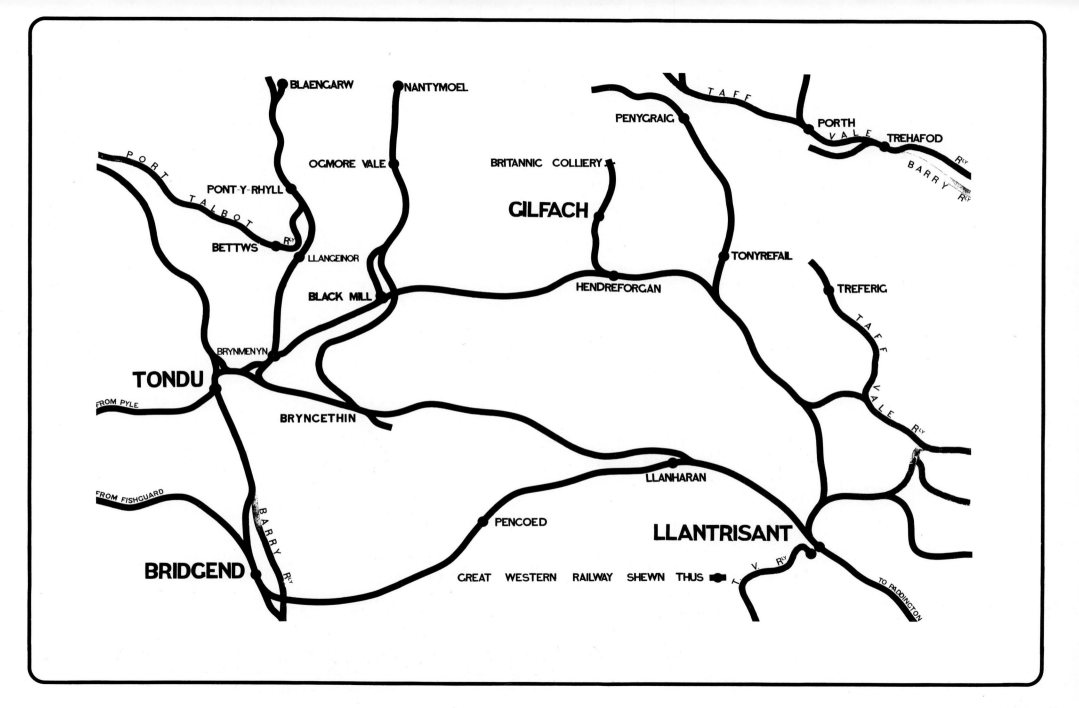

BLAENGARW
NANTYMOEL
PORT TALBOT Rʸ
PENYGRAIG
PORTH
TAFF
VALE
TREHAFOD
BARRY Rʸ
OGMORE VALE
BRITANNIC COLLIERY
PONT-Y-RHYLL
GILFACH
BETTWS Rʸ
LLANGEINOR
TONYREFAIL
BLACK MILL
HENDREFORGAN
TREFERIG
BRYNMENYN
TAFF VALE Rʸ
TONDU
FROM PYLE
BRYNCETHIN
FROM FISHGUARD
LLANHARAN
BARRY Rʸ
PENCOED
LLANTRISANT
BRIDGEND
GREAT WESTERN RAILWAY SHEWN THUS ■
T. V. Rʸ
TO PADDINGTON

Page 275

COMPLETE STOCK LIST (Absorbed Engines) 1925

TYPE	RAILWAY	CYLINDERS		ENGINE NOS.	WHEEL DIA.	TRACTIVE EFFORT LBS.	TOTAL WEIGHT FULL		WEIGHT ON COUPLED WHEELS		ADHESION FACTOR	POWER UNIT	COLOUR	LETTER
		CLASS	SIZE				T	C	T	C				
0-4-0T	S.H.T.	Outside	15" x 22"	943.	3'—4"	16830	28	15	28	15	3.82	25.05		A
,,	,, -	,,	15" x 21"	968, 1098.	3'—7"	14945	33	10	33	10	5.02	23.92		A
,,	Cardiff	,,	14" x 21"	1338, 1339.	3'—2½"	14540	25	10	25	10	3.92	20.83		A
,,	S.H.T.	,,	14" x 22"	701.	3'—5"	14305	28	0	28	0	4.38	21.81		
,,	,,	,,	15" x 21"	929.	3'—7"	14010	33	10	33	10	5.35	22.42		
,,	,,	,,	14" x 22"	974.	3'—6"	13090	26	17	26	17	4.59	20.45	Yellow	
,,	,,	,,	14" x 20"	933.	3'—3"	12815	24	10	24	10	4.28	18.59		
,,	,,	,,	,,	150.	3'—3½"	12650	27	15	27	15	4.91	,,		
,,	,,	,,	,,	886, 926, 930.	3'—3"	11960	24	10	24	10	4.58	17 36		
,,	P. & M.	,,	14" x 18"	925.	3'—0"	11245	26	11	26	11	5.29	15.05		
,,	Alexandra Docks	,,	14" x 20"	1340.	,,	11100	22	10	22	10	4.54	14.87		
,,	,,	,,	12" x 19"	1341.	3'—2"	7345	19	8	19	8	5.91	10.39		
,,	Taff Vale	,,	10" x 16"	1342.	2'—11"	5050	16	7	16	7	7.25	6.57		
,,	P. & M.			696.										
,,	,,			779.										
,,	,,	Outside	14" x 20"	795, 921.	3'—6"									
,,	,,			927.										
,,	,,			928.										
,,	,,			935.										
,,	,,	Outside		942.										
0-4-2T	Alexandra Docks	Inside	16" x 24"	1426.	5'—2"	12635	36	9	24	12	4.36	29.14		
0-4-4T	Barry	,,	17½" x 26"	3, 4, 9.	5'—8"	15925	56	5	35	1	4.93	40.28	Red	A
,,	Cambrian	,,	17" x 24"	10, 19, 20.	5'—3"	14970	45	13	28	16	4.30	35.10	Yellow	A
,,	M. & S.W.	,,	,,	23.	5'—2"	13310	47	2	30	13	5.15	30.70	,,	
2-4-0T	P.T.	,,	,,	1189.	5'—3"	15440	40	17	28	18	4.19	36.18		A
,,	N. & B.	,,	,,	1400.	,,	14970	41	2	31	2	4.65	35.10	Blue	A
,,	Cambrian	,,	14" x 20"	1192, 1196, 1197.	4'—6"	9255	33	3	24	16	6.00	18.59		
2-4-0	,,	,,	17½" x 24"	1328.	6'—2"	13930	35	5	23	3	3.72	38.30		
,,	,,	,,	17" x 24"	1329.	,,	11950	33	16	22	6	4.18	32.86		
,,	M. & S.W.	,,	,,	1334-1346	5'—6"	14740	35	5	23	14	3.60	36.19		A
2-4-2T	R. & S.B.	,,	18" x 26"	1307, 1309.	5'—3"	18755	50	15	26	13	3.18	43.94		A
,,	,,	,,	,,	1310.	,,	,,	51	19	27	0	3.22	43.94		A
,,	Barry	,,	17½" x 26"	1311-1321.	5'—8"	15925	56	7	34	11	4.86	40.28	Red	A
,,	,,	,,	,,	1311-1321.	,,								,,	
,,	Rhymney	,,	17½" x 24"	1324, 1325.	5'—0"	15620	54	8	32	16	4.81	34.87	Blue	A
,,	Barry	,,	17" x 24"	1322.	5'—3"	15440	47	2	29	13	4.30	36.18	,,	A
,,	P.T.	,,	,,	1326.	,,	,,	47	2	29	13	4.30	,,		A
,,	Barry	,,	,,	1323.	,,	14040	50	15	29	10	4.70	32.91	,,	
4-4-0T	N. & B.	Outside	17" x 24"	1392.	5'—0"	13755	45	11	32	9	5.28	30.70	,,	
4-4-0	Cambrian	Inside	18½" x 26"	1014, 1029, 1035, 1043.	6'—0"	17860	45	5	29	13	3.71	47.84	Yellow	A
,,	M. & S.W.	,,	18" x 26"	1119-1126, 1128.	5'—9"	16600	45	5	29	5	3.94	42.61	,,	A
,,	,,	,,	,,	1119-1126, 1128.		17120	46	17	30	12	4.00	43.94	,,	A
,,	Cambrian	,,	18" x 24"	1082, 1088, 1090, 1091, 1093, 1097, 1100, 1106, 1108.	6'—0"	13770	40	5	27	5	4.43	36.89	,,	
,,	,,	,,	17" x 24"	3521, 3546.	5'—2"	17120	41	16	28	16	3.77	39.40	,,	A
,,	,,	,,	,,	1112, 1118.	5'—6½"	13300	35	8	23	15	3.99	32.91	,,	
4-4-2T	Taff Vale	,,	17½" x 26"	1301-1305.	5'—3"	17200	54	6	30	6	3.94	40.31	,,	A
4-4-4T	M. & S.W.	,,	17" x 24"	27.	,,	15440	61	11	31	4	4.52	36.18	,,	
,,	,,	,,	,,	25.		14040	59	19	30	19	4.93	32.91	,,	

TYPE	RAILWAY	CYLINDERS CLASS	CYLINDERS SIZE	ENGINE NOS.	WHEEL DIA.	TRACTIVE EFFORT LBS.	TOTAL WEIGHT FULL T	C	WEIGHT ON COUPLED WHEELS T	C	ADHESION FACTOR	POWER UNIT	COLOUR	LETTER
0-6-0T	Rhymney	Inside	18" x 26"	604-606.	4'-4½"	23870	56	8	56	8	5.29	46.63	Red	C
"	"	"	"	608-611.	"	"	55	6	55	6	5.18	"	"	C
"	Cardiff	"	18" x 24"	681-684	4'-1½"	23365	49	0	49	0	4.69	43.02	Blue	C
"	"	"	17½"x 26"	685.	4'-6"	21305	47	1	47	1	4.94	42.80	"	C
"	Barry	"	"	699, 700, 702, 703, 706.	4'-3"	21230	45	8	45	8	4.79	40.28	"	C
"	"	"	"	708, 710-726, 729, 742, 747.	"	"	46	9	46	9	4.90	"		C
"	"	"	"	754, 776-778, 780, 807.	"	"	46	18	46	18	4.94	"		C
"	Alexandra Docks	"	18" x 24"	664, 665.	4'-0"	20655	46	11	46	11	5.05	36.88		B
"	Cardiff	"	17½"x 26"	688, 690-692.	4'-6"	20055	44	7	44	7	4.95	40.28	Yellow	B
"	Alexandra Docks	Outside	17" x 24"	666, 667.	4'-0"	19650	49	4	49	4	5.60	35.10	Blue	B
"	B. & M.	"	"	2161.	"	"	49	4	49	4	5.60	"	"	B
"	Taff Vale	Inside	17½"x 26"	786-791.	4'-6½"	18620	50	0	50	0	6.01	37.76	"	A
"	B.P. & G.V.	Outside	16" x 26"	2162, 2164-2168.	3'-9"	18570	44	0	44	0	5.30	31.09	Yellow	A
"	"	"	"	2163.	"	"	42	8	42	8	5.11	"	"	A
"	Cardiff	Inside	17" x 26"	1667.	5'-2"	18545	46	17	46	17	5.66	42.77	Blue	A
"	Alexandra Docks	"	"	1683.	"	"	46	17	46	17	5.66	"	"	A
"	B. & M.	"	"	1685, 1693, 1694.	"	"	46	17	46	17	5.66	"	"	A
"	Alexandra Docks	"	18" x 24"	668.	4'-6"	18360	46	15	46	15	5.70	36.89	"	A
"	"	"	"	670.	"	"	48	17	48	17	5.95	"	"	A
"	C.M. & D.P.	Outside	16" x 22"	28.	3'-6"	18240	37	19	37	19	4.66	28.49	Yellow	A
"	"	"	"	29.	"	"	37	18	37	18	4.66	'	"	A
"	Cardiff	Inside	17" x 26"	1676.	5'-2"	18025	47	18	47	18	5.94	41.56	Blue	A
"	R. & S.B.	"	17" x 24"	799, 801, 802, 805, 806.	4'-6"	18015	43	0	43	0	5.34	36.18	Yellow	A
"	Alexandra Docks	"	17¾"x 24"	671.	"	17855	50	1	50	1	6.28	35.86	Red	A
"	P.T.	"	16" x 24"	808, 809, 811-814.	4'-0"	17410	44	0	44	0	5.66	31.09	Yellow	A
"	N. & B.	"	17" x 24"	2174, 2175.	4'-7"	17160	46	8	46	8	6.05	35.12	"	A
"	Rhymney	"	17½"x 24"	612, 614, 631, 657.	"	17040	45	11	45	11	5.98	34.86	Blue	A
"	B. & M.	"	17" x 24"	2169-2173.	4'-7½"	16990	48	4	48	4	6.35	35.10	"	A
"	"	"	"	2169-2173.	"	"	48	5	48	5	6.35		Red	A
"	B.P. & G.V.	Outside	15" x 22"	2196.	3'-6½"	16830	38	0	38	0	5.05	26.62		A
"	"	"	"	2176.	"	"	39	1	39	1	5.19		Yellow	A
"	S.H.T.	Inside	16" x 22"	937, 1085, 1086.	3'-10"	16650	40	0	40	0	5.38	28.49		A
"	B.P. & G.V.	Outside	16" x 24"	2192.	3'-8"	16620	41	12	41	12	5.60	27.20	Yellow	A
"	B. & M.	Inside	17" x 24"	2177, 2179-2184, 2186, 2188.	4'-2"	16500	44	13	44	13	6.06	30.70	Blue	A
"	Alexandra Docks	"	16" x 24"	674-677.	4'-0"	16320	40	0	40	0	5.49	29.14	Yellow	A
"	N. & B.	"	17" x 24"	2189.	4'-7"	16080	45	13	45	13	6.36	32.91	"	A
"	"	"	"	2199.	"	"	47	7	47	7	6.59		Blue	A
"	Alexandra Docks	"	16" x 24"	993.	4'-1½"	15825	40	10	40	10	5.73	29.14	Yellow	A
"	"	"	17" x 26"	1679.	5'-2"	15450	47	18	47	18	6.93	35.60	Blue	A
"	Cardiff	"	"	1689.	"	"	45	18	45	18	6.65	"	Yellow	A
"	S.W.M.	"	17" x 24"	817.	4'-10"	15245	47	0	47	0	6.90	32.88	"	A
"	"	"	"	818.	"	"	42	12	42	12	6.26	"	"	A
"	P.T.	"	16" x 24"	815, 816.	4'-0"	15230	39	12	39	12	5.82	27.19		A
"	Taff Vale	"	17½"x 26"	792-794.	5'-3"	15040	44	15	44	15	6.66	35.25	Yellow	A
"	M. & S.W.	"	17" x 24"	825, 843.	4'-7"	15010	44	0	44	0	6.56	30.72	"	A
"	Cardiff	"	15½"x 22"	694, 695.	4'-0"	14975	35	0	35	0	5.23	26.74		A
"	B.P. & G.V.	Outside	15" x 22"	2197.	3'-9"	14960	36	10	36	10	5.46	25.05		A
"	"	"	"	2198.	"	"	37	11	37	11	5.62		Yellow	A
"	B. & M.	Inside	17" x 24"	2190, 2191.	4'-7½"	14870	38	0	38	0	5.72	30.71		A
"	B.P. & G.V.	Outside	15" x 22"	2193.	3'-6"	14025	35	12	35	12	5.68	21.91		
"	Taff Vale	Inside	17" x 24"	796.	4'-7½"	13800						28.49		
"	B.P. & G.V.	Outside	15" x 20"	2194, 2195.	3'-6"	13660								
"	Taff Vale	Inside	16" x 24"	798.	4'-3"	13300						25.24		
"	Barry	"	14" x 20"	781-785.	3'-6½"	11760	31	16	31	16	6.05	18.60		
"	"	"	"	781-785.	"	"						"		
"	Alexandra Docks	Outside	14" x 20"	679, 680.	3'-6"	11105	27	1	27	1	5.45	17.34		

TYPE	RAILWAY	CYLINDERS CLASS	SIZE	ENGINE NOS.	WHEEL DIA.	TRACTIVE EFFORT LBS.	TOTAL WEIGHT FULL T	C	WEIGHT ON COUPLED WHEELS T	C	ADHESION FACTOR	POWER UNIT	COLOUR	LETTER
0-6-0T	Cambrian	Outside	13" x 18"	819.	3'—6"	9235						14.43		
"	"	"	12" x 20"	820, 821.	3'—7"	8540	24	6	24	6	6.37	13.67		
"	"	Inside	12" x 17"	824.	3'—1"	7870	18	9	18	9	5.25	10.83		
"	G.V.			26.										
"	L. & M.M.			312.										
"	"			339.										
"	"			359.										
"	"			704.										
"	"			805.										
"	"			944.										
"	Welshpool & Llanfair	Outside	11½"x 16"	822, 823.	2'—9"	8175	19	18	19	18	5.45	10.04		
2-6-0	M. & S.W.	Outside	18" x 26"	24.	4'—0"	20885	41	12	33	6	3.57	37.29		B
0-6-0	Cambrian	"	18" x 26"	875, 876, 878-885.	5'—1½"	18630	39	3	39	3	4.70	42.63		A
"	"	"	"	875, 876, 878-885.	"	"	39	3	39	3	4.70	"		
"	"	"	"	844, 849, 855, 864, 873, 874, 887, 892-896.	"	"	41	13	41	13	5.00	42.63	Yellow	A
"	"	"	"	844, 849, 855, 864, 873, 874, 887, 892-896.	"	"	38	17	38	17	4.67	"	"	A
"	Taff Vale	"	17½"x 26"	912, 919.	4'—6½"	18620	36	10	36	10	4.39	37.76		A
"	"	"	"	915, 917, 920, 922, 924, 1001.	"	"	38	0	38	0	4.57	37.76		A
"	M. & S.W.	Inside	18" x 26"	1003-1011, 1013.	5'—2½"	17185	37	12	37	12	4.89	39.96		A
"	"	"	"	1003-1011, 1013.	"	"	40	19	40	19	5.33	"	Yellow	A
"	Cambrian	"	16" x 24"	898, 900, 908, 910.	4'—6"	14505	31	9	31	9	4.85	29.14		A
0-6-2T	Barry	Outside	18" x 26"	194, 196.	4'—3"	24570	61	18	54	1	4.92	46.62	Red	D
"	B. & M.	Inside	18½"x 26"	11, 21, 332, 504, 698, 888, 1084, 1113.	4'—6"	24510	63	10	53	10	4.88	49.25	"	D
"	"	"	"	11, 21, 332, 504, 698, 888, 1084, 1113.	"	"	62	10	52	5	4.79	"	Blue	D
"	Rhymney	"	"	30, 31, 32, 34, 46.	"	"	66	19	54	1	4.93	"	Red	D
"	"	"	"	30, 31, 32, 34, 46.	"	"						"	"	D
"	"	"	"	33, 47-51.	"	24510	62	11	51	15	4.72	49.25	Blue	D
"	"	"	"	35-44.	"	"	66	0	53	8	4.87	"	Red	D
"	N. & B.	"	18" x 26"	1371.	"	23870						47.96		
"	P.T.	"	"	184, 187, 188.	"	"						"		
"	R. & S.B.	"	"	180, 182.	"									
"	Rhymney	"	"	52-54, 56, 62-70, 73.	4'—4½"	23870	64	13	53	11	5.02	46.63	Red	C
"	"	"	"	55, 57-61, 71, 72, 74, 75.	"	"	64	3	53	0	4.97	"	"	C
"	N. & B.	"	18½"x 26"	1114, 1117, 1277.	4'—6"	23110	58	13	49	1	4.75	46.43	Blue	C
"	Cardiff	"	18" x 26"	151, 152, 161.	"	22540	54	17	45	12	4.55	45.29	Yellow	C
"	Barry	Outside	"	193, 195, 197.	4'—3"	22470	58	18	49	17	4.96	42.63	Red	C
"	R. & S.B.	Inside	19" x 26"	164-167	4'—9"	22395	58	4	45	14	4.57	47.50	Blue	C
"	Alexandra Docks	"	18" x 26"	663.	4'—0"	22375	51	18	45	14	4.57	39.95	Yellow	C
"	Rhymney	"	18½"x 26"	76, 77.	5'—0"	22060	60	15	50	10	5.12	49.25	Red	C
"	"	"	"	78-81.	"	"	64	0	53	7	5.41	"	"	C
"	Cardiff	"	18" x 26"	160.	4'—6"	21880	54	18	46	2	4.71	43.96	Yellow	C
"	R. & S.B.	"	"	168-176.	"	"	50	12	40	7	4.13	"	"	C
"	"	"	"	177, 179.	"	"	52	0	42	0	4.29	"	"	C
"	R. & S.B.	"	"	178.	"	"	51	6	42	9	4.34	"	"	C
"	Taff Vale	"	17½"x 26"	236, 278-302, 310, 311, 313-315, 317-321, 324.	4'—6½"	21730	65	5	52	19	5.45	44.07	Red	C
"	"	"	"	333, 409, 414, 420.	"	"	65	5	52	19	5.45	"	"	C

TYPE	RAILWAY	CYLINDERS CLASS	SIZE	ENGINE NOS.	WHEEL DIA.	TRACTIVE EFFORT LBS.	TOTAL WEIGHT FULL T	C	WEIGHT ON COUPLED WHEELS T	C	ADHESION FACTOR	POWER UNIT	COLOUR	LETTER
0-6-2T	Taff Vale	Inside	17½"x 26"	333, 409, 414, 420.	4' — 6½"	21730	61	0	50	6	5.18	44.07	Blue	C
"	Barry	"	"	198-200, 203, 204, 206-214, 223-232.	4' — 3"	21230	51	15	42	12	4.49	40.28	Yellow	C
"	"	"	"	198-200, 203, 204, 206-214, 223-232.	"	"	50	2	41	3	4.34	"	"	C
"	"	"	"	233-235, 238, 240-277.	"	"	53	9	43	19	4.63	"	"	C
"	"	"	"	233-235, 238, 240-277.			53	9	44	12	4.70	"	"	C
"	N. & B.	"	18" x 26"	1327.	4' — 6"	21215	53	9	44	7	4.65	42.61	"	C
"	P.T.	"	"	183, 185, 186, 189.	"	"	55	14	44	4	4.66	"	"	C
"	R. & S.B.	"	"	180, 182.	"	"	55	12	45	2	4.76	"	"	C
"	Alexandra Docks	Outside	"	190-192.	4' — 3"	21060	52	13	46	18	4.99	39.96	Blue	C
"	Cardiff	Inside	"	153-155.	4' — 6½"	21020	63	14	53	0	5.64	42.62	Red	C
"	Taff Vale	"	18½"x 26"	335, 337, 343-349, 351, 352, 356, 357, 360-362.	5' — 3"	21000	69	1	56	11	6.03	49.21	"	C
"	"	"	"	364-368, 370-391, 393, 394, 397-399.	"	"	69	1	56	11	6.03	"	"	C
"	"	"	"	401-404, 406, 408, 438-441.	"	"	69	1	56	11	6.03	"	"	C
"	"	"	"	401-404, 406, 408, 438-441.	"	"	65	14	53	10	5.70	"	"	C
"	B. & M.	"	18" x 26"	1372-1375, 1668, 1670.	5' — 0"	20885	57	12	51	0	5.47	46.62	Blue	B
"	Rhymney	"	"	82, 83.	"	"	60	5	52	5	5.60	"	Red	B
"	R. & S.B.	"	17½"x 26"	181.	4' — 6"	20680	49	10	39	5	4.25	41.56		B
"	Cardiff	"	"	156, 159, 162.	"	20055	48	2	39	2	4.36	40.28		B
"	"	"	"	157, 158.	"		50	0	40	9	4.51	"		B
"	Taff Vale	"	"	412, 413, 415, 419, 421, 423-426.	4' — 6½"	19870	61	10	48	16	5.49	40.30	Blue	B
"	"	"	"	410, 411, 416-418, 427-435, 436.	"	"	63	0	50	0	5.63	"	"	B
"	"	"	"	443, 445, 466, 481-484, 487, 491-493.	"	18620	52	5	41	7	4.97	37.76	Yellow	A
"	"	"	"	506, 507, 511, 513, 520, 552, 567, 573, 577-579.	"	"	52	5	41	7	4.97	"	"	A
"	"	"	"	582-585.	"	"	52	5	41	7	4.97	"	"	A
"	"	"	"	582-585.	"	"	48	5	39	13	4.76	"	"	A
"	"	"	"	485, 486, 494-496, 498, 502.	"	"	54	4	43	5	5.20	"	"	A
"	"	"	"	446, 448, 453, 481.	"	"	56	6	44	6	5.32	"	"	A
"	"	"	"	449, 450, 454, 455, 471, 473-475, 477, 480.	"	"	56	8	44	8	5.34	"	"	A
"	Cardiff	"	"	163.	4' — 6"	17545						35.24		A
"	Taff Vale	"	"	587, 589, 590, 591, 593, 595-597.	5' — 3"	17190	63	0	50	15	6.61	40.28	Blue	A
"	"	"	"	588, 592, 598, 599, 600, 602, 603.	"	"	62	18	50	15	6.61	"	"	A
"	Rhymney	"	17½"x 24"	84-91, 97-101, 106-109, 112-115, 117-119, 122.	4' — 7"	17040	53	8	44	13	5.86	34.86	"	A
"	"	"	"	127, 129-131, 133-145, 147, 148.	"	"	53	8	44	13	5.86	"	"	A
"	B. & M.	"	17" x 24"	1677.	4' — 7½"	15935	44	12	37	14	5.30	32.90		A
0-6-4T	Alexandra Docks	Inside	20½"x 26"	1346.	4' — 7"	27020	66	10	51	6	4.25	55.30	Red	D
"	Barry	"	18½"x 26"	1347, 1349, 1351, 1357.	"	24755	75	6	56	10	5.11	50.65	Red	D
"	"	"	"	1348, 1350, 1352-1355.	"	"	72	11	55	9	5.01	50.65	"	D
2-6-2T	Alexandra Docks	Outside	18½"x 26"	1201, 1207-1209, 1211.	4' — 7½"	24530	62	3	44	10	4.06	50.65	Yellow	D
"	"	"	"	1201, 1204, 1207-1209, 1211.	"	"	62	11	44	10	4.06	"	"	D
"	"	"	19½"x 26"	1199.	4' — 6"	24900	63	1	44	4	3.97	50.02	"	D
"	"	"	19" x 26"	1205, 1206.	4' — 7"	23210	65	0	44	5	4.27	47.50	"	C
"	Vale of Rheidol	"	11½"x 17"	7, 8, 1213.	2' — 6"	10510	25	0				11.73		
"	"	"	11" x 17"	1212.	"	8740	25	0				9.75		
0-8-0	Barry	"	20" x 26"	1387, 1388.	4' — 4"	27200	48	10	48	10	3.99	52.62		D
"	"	"	19" x 26"	1389, 1390.	"	24550	48	10	48	10	4.42	47.50		D
0-8-2T	P.T.	"	20" x 26"	1358-1360.	4' — 3"	31200	75	17	63	1	4.52	59.21	Blue	E
"	"	"	19" x 24"	1378, 1379.	4' — 4"	28325	72	3	63	3	4.99	54.79	Red	D
"	Barry	"	20" x 26"	1380, 1382-1386.	"	27200	73	0	59	13	4.91	52.62	Blue	D

Yesterday's scene on the Taff Vale showing Nos. 796 and 481 at Cardiff West
yard in 1926. All things pass . . .

NOTES